MW00743421

MASTERING
MICROSOFT WORD
ON THE IBM PC

MASTERING MICROSOFT® WORD ON THE IBM PC

Fourth Edition

Matthew Holtz

 SAN FRANCISCO • PARIS • DÜSSELDORF • LONDON

Acquisitions Editor: Dianne King
Supervising Editor: Joanne Cuthbertson
Copy Editor: Nancy O'Donnell
Technical Editor: Jeff Green
Word Processors: Deborah Maizels and Chris Mockel
Book Designer: Julie Bilski

Chapter Art: Suzanne Albertson
Technical Art and Screen Graphics: Jeffrey Giese
Typesetter: Bob Myren
Proofreader: Ed Lin
Cover Designer: Thomas Ingalls + Associates
Cover Photographer: Michael Lamotte

AutoCAD is a trademark of Autodesk, Inc.
Epson is a registered trademark of Epson America, Inc.
Excel, Microsoft Windows, Multiplan, and OS/2 are trademarks of Microsoft Corporation. Microsoft, MS, and MS-DOS are registered trademarks of Microsoft Corporation.
Genius is a trademark of Micro Display Systems.
Hercules Graphics Card and Hercules Plus Card are trademarks of Hercules Computer Technology.
IBM PC/AT and PS/2 are trademarks of International Business Machines Corporation. IBM is a registered trademark of International Business Machines Corporation.
LaserJet and LaserJet Series II are trademarks of Hewlett-Packard Corporation.
Lotus and 1-2-3 are registered trademarks of Lotus Development Corporation.
MultiMate Advantage is a trademark of Ashton-Tate Corporation. dBASE, dBASE III, and MultiMate are registered trademarks of Ashton-Tate Corporation.
Reflex and Quattro are trademarks of Borland International, Inc.
Tandy is a registered trademark of Tandy/Radio Shack.
ThinkTank is a trademark of Living Videotext, Inc.
Ventura Publisher is a trademark of Ventura Software, Inc.
Word Exchange is a trademark of Systems Compatibility Corporation.
WordPerfect is a registered trademark of WordPerfect Corporation.
WordStar is a registered trademark of WordStar International.
Xerox is a trademark of Xerox Corporation.

Nonsmoking policy in Figure 9.20 excerpted from *A Smokefree Workplace*, copyright © 1985 by American Nonsmokers' Rights Foundation, Berkeley, California.

The text of this book was originally entered with Microsoft Word.

SYBEX is a registered trademark of SYBEX, Inc.

SYBEX is not affiliated with any manufacturer.

Every effort has been made to supply complete and accurate information. However, SYBEX assumes no responsibility for its use, nor for any infringements of patents or other rights of third parties which would result.

First edition copyright © 1985, second edition copyright © 1987, third edition copyright © 1988, SYBEX Inc.

Every effort has been made to supply complete and accurate information. However, SYBEX assumes no responsibility for its use, nor for any infringements of patents or other rights of third parties which would result.

Library of Congress Card Number: 89-61529
ISBN 0-89588-597-2
Manufactured in the United States of America
10 9 8 7 6 5 4 3 2 1

To my mom and dad: Helen and Leslie Holtz

I rarely think in words at all.
                                    —*Einstein*

ACKNOWLEDGMENTS

For this edition, once again thanks and acknowledgment go to Barbara Gordon, who taught me so much. I keep hearing your voice when I write. Thanks especially to Nancy O'Donnell for her careful edit and to all those at SYBEX who have collaborated in the creation of this book. My gratitude extends to all of you.

Special thanks to Gene Brott for all the help and encouragement.

CONTENTS AT A GLANCE

TABLE OF CONTENTS

P A R T II **ENHANCING YOUR WORD PROCESSING SKILLS**

P A R T IV DESKTOP PUBLISHING IN WORD

C H A P T E R 16: ORGANIZING YOUR MATERIAL WITH THE OUTLINER

INTRODUCTION

BECAUSE OF MICROSOFT WORD'S ADVANCED DESIGN, many consider it the finest word processor available for desktop publishing. Microsoft Word works with your IBM or IBM-compatible personal computer, and together they allow you to deliver first-class documents for business or personal use.

As with any piece of software, you have to learn the rules of Word's game before you can play. Once you have mastered the rules, you can use them in various ways to accomplish numerous tasks. *Mastering Microsoft Word on the IBM PC* will teach you the rules and show you how you can use them to your advantage.

Since people generally learn best by example, I explain features in general terms and follow these explanations with examples that demonstrate the feature being discussed. You can read through the book or use the examples, which are accompanied by illustrations, as a hands-on tutorial.

My goal is to provide a thorough, practical approach to learning Word. I present instructions on how to perform different procedures in a step-by-step fashion that makes them easy to follow. Examples are carefully constructed: kept simple to highlight the principles being taught, they are at the same time thorough in demonstrating Word's operations.

M O U S E

A note such as this in the margin provides the methods of performing operations using the mouse. Its steps correspond to those listed next to it in the text for the keyboard. I discuss some of the more extensive mouse procedures more fully in the text.

In those instances when Word provides more than one way to accomplish the same task, we'll look at the advantages of each approach. I give directions for using the keyboard in the text, while those for the mouse are generally in the margin, as shown here. Although you don't have to use the mouse at all, if you are accustomed to using it with other programs or have an oversized screen, you'll find the mouse a handy tool with Word; some procedures are quicker when performed with the mouse than with the keyboard.

In addition to the standard keyboard methods, Word 5 has several function-key shortcuts for procedures and commands. Look for this box

Shortcut:

to the right of numbered steps in the text. It will contain the key combination you can substitute for the associated steps. These key combinations are often *toggles,* allowing you to turn a feature on and off; this will also be indicated in the box when applicable.

WHO THIS BOOK IS FOR

I have geared this book toward Word 4 and 5 users who have a hard disk and an IBM PC or compatible, with either a monochrome or color/graphics monitor. Other configurations are discussed in Appendix A. For the keys, I use the names and locations on the enhanced keyboard, the latest keyboard sold with PC/ATs and compatibles. Although I developed all examples and operational instructions using Word release 5, I have made it clear when the procedures differ for Word 4 so that Word 4 users can follow along easily.

5 New in Word 5

To identify the features introduced in Word 5, I have included a flag in the margin, which you can see here, whenever I discuss a new feature. If you are already familiar with Word and have just acquired release 5, you can scan for this flag to get to the new features quickly.

Beside adding new features, such as automatic pagination, Microsoft has also changed several function keys' assignments, renamed one or two command options, and reorganized some commands in Word 5. For instance, Word 4's General Options and Window Options commands are grouped together as one command, Options, in Word 5. Table 1.1 (in Chapter 1) summarizes Word's features, indicating which are new or substantially improved with release 5.

Regardless of your prior experience with Word, this book will increase your understanding of how Word operates. For the beginner, the book requires no previous experience with word processing. I explain all concepts fully, using practical examples and step-by-step instructions. If you've recently acquired Word, this book shows you how to prepare Word for use on your system (see Appendix A).

For intermediate users, detailed explanations of all areas of the program allow you to explore and understand more of its features. If you've worked with other word processing systems, you'll undoubtedly appreciate the examples and figures. They enable you to see Word in action and learn the unique methods Word uses to accomplish word processing tasks.

Advanced users will find sophisticated techniques for working with Word. The book presents numerous exclusive methods and approaches that I discovered while exploring the program and searching for solutions to real problems. Part 4, "Desktop Publishing in Word," will particularly interest the advanced Word user.

T I P

The tip notes in the margin provide you with tips and tricks that can enhance your use of Word, regardless of your level of expertise. For instance, I often add a note to direct you to one of Word's supplied macros when it expedites the procedure under discussion. The notes also present pitfalls to watch out for.

A PREVIEW OF THE BOOK'S CONTENTS

This book has been constructed so that the simplest and most frequently used features are explained in the earlier chapters. Within the chapters, I present the method that's quickest and most easily implemented first. I then discuss variations on that approach, incorporating the use of other techniques in the example when necessary.

The Fast Track section at the beginning of each chapter summarizes the chapter's contents, lists the steps or keystrokes needed to complete specific tasks, and points you to the page where you can find a tutorial presentation or more detailed explanation. In some cases, the Fast Track entry will be all you need to get going, especially if you have some computer experience. In other cases, you can use the Fast Track to pick out the points you are interested in and then go directly to the information you need. But note that Fast Tracks cover the chapters' primary topics; they do not cover every option, exception, or caveat discussed in the text.

In addition to the information I provide in the chapters, I have included reference tools on the pages inside the front and back covers. In the front you'll find an alphabetical guide to Word operations, complete with page numbers indicating where I discuss them in the text. In the back you'll discover several useful tables listing Word's display symbols and cursor-movement keys. The comprehensive index also makes it easy to find "how-to" information for numerous procedures. Finally, you can use the form at the back of the book to order a disk containing the examples shown in this book, so that you don't have to type them yourself. The disk also includes ALPHA-MAC, a glossary of macros that provide quick and easy alphabetical access to Word's operations.

The following is an overview of the book's contents, chapter by chapter.

PART I: BEGINNING WITH THE BASICS

Chapter 1 provides a general discussion of word processing with Word, including a brief look at some of the features that make Microsoft Word special. In it you'll learn how Word uses your computer system's keyboard, printer, monitor, and disk drive.

Chapter 2 introduces Word itself. First, we take an in-depth look at the Word screen, in effect the game board you use to move about in Word. You'll then get a chance to type some simple material and see how to correct mistakes. After saving the document, you'll learn how to use Word's Help feature to get extra assistance if needed. Finally, I explain briefly how you can customize certain aspects of Word's operation.

In Chapter 3 we turn our attention to the end product of word processing: the printed document. Microsoft Word's Print commands allow you to print quickly with little adjustment, but their options also give you the ability to meet special printing needs. You'll see how you can print all or just part of a document, as well as how you can print while you work.

In Chapter 4 we examine how Word uses your computer's temporary memory (RAM) and disk storage capability to manipulate and preserve your documents in electronic form. You'll learn how to retrieve documents, clear the screen for new documents, and even combine documents.

Chapter 5 is the first to discuss formatting, which changes the look of your document as opposed to its content. Practical examples illustrate the difference good formatting makes as well as how to implement it. You'll look at the Alt codes—shortcuts to formatting—as well as at how to change Word's switchboxes of format settings.

PART II: ENHANCING
YOUR WORD PROCESSING SKILLS

Chapter 6 shows you how to manipulate blocks of text in your document. You'll see how to delete text, relocate it elsewhere, and copy it to other positions, observing how Word's unusual scrap area plays a central role in these operations. You'll also examine Word's redlining feature, which you can use to keep track of changes you make to your documents.

Chapter 7 covers the use of fonts, a topic of great interest in desktop publishing. In it I present some fundamental concepts of typography and introduce you to printing fonts with sophisticated printers, such as the LaserJet.

Chapter 8 introduces Word's windows. By using windows, you can subdivide the computer screen to display parts of one or more documents. After practicing with windows, you'll explore the various views that you can use to work with your document, including Word's new Print preView command, which allows you to check your document's appearance before you print it. You'll also glance at Microsoft Windows.

Chapter 9 focuses on page layout—setting margins, repeating headings at the top or bottom of your pages, and creating footnotes. You'll also see how to adjust Word for all kinds of paper sizes and margins, even when a single document contains several page formats.

Chapter 10 demonstrates the use of Word's search and replace capabilities for locating text as well as formats (such as boldfacing or underlining) in context. I discuss when and why you'd want to use these techniques, both for simple and more sophisticated operations. This chapter also presents methods of searching for documents on disk.

PART III: USING WORD'S
SPECIALIZED FEATURES

Chapter 11 investigates the types of columns that Word can create, discussing when to use each type. You'll learn how to set tabs to create tables and how to compose newspaper-style columns. You'll also see how to draw lines on the page and create sophisticated page layouts.

In Chapter 12 you'll see how you can use Word to perform math calculations and alphabetize or number material. You'll also examine Word's new cross-referencing feature, which ensures that your readers will find the material that you direct them to.

Chapter 13 shows you how to use the Spell program to check your documents for misspellings and correct them. This chapter also demonstrates how Word can automatically hyphenate words to fill in distracting gaps and how you can use Word's thesaurus, Word Finder, to find synonyms.

Chapter 14 examines the role of Word's Print Merge command in the production of personalized form letters. I show you how you can set up the print merge operation to personalize the letters or to print letters to selected names in the database. You'll also look at printing mailing labels.

Chapter 15 explains how you can specify glossary abbreviations for passages of text that you would otherwise type repeatedly and have Word substitute the full text in place of the abbreviations. You'll also examine macros, an advanced glossary feature that enables you to create shortcuts for procedures you perform repeatedly. With macros, you can accomplish complex processing with push-button efficiency.

PART IV: DESKTOP PUBLISHING IN WORD

Chapter 16 begins our look at several Word features that work in concert with one another, allowing you to develop professional desktop-published applications. With Word's outline processor, you can organize your material as you compose the document. You can also use it to move quickly from one topic to another and to relocate topics and supporting material as appropriate.

Chapter 17 examines a special capability of Word: the ability to accommodate desktop-publishing applications with style sheets. Style sheets enable you to customize formats consistently, according to your needs and wishes. Through Word's gallery, style sheets access all of Word's exceptional formatting features and store your format specifications separately from documents for maximum flexibility.

Chapter 18 examines Word's enhanced importing capabilities, which allow you to include spreadsheets, graphics, and other Word documents in your document and update its content quickly. You'll also see how easy it is to convert documents you create with Word for use with other applications.

Chapter 19 discusses features that round Word out for use with desktop publishing. You'll learn how Word can compile an index and a table of contents for your document. You'll also see how it can compile other lists as well, such as figures or case citations.

APPENDICES

In the appendices the focus shifts from how to use Word's features to how Word interacts with your particular computer setup.

Appendix A tells you how you can set up and load Word. For instance, you'll see how you can have Word automatically load a document when you start it up. It also describes how to set up Word to work with different hardware configurations—including a serial printer or a RAM drive.

Appendix B explains how to manage your directories so that you can make the most of your hard disk configuration. It also discusses several system commands you might find useful for file operations you can perform outside of Word.

Appendix C contains a listing of the supplied macros that Word provides to augment its operations. You can refer to this appendix to learn how to use a particular macro, or you can use it as a guide for constructing your own macros.

Appendix D, another reference tool, lists the standard character sets you can use to create symbols that don't appear on your keyboard.

By using *Mastering Microsoft Word on the IBM PC* as an in-depth tutorial or as a reference guide, you can gain a solid understanding of Word and its capabilities. Welcome to the world of word processing and desktop publishing. To begin, go directly to Chapter 1.

PART I

Beginning with the Basics

1

Welcome to Microsoft Word

Fast Track

TRADITIONALLY, WORD PROCESSING INVOLVED THE use of a computer to write, revise, and print your words. In the end, all it did was make good typing easier.

With a state-of-the-art program such as Microsoft Word, however, today's word processor goes far beyond such fundamentals, encompassing abilities in an area that has become known as *desktop publishing*. Word's capabilities with the laser printer are legendary, and with the right printer, such as a Hewlett-Packard LaserJet, you can produce a variety of type styles, page layouts, and graphics not possible with a typewriter or many other word processing programs. This ability to create typeset-quality output with a personal computer is a hallmark of desktop publishing.

WHAT MAKES WORD SPECIAL?

Word is one of the finest word processing programs available. It has many features that can't always be found in such software. Naturally, it also includes features that we've come to expect from a word processor, such as displaying underlining and boldface on the screen. Table 1.1 lists some of the remarkable things you can do with Word. As indicated, several features are new with Word 5.

Table 1.1: Features of Microsoft Word

FEATURE	DESCRIPTION
Annotation *	Inserts comments into a document, which can be used for revisions or review by others.
Autosave *	Backs up your documents to disk automatically at an interval that you specify.
Color *	Assigns colors for printing and can also be assigned to represent varying font sizes or other formats (such as boldface).

Table 1.1: Features of Microsoft Word (cont.)

Column	Creates newspaper-style columns, tabular columns, or side-by-side paragraphs.
Cross-reference *	Allows you to cross-reference page numbers, paragraph numbers, and footnotes. When you print, Word updates and prints the correct cross-references automatically.
Date/time stamping	Automatically inserts the correct date or time when you prepare the document or print it.
Footnote	Places automatically numbered footnotes at the bottom of the correct page or at the end of the document.
Form	Allows you to create blank forms that you can fill later in a semiautomatic fashion.
Frame *	Allows you to position text or graphics on the page easily. You can even have text flow around the frame.
Glossary/macro	Allows you to create customized "shorthand" for text you enter or procedures you perform repeatedly. Word also supplies macros already set up for you.
Help	Provides online information as you are performing an operation, without interrupting your work.
Hidden text	Enables you to place text in a document that can be suppressed when you print the document.
Hyphenation	Scans the document and correctly hyphenates words to improve alignment.
Indexing	Generates an index from specified text.
Line/shading *	Enables you to create lines and shading by drawing them or assigning them to paragraphs automatically.
Linking *	Allows you to incorporate data, graphs, and pictures from Lotus 1-2-3 and other programs into Word documents easily.

Table 1.1: Features of Microsoft Word (cont.)

Math	Performs five math operations on text in the document.
Networking *	Provides access to Word documents from a pool of computers.
Numbering *	Numbers and renumbers a document's pages, lines, or sections by number, letter, or other format.
Outliner	Allows you to organize your document, examine its structure, focus on different levels by collapsing the text, move quickly through it, and rearrange sections.
Print Merging	Creates an electronic stack of names and addresses for personalized form letters or mailing labels.
Print preview *	Accurately shows columns, fonts, running heads, and footnotes on the screen as they will appear in the final printed version of the document.
Queued printing	Allows you to continue working with Word as you print your documents.
Red-lining	Indicates changes to the previous version of the document; these can be accepted or rejected individually.
Running head	Allows you to provide text that appears at the top or bottom of each page.
Search and Replace	Find specified text or format and replaces it as indicated.
Sorting	Rearranges material into numeric and alphabetical order.
Speller	Checks documents for misspelled words and incorrect punctuation. Word proposes correct spellings and lets you edit the misspellings.
Style sheet	Helps guarantee that your documents are formatted consistently, including their spacing, font size, and line length, and lets you make changes easily.

Table 1.1: Features of Microsoft Word (cont.)

Summary sheet	Allows you to record information about a document, so it's easier to locate later.
Table of contents	Generates a table of contents for your document from its headings.
Thesaurus	Finds synonyms for words, making substitutions as you indicate.
Undo	Allows you to immediately reverse the effects of whatever procedure you just performed.
Window	Splits the screen to enable you to work on more than one document or different parts of the same document, and to transfer material between them.

* New or significantly improved with release 5.

LEARNING WORD

Don't feel daunted by the many features that Word makes available to you. Fortunately, the basics are not difficult to grasp. And thanks to a consistency of approach throughout the program, Word becomes progressively easier to learn. As you use Word, you will recognize the common sense that underlies its structure. In fact, you may even begin to second-guess it.

Perhaps best of all, Word has an Undo command. If you accidentally perform some action (such as deleting the wrong chunk of text), it is possible to retrieve—or *undo*—your mistake. If you don't like the results of the Undo command, you can take it back by "undoing" the Undo. Thanks to the Undo command, you may find that you become bold in experimenting with Word.

To learn Word, we must begin by looking at its contents.

THE WORD PACKAGE

When you purchase Microsoft Word release 5, you receive thirteen 5¼-inch floppy disks. Let's take a moment to survey the contents of those disks.

The two Program disks contain the main chunk of the Word package. The instructions on these disks tell the computer what to do and how to interact with you.

The three Utilities disks (and one Utilities/Printers disk) are used with the Setup program to get Word ready to work on your computer. The setup process is quite simple, and you'll need to perform it if your copy of Word isn't up and running yet (see Appendix A).

The two Printers disks (and the Utilities/Printers disk) are also used by the Setup program. These disks contain the technical specifications, called *printer drivers* or *.PRD files*, for a variety of individual printers. Running the Setup program will provide Word with the information it needs to print your documents.

The Spell disk is essentially a dictionary on a disk. Word uses it when you check your documents for misspelled words. Chapter 13 explains in detail how to use the Spell program to check your documents. The same chapter shows you how to use the thesaurus on the Thesaurus disk to find synonyms.

In addition, Word includes three disks for learning Microsoft Word. One disk covers the essentials for the keyboard, one covers the mouse, and the last one covers advanced lessons for both. These disks are interactive tutorials; that is, they teach some of the uses of Word by working with you on the screen. You can also use them for review. This book does not assume that you have worked with these disks (or that you have studied Word in any other way). If you have, however, reading this book will enhance your knowledge of Word.

Finally, Microsoft Word is also available on 3½-inch disks. These contain the same information provided on the 5¼-inch disks and are for computers that use them, such as laptops and the IBM PS/2.

HOW WORD AND YOUR COMPUTER SYSTEM WORK

You, your computer, your printer, and the information on your Word disks act as collaborators in building documents. Let's look at how your computer and the program complement each other. (An underlying component of your computer is its operating system, which is examined in Appendix B.)

Your system is composed of five main parts:

- the system unit (containing the disk drives and the computer circuitry)
- the keyboard
- the monitor
- the printer
- the mouse (which is optional)

Each of these hardware components has an important role to play in creating documents with Microsoft Word.

USING WORD WITH A HARD DISK

Within the system unit, we'll assume that your computer contains a hard disk (also called a *fixed disk*), in addition to one or more floppy drives. Once prohibitively expensive, hard disks are now standard equipment, and sophisticated programs such as Word are increasingly designed to take advantage of their capabilities.

In most setups, the hard disk (that is, the first hard disk installed) is drive C. Even if you have only one floppy disk drive, generally the hard disk is still drive C; the single floppy performs double duty as either drive A or drive B when necessary. (With some laptops, drive C is used by the built-in operating system, and the hard disk uses drive D.)

When you set up Word with this arrangement, a copy of the Word program is placed on the hard disk. As a hard disk has lots of storage space, you can store your documents on it, alongside the Word program. You could also store the documents on floppy disks, but it is quicker to access the files on the hard disk.

Storage space in a hard disk is usually divided into various sections called *directories*. This arrangement makes it easier for you to locate material. You can think of a directory as one drawer of a filing cabinet. To find out how to look in that directory drawer for the files that contain your documents, see Appendix B.

As Word operates, it takes (or *reads*) information off the disk. It stores the information in the electronic circuitry of the computer (also within the system unit), called RAM (random-access memory). The material that you type is also initially stored in RAM and then stored to the disk drive when you save it. Release 5 of Word requires that your computer have at least 384K of RAM, while you can get by on 320K with release 4.

USING WORD WITH TWO FLOPPY DISK DRIVES

Using Word 5 with two standard 320K floppy disk drives is awkward at best, requiring you to swap disks often. The Setup program creates two Program disks for use in drive A; you use one to load (start up) Word, and the other as Word is running. In addition, when you print, your document disk in drive B must contain the printer specification (.PRD) file. Running Spell, using the thesaurus, and hyphenating necessitates that you swap the appropriate disks into drive A, as prompted.

In this book, I assume that you use Word with a hard disk drive. (I discuss using Word without a hard disk in Appendix A.) If you do not have a hard disk, I recommend you consider installing one to word process with Word 5.

USING 3¹/₂-INCH DISKS

As mentioned, laptops and the IBM PS/2 use 3¹/₂-inch floppy disks instead of 5¹/₄-inch disks. IBM made them its standard because they are more durable, are smaller, and hold more information. Because the 3¹/₂-inch disks hold more information, swapping is not as extensive with them as it is with the larger disks.

THE KEYBOARD

The keyboard is another component and is separate from the system unit on most computers. Figure 1.1 shows the IBM keyboard in its various incarnations. We'll refer to the enhanced keyboard as we discuss the keys. However, if you have one of the other keyboard types, you should be able to follow along. Consult this figure for the differences, if necessary.

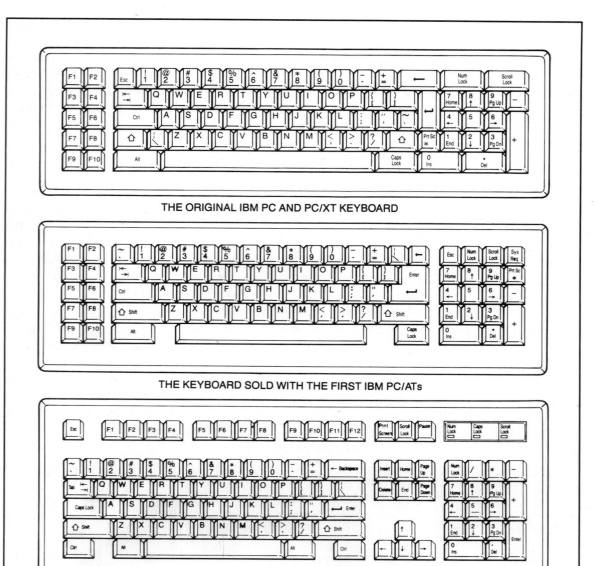

THE ORIGINAL IBM PC AND PC/XT KEYBOARD

THE KEYBOARD SOLD WITH THE FIRST IBM PC/ATs

THE "ENHANCED" IBM KEYBOARD, SOLD WITH MOST IBMs (INCLUDING PS/2s) AND MOST COMPATIBLES. IN SOME CASES, THE THREE INDICATOR LIGHTS AT THE TOP RIGHT ARE OMITTED.

Figure 1.1: Keyboards for the IBM and compatibles

The main group of keys on the enhanced keyboard are the alphanumeric keys. To the right of these keys are the keys that you use for moving around the screen and within documents. I call them the *directional keys*. We'll be working with the directional keys when we create a document in the next chapter. On the right is the *numeric keypad*. Its keys can perform double duty as either numbers or directional keys, depending on the status of the NumLock key.

In Word, the function keys (F1 to F12) perform frequently used word processing functions. We will study these keys in more detail as we come across them in our work.

Note that Word enables you to perform many more than twelve functions by providing key combinations for other common operations. For example, you can start a new page by pressing Ctrl-Shift-Enter. These key combinations are listed on the pages inside the back cover.

THE MONITOR

What you type at the keyboard shows up on the monitor at a spot indicated by a highlighted rectangle, which is commonly called the *cursor* or *highlight*. You can use the directional keys, as well as some function keys, to move the cursor to where you want in the document.

You now have a wide variety of monitors from which to choose. To examine monitors, we must first look at the two basic display modes in which the PC can operate, as the mode capabilities you want determine the type of monitor you should get.

TEXT MODE AND GRAPHICS MODE   IBM created the Text and Graphics modes when it designed the PC. Generally, only alphanumeric characters appear in Text (or Character) mode. Boldface and underline are available, but graphics are not (no italics, strike-through, superscript, and so on). In Graphics mode, you can see the graphics in place. With Word's Print preView feature, you can even see different-sized fonts displayed correctly. Depending on the hardware, however, you may find that some Word operations, such as editing, are slower in Graphics mode than in Text mode.

When you set up Word, you specify the mode in which Word initially operates. In this book I assume you are in Graphics mode.

Once Word is running, you'll learn how to change modes with the Options command or Alt-F9.

TYPES OF MONITORS Originally, IBM provided two choices of monitors (and the corresponding cards that supported them): MDA (monochrome display adapter) and CGA (color graphics adapter). Monochrome monitors displayed Word only in Text mode, whereas CGA showed colors when it operated in Text mode and black-and-white graphics in Graphics mode. However, many characters displayed in the CGA Graphics mode were difficult to read.

Later, adding a Hercules graphics card (HGC) to a monochrome monitor allowed the monitor to operate in either Text mode or a cleaner Graphics mode. A more recent addition, EGA (enhanced graphics adapter) cards, provided both color and crisp graphics in Graphics mode.

Today, VGA (video graphics array) and Super VGA monitors improve on the EGA standard, providing even higher resolution. In addition, full-page displays, such as the Genius, allow you to see up to 66 lines on the screen at once, as opposed to the standard 25. There are also two-page displays.

Word supports a whole host of these monitor types. When you set up Word, it normally detects the type of monitor installed and automatically makes the full capabilities of the monitor available to you, whether you have an old MDA card or a full-page display.

As you work with Word, you'll see how it responds to your particular monitor. You can compare this to the screen examples you encounter in this book.

Most monitors have both brightness and contrast controls, and you should adjust these to your comfort. Be sure not to neglect these adjustments—they can make a world of difference in your word processing performance. As you look at the monitor, the top edge should be at eye level, so that you look down slightly to view the screen.

If nothing appears on the screen when you try to run the computer, be sure to check the monitor and your other computer equipment before you place a service call. Check that the brightness and contrast controls are not turned down all the way, that the power cord is plugged in, that the signal cord is plugged into the computer, and that the monitor's power switch is turned on.

THE PRINTER

Printers, too, vary a great deal in setup. Be prepared to experiment. This is especially true if you are dealing with material that calls for precise placement, such as a letterhead or mailing labels.

In this book, we'll use the Hewlett-Packard LaserJet Series II as our sample printer. Let's take a moment to look at some of the switches and indicators that you might find on the printer (see Figure 1.2). Note that your printer may be different.

THE ONLINE SWITCH This switch might be labeled Select or Sel, On Line (or On-line or OL), or Start/Stop. When it comes time to print one of your documents, the printer must be *online*, which simply means it is ready to receive information. One press turns the switch on; another turns it off. This is usually an indicator light near the switch that glows when the switch is on. When it's on, the printer accepts signals from the computer for printing; in other words, the

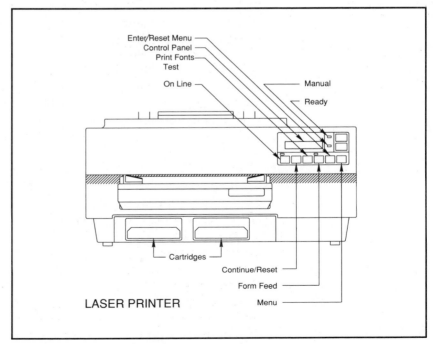

Figure 1.2: Printer switches and indicators

printer is connected to the computer. When it's off, the printer and the computer are, in effect, "unplugged" from each other.

You might need to turn the online switch off to stop the printing—should the paper jam, for example. To start up again, you turn it on. Some printers, such as the LaserJet, go offline automatically when the paper jams. You must clear the paper's path before you can place the printer online again.

THE FORM-FEED SWITCH This might be labeled FF (form feed), TOF (top of form), or Page Advance. When you push this button, it ejects the paper so that you start on a fresh sheet. Form-feeding is handled automatically with Word, so you don't generally need to use this button. However, if you ran another program before using Word, you may find you need to eject a partially used piece of paper before you start printing. You may have to turn off the online switch for the form-feed switch to operate.

THE PRINTER CONTROL PANEL Sometimes, a problem with your printer may occur that requires your attention. The printer may be out of paper, the paper-feed path may be jammed, or the printer's cover may be open.

Some printers, like the LaserJet, tell you exactly what the problem is by displaying a message on the printer's control panel. Others may sound an alarm or light a special indicator.

Correct the condition. Generally, the online switch is automatically turned off when the alarm is triggered, so you have to turn it on again. Once you've corrected the condition, the LaserJet reprints the problem page, if necessary, before continuing.

If while using your printer, you find that it begins to behave in a way you can't understand (strange characters or margins, for example), you might just try turning it off, pausing for a moment, and turning it back on. Often, this kind of clearing out will work wonders. Of course, you should read your printer manual carefully to learn the specifics of your printer.

THE MOUSE

The mouse is an optional piece of hardware manufactured by Microsoft (among others) to complement its products, including Word, on the PC. This electronic critter is a device the size of your palm, designed to be moved around on a flat surface. As you move the mouse, a corresponding pointer moves around on the screen. You can use the mouse instead of the keyboard to select text and issue commands in Word.

A typical mouse has two control buttons on the top. (Your mouse may have anywhere from one to three buttons; if you don't have a two-button mouse, which is the type of mouse Word supports, refer to the mouse's manual for instructions.) As you rest your hand on the mouse, you use your fingers to press and release the buttons. This action is called *clicking* the mouse. To make a selection, you roll the mouse on the desktop to move the pointer to something on the screen. Then you click one or both buttons to indicate your choice.

As you move the pointer about the screen, it will change in size and/or shape. A change indicates that the mouse is ready to perform a particular task. The exact nature of the change will be determined by the task, your monitor, and the display mode. Table 1.2 lists the various shapes of the mouse pointer as it appears when you use Word in Graphics mode. In Text mode, the mouse pointer is generally a flashing box that changes size.

You can also use the mouse by pressing and holding a button, moving the mouse pointer to a new location, and then releasing the button. This process is often called *dragging* the mouse.

Almost all the mouse commands can be duplicated with the keyboard. The operations in this book that can be performed with either the keyboard or the mouse will be listed side by side or explained within the text. If you have a mouse, you'll want to learn both the keyboard and mouse methods, to decide which works best for a particular circumstance.

Once you have run the Setup program to prepare Word for use on your system (which is described in Appendix A), the computer will automatically know whether you have a mouse installed in your computer.

In the next chapter, we'll actually run the Word program and begin to work with it. You'll get a feel for how it operates and work with some new keys on the keyboard. Then we'll create a short document and modify it slightly.

Table 1.2: Mouse Pointer Shapes, Graphics Mode

SHAPE	POSITION	ACTION
⬆	Text area	Moves cursor, highlights.
⬆	Command area	Activates commands, registers choices.
⬆	Inside window, far left	Highlights.
⬍	Left window border	Ready to scroll up or down.
⬆	Left window border	Scrolls up.
⬇	Left window border	Scrolls down.
⬌	Bottom window border	Ready to scroll left or right.
⬅	Bottom window border	Scrolls left.
➡	Bottow window border	Scrolls right.
□	Top or right window border	Ready to split or close a window.
⊟	Right window border	Splits a window horizontally.
⊞	Top window border	Splits a window vertically.
⊠	Top or right window border	Closes a window.
‖‖	Upper-right corner of window	Turns ruler line (at top) on and off.
✥	Lower-right corner of window	Moves a window's border.
►	Left window border	Jumps.
Y	Command area	Confirms command.
X	Command area	Cancels command.

2

Getting
Started
with Your
First
Document

Fast Track

BEFORE WE GET STARTED, YOU'LL WANT TO MAKE sure you have copied Word to your hard disk by using the Setup program. This process is described in Appendix A.

Once Word is prepared, you can use it to create and revise your documents easily. The process of revision, truly the heart of word processing, is generally known as *editing*.

In this chapter, we'll create a document from scratch and make some simple revisions in it. This will give you a basic idea of what editing with Word is all about. We will

1. Load Word into the computer's RAM area

2. Type in a short document

3. Correct mistakes and revise the document

4. Save the document for future use

We'll be exploring a number of Word's features as we walk through these steps.

STARTING UP WORD

Start up your computer. Once you see the DOS (or OS/2) prompt, change to the directory where the Setup program has placed Word, unless the directory is specified in the PATH command. (For a discussion of directories and paths, see Appendix B.)

Next, simply type

WORD

and press the Enter key. With this action, you load Word into the computer's RAM area, and its power is at your fingertips.

There are other methods you can use to start up Word from the prompt. For instance, you can instruct Word to load a specific document. As you become more familiar with Word, you'll probably want to become acquainted with these alternative start-up methods, which are discussed in Appendix A.

EXAMINING THE WORD SCREEN

Once you've started Word, you see an almost empty screen with a few words down at the bottom. Before going any farther, take a moment to look at the screen. If your screen doesn't look like Figure 2.1, your Word setup may have been modified by another user. We'll see how you can customize Word with the Options command later in this chapter.

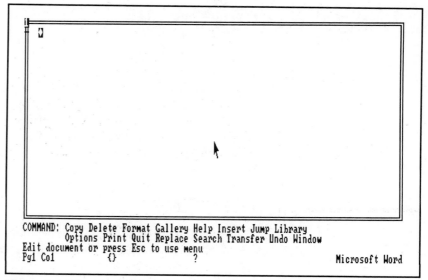

```
COMMAND: Copy Delete Format Gallery Help Insert Jump Library
         Options Print Quit Replace Search Transfer Undo Window
Edit document or press Esc to use menu
Pg1 Co1              {}                  ?                    Microsoft Word
```

Figure 2.1: The Word screen

THE WINDOW

The area with the border around it is called the *window*. This is where you type your words. You use this window to view your documents. By splitting the screen (a technique you'll learn in Chapter 8), you can fragment it into additional windows. Your screen can have up to eight windows for displaying different document areas.

Within the window, notice the highlighted rectangular box the size of a letter. This glowing box contains a black diamond. These are actually two figures, superimposed on one another for the moment.

The box is the *cursor*. It is the central actor in word processing. The cursor indicates the exact spot where your typing will appear. Right now the cursor is the size of one character, but you can make Word expand the cursor to designate text for alteration. Such text is then *highlighted* by the expanded cursor. For this reason, we will sometimes refer to the cursor as the highlight, especially if it's expanded. These terms are synonymous. In addition, highlighted text is also called selected text or simply the *selection*.

Type two or three letters and watch the cursor move as you type. Then use the Backspace key to erase what you've just typed.

The diamond, superimposed on top of the cursor at this point, is the *end mark*. It always indicates the end of your documents.

THE COMMAND AREA

The area beneath the window is the *command area*. Each command (Copy, Delete, Format, and so on) represents one or more word processing tasks that you can command Word to perform. In the course of this book we will examine each of these commands in depth. The commands are pathways to the power behind Word.

Notice that each command begins with a different letter:

Copy Delete Format Gallery Help Insert Jump Library
Options Print Quit Replace Search Transfer Undo Window

You'll use these initial letters to select the command you desire. (Note that if two commands started with the same letter, one of them would have another letter capitalized within it, which you would type to select that command.)

The command panel is activated by pressing the Escape key (labeled Esc). When you do this, the computer enters *Command mode*. While in Command mode, you cannot use the letters on the keyboard to type material into the document window. Instead, you use them to issue commands to Word. That is, by typing a command's capitalized letter, you activate (or *invoke*) that command.

To go back to typing your document (*Document mode*), you press the Esc key a second time.

Now is a good time to try your hand at issuing commands.

1. Press the Esc key to enter Command mode.
2. Notice that Copy is highlighted.
3. Press the Esc key again to reactivate Document mode.

You can now type material into the window again.

SELECTING COMMANDS WITH THE MOUSE   If you have the optional mouse, you can use it, as well as the Esc key, to issue commands. Your mouse pointer will initially appear in the center of the screen. To use the mouse, you move the pointer so that it hovers over the name of the command that you desire. Notice that the shape or size of the pointer changes as you move the mouse. When the pointer is on the command you want, click the mouse's left button; that is, press it and release it. When I tell you to do this, I'll simply use the phrase "click left on" the given command.

The mouse's right button sometimes provides shortcuts to the commands' branches (subcommands). We'll examine the right-button shortcuts as we go along. There are other times when the right button does the same thing as the left button. In those cases I'll tell you to click either button.

To use the mouse to return to Document mode, position the pointer in any area below the window border and press both of the mouse's buttons. Be sure to click the buttons simultaneously.

COMMAND BRANCHES   Many of the listed commands branch into additional commands. For example, the Transfer command branches into nine other commands (the Transfer Save command, the Transfer Load command, and so on). When you activate the Transfer command, the word COMMAND (below the left edge of the window) changes to the word TRANSFER, as shown in Figure 2.2. The nine words to the right of TRANSFER are the Transfer subcommands.

While the computer displays one of the subcommands, pressing Ctrl-Esc or Shift-Esc will cause Word to back up to the main command level. Press the Esc key to get back to editing your document.

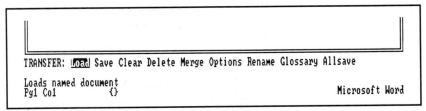

Figure 2.2: The Transfer command

With the mouse, you can also enter Document mode directly from the branch levels. Just click both buttons at any point below the window border.

Let's try this procedure with the Transfer command. To activate the Transfer command,

*M*OUSE
Activate the Transfer command by clicking left on it (see Figure 2.3).

1. Press the Esc key to enter Command mode.

2. Press T for Transfer. Notice that the word COMMAND changes to TRANSFER and its subcommands appear in the command area.

To return to Document mode, press the Esc key.

*M*OUSE
To return to Document mode, click both buttons on any spot below the window border.

For most commands, these are the normal ways to reenter Document mode. A couple of the main commands behave differently: the Gallery and Help commands. Both commands require you to choose their Exit subcommand to return. Let's look at the Gallery command as an example.

THE GALLERY COMMAND The gallery is a collection of formatting styles for style sheets, an advanced use of Word (see Chapter 17). When you type G to activate the Gallery command, anything you have

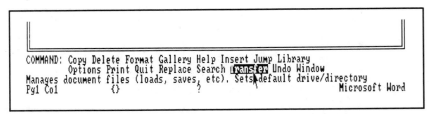

Figure 2.3: Using the mouse to issue the Transfer command

typed on the screen disappears momentarily. The Esc key does not reactivate Document mode. However, you will see the message

Select style or press Esc to use menu

The clues that you've chosen the Gallery command are this message and the word GALLERY that appears in the bottom-left corner of the screen (see Figure 2.4). To return to editing, you must select the Exit command. When you do, your document will reappear.

It would be a good idea to visit the gallery now, so you can view what's on exhibit and, most important, learn how to get out. To activate the Gallery command,

1. Press the Esc key.

2. Type G for Gallery. Notice how the screen changes.

To return to Document mode, type E for Exit.

THE UNDO COMMAND   One last command we want to practice using now is a powerful but benevolent command: the Undo command. You invoke it by

1. Hitting the Esc key

2. Typing U for Undo

Shortcut:

Shift-F1

The Undo command will correct a wide variety of command errors (accidental deletions, for instance) or editing changes you decide you don't like after all. If you ever find yourself saying "Oh no," try the Undo command immediately. It will probably work.

M O U S E

Click either button on Gallery to activate it. To leave the gallery, click either button on Exit.

M O U S E

Invoke Undo by clicking either button on it.

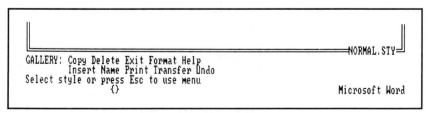

Figure 2.4: The Gallery command

If you have not made any changes, attempting an Undo will cause Word to display the message

No edit to Undo

There are some commands on which you can't use the Undo command (see Table 2.1). With those, the chance of error is less, because they either ask you for confirmation before they are executed or perform an action of no great consequence.

Because the Undo command highlights material that it undoes, you can use it to highlight even when you don't have an error to fix. For instance, to highlight some material you just typed, invoke the Undo command twice. The first Undo will remove what you typed,

Table 2.1: Commands and Undo

COMMAND	UNDO IT?
Copy	Yes
Delete (Delete key)	Yes
Format	Yes
Gallery	No, use Exit
Help	No, use Exit
Insert (Insert key)	Yes
Jump	No
Library	Yes, except Library Run
Options	No
Print	No
Quit	No
Replace	Yes
Search	No
Transfer	No, except Transfer Merge
Undo	Yes (you can undo the Undo)
Window	No

and the second one will restore the material and highlight it. You may find it easier to evaluate your changes this way—you'll get the "before and after shots" of an edit.

THE MESSAGE AREA

Below the command area resides a line known as the *message area*. It's the mailbox that contains messages from Word to you. When you press Esc to activate Command mode, Word displays the message

Copies selected text to scrap or to a named glossary entry

This message is a description of the Copy command. It appears because the Copy command is the one initially highlighted. The message changes to explain whatever command is highlighted. To move the highlight from command to command, you can use the arrow keys on the directional keypad. You can also use the Tab key to move the highlight forward and Shift-Tab to move it backward. The Home and End keys move the highlight to the beginning (the Copy command) and end (the Window command), respectively. Note that the commands are arranged in alphabetical order.

Highlight the Undo command that we just examined by pressing the End key and then the ← key. The explanation

Undoes last edit or command

then appears in the message area.

As you work with Word, keep an eye on this message area. Besides providing descriptions, it will often let you know what you need to do next.

THE PAGE AND COLUMN NUMBERS

T IP

Word provides you with two macros, **next_page.mac** and **prev_page.mac**, that allow you to display the next and previous pages quickly (see Appendix C).

The page number of the document on display is located in the bottom-left corner of the screen. If you instruct Word not to paginate automatically as you edit (which it normally does in release 5), Pg1 will be displayed here. We will cover the numbering process when we look at printing in Chapter 3. The column number (Co1) for the cursor's postion appears next to the page number. This indicates the cursor's location on the screen from left to right (usually 1 to 60) and adjusts as you move the cursor. Word defines a column as the width of one standard alphanumeric character.

THE SCRAP AREA

The area identified by the curly braces below the message area is the *scrap area*. Word uses it to hold scraps of text that you have deleted or are moving from one place to another. We'll see how this area works a little later in this chapter.

THE HELP QUESTION MARK

If you have a mouse, a question mark appears at the bottom center of the screen. You can use the mouse to point to it when you need help with a command. We'll examine Word's Help feature, with and without the mouse, toward the end of the chapter.

THE LOCK AREA AND THE LOCK KEYS

To the left of the words Microsoft Word in the lower-right corner of the screen is an area that is probably blank. This is the *lock area*. Release 5 has twelve abbreviations that can appear in six positions in the lock area (see Figure 2.5); they indicate the status of the lock keys. (There's also one command that behaves like a lock key.)

Lock keys operate much like the Shift Lock key on a typewriter; that is, you push them once to lock them (turn them on), and you push them again to release them (turn them off). Keys that are activated and deactivated in this way are also called *toggles* or on/off keys.

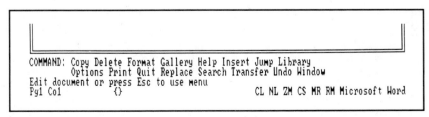

Figure 2.5: Codes in the lock area

Generally, I recommend that you keep the locks turned off, toggling them on only when you need them. After you use them to accomplish a task, it's a good idea to turn them off again immediately. There is one exception, however: NL. See the ''Num Lock (NL)'' section, which follows.

Since you haven't begun to use the lock keys, the screen's lock area should be blank. If any codes do appear there, consult Table 2.2 and turn them off by pressing the appropriate keys.

Table 2.2: Lock Codes and Their Meanings

POSITION	DISPLAY PRIORITY	CODE	MEANING	CHANGE WITH
1	High	LY	Layout	Alt-F4
	Low	CL	Caps Lock	Caps Lock key
2	High	LD	Line Draw	Ctrl-F5
	Low	NL	Number Lock	Num Lock key
3	High	ZM	Zoom window	Ctrl-F1
	Low	SL	Scroll Lock	Scroll Lock key
4	High	CS	Column Selection	Shift-F6
	Low	EX	Extend	F6
5	High	MR	Mark Revisions	Format revision-marks Options command, add revision marks setting
	Low	OT	Overtype	F5
6	High	RM	Record Macro	Shift-F3
	Low	ST	Step Macro	Ctrl-F3

You can see up to six of the twelve lock codes at a time, as shown in Figure 2.5. Each code is assigned to one of the six positions from left to right, as listed in Table 2.2. Each position only displays one of its two assigned codes at a time. If you turn on both locks assigned to the same position, only the lock with high priority will appear.

Let's look at some of the most commonly used lock keys. We'll study others as we need to use them. While reading about a lock key, you may wish to lock and release it so you can observe its abbreviation in the lock area.

CAPS LOCK (CL)   The Caps Lock key is almost the same as the Shift Lock key on a typewriter. Unlike a Shift Lock, however, it locks only capital letters; the number keys on the top row will still type numbers, and the punctuation keys will also type their lower symbol. To type the upper symbols on these keys, you must use one of the two Shift keys, even when Caps Lock is on.

Look at the screen and press the Caps Lock key once; you will see the CL appear in the lock area, indicating that Caps Lock is on. Press the key again and the CL disappears, indicating that Caps Lock has been released.

When Caps Lock is on, a "shifted" letter produces a lowercase version of the letter. For example, if you press Shift-Q (holding the Shift key down while you press the Q key), with Caps Lock on, you will get a "q."

Experiment with the Caps Lock key. Type a few letters, with Caps Lock on and with it off. You can use the Backspace key to erase what you create.

NUM LOCK (NL)   The white keys on the right side of the keyboard make up the numeric keypad. They are numbered 0 through 9, plus the decimal point, and they include arrows and other directional indicators. The Num Lock key changes the operation of these keys.

Each number key, except the 5 key, has a directional function ($\rightarrow$, $\leftarrow$, Del, End, and so on) below its number. If you press these keys when the Num Lock key is off, these functions are performed. When Num Lock is on, NL appears in the lock area on the screen, and pressing the keys types their numbers instead. In addition, using

Shift with these keys reverses the effect. That is, a shifted key with Num Lock on is the same as having Num Lock off.

If you have an enhanced keyboard, you can leave Num Lock on, since you can use the directional keys that are between the alphanumeric keys and the keypad. Otherwise, Num Lock should be off.

SCROLL LOCK (SL)   The Scroll Lock key also alters the way that the keypad operates. The keys continue to operate as directional keys, but they position the text differently as you move through it. We will look at this scrolling action when we work with additional windows. Because you won't normally want Scroll Lock on, SL should not show in the lock area.

EXTEND (EX)   You lock and release Extend by pressing the F6 key. If you see EX on the screen in the lock area, it means Extend is on. Press the F6 key to turn it off.

Many Word operations, such as deleting text, are accomplished by first designating your chosen text with the highlight. Turning Extend on anchors the highlight at the chosen point. From there you can extend or stretch the highlight with any directional key.

Unlike other lock keys, once Extend has accomplished a task, it turns off automatically. You can also release this lock without issuing a command, by pressing the F6 key a second time. If you see your cursor stretching as you try to move it, check the lock area to make sure the EX code isn't listed there.

OVERTYPE (OT)   Overtype is turned on and off by pressing the F5 key. It, too, should be off.

Normally, as you insert characters in your document, anything you add will cause material after it to be moved to the right and down in the document. If Overtype is on, however, anything you type will replace what is already on the screen, character by character.

Turning on Overtype also causes the Backspace key to operate differently: it highlights material in reverse, starting with the spot where you turned the lock on. Since you will rarely need to type over material or use the Backspace key in this fashion, the normal condition for Overtype is off.

Keep an eye on the lock area. If something unusual occurs when you press a key, check to see that you haven't accidentally turned on one of the lock keys. If you have, just turn off the lock key indicated by the abbreviation.

OUTLINE LOCKING

Microsoft has provided an outline processor built into the word processor. Two function keys operate as lock keys with regard to outlines. However, Word does not use the lock area to indicate that you've activated these keys. Instead, it uses the bottom-left corner of the screen.

The Outline View key (Shift-F2) switches the screen's window from Document mode to Outline view. If Outline view is on, the page and column numbers in the bottom-left corner of the screen are replaced by the highlighted word ''Text'' or ''Level'' followed by a number (see Figure 2.6). If the Outline Organize key (Shift-F5) is on, the word ''Organize'' will appear instead. Until we work with the outliner in Chapter 16, these keys should be off and you should see the regular page and column numbers in the bottom-left corner of the screen.

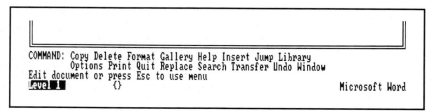

Figure 2.6: Outline view turned on

TYPING A DOCUMENT

You should now be familiar with the Word screen's window, command area, message area, page and column number area, scrap area, ? symbol, and lock area. As we proceed, remember to keep an eye on the message area for messages from Word. In addition, double-check occasionally that the lock area is blank and the page and column numbers are displayed on the bottom left.

Before you begin creating your first Word document, the screen should be clear. If you have experimented with some text, use the Backspace key to erase your experiments from the Word window.

We will be typing the announcement that appears in Figure 2.7. Please follow the directions here for typing it.

If, as you type, you find that your typing does not match the examples (odd indents, spacing, and so forth), it may be that another user has made some changes in Word's standard style elements. The margins or the NORMAL.STY style sheet may have been altered in your copy of Word. To correct such problems, see Chapters 9 and 15.

TABBING TO INDENT

Look at the example. The first thing you'd want to do is indent the paragraph. Although you could use the Spacebar to do that, it's easier to use a tab. Word accommodates you in that it has already set tab stops, one at every five spaces. The settings can be changed, and we will study tabbing methods in Chapter 11. For now, all you need to know about the Tab key is that by pressing it you will move to the first preset position.

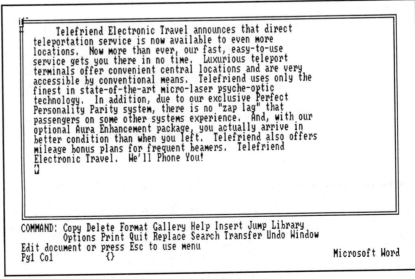

Figure 2.7: Telefriend's service announcement

Press the Tab key once to indent the first line of the paragraph. (There's yet another way to perform a first-line indent; you'll learn how when we study formatting in Chapter 5.) The cursor should move to the right five spaces. If it does not, the Options command's default tab width setting may have been changed (see Chapter 11).

WORD WRAP

To enter the document's text, begin by typing the first line. Use the Shift key to type the capital "T" in "Telefriend." Stop after you type the "t" in "direct":

Telefriend Electronic Transport announces that direct

When you type in the next word, watch the screen as you type it one letter at a time. Type the word

teleportation

It jumps to the next line! Word automatically moves the cursor and the word you're typing when you reach the right margin. This feature is called *word wrap,* because the words "wrap" down to the next line.

As you process words with Word, you should allow word wrap to handle line endings whenever possible, so that you press the Enter key only to end a paragraph. When you press the Enter key, you create a carriage return— sometimes called a *hard return.* This has a special purpose in Word. If used unnecessarily, it can produce unwanted effects in subsequent edits. The return that Word puts in when it wraps words is called a *soft return.*

Now continue typing the material you see in Figure 2.7, pressing the Enter key only at the end of the paragraph.

CORRECTING MISTAKES

If you catch a mistake just after you make it, you can use the Backspace key to erase back to the error. Then just retype.

If you don't catch an error right away, leave it in place for now. Once you're done, you'll learn how to correct mistakes without retyping: by editing the material.

CHANGING WHAT YOU'VE TYPED

Now that you've typed in the material in Figure 2.7, the truly productive advantage of word processing—editing—begins. With computers, *editing* is the name for the process of changing text that has already been typed.

THE DIRECTIONAL KEYPAD

To revise anything in the text, you must first move the cursor to it so you can tell Word where you want to make the change. Right now, your cursor should be on the line below the paragraph, just below the "E." To move it anywhere else, you can use the directional keypad or the mouse.

The keys labeled ↑, ↓, ←, and → move the cursor one character or one line in their respective directions. The Home and End keys move the cursor to the beginning and end of a line, respectively. The Page Down and Page Up keys move the cursor forward and backward one window of material at a time. When these keys are used with Extend, they expand the cursor. The pages inside the back cover provide a quick reference to the various operations of the directional keys.

Let's say that on rereading the announcement, you decide it would be more effective if you added the word "even" before "better condition" on the third line from the end.

First make sure that none of the lock keys are on by checking the lock area on the screen. Then use the ↑ key to move the cursor to the appropriate line. Tap it three times so that the cursor lands on the "b" in "better." (Never loiter on keys. Tap and release them quickly.) To move the cursor with the mouse, click left on "b."

Now watch the screen and type the word "even." As you do, notice that the rest of the line moves to the right. Not only that, but the word "offers" is pushed over to the next line. This feature is called *automatic reform.* (Some word processors do not perform this job automatically.) Automatic reform keeps material within the preset margins.

Press the Spacebar once after typing the word ''even'' to separate it from ''better.'' At this point your screen should look like the one shown in Figure 2.8.

Now let's make another change in our paragraph. Let's change the period after ''Travel'' in the last line to a colon, so that the sentence reads

Telefriend Electronic Travel: We'll Phone You!

With the mouse, you can move the cursor to the period quickly by clicking left on it. With the keyboard, begin by tapping the ↓ key twice to bring the cursor down to the bottom line.

MOVING WORD BY WORD

Now you could use the → key to get to the period after ''Travel.'' But there are quicker ways to get there. We'll move the cursor one

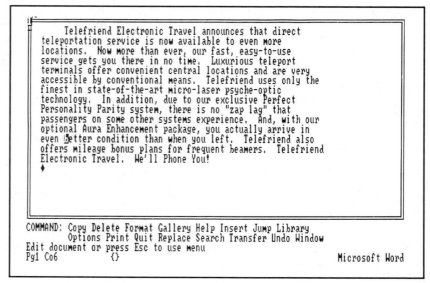

Figure 2.8: Adding a word

word at a time rather than one letter at a time. To do that, we use the Next Word key (F8) or Ctrl-→.

USING THE NEXT WORD KEY   Press F8 once, and the cursor expands to include the entire word "Electronic." Press F8 again, and the word to its right, "Travel," is highlighted. These moves demonstrate how the Next Word key works. On the first stroke, it highlights whatever word the cursor is on (even if most of the current word is actually to its left). With the second stroke (and all that immediately follow), the highlight moves to the next word to the right.

Lastly, press the → key. We don't use the Next Word key here because it would highlight too much material for our purposes. As you work with Word, you'll come to understand how it determines a word. In the meantime, just keep an eye on the cursor as you use the keys.

USING THE CTRL-→ COMBINATION   Word provides another means of moving one word at a time. You can use Ctrl-→, which moves the cursor to the first character of the next word. Thus, once the cursor is on the "E" in "Electronic," we could also reach the period by pressing Ctrl-→ two times: the first time brings the cursor to the "T" in "Travel," and the second time brings the cursor to the period, which it is treating as the next "word." Unlike F8, Ctrl-→ does not highlight the words as the cursor is moved. Your cursor should now be over the period, which we want to change into a colon.

DELETING WITH THE DELETE KEY

You have already experimented with the Backspace key, which erases as it backs up. Just as there are other ways to move, there is another way to delete, and that's by using the Delete key.

Press the Delete key now, and the period is deleted. (With the mouse, click right on the Delete command.) Now just type the colon. Your screen should look like Figure 2.9.

The period has not completely disappeared, however. If you look at the bottom of the screen, you'll see it in the scrap area, between the braces:

{.}

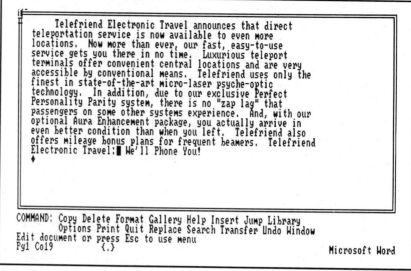

Figure 2.9: Using the Delete key

The Delete key deletes whatever is highlighted and places it in the scrap area. This can be any amount of material—a single character, a sentence, a paragraph, or more. Large amounts of material are abbreviated with ellipses (...). Material erased with the Backspace key is not placed in the scrap area.

Once in the scrap area, deleted text can be inserted somewhere else by using the Insert key. Let's try that.

INSERTING WITH THE INSERT KEY

Pressing the Insert key inserts whatever is in the scrap area to the cursor position. To see this, let's first use the Delete key to delete a word (and thereby replace the period that is currently in scrap). Let's say that we want to move the word ''some,'' which appears about two-thirds of the way down the example. We'll change the sentence that reads

passengers on some other systems

to read

some passengers on other systems

Here are the steps:

1. Press the ↑ key four times to bring the cursor up to the word "some."

2. Press the F8 key to highlight the word "some" and the space that follows it.

3. Press the Delete key. The word "some" and the space are deleted and pop into the scrap area, replacing the period that was there.

4. Now you want to move to the word "passengers." You could use the ← key, but once again, there's a quicker way. The Next Word key has a sister key—the Previous Word key (F7). Push it twice, and the highlight moves word by word to the left, highlighting the word "passengers."

Now watch the screen carefully. With the word "passengers" still highlighted, press the Insert key. Your screen should look like Figure 2.10. As you can see, when you insert from the scrap area, there might be enough room at the end of the previous line for some of the scrap words. (There was enough room there for "some," even though there had not been enough for "passengers.") If any can fit there, that's where they'll be sent. The cursor ends up on the character following the newly inserted material.

Notice that when you insert from the scrap area an identical copy of the inserted material remains behind in scrap. Thus, it could be inserted in another spot as well. Material will remain in scrap until you send some other material to scrap or until scrap is cleared—by quitting Word, for instance.

MAKING TWO PARAGRAPHS OUT OF ONE

Suppose we decide to start a new paragraph at the point in the text that begins "Telefriend uses only." How do we split this single paragraph into two?

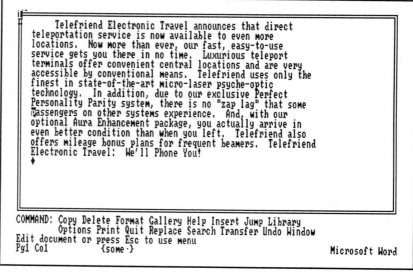

Figure 2.10: Inserting from the scrap area

First, bring the cursor to the "T" in "Telefriend," by following these steps:

MOUSE

Click left on the "T" in "Telefriend" to move the cursor to this character and press Enter to make a new paragraph.

1. Press the ↑ key four times to move the cursor to the correct line.

2. Press Ctrl-→ five times and the cursor is in position.

3. Press the Enter key to insert a hard return between the words "means" and "Telefriend."

Now, with the cursor still on the "T," press the Tab key. A tab is inserted, creating the indent for the second paragraph (see Figure 2.11).

INSERTING
NEW MATERIAL AT THE BEGINNING

Documents always need a title, so let's add one to ours. First you need to get to the top line in the window. To do this, we'll use one of the directional key combinations. Press Ctrl-Home to bring the

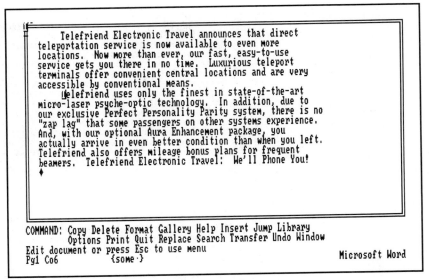

Figure 2.11: Making two paragraphs out of one

cursor to the top-left corner of the window. (In this case, pressing Ctrl-Page Up would accomplish the same thing.) To use the mouse to reposition the cursor, click either button on the top-left corner of the window (at the tab indent).

Notice how the cursor has expanded to include the entire tab area. The tab is a character: just like letters or numbers, it was created by pressing one key, so it is one character. The cursor is still highlighting one character, albeit a large one.

Turn on the Caps Lock key. Then start typing the title

MORE DIRECT SERVICE AVAILABLE

Remember that as you type, the tab character remains between the material you are typing and the word ''Telefriend.''

When you finish typing the ''E'' in ''AVAILABLE,'' turn off the Caps Lock key. Then press the Enter key. (The order of these last two actions is not important. However, it is always a good idea to turn off the lock keys as soon as you are done with them.) Voilà! Your screen should now look like Figure 2.12. By hitting the Enter key, you inserted a hard return between the word ''AVAILABLE'' and the tab character.

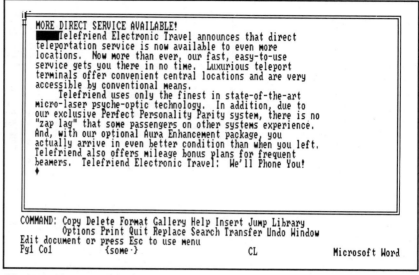

Figure 2.12: Adding a title

Using this technique, you can add any amount of material to the beginning of a document: a word, a sentence, a paragraph, or more. Simply move the cursor to the beginning of the document and type.

SAVING A DOCUMENT

When you type material, the information is entered into the electronic area of the computer's memory, called RAM (random-access memory). RAM storage, however, is only temporary. When you turn off the computer (or if the power fails), everything that was in RAM disappears (much like one of those "magic" slates, where lifting the top sheet causes all your images to vanish). If this were to happen, you would lose the material you've typed in so far. So it's important to *save* documents to disk regularly. Follow these steps to save your document with the Transfer Save command:

1. Press the Esc key.

2. Type T for Transfer.

M<u>OUSE</u>

To save your document, click left on Transfer. Then click left on Save. After typing in a name as prompted, click right on TRANSFER SAVE.

Shortcut:

Ctrl-F10

3. Type S for Save. The computer responds with

TRANSFER SAVE filename:

4. Type in a name to assign to the document; in this case let's use the name ANNOUNCE. Type ANNOUNCE with either lowercase letters or capitals.

5. Register the command by pressing the Enter key.

T IP

Word 5 allows you to save documents in different formats, so you can exchange them with other systems (see chapter 18).

Word will then present you with the summary sheet (Figure 2.13). Word's summary sheets allow you to provide information about your documents that you can later tap for retrieval purposes. However, they are entirely optional. We won't work with the summary sheet at this time. To bypass the summary sheet, simply press Enter or Esc. (To bypass summary sheets with the mouse, click either button anywhere on the words SUMMARY INFORMATION.) We'll study summary sheets in Chapter 10.

If you attempt to save and get the message

File already exists. Enter Y to replace or Esc to cancel

```
MORE DIRECT SERVICE AVAILABLE!
   Telefriend Electronic Travel announces that direct
teleportation service is now available to even more
locations. Now more than ever, our fast, easy-to-use
service gets you there in no time. Luxurious teleport
terminals offer convenient central locations and are very
accessible by conventional means.
   Telefriend uses only the finest in state-of-the-art
micro-laser psyche-optic technology. In addition, due to
our exclusive Perfect Personality Parity system, there is no
"zap lag" that some passengers on other systems experience.
And, with our optional Aura Enhancement package, you
actually arrive in better condition than when you left.
Telefriend also offers mileage bonus plans for frequent
beamers. Telefriend Electronic Travel: We'll Phone You!

SUMMARY INFORMATION
   title:                                  version number:
   author:                                 creation date: 04/04/89
   operator:                               revision date: 04/04/89
   keywords:
   comments:
Enter text
Pg1 Col          {some ·}                            Microsoft Word
```

Figure 2.13: Summary sheet

it indicates that you already have a file on the disk with the same name as the one you're trying to save. By typing Y you'll destroy the file on the disk, and the file in the window will be saved under that name. N will cancel the save and activate Document mode. Pressing the Esc key also cancels the save but returns you to Command mode.

As Word is saving, you'll see the message

Saving file

Once the save is successful, a message displays the number of characters in the file you've just saved.

A document name can be up to eight letters or numbers long. Word automatically adds the extension .DOC for document. This indicates that Word (and you) created the file. Hence, this file is named ANNOUNCE.DOC on the disk. You can tell this because the full name now appears in the bottom-right corner of the window border. (Other programs that create files sometimes have naming conventions, too. For instance, dBASE adds .DBF to its data files.)

The name you assign should be a simple file name that relates directly to your document's subject matter. Avoid clever abbreviations such as SY07BE6X, since the simpler names are always easier to spot and recall.

In addition, it's a good idea to use only letters and numbers. Some of the symbols and punctuation marks, such as ! and -, are also usable, but some are not. Letters and numbers, however, are always accepted.

Saving is an important step in creating a document. As you work through this process, Word is standing by to assist you in two ways— by offering help on the screen and by giving you the ability to customize Word itself. Let's look at these two features and then finish the chapter, appropriately enough, with the Quit command.

T IP

The supplied macro **save_selection.mac** allows you to save a highlighted chunk of the displayed document as a separate document. See Chapter 15 and Appendix C for more on macros.

GETTING HELP

When you are at the main command level, you can get help by invoking the Help command or by selecting the ? symbol at the bottom of the screen with the mouse. Because this provides you with Help screens for all the Word features (the first screen tells you how to use Help), it is most useful when you can't remember the exact name of the command you want to use or are unsure which command would be the most appropriate for the task you want to do.

Word also provides another means of accessing help when you are already working with a command and find that you need reminders on how to use it. For example, suppose you need some more information as you are performing the Transfer Save command. The Help command in the command menu is not available at this point, because you're using the Transfer Save command. But you can still get help now by pressing Alt-H. That is, press the Alt key, hold it down, and tap the H key. If you have a mouse, you can get help by clicking either button on the question mark at the bottom of the screen. Word then displays information for the particular command with which you're working. Since you just finished saving your document, let's try out Alt-H on the Transfer Save command.

M O U S E
Click left on Transfer and click left on Save to invoke the Transfer Save command. To get help on this command, click either button on the question mark.

1. To invoke the Transfer Save command, press the Esc key and type T for Transfer and S for Save.

2. Access Help for the Transfer Save command by pressing Alt-H.

At this point you should see the screen shown in Figure 2.14. This screen gives you information on the Transfer Save command. Thus,

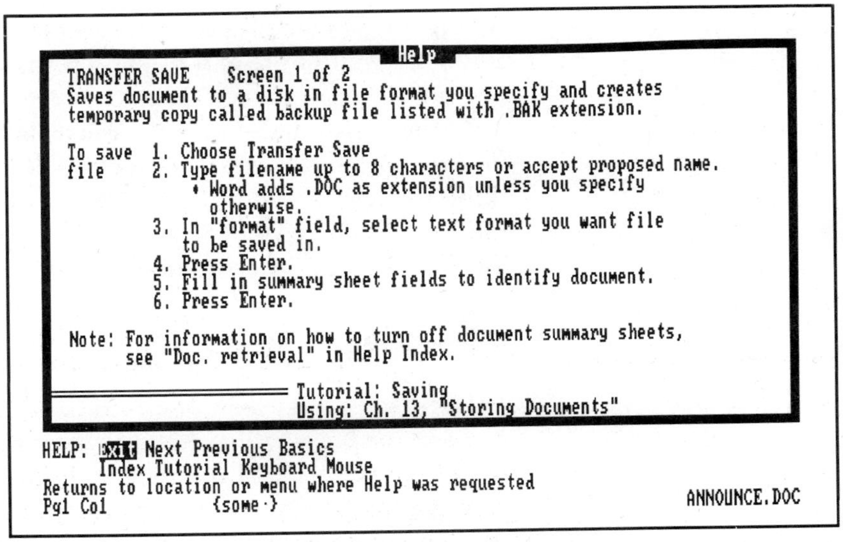

```
                              ═Help═
 TRANSFER SAVE      Screen 1 of 2
 Saves document to a disk in file format you specify and creates
 temporary copy called backup file listed with .BAK extension.

 To save  1. Choose Transfer Save
 file     2. Type filename up to 8 characters or accept proposed name.
              • Word adds .DOC as extension unless you specify
                otherwise.
           3. In "format" field, select text format you want file
              to be saved in.
           4. Press Enter.
           5. Fill in summary sheet fields to identify document.
           6. Press Enter.

 Note: For information on how to turn off document summary sheets,
        see "Doc. retrieval" in Help Index.

                            ═══════ Tutorial: Saving
                                    Using: Ch. 13, "Storing Documents"

 HELP: Exit Next Previous Basics
        Index Tutorial Keyboard Mouse
 Returns to location or menu where Help was requested
 Pg1 Co1          {some·}                                  ANNOUNCE.DOC
```

Figure 2.14: The Transfer Save Help screen

you get help specific to the command you are performing (sometimes referred to as *context-sensitive* help). This contrasts with typing Esc H, which just introduces the initial Help screen from the main command level.

When you call for help, you move into Help's unique structure. There are two basic components to Help: Help screens and the tutorial.

THE STRUCTURE OF THE HELP SCREENS

At the bottom of this Help screen, you see a line of words that is displayed on all Help screens in Word 5:

HELP: Exit Next Previous Basics

You can select one of these Help commands by typing its initial letter (E, N, P, or B) or by clicking either button on it. Also, pressing the Page Down key performs the same action as the Next command, and the Page Up key is the same as using the Previous command.

New in Word 5

Help screens operate much like a Rolodex card file. That is, each of the numerous Help screens follows one after the other, just like cards in the file. If you select Exit on this line (or Resume for Word release 4), Word will redisplay the screen exactly as it was when you asked for help. If you select either Next or Previous, you advance through the circular file in one direction or the other. If you were to go all the way to the end of the screens using the Next command, pressing Next again would return you to the beginning.

For example, let's say you issued the Help command from the main command menu (or selected Basics) and then proceeded through Help screen by screen by typing N for Next or using the Page Down key. With release 5, you would see Help screens on the following topics in this order:

Help

Commands

Selecting

Editing

All commands, listed alphabetically, Copy through Window

Bulleted List

File Formats

Calculating with Word

Columns

Cross-Referencing

Keyboard

Mailing Labels

Macros

Mouse

Networks

Outlining

Show Layout

When you reached the last Help screen and pressed the Page Down key or issued the Next command, you would see the first screen again, which is simply titled Help. (This is the screen that explains how to use Word's Help feature.)

Of course, it isn't practical to page through the Help screens each time you have to find information on a particular topic. Fortunately, in addition to context-sensitive help, Word provides another way to reach these topics. On the second line of commands toward the bottom of the Help screens, you'll see the words

Index Tutorial Keyboard Mouse

If you choose Index, Word will display a listing of the topics given previously as well as others that simply cross-reference those topics under other names. You can then choose a topic from the listing and proceed directly to its Help screen.

USING THE TUTORIAL

Choosing Tutorial activates Word's interactive tutorial, which requires 384k of available memory to run. Then you can choose either Lesson or Index. Use Lesson to learn about the particular command you were working on when you entered Help. Use Index to look at a listing of all the lessons and pick from among them.

Once you make your choice, Word may ask you to insert the "Word Essentials" disk. This will happen if you don't have a hard disk or if you haven't copied the tutorial lessons to your hard disk. The lessons take up too much room to fit on the Word Program disk. When you've completed the lesson or lessons in which you are interested, choose Quit to redisplay the initial Help screen, leaving the tutorial.

As you can see, pressing Alt-H (or selecting the ? symbol with the mouse) provides you with a direct path to the particular Help screen or tutorial lesson you require at the moment. When working with a Help screen, you may want to flip through the adjacent screens for related material.

Using Help's Keyboard command is especially handy. It summarizes the operations of the function keys (see Figure 2.15). You can select this command after invoking the Help command or pressing Alt-H.

*M*OUSE

Click left on Help's Mouse command to review the use of the mouse with Word.

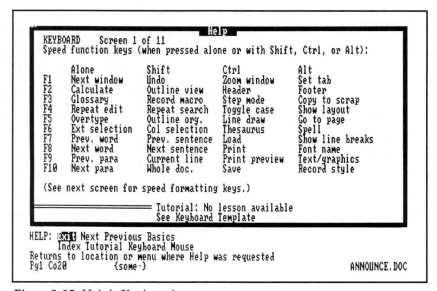

Figure 2.15: Help's Keyboard screen

RETURNING FROM HELP

To get out of Help, invoke the Exit command. No matter where you were or what you were doing when you entered the Help structure, everything is exactly as you left it.

Now let's look at a second way Word can assist you—by allowing you to tailor the program so you feel most comfortable.

CUSTOMIZING WORD

With the Options command you can customize your copy of Word to suit your taste. When you invoke the Options command (by pressing the Esc key and then typing O for Options, or by clicking either button on Options), the screen shown in Figure 2.16 appears on your monitor.

From here, you can use the Tab key or the directional keys to reach one of the options (show borders, paginate, default tab widths, colors, mute, and so on). Once at an option, you indicate your choice

MOUSE

With the mouse you can both make a choice and register the command simultaneously by clicking right on the choice.

```
MORE DIRECT SERVICE AVAILABLE!
Telefriend Electronic Travel announces that direct
teleportation service is now available to even more
locations.  Now more than ever, our fast, easy-to-use
service gets you there in no time.  Luxurious teleport
terminals offer convenient central locations and are very

WINDOW OPTIONS for window number: 1        show hidden text:(Yes)No
          show ruler: Yes(No)      show non-printing symbols:(None)Partial All
         show layout: Yes(No)               show line breaks: Yes(No)
        show outline: Yes(No)                 show style bar: Yes(No)

GENERAL OPTIONS mute: Yes(No)                 summary sheet:(Yes)No
             measure:(In)Cm P10 P12 Pt         display mode: 3
            paginate:(Auto)Manual                    colors:
            autosave:                       autosave confirm: Yes(No)
           show menu:(Yes)No                    show borders:(Yes)No
         date format:(MDY)DMY              decimal character:(.)
         time format:(12)24                default tab width: 0.5"
        line numbers: Yes(No)              count blank space: Yes(No)
        cursor speed: 3                   linedraw character: (|)
        speller path: C:\WORD\SPELL-AM.LEX
Enter number
Pg1 Col          {some·}                                  Microsoft Word
```

Figure 2.16: Selecting the Options command

by using one of the following methods:

- Typing its initial letter.

- Pressing the Spacebar until it is highlighted.

- Clicking left on it.

- Entering a value.

- Pressing F1 or clicking right to display the list of possible choices and selecting the choice you want from it.

Your choices are not registered, however, until you press the Enter key or click either button on the word Options.

Once your choices for these settings are registered, they remain in place until you change them again. When you use the Quit command to leave Word, your choices are recorded in Word's MW.INI file.

We'll examine most of these options in detail as we need them, but let's look at a few of the important ones now.

SHOWING NON-PRINTING SYMBOLS

Initially, show non-printing symbols is set to None. (This was called the visible option before release 5.) By changing it to Partial or All, you can see some normally invisible codes displayed on the screen. For instance, when it is set to Partial you can see where you pressed the Enter key (indicated by a paragraph mark). When you set it to All, you can also see where you pressed the Tab key (shown with a small right arrow) and where you pressed the Spacebar (indicated with a suspended dot). Table 2.3 lists all the codes that can be made visible, along with their meanings. Those that are unfamiliar will be explained as they come up later in the book.

The window in Figure 2.17 shows how the document we've typed looks when show non-printing symbols is set to All. Set yours the same way and compare your document. Verify that you only pressed the Enter key at the end of each paragraph (not at the end of each line), used the Tab key in the right spots, and haven't included any unnecessary spaces.

Table 2.3: Codes You Can Make Visible with Show Non-printing Symbols

SYMBOL	MEANING	HOW CREATED
Codes Shown with Partial		
↓	New line code	Shift-Enter
¶	Paragraph return	Enter key
-	Optional hyphen	Ctrl-hyphen
↔	Hidden text	Alt-E
Additional Codes Shown with All		
→	Tab character	Tab key
• (suspended dot)	Space	Space bar

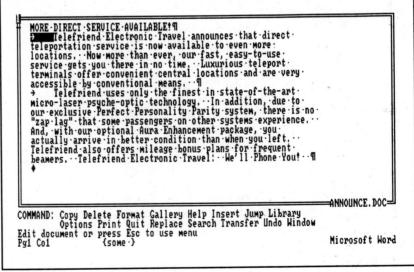

Figure 2.17: Text with show non-printing symbols set to All

DISPLAYING MORE OF THE DOCUMENT

The show menu setting controls the display of the command menu. Selecting No hides the menu until you press the Esc key. If you are using a mouse, you can display the menu by clicking either button somewhere on the bottom line of the screen (except on the question mark).

By turning the menu off, you gain an extra three lines of document display (see Figure 2.18). Messages appear on the bottom line until you type something or use the mouse. Three lines may not seem like a lot of extra room, but when you are editing large documents or split the screen, those few additional lines are truly a blessing.

You can also display more of the document by removing the border that surrounds the document window. Doing so will show two more lines of the document as well as two more columns of characters in each line. To turn off the borders, change show borders to No. Figure 2.19 shows the screen with both the menu and the screen borders turned off.

Note that you can have the screen borders off only when there is just one window showing. Should you turn off the borders and then

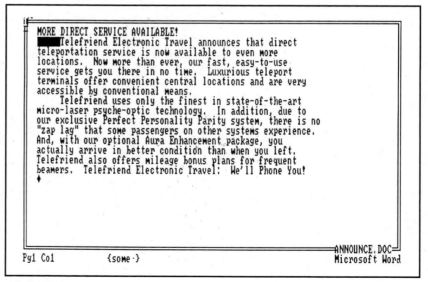

Figure 2.18: The screen with show menu set to No

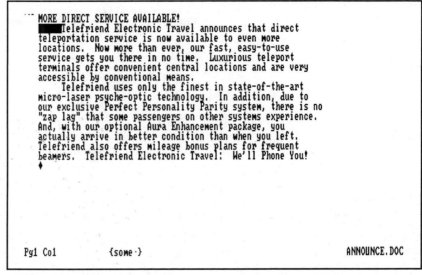

Figure 2.19: The screen with show menu and show borders set to No

split the window into additional windows (Chapter 8), the borders will reappear. They disappear again when you go back to using only one window.

If you have a mouse, be aware that it uses the borders to perform some operations (such as scrolling and splitting windows). If you remove the borders, you will have to use the keyboard to perform these operations.

SILENCING THE BEEP

You may have heard the beep on your computer, usually indicating an error. Changing the mute setting in the Options command to Yes will silence that beep in Word. If you are annoyed or embarrassed by this audible indication of your errors, you may want to turn it off.

DISPLAYING LINE NUMBERS

Sometimes users like to know their position on the page from top to bottom. This can be helpful, for instance, when you're trying to fit everything on one page. You can make Word display the number of the line where the cursor is located. To do this, change the line numbers setting to Yes. Word will then show the line number in the bottom-left corner of the screen between the page number and the column number. For instance, when the cursor is at the very beginning of the document, the bottom-left corner will show

Pg1 Li1 Co1

Although the line number will be displayed correctly in Word 5 (unless you have turned off automatic repagination), Word 4's line number will not necessarily be accurate until you print or repaginate the document. Also be aware that displaying the line number may slow down the operation of the program slightly.

New in Word 5

As we work with Word, you'll see that it sometimes inserts blank lines into which you cannot type text; it does this when automatically double-spacing, for instance. Normally, Word does not count such blank lines when displaying line numbers. If you want Word to include these blank lines, change count blank space to Yes.

ADJUSTING THE CURSOR SPEED

Depending on your computer and your preference, as you move through your document, you may find that the cursor travels too quickly or slowly. To adjust the speed of the cursor, use the cursor speed setting. Initially set at 3, it can be a number from 0 to 9 (slow to fast).

SAVING AUTOMATICALLY

New in Word 5

With release 5, Word will automatically back up your documents as you work. This can prove to be a valuable safety net for you, should your computer crash in the middle of your work (due to a power outage, for instance). If you want Word to provide this service for you, decide how often you want Word to save. Enter a value for the number of minutes into the autosave field. If you want Word to check with you just before each save, set autosave confirm to Yes.

Be aware that autosave is a form of backup saving, creating only temporary files in the Word directory. Do not use it in place of standard saving with the Transfer Save command (Ctrl-F10).

T IP

You can set up several versions of Word, customizing each in a different way. For example, you could have one with the menu displayed and the beep sound on, and another with those features turned off. Place each copy of Word in its own directory and change to the appropriate directory to begin the program (see Appendix A).

ADDITIONAL CUSTOMIZING

In addition to the Options command's remaining settings, you can customize other features of Word by using the Format Division Margins command and by editing the NORMAL.STY style sheet. I discuss margins in Chapter 9 and style sheets in Chapter 17.

With this command and style sheet, you can change the standard setup for margins, paper size, typeface size and style, and the spacing between paragraphs. You can also set up right-justified, double-spaced, numbered pages (or some other combination) as standard, if you so desire. You can even create several standard setups and choose one of them by making the disk or directory that it is in active when you start up Word.

QUITTING WORD

We've covered a lot of material in these two chapters, and you probably feel like taking a break before you go on. (You should practice quitting now even if you plan to continue.) Before you end a session with Word, you should always save the file you're working on. Then leave the program by performing these steps:

MOUSE

Click left on Quit to leave Word.

1. Press the Esc key.

2. Type Q for Quit.

When quitting Word, you may receive the message

> Enter Y to save changes to document, N to lose changes, or Esc to cancel

T IP

The Quit command stores customized settings, set with the Options and Print Options commands, in the MW.INI file. It also stores the status of the locking keys. That way, the settings are the same when you next use Word.

This indicates that you neglected to save before issuing the Quit command. Type N if you do not wish to save your work or press the Esc key to cancel the Quit command. Typing Y will activate the Transfer Save command before quitting. (Before release 5, specifying Y only works if you've already assigned a name to the document, generally by a previous save.)

With the mouse, you can quit and save at the same time by clicking right instead of left on the Quit command.

Now that your document is safely stored on disk, you've completed an important phase en route to your mastery of Microsoft Word. You've created a document from scratch, made changes to it, and saved it on the disk for future use.

The process of saving a file on disk is called a file operation. In the next chapter, we will look at other file operations. We will also get our first taste of printing and learn about all the printing options Word offers.

3

Printing Your Document

Fast Track

- Copies: the number of copies you want to print
- Draft: the quality of the printed document
- Hidden text and summary sheet: the instruction to print these features or not
- Range and page numbers: the portions of the document to print
- Widow/orphan control: the instructions to print stranded lines or not
- Queued: documents printed in succession while you edit
- Paper feed: the instructions for feeding paper to your printer or the paper tray to use
- Duplex: double-sided printing

To print while you edit,   75

invoke the Print Options command, set queued to Yes, and then issue the Print Printer command. To interrupt queued printing if necessary, use the Print Queue Stop or Pause command.

To print directly from the keyboard,   77

use the Print Direct command.

To change to manual pagination,   78

use the Options command. You can then use the Print Repaginate command to preview page breaks. You can also insert permanent page breaks in your document by pressing Ctrl-Shift-Enter.

To send the printed output to disk,   79

issue the Print File command.

IN THIS CHAPTER WE WILL USE THE TRANSFER LOAD command to retrieve our previously saved document so we can explore a variety of ways to print this document. In Chapter 4, we will examine the rest of the Transfer subcommands.

There are many printing options that are available to you with Microsoft Word. With them, you can print part of a document, work on one document while you print another, do a quick draft, or produce finished documents.

RETRIEVING YOUR DOCUMENT

In Chapter 2 you typed a simple document, made some changes to it, and saved it on the disk for later use. You saved it by using the Transfer Save command.

When you perform the Transfer Save command, Word transfers an exact image of your document to the disk. An identical copy of the document also remains in RAM. When you quit Word, however, the image of the document in RAM fades away. The image of your document on the disk, on the other hand, remains there indefinitely.

To print a document, Word requires that you reintroduce the document into RAM; that is, you must *load* a copy of it from disk so it appears in the window. You load with another of the Transfer commands, the Transfer Load command.

To issue the Transfer Load command, follow these steps:

M O U S E

Click right on Transfer to select the Transfer Load command.

1. Press the Esc key.

2. Type T for Transfer.

3. Type L for Load.

Shortcut:

Ctrl-F7

This shortcut, Ctrl-F7, and most of the function-key shortcuts, will work in either Command mode or Document mode. However, it won't work if you are in the middle of another command (if you've invoked the Options command, for instance).

The mouse method I just gave demonstrates a mouse shortcut. Because Load is the first choice on the Transfer menu, clicking right on Transfer invokes the Transfer Load command. Other mouse shortcuts operate in the same manner, working on the first subcommand. Load is the only Transfer command for which the right-button shortcut is available. The other Transfer commands require that you click left on Transfer and click left again on the command you need in the Transfer menu.

When you issue the Transfer Load command, Word responds by asking you for the name of the document you want. In many instances—when Word asks you for information like this—there are at least two ways to answer. The first is simply to type in your choice. The second is to use the F1 key or click right to choose from a list. If you have difficulty loading the document by typing the name, you may have mistyped it. If so, try using the second method of choosing the document name.

SPECIFYING THE FILE TO LOAD

T I P

Word allows you to convert files created with other programs so you can load them as Word documents (see Chapter 18).

The command area now displays

   TRANSFER LOAD filename:

indicating that Word has branched to a subset of the Transfer command. Notice that a highlighted box, like a second cursor, appears after the word filename. This box indicates a field where Word is asking you for the name of the file you want it to load. Also note that the message area says

   Enter filename or press F1 to select from list

This refers to the two methods of specifying the document you want Word to load. Let's discuss the first method now but wait to load our file with the second method.

ENTERING A FILE NAME   If you were to use the first method at this point, entering a file name, you would type the name of the document you wanted to load

   ANNOUNCE

using either capitals or lowercase letters.

With a field such as this, you can edit what you've typed (or what Word presents for you). The F7 and F8 keys move the highlight one word, left and right respectively, just as they do in a document. The F9 and F10 keys, which are directly below these keys, move the highlight one character left and right. The Delete and Backspace keys also operate as they do with a document. You may wish to experiment with these keys now, but don't press Enter yet.

If, after you type a name and press Enter, you see the message

File does not exist. Enter Y to create or Esc to cancel

it means that Word is unable to locate the file as you've typed it. If you know that the file exists, press the Esc key and try selecting it with the second method. (Typing Y would tell Word to create a blank file using the name you just typed.)

SELECTING FROM A LIST   Let's try loading our sample file by selecting it from a list. Here are the steps for doing this:

M O U S E

Click right on filename to display a list of files.

1. Make sure that nothing appears in the filename field. (Use the Delete or Backspace key if necessary.)

2. Display a list of files by pressing F1.

At this point, with Word 5, you'll see a listing that looks something like Figure 3.1. The exact display will depend on how your system is configured. You should see our document's name, ANNOUNCE. If not, you may have the wrong directory; just read on.

You can select the file you want from among those listed. Word screens your files and normally shows only files it created; those with a .DOC ending (more on this in Chapter 10).

M O U S E

To select the ANNOUNCE file, click right on it.

Make your selection and register your choice:

1. Use the arrow keys to highlight ANNOUNCE.

2. Press the Enter key. The document is now loaded and appears on the screen.

New in
Word 5

You can also use this display to change directories or disk drives temporarily, which allows you to load a document from a different

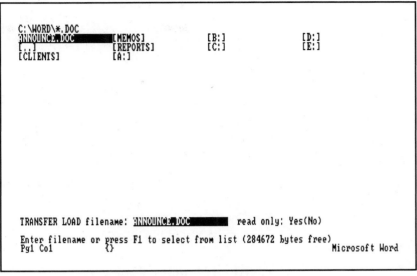

Figure 3.1: Selecting ANNOUNCE.DOC from a list

location. At the top of the screen is the current path. The bracketed letters with colons, such as

[A:]   [B:]   [C:]

indicate the drives Word has detected in your system. Bracketed words, such as

[CLIENTS]   [MEMOS]   [REPORTS]

T IP

You can also press F1 instead of Enter to select a new drive or directory.

indicate subdirectories of the current directory, which is WORD in Figure 3.1. The bracketed double dots [..] stand for the parent directory of the current directory. To change drives or directories, follow the same procedures as with selecting a file: use the arrow and Enter keys or the mouse's right button. For example, to select the parent directory, move the highlight to the bracketed dots and press Enter or click right on it.

To change directories for your entire Word session, use the Transfer Options command (see Chapter 4 for more information).

WRITE-PROTECTING YOUR LOADED DOCUMENT

When you issue the Transfer Load command, the words

read only: Yes (No)

appear on the right side of the screen. If you are only interested in looking at a document without making any changes in it, you might want to make it read only. For example, if you are printing someone else's file, you can write-protect it so that you won't change it accidentally. To do this, you first type the file name. Then, instead of pressing the Enter key, press the Tab key or the → key. Then type Y for Yes and press Enter. (With the mouse, type the file name and then click right on Yes.)

Once you have write-protected a file, you can make changes on the screen. However, if you later try to save the edited document, Word 5 will present the Transfer Save command without a document name, allowing you to make a copy of the protected file under a new name. Should you attempt to use the same file name for the copy, Word will display the message

Read-only file must be saved with a different name

To remind you that the loaded document has read-only status, Word places an asterisk (*) in front of its displayed name at the bottom-right corner of the window.

For practice, quit Word and start it up again. Then try loading ANNOUNCE.DOC again and make it read only since we just want to print it. Now that we have ANNOUNCE.DOC before us, let's print it.

5 New in Word 5

BASICS OF PRINTING

T I P

If you only specified one .PRD file during setup, you can skip this step and print your file.

When you prepare Word with the Setup program, it copies one or more of the .PRD (printer driver) files to your hard disk along with your Word program. Before you can print, you must specify which of these copied .PRD files you wish to use. You do this with the Print Options command.

Word will record the choice you make now for use whenever you print, unless you change the Print Options' printer setting again. (This and other customizing specifications are kept in a file named MW.INI.) To specify or change your choice of printers, you use the Print Options' printer option. Let's examine this command more closely.

SELECTING YOUR PRINTER

Since choosing your printer's .PRD file is an essential step in printing when you have several .PRD files, do this now.

M_O U S E_

Click left on Print to select it. Then click left on Options to activate this subcommand.

1. Issue the Print command by pressing Esc and typing P. The screen shown in Figure 3.2 will then appear.

2. Activate Print's Options subcommand by typing O.

At the upper left of the command area appears

PRINT OPTIONS:

in capitals, indicating that you have activated the Print Options command. Following this is the word

printer:

and then the name of the current printer. The message in the message area prompts you to

Enter printer name or press F1 to select from list

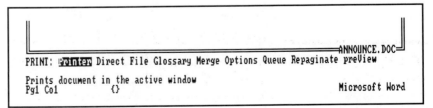

```
                                                              ═ANNOUNCE.DOC═
PRINT: Printer Direct File Glossary Merge Options Queue Repaginate preView
Prints document in the active window
Pg1 Co1          {}                                     Microsoft Word
```

Figure 3.2: The Print command

M O U S E

Click right on printer
to display the list.
Then click right on
your printer's name to
select it.

We'll select a name from the list to tell Word which .PRD file to use.

1. Display the list by pressing F1. It will resemble that shown in Figure 3.3.

2. Using the directional keys, highlight the name of the printer you wish to use and press the Enter key to select it.

The .PRD files that are listed will vary according to what you selected with the Setup program (Appendix A). Once you make your selection, Word duplicates your printer's .PRD file in RAM.

Now Word is prepared to print. At this point, neither Document mode nor the initial command level is active; the Print command remains in effect instead. Word generally reverts to Document mode when you are finished with a command. After the Print Options command, however, the Print menu (Figure 3.2) is displayed because Word assumes that you want to print now.

If you did want to reactivate Document mode, you could do so by pressing the Esc key. With the mouse, you could click both buttons at any point in the command area.

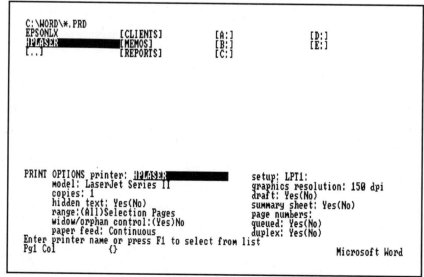

Figure 3.3: Selecting a printer name from the Print Options list

PRINTING YOUR FIRST DOCUMENT

Now that the printer is specified, let's go ahead and print. First verify that your printer is ready. It should be plugged in, turned on, connected to the computer, and online. It should have paper inserted and the cover should be closed.

Once you have checked that your printer is ready, type P or press the Enter key to choose Printer. This instructs Word to print the ANNOUNCE.DOC file. Remember, pressing Enter gives the command because Printer was already highlighted.

If the printer had not been properly prepared, Word would display the message

Printer is not ready

followed by

Enter Y to continue or Esc to cancel

You would either have to prepare the printer and type Y or abort the printout with N or the Esc key.

However, this is not the case here, so Word treats the Printer command as its go-ahead signal, using the options you have established. With impact printers (typically, printers that use a daisy wheel), you may receive a message that begins

Enter Y after mounting

If you do, just type Y to start printing.

If you're using a driver with downloadable fonts, you'll see the message

Enter Y to download New Fonts, A to download All Fonts, N to Skip

For now, you can press A for All. You'll get to examine the individual fonts in Chapter 7.

Assuming all goes well, Word displays the Print Printer command level (Figure 3.4), the document is printed, and you are the proud parent of your first printout from Word.

M O U S E

Click either button on Printer to send ANNOUNCE.DOC to the printer.

```
PRINT PRINTER:

Printing page 1 of ANNOUNCE.DOC
Pg1 Co1              {}                           Microsoft Word
```

Figure 3.4: The Print Printer command

PRINTING QUICKLY

Now that you have set up your printer and printed your first document, you can print documents quickly by using the options you have already established. To run the Print Printer command directly, you simply do this:

MOUSE

Click right on Print to send the displayed document to the printer.

1. Press Esc and type P for Print.

2. Type P or press Enter for Printer.

Shortcut:

Ctrl-F8

As it prints, Word counts the number of lines and words in the document. The results appear in the message area. Blank lines are not counted, and neither are lines containing running heads, footnotes, and page numbers, features that we'll study later in the book.

If there is a problem (for instance, if you forgot to insert the paper in the printer), press the Esc key to interrupt the printing. Press Esc a second time to confirm that you want to cancel the printing. Then follow the instructions in the message area. You may also want to check Chapter 1 for hints on how the printer operates.

When you look at the printed copy, you may see slight differences between the printed version and its electronic counterpart in the window. Specifically, there may be more or fewer words on each line. This would happen if your printer's pitch is something other than pica (10 pitch, or 10 characters to the inch). In Chapter 8 we'll see the various ways you can get Word's screen display to match the printed version of your documents.

MORE PRINT COMMANDS

As you work, you will probably find a variety of circumstances that demand flexibility in the printing capabilities of your word processor.

Word provides that flexibility. In fact, Word's printing capabilities are among its finest features.

EXAMINING PRINT OPTIONS

Earlier in this chapter, you used the Print Options command to tell Word which printer you are using. Let's look at some other features of the Print Options command and discuss why you might want to change the options from their usual settings.

First, issue the Print Options command again by pressing Esc, typing P, and typing O. (With the mouse, select it by clicking left on Print and then clicking either button on Options.)

Notice the many settings that follow the name of your selected printer (see Figure 3.3). Remember that you gain access to a command's options and settings by moving the highlight with the directional keys or the Tab key, or by clicking left on the setting you want.

Practice moving the highlight now. As it moves, it highlights an option (one or several words together) or it lands on a word that is in parentheses (and the parentheses disappear). These choices in parentheses represent the current settings and are the standard choices for the various options.

You can change the settings by typing the initial letter of your choice, for instance, Y for Yes or N for No. With some blank fields, you can see and select choices by using the F1 key. If you're unsure of how to change a particular option's setting, check the message line for a prompt after you move to that option.

When you press the Enter key, you register the settings displayed on the screen. If you press the Esc key instead, you will be returned to the Print command level, and the settings will be left the way they were.

With the mouse, you can change the settings by clicking left on a new choice—such as Yes or No. You can register your choices in two ways:

- To change just one of the settings, you can choose it and register the Print Options command (returning to Print) by clicking right on the setting. (You can also use this method for the last setting after you have made all the other changes you want.)

- After changing all the settings, click either button on PRINT OPTIONS.

Let's examine each option of the Print Options command in turn and discover how they work.

SETUP   The setup option normally reads

LPT1:

This setting indicates into which connection (*output port*) of your computer the printer is plugged. (Some computers have more than one place to connect a printer.) You can change the setting if you have more than one printer connected to the computer at the same time or if you have a serial printer. You can view the other choices for this option by pressing F1 or clicking right on setup. For example, if you have a serial printer, press F1 and select

COM1:

so that Word knows to direct output for the printer to the serial port.

5 New in Word 5

MODEL   The model option provides the name of the printer for which the .PRD file listed as the printer setting is designed. For example, it may show

LaserJet Series II

if the printer option is set to HPLASER. This helps keep you from accidentally using the wrong .PRD file for the printer. As we'll see when we examine the use of fonts in Chapter 7, the same printer can have more than one .PRD file available for its use.

5 New in Word 5

GRAPHICS RESOLUTION   Release 5's graphics resolution option allows you to specify how sharp the pictures you import should be. Pressing F1 or clicking right on the option displays a list of the resolution settings that are available for your printer. You'll learn how to insert pictures in Chapter 18.

COPIES   Let's say it's 4 P.M. when you complete a report and you have a meeting to go to in fifteen minutes. Tomorrow morning you will need twelve "originals" of the report for twelve board members. Just specify 12 for the copies setting, check that you have enough paper, and start the printing. Once you have made sure the printer is printing correctly, you can go to your meeting, leaving Word and your printer to do the rest. The entire document will be printed out once, and then the printing process will be repeated eleven more times.

DRAFT   Now imagine that you have created an exquisite document on the disk. It is a solicitation for attracting first-rate clients. Your document will have a number of fine features, including *microjustification,* which places minute spaces between letters and words to create even right margins.

No matter how fast your printer is, fancy features like microjustification can slow it down. By requesting a draft-quality document, you tell Word to ignore some features for the printout. The features remain in the document, and you can have them back just by changing the draft setting. If you wish to have the printer print a draft-quality version of one of your documents, type Y for Yes when the draft option is highlighted. Printing may be faster, but it will not look as nice. Usually, No is highlighted, indicating that you want the print in your document to be of the standard higher quality.

HIDDEN TEXT/SUMMARY SHEET   We'll examine the use of these options when we study the hidden text and summary sheet features in Chapter 18 and 10, respectively. For now, you can leave them set to No.

RANGE/PAGE NUMBERS   Suppose that after you've printed a long document, you find errors on pages 16, 21, and 30 through 33. Instead of reprinting the entire document, you can tell Word to print only part of the document after you fix the errors. To specify that you want to have only certain pages printed, move the highlight to the range option and type P for Pages. Then move to the page numbers option and type in the pages you want to reprint. Use commas to separate pages and dashes to indicate page ranges. In this example, you would type

16, 21, 30–33

T I P

Once you've chosen
Pages for the range
setting, you *must*
specify some page
number. You will be
unable to move the
highlight out of the
page numbers field
until you do. If you
decide not to print
pages, type any page
number to leave the
field and then change
the range setting.

You can also indicate page ranges with a colon (:) instead of a dash. If
you want to print to the end of the document but are unsure of the
last page number, just type a very high number—one you're sure is
greater than the last page number.

Choosing Selection as the range setting will cause Word to print
only the part of the document that you have designated by highlighting. We've seen how to highlight one word and we'll see how to highlight more than that in Chapter 5.

WIDOW/ORPHAN CONTROL Many word processors avoid
separating the first or last lines of a paragraph on one page from the
rest of the paragraph on the subsequent or previous page. Such
stranded lines are referred to as *widows* and *orphans*. Normally, Word
will automatically keep this from happening with its default Yes for
this setting. Change the setting to No if you don't want Word to prevent such occurrences (perhaps for a draft version of a document, for
instance).

QUEUED Let's assume that just when you are about to print a
long document, you realize that you also need to do rush edits on a
different document. Both jobs need to get done. Specifying Y for Yes
as the queued setting will allow you to do one job while the printer
does the other.

Queued printing can require quite a bit of free disk space, as Word
must make a copy of the file being printed. The copy is automatically
deleted once the printing process is complete.

The default setting is No. We will demonstrate queued printing in
a moment, so specify Y for Yes now.

PAPER FEED/DUPLEX Word can deal with the variety of ways
that today's printers handle paper. The paper feed option's Continuous choice, which stands for continuous paper, is the default. If your
printer requires you to hand-feed pages one at a time, you should
specify Manual. Manual stops the printer before each new page
(including the first one). Word then displays the message

Enter Y to continue or Esc to cancel

Insert the next sheet and type Y. If you wish to stop printing, press the Esc key instead.

Your printer might have one or more paper trays that feed the printer. Bin1, Bin2, and Bin3 designate the respective trays. Selecting Mixed causes the printer to take a sheet from Bin1 only for the first page; the sheets for all other pages come from Bin2. If you are printing reports, for example, you could place letterhead or some kind of cover stock in the first tray (Bin1), and use plain paper in the second tray (Bin2). Bin3 is not used by the Mixed setting. Often, it contains 14-inch paper.

If your printer has an envelope feeder, you will also have the Envelope option available. Use it to feed envelopes to your printer.

5 New in Word 5

In addition, Word 5 has a duplex option to support printers that print on both sides of a sheet. Set it to Yes when you want to take advantage of this handy feature.

5 New in Word 5

Once you have set your choices in the Print Options command, use the Enter key to register them. With the mouse, click either button on PRINT OPTIONS.

As you can see, Word has powerful printing capabilities. Potentially, one of its greatest time-saving features is its ability to allow you to queue files to be printed. Let's take a closer look at queuing now.

PRINTING WHILE EDITING

When you print a document, the computer normally focuses all of its attention on printing to get the job accomplished efficiently. It will not allow you to edit anything while the printer is printing. This is fine for short documents or if you can leave the computer and do other work.

When you need to print and edit simultaneously, however, you can specify queued printing with the Print Options command. This feature, which is also called *background printing,* is especially useful if the computer will be tied up with printing a long document. In general, I recommend you use queued printing if you spend much time at your computer.

Although printing in this way requires more disk space than printing without the queued option (since queued printing creates a temporary file on the disk), this should not be a problem unless you are running out of room on your hard disk. If queued printing does not work, you could still print in the normal fashion.

Let's try a queued printing with our ANNOUNCE.DOC file (suppose you want to start working on a memo you need to get out right away). Make sure you have specified Yes for the queued setting in the Print Options command and that the printer is ready. The Print menu should be displayed. If the Print Options menu is still on the screen, register the settings, which returns you to the Print menu. If you're in Document mode, press Esc to activate Command mode and issue the Print command.

Once you have the Print menu displayed, type P for Printer (or with the mouse, click left on Printer). After you issue the command, you are in Document mode and can continue editing ANNOUNCE-.DOC (note that these changes will not be printed) or clear the window to start your urgently needed memo.

When printing without queuing, you use the Esc key to stop printing. With queued printing, however, pressing the Esc key will simply take you into Command mode. To stop a print job, you use the Print Queue command instead (see Figure 3.5).

TIP

Be careful not to confuse Print Queue Continue with Print Queue Restart.

Use Print Queue Stop to halt the operation completely. Use Pause if you just want to pause temporarily; then specify Continue when you're ready to go on. Use Restart to start the printing all over again from the beginning of the document.

You can also use queued printing to print one document after another automatically. Let's say that you have completed ten letters to various customers and colleagues. It's time to print them, and you want to set up the computer and forget about it. You can "queue up" (that is, line up) the documents to be printed, one after another. You don't have to wait for each document to be printed, but you do have to wait for all of them to be formatted, a process that prepares them for printing.

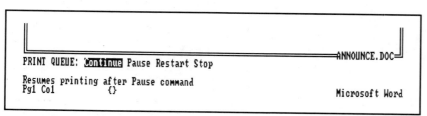

Figure 3.5: The Print Queue command

T *IP*

Word supplies the **chainprint.mac** macro, which you can use to create a document that lists files for printing. The macro prints those files one after another with consecutive page numbering (see Chapter 15).

To queue up documents, follow these steps:

1. Load the first document.

2. Set the Print Options queued option to Yes.

3. Issue the Print Printer command.

4. Wait for Word to finish formatting the first document (check the message area).

5. Repeat the procedure for subsequent documents.

Once all the documents are formatted and queued, you can let the computer handle the printing.

To recap, when you print without queued printing, the computer is off and running. There is nothing it can do except print. Queued printing allows you to send several documents to the printer at once and continue working, but it requires additional storage space on the disk.

PRINTING DIRECTLY FROM THE KEYBOARD

Suppose you don't want to store what you are printing at all? You can use the Print Direct command to print text without making a copy of it on the screen or disk.

If you have a form to fill in, such as a COD tag or something else that demands precise placement, with the right type of printer you can insert the form, position it carefully, and issue the Print Direct command (see Figure 3.6). This command sends whatever you type directly to the printer. Line by line or character by character (depending on your printer), it prints what you type. In effect, it turns your computer into a typewriter. The typed material is not stored anywhere by the computer.

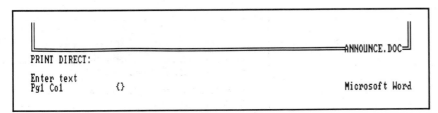

Figure 3.6: The Print Direct command

T *I P*

With some printers, like the LaserJet, this command works poorly, if at all. Instead of using the Print Direct command, print a selected portion of text (as discussed under "Examining Print Options") or clear the window (Chapter 4), enter text, edit, and print.

New in Word 5

Unfortunately, this command makes your computer behave a bit too much like a typewriter. For example, if you make an error and have a character-by-character printer, the Backspace key does not delete as it goes back; instead, one character will be printed on top of the other and you will have to reenter the entire text. In addition, your typing does not appear on the screen at all.

To end the Print Direct mode, press the Esc key. The computer will be returned to Document mode.

SPLITTING THE DOCUMENT INTO PAGES

When you print a document, Word calculates how many lines fit on the page. It tells the printer when to move the paper to the next page. This process is called *pagination.*

Word 5 paginates documents automatically, calculating page breaks as you work. It indicates a page break—that is, the point where one page ends and another begins—by widely spaced dots, like so:

. . . .

However, Word still provides you with the option of having it paginate only on demand. Thus when you get documents back from your boss or editor with revisions marked, you can rig Word so the page numbers on the screen continue to agree with those of the original document, even as you edit the changes on your computer. This makes it quick and easy to locate material, especially if you use the Jump Page command (see Chapter 10).

To configure Word in this fashion, activate the Options command and change the paginate setting to Manual. With manual pagination (or with earlier versions of Word), if you ever want to see where your pages will break or how many pages your document has *before* you print, you use the Print Repaginate command (see Figure 3.7). When you issue the Print Repaginate command, Word will ask you if you want to confirm the page breaks. If you are fussy about where you want them in the document, specify Y for Yes. To let Word break the pages where it sees fit, specify N for No and press the Enter key.

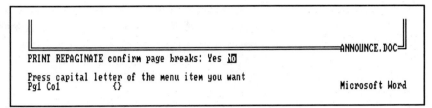

```
PRINT REPAGINATE confirm page breaks: Yes NO

Press capital letter of the menu item you want
Pg1 Col              {}                              Microsoft Word
```

Figure 3.7: The Print Repaginate command

T *IP*

Word supplies you with **next-page.mac** and **prev-page.mac**, two macros that allow you to move to the next or previous page of a document (see Chapter 15).

When you indicate that you want to have a say in how the pages break, Word first displays the upcoming printout accurately. Then, one page at a time, Word highlights the spot it suggests for starting a new page. The message

Enter Y to confirm page break or use direction keys to reposition

appears in the message area.

You can use the ↑ and ↓ keys to adjust the page break symbol. Since you can't lengthen the paper (at least not at this point), you can only have the page break placed prior to the locations suggested by Word. Position the highlight as you desire and type Y.

As you type your document, you can also insert permanent page breaks by pressing Ctrl-Shift-Enter. For example, you might want to do this to create a title page for your document. You can easily distinguish these page breaks from Word's automatic ones since the dots representing the permanent page breaks are spaced together more closely. When you perform the Print Repaginate command, Word says

Enter Y to confirm or R to remove page break

when it encounters these permanent page breaks. This gives you an opportunity to check these breaks as well.

You can cancel the Print Repaginate command at anytime by pressing the Esc key.

PRINT FILE/PRINT MERGE/PRINT PREVIEW

These final features make advanced use of Word. The Print File command is used to send the formatted version of your document that is ready for your printer to a file on the disk. This way, even without Word, you (or anyone) can later print the document on paper by using the operating system commands. If you use this command, you'll be asked to give the output a file name. See Chapter 14 for more on the use of this command in translating documents.

I discuss the Print Merge command in detail in Chapter 14. Let's glance at it here, though, to become more familiar with Word's terminology for its commands.

The main use for Print Merge is in the production of personalized form letters. You type a list of names and addresses into one file and a form letter into another file. When you print, the two files are *merged,* resulting in a letter for each person that appears to be individually typed to him or her.

Note that this result is quite different from the result you get using the Transfer Merge command. Transfer Merge brings a copy of an entire document permanently into another.

As you can see, some of the command words used by Word have a variety of meanings. Used in one place, a word means one thing; used in a different place, it has a completely different purpose. It helps to associate the entire command phrase with its respective operation.

Finally, Print preView allows you to see documents as they will appear in print. We'll examine this command in Chapter 8.

We have now studied the creation of a document in its entirety— you typed it, fixed minor errors, and printed it. In the process, you have discovered a variety of ways that documents can be printed. When you used the Transfer command to save your file, load it again, and print, you probably noticed the other Transfer commands listed on the Transfer menu. We'll look at those commands in the next chapter, creating a new sample document to demonstrate their use.

4

File
Fundamentals

Fast Track

IN THE LAST CHAPTER, WE LOOKED AT THE METHODS for going from disk back to RAM, the computer's ephemeral storage, using the Transfer Load command. Load, the first subcommand on the Transfer menu, precedes the following subcommands in release 5:

Save Clear Delete Merge Options Rename Glossary Allsave

We will examine Transfer commands in this chapter.

The Transfer commands concern themselves with entire documents, and their storage on disk. Using them, you can combine documents, move them, erase them, or change their names. We will also examine the ways in which related Transfer activities can be put to use. Let's begin by working with a new document. (You can also use Word's Library Document-retrieval system, as we'll see in Chapter 10.)

CREATING A NEW DOCUMENT

First of all, we need a clear screen, the equivalent of a clean desktop, so that we can create our new document. When you start up Word, the screen is clear (unless you use one of the alternative startup methods, described in Appendix A). If you've been working on another document, though, you need to remove it before creating a new one. To do this, you use the Transfer Clear command. In the process, you can save the document with which you've been working.

CLEARING THE SCREEN

The Transfer Clear command clears the screen so that you can work on a new document. As long as you save or have saved the document you are clearing, clearing the screen will not eliminate the document on the disk.

When you perform a Transfer Clear command, you can choose All or Window (see Figure 4.1). What does it mean to clear "All"? That is, what can Word clear besides the window? For one thing, the scrap area will be cleared if you select All but will not be cleared if you select Window. More important, you can use All to clear out some of

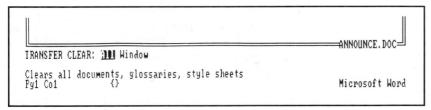

```
TRANSFER CLEAR: ▓█▌ Window                                          ═ANNOUNCE.DOC═

Clears all documents, glossaries, style sheets
Pg1 Co1              {}                                     Microsoft Word
```

Figure 4.1: The Transfer Clear command

the features we will work with later—style sheets and glossaries—right along with the window. Choosing Window with this command will allow these features to be carried forward to the next document. Since clearing just the window is quicker than clearing everything and you haven't used the more advanced features yet, let's simply clear the window for now.

To issue the Transfer Clear Window command, follow these steps:

M *O U S E*

Click left on Transfer. Then click left on Clear to select this subcommand.

1. Press the Esc key.

2. Type T for Transfer and C for Clear.

The screen now reads

TRANSFER CLEAR: All Window

indicating that we are at Transfer Clear command's level, with the All option highlighted. Since we just want to clear the window, type W or click left on Window.

At this point either the window will clear immediately or you will see the message

Enter Y to save changes to document, N to lose changes, or Esc to cancel

if you have not saved your changes to the document since you loaded it. Even if you only hit a letter on the keyboard accidentally while Word was in the Document mode, Word paid attention and alerts you that you made a change.

When you get this message, decide if you want to save the changes you've made to your document. If you do, type Y for Yes. If you don't wish to save the changes, type N for No.

ENTERING THE TEXT

With our screen cleared, we are now ready to type some new material. Type in the note you see in Figure 4.2. To create the blank lines, just press the Enter key. That is, start by typing

    Steve –

Then press the Enter key twice and continue to type in the body of the note.

Remember to use the Enter key only at the end of the paragraph, not after lines within it. After you type your name at the end, press the Enter key so that the cursor is positioned as it is in the figure.

ADDING TEXT BY EDITING

Now let's say that after you have read the note on the screen, you decide to add some material to it. To do this, we'll edit the note so that it looks like Figure 4.3. Bring your cursor to the word ''within''

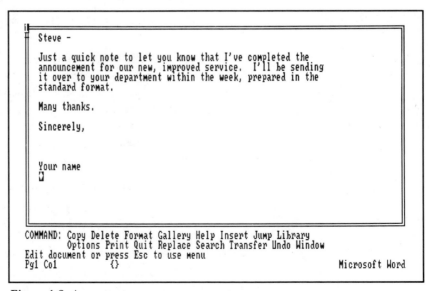

Figure 4.2: A new note

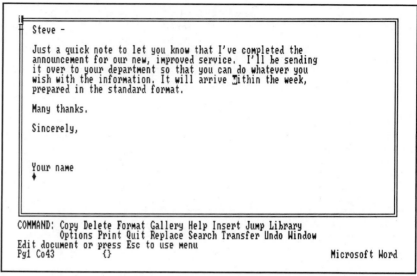

Figure 4.3: The revised note

toward the end of the paragraph by following these steps:

M*O U S E*

Click either button on the "w" in "within." By using the left button, you highlight the character. By using the right button, you highlight the word.

1. Press the ↑ key repeatedly until the cursor lands on the word "it."

2. Press the Next Word (F8) key or Ctrl-→ so that the cursor reaches the word "within." (Use the F8 and F7 keys or Ctrl-→ and Ctrl-← when you want to jump from word to word. Many users of word processing systems get into the unfortunate habit of using only the cursor-movement arrows. Instead, remember to use these "word-movement" keys to speed up your editing.)

3. Now without pressing Enter, type the words

   so that you can do whatever you wish with the information. It will arrive

Then press the Spacebar once to place a space between "arrive" and "within." Watch how Word automatically reformats your paragraph as you type.

SAVING WHAT YOU'VE DONE SO FAR

It's a good idea to save your documents regularly. Remember that the material on the screen is in constant jeopardy due to a possible power failure or other problems you may encounter, such as a full disk. Your documents are safe only when they are successfully saved on a disk.

MO U S E

Click left on Transfer. Then click left on Save to select this command. After entering the file name NOTE, click either button on TRANSFER SAVE to register the command.

1. Activate the Transfer Save command by pressing the Esc key, typing T for Transfer, and typing S for Save.

Shortcut:

Ctrl-F10

2. Respond to the prompt

   TRANSFER SAVE filename:

   with a document name. This time, let's use the name NOTE. Type NOTE using lowercase or capital letters (the computer always stores the file name as capitals in any case).

3. Register the command by pressing the Enter key.

If you are trying to save a file and Word displays the message

   Not a valid file

it means that the name you are using is violating one of the operating system's rules for naming files: it may have a space or more than eight letters in it. Your error will be highlighted. You can remedy the error by pressing the Delete key and then pressing Enter.

You could also get a message that says

   File already exists. Enter Y to replace or Esc to cancel

This indicates that the name you've specified is already being used by another file in that directory. A Y response would replace that file with the one you're saving. The earlier file becomes the backup (.BAK) version of the file. (We'll discuss backup files later in this chapter.) Unless you intentionally want to overwrite an existing file with a new file, press Esc to abort the save.

SAVE INDICATOR   If you neglect to save your document for a long period of time, Word may remind you to save by displaying the word

> SAVE

on the bottom line of the screen. Word is telling you that it is starting to run out of available memory (RAM). Always save when you see this signal. If you don't, you could place your document in danger. If you ignore the warning, eventually the word will begin to flash in an attempt to get your attention.

If you save the document and the warning doesn't go away, or if you get the message

> WORD DISK FULL

you must quit Word and start it up once again, or issue the Transfer Clear All command. If your hard disk is full or nearly full, doing so will free up space on it, but it will be a temporary measure. You will probably need to delete unused files and directories.

If you've been having this problem and you forgot to quit Word before you turned off your computer, you can get rid of some files by erasing files that end with .TMP from your Word directory. For example, you could enter the DOS command

> DEL C:\WORD*.TMP

to erase temporary files that Word creates as it works. (It normally erases these files when you quit.) See Appendix B for more on working with the operating system.

MERGING DOCUMENTS

Assuming that your save has proceeded smoothly, let's say that you decide it would be appropriate to include a copy of the announcement as part of the actual note. With Word, it's easy to merge one document with another.

This is an instance that calls for the use of the Transfer Merge command. Transfer Merge can insert the announcement into the note wherever you position the cursor. By executing Transfer Merge, you both load a document from the disk and merge it into the displayed document at the cursor position.

PREPARING TO MERGE

Before we perform the merge operation, we should add a short line to the note introducing the announcement.

M_OUSE_

Click either button on the "M" in "Many" to move the cursor to it.

1. Position your cursor on the "M" in "Many" by pressing the ↓ key three times and then pressing the Home key.

As the cursor has not left the word "within," pressing the ↓ key initially moves the cursor to the paragraph mark (carriage return) at the end of the first paragraph, which is down one line and to the left of "within." On the next line, you have typed only a paragraph mark; pressing ↓ again moves the cursor to it since you have not typed anything to its right. When you press ↓ a third time, the cursor jumps down one line and back to the right, to the end of the line. Because the cursor is at the end of the line and "Many" is at its beginning, you press the Home key. This key always moves the cursor to the far-left position in the current line.

2. With the cursor on the "M" in "Many," type the line

   Here is the information that will be included:

   and press the Enter key twice. This positions the cursor exactly where we want the note to be inserted.

USING THE TRANSFER MERGE COMMAND

To get the announcement into the note on the screen, you must tell the computer to display a copy of the announcement in its new context. The announcement is still recorded on the disk, under the name ANNOUNCE.DOC. With the Transfer Merge command (see Figure 4.4), the computer can look up that file and insert its contents in the displayed document. The file is placed where the cursor is, splitting

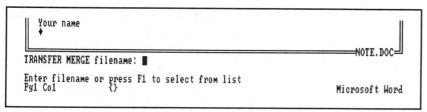

Figure 4.4: The Transfer Merge command

material that precedes and follows the cursor. (Sometimes, this look-up and display process is called *reading* the file from the disk into the current document.) Let's issue this command now.

M*OUSE*

Click left on Transfer and then click left on Merge to invoke the Transfer Merge command. To choose ANNOUNCE.DOC from the list, click right on filename to list the files and then click right on the displayed file name.

1. Make sure the cursor is where you want the file to be inserted (that is, on the "M" in "Many").

2. Issue the Transfer Merge command by pressing the Esc key, typing T for Transfer, and typing M for Merge.

3. Press F1 to display the list and use the directional arrows to select the file name from the list.

4. Press the Enter key to register your choice. Word then loads the document.

5. Press Enter again to insert a blank line between the merged document and "Many Thanks." Your NOTE.DOC file now contains the material shown in Figure 4.5.

T*IP*

You cannot use Transfer Merge to insert *part* of one file into another. For that, you have to split the window and then look into the other file. We'll explore the use of windows in Chapter 8.

The Transfer Merge command can insert one file anywhere within another file. You can insert the file at the beginning, somewhere in the middle, or at the end of the displayed file.

You can have more than one character highlighted when performing a Transfer Merge command. That is, this merge also would have worked with the word "Many" highlighted. The transferred file is inserted beginning at the spot occupied by the first character in the highlight, pushing the highlighted material below it.

SCROLLING YOUR DOCUMENT

When the merge operation is complete, you will notice that the top portion of the note has disappeared (see Figure 4.6). Because your

```
Steve -

Just a quick note to let you know that I've completed the
announcement for our new, improved service.  I'll be sending
it over to your department so that you can do whatever you
wish with the information.  It will arrive within the week,
prepared in the standard format.

Here is the information that will be included:

MORE DIRECT SERVICE AVAILABLE!
     Telefriend Electronic Travel announces that direct
teleportation service is now available to even more
locations.  Now more than ever, our fast, easy-to-use
service gets you there in no time.  Luxurious teleport
terminals offer convenient central locations and are very
accessible by conventional means.
     Telefriend uses only the finest in state-of-the-art
micro-laser psyche-optic technology.  In addition, due to
our exclusive Perfect Personality Parity system, there is no
"zap lag" that some passengers on other systems experience.
And, with our optional Aura Enhancement package, you
actually arrive in even better condition than when you left.
Telefriend also offers mileage bonus plans for frequent
beamers.  Telefriend Electronic Travel:  We'll Phone You!

Many thanks.

Sincerely,


Your name
```

Figure 4.5: Note with merged text

M_OUSE_

Point to the bottom-left corner of the window. When you do this, the pointer becomes a two-directional arrow (see Figure 4.7). Click left to move the window up or click right to move the window down. When you use the mouse to scroll a full window, lines do not overlap.

document is longer than your screen, you can view only part of it at any one time. To see the top part of a large file, you need to move the window *up* in the document. Then, if you want to go back to the bottom part, you would need to move the window *down*.

This process of moving the window up and down in the document is called *scrolling*. The name is derived from the word for a roll of continuous paper or parchment, a "scroll." You can use either the keyboard or the mouse to scroll the window. Practice these steps:

1. To move the window up through the document, press the Page Up key on the directional keypad. Notice that the window now displays the top of the note, as shown in Figure 4.8.

2. To move the window down, press the Page Down key. As you scroll, notice that a couple of the lines overlap. That is, they appear in your views of both the upper and the lower portions of the document.

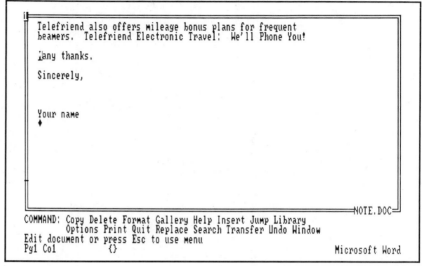

Figure 4.6: Screen display after the Transfer Merge command

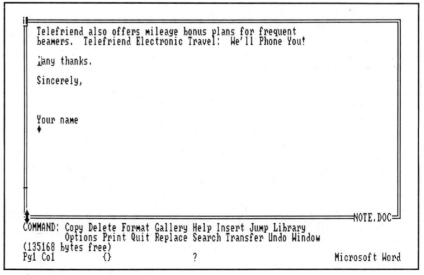

Figure 4.7: Positioning the mouse for scrolling

```
┌──────────────────────────────────────────────────────────────┐
│ ┌──────────────────────────────────────────────────────────┐ │
│ │ prepared in the standard format.                          │ │
│ │                                                            │ │
│ │ Here is the information that will be included:             │ │
│ │ ▌ORE DIRECT SERVICE AVAILABLE!                             │ │
│ │      Telefriend Electronic Travel announces that direct    │ │
│ │ teleportation service is now available to even more        │ │
│ │ locations.  Now more than ever, our fast, easy-to-use      │ │
│ │ service gets you there in no time.  Luxurious teleport     │ │
│ │ terminals offer convenient central locations and are very  │ │
│ │ accessible by conventional means.                          │ │
│ │      Telefriend uses only the finest in state-of-the-art   │ │
│ │ micro-laser psyche-optic technology.  In addition, due to  │ │
│ │ our exclusive Perfect Personality Parity system, there is no│ │
│ │ "zap lag" that some passengers on other systems experience.│ │
│ │ And, with our optional Aura Enhancement package, you       │ │
│ │ actually arrive in better condition than when you left.    │ │
│ │ Telefriend also offers mileage bonus plans for frequent    │ │
│ │ beamers.  Telefriend Electronic Travel:  We'll Phone You!  │ │
│ │                                               ═NOTE.DOC═   │ │
│ │ COMMAND: Copy Delete Format Gallery Help Insert Jump Library│ │
│ │          Options Print Quit Replace Search Transfer Undo Window│ │
│ │ Edit document or press Esc to use menu                     │ │
│ │ Pg1 Co1              {}                    Microsoft Word  │ │
│ └──────────────────────────────────────────────────────────┘ │
└──────────────────────────────────────────────────────────────┘
```

Figure 4.8: Scrolling the document

SCROLLING AND THUMBING WITH THE MOUSE

Scrolling with the mouse, unlike scrolling with the keyboard, does not move the cursor. The cursor remains with the text where it was, even if that text is now out of sight. If you were to start to type, the window would again display the stranded cursor's location. After scrolling, to move the cursor to where you can see it, click one or both buttons on any spot in the window.

With the mouse, you aren't confined to scrolling a set amount each time. To use the mouse for incremental scrolling, position the pointer somewhere on the left window border. To scroll up, click left; to scroll down, click right. The amount of scrolling you do will be determined by the pointer's position on the border. The border acts as a sort of yardstick. The lower you position the pointer, the more the window will scroll; the higher the pointer, the less the scroll. Far to the bottom approaches one window scroll; to the top, only one line. Thus, the spot you point to does not determine which *direction* you go, but rather *how far*.

Now notice the sliding marker on the left window border in Figure 4.8. It appears immediately to the left of the heading

MORE DIRECT SERVICE AVAILABLE!

This marker indicates the position of the displayed text in your document. When the window shows the beginning of the document, the marker is at the top of the border. When the window shows the end of the document, the marker is positioned at the bottom of the border. When the window displays text in between, the marker's position on the border reflects the text's position relative to the beginning and end of the document.

With the mouse, you can move this marker, and hence the window, to a general area of your document. Just as you can pick up a book and thumb through it, this operation, called *thumbing,* is designed to get you to a general area quickly.

Note that this is perhaps the only Word procedure for which there is no direct keyboard equivalent. Follow these steps to thumb through a document:

1. Move the mouse pointer to the left border of the window.

2. Position the pointer where you want to go in the document. If you wish to go, say, two-thirds of the way through the document, you'd position the pointer two-thirds of the way down the border.

3. Click both mouse buttons. The marker moves to where the pointer is, and the appropriate text is displayed.

BACKUP FILES

Now that you've changed the note significantly, it would be good to save it again. Since you've already provided a name, you can save the file quickly by pressing Esc, typing T for Transfer, typing S for Save, and pressing Enter. With the mouse, you can click left on Transfer and click right on Save. On this second save, Word creates a backup file to safeguard your document.

Backup files are created by Word every time you save a file under the same name. As a result of this save, the first version of our sample, NOTE.DOC, is renamed NOTE.BAK. On the third save, the first version will be erased and the second version will become NOTE.BAK, and so on (see Figure 4.9).

Backup files are valuable for retrieving the previous version of a file. You may need to use one if you have a problem saving your document or if you accidentally delete a document file from the disk.

Although files ending with .BAK do not normally appear on Transfer Load lists, you can load a backup file by typing its full name, including the .BAK extension. Also, you can display the backup files' names on the list by using a wild card—a symbol that stands for one or more characters in the names (see Chapter 10).

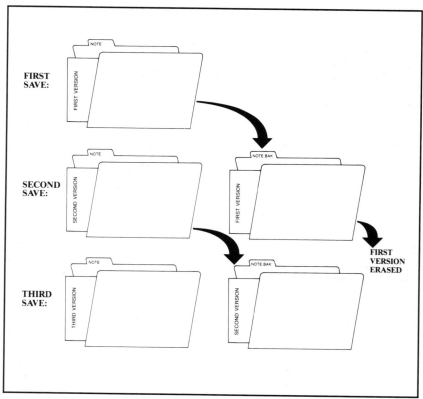

Figure 4.9: Backup files

Word's system of automatically generating backup files is good insurance. However, it won't protect against physical damage to your disk. For added protection, I recommend you back up your hard disk on a regular basis.

If you run out of space on your hard disk or it starts running noticeably slower, you may find that you need to erase .BAK files belonging to documents that are not currently in use. Let's take a look at this process of deleting unwanted files.

DELETING FILES ON DISK

The main reason for deleting files, especially with floppy disks, is that files take up disk space: only so much information can be stored on a disk. Even though the need is less acute with a hard disk, searching through a lot of inactive files can be inefficient and irritating. Erasing files that you no longer need is a housekeeping chore you will want to do fairly regularly.

To delete files, you use the Transfer Delete command (see Figure 4.10). In general, you should not delete backup files, at least not those belonging to active files. Experienced word processors will recount how they have been saved by backup files. If you should get a disk full message when you try to save, however, you might have no other choice.

You can display the list of file names for the current drive and directory with the Transfer Delete command. If you need to delete files from another directory or drive, you can change the current drive and directory with this command or by using the Transfer Options command before using Transfer Delete. You'll notice that the .BAK file names are displayed. You will also see your original document files with their .DOC extension. As a safety measure,

 New in Word 5

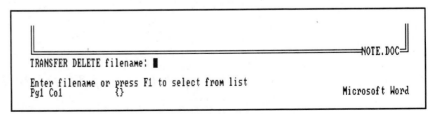

TRANSFER DELETE filename: ▮

Enter filename or press F1 to select from list
Pg1 Co1   {}   Microsoft Word

Figure 4.10: The Transfer Delete command

M_O U S E_

Click left on Transfer
and then click left on
Delete. To display the
list of file names, click
right on filename.

when you delete a file by entering the file name rather than by selecting it from the list, Word requires that you use the entire name,
including its extension.

Try these steps to display a list of files for deletion:

1. Activate the Transfer Delete command by pressing the Esc
   key, typing T for Transfer, and typing D for Delete. The
   computer then displays

   TRANSFER DELETE filename:

2. To display the list of files, press F1.

Be careful to select the correct file for deletion. The Undo command
does not reverse the effect of Transfer Delete.

Go ahead and delete NOTE.BAK. As a safety precaution, Word
displays the message

   Enter Y to confirm deletion of file

You must type Y to indicate that you are certain you want the file
removed.

There are other Transfer Delete situations that could provoke
messages such as

   Cannot delete file

or

   File or directory does not exist

T_I P_

You cannot use the
Transfer Delete com-
mand to delete more
than one file at a time.
To delete several files
simultaneously, use
the Library
Document-retrieval;
Delete command (see
Chapter 10).

For example, you might have typed the name of a file that is not in
the directory, or you might have mistyped the file name. Correct the
situation and try again.

Deleting unneeded files is not the only housekeeping chore you will
need to do. From time to time, you may also find it necessary to
change inappropriate file names.

RENAMING AND MOVING FILES

Suppose you decide that the name of our currently loaded sample
document (NOTE) is too vague, since you will soon have to write a

number of notes to various people. Because the note is addressed to Steve, let's rename it STEVNOTE. Notice that we must leave out the "e" in "Steve"—the maximum length of a file name in Word is eight characters. (Some of the symbol characters are permitted, but others are not. To be on the safe side, it's a good idea to use only letters and numbers.) You can also add a period and up to three more characters as an extension, but it's best not to since Word automatically adds the appropriate ending, such as .DOC.

Anytime you find that the name of a file does not quite suit its contents, it is wise to change it. You can change the name of the displayed (loaded) file by using the Transfer Rename command (see Figure 4.11).

1. Activate the Transfer Rename command by pressing the Esc key, typing T for Transfer, and typing R for Rename.

2. Type the new name

    STEVNOTE

3. Register the new name by pressing the Enter key.

You can also use this procedure to move a file from one directory to another on the same drive. Word copies the file to the new directory you specify and then deletes the file from the old directory. Remember, you can use the following function keys to edit the path and file name that appear, rather than retyping them:

F7   Previous Word

F8   Next Word

F9   Previous Character

F10   Next Character

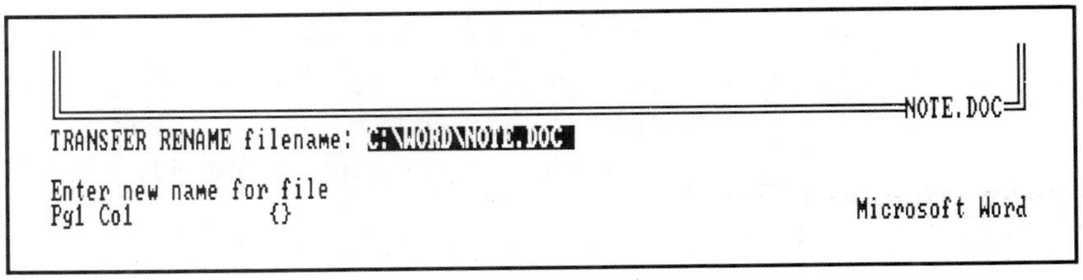

Figure 4.11: The Transfer Rename command

You can also use the Delete and Backspace keys to edit.

You cannot use this method to move a file from one drive to another. Attempting to do this will cause the message

Cannot rename file

to appear. You could also get this message if there's already another file with the name you're trying to assign, if the file is write-protected, or if the name doesn't abide by the operating system's rules for file names.

OTHER TRANSFER COMMANDS

Let's take a moment to review our accomplishments in this chapter. If you look at the Transfer menu on your screen, you will notice that we have examined most of the commands listed there. As mentioned at the beginning of this chapter, the Transfer commands manipulate entire documents, to and from the disk. Transfer Clear wipes the window, saving the current document if necessary, so you can create a new document. With Transfer Merge we were able to bring an entire file into another, and we learned how to erase a document from the disk with Transfer Delete. Lastly, we performed the Transfer Rename command to give a more specific name to a displayed file.

There are only three remaining Transfer commands: Glossary, Allsave, and Options. Briefly, Transfer Glossary merges, saves, and clears glossaries just as equivalent Transfer commands merge, save, and clear documents. We will study this command when we look at glossaries in Chapter 15.

5 New in Word 5

The Transfer Allsave command saves all current files that affect Word's displayed document: the document itself, the glossary, and the style sheet. As you begin to use these features, you may wish to expedite your saving by using this command. It also helps ensure the most up-to-date versions of these files are on disk, should you run into a problem.

Although you may not need these last two commands yet, you are probably ready for the Transfer Options command. Let's examine it more closely.

SPECIFYING A DRIVE AND DIRECTORY

You can use the Transfer Options command (Figure 4.12) to specify the disk drive and directory for Word to use for documents during the current session (until you quit). Initially, the drive and directory that were active when you started Word will appear here. Simply provide a new path (the exact location of the new directory). Don't forget that rather than retyping, you can use the F7 to F10 keys and the Delete and Backspace keys to edit the path that appears.

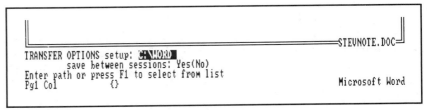

Figure 4.12: The Transfer Options command

Alternatively, as we saw, you can change drives temporarily as you use the Transfer commands. You can also simply precede the names of the files with the drive and a colon (and a path) when you perform various Transfer commands. For example,

C:\WORD\ANNOUNCE

tells Word that ANNOUNCE is on drive C in the WORD directory.

New in
Word 5

You can now indicate whether you want to save and use the path information between Word sessions. To do so, use the Tab key, the ↓ key, or the mouse to set save between sessions to Yes. If you leave this option set to No, Word will continue to use whatever drive and directory is active when you start the program.

There is more to Word than typing, storing, combining, and printing. Word provides many ways to improve the look of your documents. The broad term for enhancing the visual appeal of a document is *formatting*. Knowing how to format is the next step to mastering Microsoft Word, and the subject of the next chapter.

5

Formatting for Emphasis and Variety

Fast Track

BEFORE WE BEGIN TO FORMAT TEXT, LET'S TAKE A moment to discuss just what formatting is. What does it mean to format with Microsoft Word? Why format at all?

The *format* of your document is the shape it takes. It is what you do with characters, words, sentences, paragraphs, and pages to give them printed form.

Formatting makes anything written more readable. It helps you win your readers and makes the document you've prepared more attractive. What is more, text that is well formatted communicates ideas better and is easier to digest. Through indenting and boldfacing, you can emphasize points. Through page layout, you can create a sense of structure and show relationships. You can focus your reader's attention by creating format contrasts, and you can help lead the reader's eye across the paper. By giving a document more white space, you can open it up and avoid the negative impact of densely written or highly technical material. In short, formatting allows you to use aesthetics as an expressive tool.

Some aspects of formatting, however, are not just a question of aesthetics. Formatting also includes the use of established conventions, such as italicizing the names of books.

Word offers a full range of formatting techniques. Some are strictly practical: they save you time by combining keystrokes or allowing you to skip some keystrokes altogether. Because it is so easy to create these formatting features, you can print out different versions and compare them side by side to see which you like best.

FORMATTING YOUR TEXT USING THE "ESCAPE" ROUTE AND THE "ALTERNATE" ROUTE

Word's formatting capability is so extensive that we won't cover every command in this chapter. Instead, we will concentrate on two important formatting commands. You use the first, Format Character, to format the look of characters—using boldfacing or underlining, for example. With this command, you change the printed shape and perhaps the size of the characters. (Word considers underlining to be a character change as well, though the character itself doesn't actually change.)

You use the second format command, Format Paragraph, to determine the printed shapes of paragraphs—creating, for example, justified, indented, and double-spaced paragraphs.

Because the Format commands are comprehensive, they can be bewildering at first: the main Format command branches into thirteen other commands (see Figure 5.1). Each of these subcommands presents other choices for you to make. Thus, to format a character or paragraph using the Format command, you first press the Esc key and then type F for Format. (With the mouse, you click left on Format.) You next have to choose whether you want to format a character or a paragraph, and then you specify the actual format. This is the "Escape" route to formatting, the method of selecting commands you have already learned.

Fortunately, however, there is an easier way to go: the "Alternate" route. This route uses the Alt key with another key. The resulting Alt code (key combination) provides for many practical formatting needs. What is more, the key combinations are easy to learn. Usually the code letter is the first letter of the feature; for example, Alt-U is used for underlining. We will study formatting by looking at both the Format command and the Alt code methods.

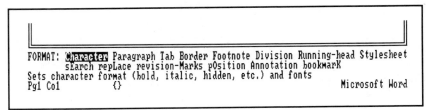

Figure 5.1: The Format command

FORMATTING CHARACTERS

Once you get a taste for formatting, you might just want to do more of it. Some of the more specialized commands that format characters and paragraphs do not have an Alt code equivalent. For these, you must use the Format commands. Later in this chapter, we will look at these Format commands. Right now, let's learn how to change character styles with the Alt key.

BOLDFACING AND UNDERLINING

To use the Alt key, you hold it down and press another key; this activates the Alt code effect you desire. You can use the Alt key to alter standard characters in two ways. The first way is to instruct Word as you're typing in the text. We'll call this "altering in progress." The second way is to alter text that you've already typed in: in other words, "altering after the fact."

Since boldface is a popular feature, let's practice boldfacing through the first method: *altering* the appearance of a character *in progress.*

BOLDFACING "IN PROGRESS" Boldfacing gives emphasis by making the characters darker than usual. To boldface while you are typing along, you first instruct Word to activate the boldface feature. As you go on typing, the characters appear in boldface on the screen. (When those characters are eventually printed, they will be boldfaced as well.) Once you reach the end of the material you want in boldface, you instruct Word to stop boldfacing. As you continue typing, you see normal characters displayed once again.

Let's try altering in progress by typing the line in Figure 5.2. Begin with your screen cleared and Word in Document mode.

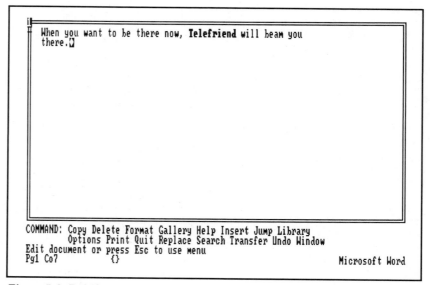

Figure 5.2: Boldfaced text

1. Type the first portion of the sentence:

   When you want to be there now,

2. To activate boldfacing, press Alt-B for boldface. (The hyphen in Alt-B indicates that you should press the Alt key and hold it down while you press the B key. You don't press the Shift key for the B.)

3. Type the word that we want printed in boldface:

   Telefriend

   Notice how the word is boldfaced as you type. (If you can't see the difference, try adjusting the brightness and contrast controls on your monitor.)

4. Now turn off boldfacing by pressing Alt-Spacebar.

5. Type the rest of the sentence:

   will beam you there.

   Notice that the characters have returned to the normal, non-bold look.

Character altering in progress can be accomplished only with the Alt codes. It cannot be performed with the mouse or the Format command.

Underlining is another popular character format. We'll use underlining to demonstrate the second way you can format characters with the Alt key: *altering after the fact*.

UNDERLINING "AFTER THE FACT"   Like boldfacing, underlining is sometimes used to emphasize words. In addition, you can use underlining in place of italics if your printer does not print italics. (Often, however, Word will automatically substitute underlining if a printer cannot print italics.)

The second method of altering characters—doing so after you type—works like this. First, you indicate the text that you want altered; that is, you designate or *select* the text for alteration by highlighting it. Second, you give Word the appropriate Alt code. The selected text will be changed as you indicate.

T I P

As you work with Word, you'll see this same general method used repeatedly. That is, when you want to change text in some fashion, you first highlight the text, and then you instruct Word to change it.

Let's try underlining "after the fact."

1. Type this sentence:

   People said it could never be done.

2. Using the Previous Word (F7) key, return to the word

   never

   which highlights it. With the mouse, click right on "never" to highlight it.

3. Underline it by pressing Alt-U.

If you can't see the underlining, move the highlight away from the word. You should then see "*never.*" When you have finished underlining selected words, turn off the underlining feature. This is only necessary when you use the alter-in-progress method of formatting characters.

If you format after the fact frequently and you prefer using the mouse to highlight text and perform commands, you can use the Format Character command rather than the Alt codes. Of course, you can also perform this command by using the keyboard.

T **I P**

Because the mouse is an efficient tool for selecting text, you may find it quicker to use it to format text after the fact than to use the keyboard in progress or after the fact.

USING THE SWITCHBOX OF CHARACTER FORMATS TO CHANGE CHARACTER FORMAT SETTINGS

Each character that you type on the screen has a register that keeps track of its format; in effect, every letter, number, and symbol has hidden switches for boldface, underline, and the other formatting features. When you change the format of characters, the settings on these switches are changed.

The Format Character command allows you to view the settings for any character's format. Once you display the Format Character "switchbox" (menu), you can make changes in a character's format, just as you can with the Alt codes.

VIEWING FORMAT CHARACTER SETTINGS
Let's issue the Format Character command to view the settings for the normal, boldfaced, and underlined characters that we've created. We will

begin by displaying the Format Character menu. First place the cursor on one of the normal (not altered) characters (the ''e'' in ''done,'' for example).

1. Press the Esc key to activate Command mode.

2. Type F for Format and C for Character. The Format Character menu is then displayed for the highlighted character.

Your Format Character menu should look similar to the one shown in Figure 5.3. You can see that it resembles a switchbox in that it displays a number of settings or indicators (mostly Yes/No). Each of these settings shows the status of one format feature. They are giving you feedback on the character or characters that you highlighted before you invoked the Format Character command.

Since you chose a normal character, all the Yes/No features read No. There's a lot to look at, but check the first feature, bold. Its No setting is highlighted. Also check the underline option: No is indicated by parentheses.

Now let's compare this with the menus for some other characters. To do this, we must exit from this menu and go back to the main command menu, where we can reposition the cursor. You don't

MOUSE

Click right on Format to activate the Format Character command (clicking left would activate only the Format command).

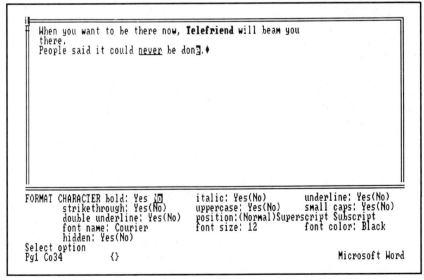

Figure 5.3: The Format Character menu

need to return to Document mode to move the cursor when you use the keyboard. Follow these steps:

M O U S E

Click both buttons on any spot in the Format Character menu to activate Document mode. Click right on the word ''never'' and then click right on Format.

1. Press Ctrl-Esc or Shift-Esc. This activates the main command menu without activating Document mode.

2. Highlight the word ''never.'' (You can use the word-movement keys, F7 and F8, to get there.)

3. Type F for Format and C for Character.

Now the settings for the word ''never'' are displayed. At this point we can change its setting. Changing them here has the same effect as changing them with an Alt code.

CHANGING FORMAT CHARACTER SETTINGS   Let's italicize the word ''never'' for emphasis instead of underlining it. To do this, we have to set underline to No and italic to Yes, and then register our choices.

M O U S E

Click left on Yes for italic and click right on No for underline. Since underline is the last option you want to set, you can use the right button, which both changes the setting and registers your choices, to complete the command.

1. Use the → or the Tab key to reach the italic setting. (When you reach the last setting, the highlight wraps back to the first one. The End or Page Down key moves the highlight to the last setting; Home or Page Up moves it to the first setting. Additionally, typing Shift-Tab generates a backtab; that is, the highlight goes backwards.)

2. Type Y for Yes to select italic. (You can also press the Spacebar instead of Y or N to reverse the setting for any option.)

3. Move to the underline setting and type N or press the Spacebar to turn off underline.

4. When you have completed your character formatting, press the Enter key to register your choices.

In Text mode, the italicized word ''never'' will still be displayed as underlined. Word will, however, print the word in italics (assuming your printer has that capability). Word may even substitute underline on the screen for all the other character formats except bold.

Many character formats are available with Word. The formats can be created by using the Alt key or the Format Character command.

T *IP*

At the computer, you can look at a listing of the Alt codes, provided for quick reference (Figure 5.4). Issue Word 5's Help Keyboard Next commands (in that order) to display this list. Select Exit to go back to the document.

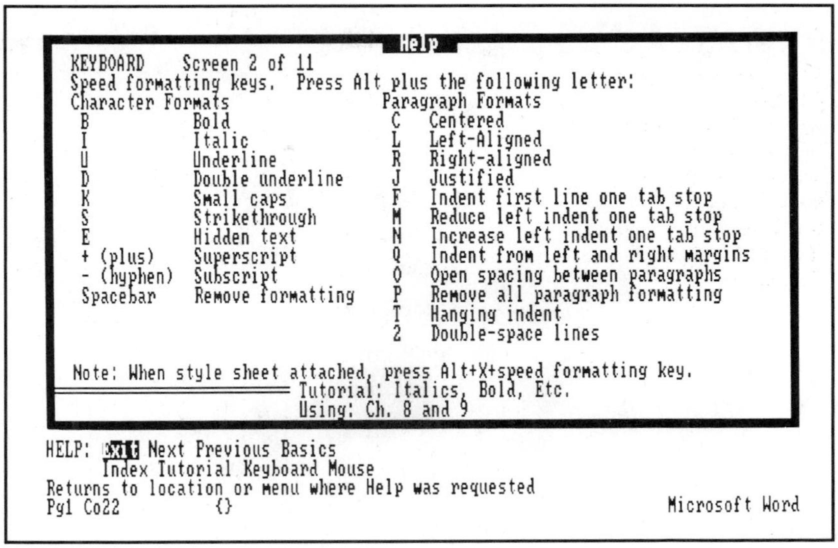

```
                                                          Help
  KEYBOARD    Screen 2 of 11
  Speed formatting keys.  Press Alt plus the following letter:
  Character Formats                 Paragraph Formats
     B            Bold               C   Centered
     I            Italic             L   Left-Aligned
     U            Underline          R   Right-aligned
     D            Double underline   J   Justified
     K            Small caps         F   Indent first line one tab stop
     S            Strikethrough      M   Reduce left indent one tab stop
     E            Hidden text        N   Increase left indent one tab stop
     + (plus)     Superscript        Q   Indent from left and right margins
     - (hyphen)   Subscript          O   Open spacing between paragraphs
     Spacebar     Remove formatting  P   Remove all paragraph formatting
                                     T   Hanging indent
                                     2   Double-space lines

     Note: When style sheet attached, press Alt+X+speed formatting key.
                        Tutorial: Italics, Bold, Etc.
                              Using: Ch. 8 and 9

  HELP: Exit Next Previous Basics
             Index Tutorial Keyboard Mouse
        Returns to location or menu where Help was requested
        Pg1 Co22         {}                              Microsoft Word
```

Figure 5.4: Help screen for Alt codes

Table 5.1 lists the available character formats, as well as the Format Character command options and Alt key codes for effecting them.

The Alt-Spacebar key combination turns off character formats. When you use it, the highlighted characters are changed to normal, regardless of whether the formatting was established with Alt codes or with the Format Character command.

USING THE ALT KEY COMBINATIONS TO ALTER A SINGLE CHARACTER

M *OUSE*

Click left on the "T" in "Telefriend." Then click right on Format and click right on bold's Yes setting to boldface it.

Not only can you establish a character format with the Alt codes, but you can also alter an existing format with them. To practice, let's suppose that you want to emphasize the name of our fictional company, Telefriend, by boldfacing its initial letter.

1. Place the cursor on the "T" in "Telefriend."

2. Boldface the "T" by typing the Alt code letter twice. That is, press Alt-B-B. (Keeping the Alt key down, type "B" twice.)

Table 5.1: The Character Formats Available in Word

FEATURE	ALT CODE	FORMAT CHARACTER OPTION	EXAMPLE
Boldface	Alt-B	bold	**Daring**
Double Underline	Alt-D	double underline	Bottom line
Hidden text	Alt-E	hidden	(invisible)
Italics	Alt-I	italic	*Mamma mia*
Small caps	Alt-K	small caps	PILLBOX
Strikethrough	Alt-S	strikethrough	You're out
Underline	Alt-U	underline	Factors
Superscript	Alt- +	position	$E = mc^2$
Subscript	Alt- –	position	$H_2 0$
Capital letters		uppercase	IDEA
Typeface	Alt-F8	font name	**varies**
Type size	Alt-F8-Tab	font size	varies

Notes:
   Alt-Z turns off character formatting except any assigned font name and font size.
   Alt-Spacebar turns off all character formatting and reassigns the default font name and font size.
   Alt-X should precede all the above Alt codes when you attach a style sheet to the document (see Chapter 17).

When you use the Alt code to format a single character, you must type the code twice. When the cursor is the size of a single character and you type an Alt code, Word assumes that you are in the process of typing text. With the first code, you're telling Word to start formatting. With the second Alt code, you tell Word that you're not typing in text right now; you just want to format a single character.

You turn off a single character's format in a similar fashion. That is, after highlighting the character, press Alt-Spacebar-Spacebar.

FORMATTING PARAGRAPHS AND THEIR TEXT

With the Alt key, you can activate paragraph formatting as well as character formatting. In the following sections, we will practice formatting both characters and paragraphs as you type. To give us something to work with, we will type the example shown in Figure 5.5. (Notice that the letter shown in this figure does not yet have a date, an inside address, or a closing. We'll add those after we have worked with the body of the letter.)

As you type these paragraphs, you won't be using the Tab key to create the paragraph indents as we did in Chapter 2. Tabs would work just fine, but using the Alt codes is more efficient.

```
Dear Mr. Esprit:
     Thank you for your communication of January 12, 2052.
In that communication, you indicate that you wish to be
additionally compensated for the recent delay you
experienced in teleportation.
     On the ticket you purchased, however, the terms of your
teleportation are clearly stated:
          On rare occasions, passengers may experience some delay
          in beaming. However, Telefriend Teleportation,
          Incorporated is not liable for any delay except as
          provided by law.
As your letter indicates, we have fulfilled our obligation
in that regard.
     While we realize that it is not pleasant to be trapped
in the suspension state, we believe that added effort on
your part may have shortened the delay.
     Before departure, beam attendants clearly inform all
passengers that the formula for relativity is E=mc$^2$.  They
give instructions in the proper use of this formula in the
event of rematerialization difficulties.
     Passengers are also instructed to look for our super
highpower ethereal searchlights to be guided to their
destination or returned to the point of departure.
     We realize that teleportation is an exciting
experience, and that your attention may not have been fully
focused on the instructions at the time. With this
explanation, we hope that you now feel adequately
compensated, and that you will continue to be our customer.
```

Figure 5.5: Indenting without using the Tab key

INDENTING THE FIRST LINE OF A PARAGRAPH

Begin the letter by typing the salutation "Dear Mr. Esprit:". After you've typed it, press the Enter key.

Now, to begin the first paragraph, *do not* press the Tab key. Instead, we'll use the paragraph shape called *first-line indented*. You activate it by pressing Alt-F. When you press Alt-F, the cursor automatically indents. Normally, the printed indent will be 1/2 inch, the distance of Word's first preset tab setting. If you've changed the tab settings (as discussed in Chapter 9), Alt-F will move the cursor to your first tab setting.

Once the Alt-F code has taken effect, the cursor will not return to the left margin when you press the Enter key at the end of a paragraph. Instead, it will be moved to the first tab setting again. Only material that you type from this point forward, however, will be affected. Previously typed material will remain the same. (The salutation, for instance, is safe.)

Type the entire paragraph now and press the Enter key at the end, after "teleportation." Paragraphs, just like characters, have a hidden switchbox that stores the settings you have established. The normally invisible *paragraph mark,* which is located at the end of the paragraph right where you pressed the Enter key, stores the settings information.

If you delete the paragraph mark (with the Delete key, for instance), the paragraph's formatting will be deleted as well. When the paragraph mark is deleted, its paragraph joins with the paragraph that follows, and they become one. The resulting single paragraph has the format settings of the one paragraph mark that ends it.

The paragraph marks do not normally appear on the screen, but you can make them visible by invoking the Options command and changing its show non-printing symbols setting to Partial. This will enable you to see paragraph marks and new-line marks (another normally invisible symbol, which is discussed later in this chapter). The behavior of the Alt-F command is the same whether the paragraph mark is visible or not.

INDENTING ENTIRE PARAGRAPHS

Now type the second paragraph. After the word "stated:", press the Enter key.

T I P

If you lose formatting by accidentally deleting a paragraph mark, you will probably notice it right away: the special format shape will disappear. Use the Undo command to retrieve the mark.

T I P

You can remember to use Alt-N to indent entire paragraphs by thinking of the sound these words begin with: N-dent N-tire.

Notice that we want the entire paragraph (beginning "On rare occasions") to be indented from the left, not just the first line. To indent the entire paragraph without increasing the indent on the first line, we must first suppress the Alt-F format. We can do this by pressing Alt-P. This code switches off the formatted paragraph shapes. The P in Alt-P stands for *plain paragraph*. To indent the paragraph as a whole, press Alt-N.

As you type this paragraph, you will need to underline text. Underline as you did before, activating the format with Alt-U and turning it off with Alt-Spacebar. Notice that Alt-Spacebar neutralizes the effect of the character alterations but does not turn off the paragraph shapes: only Alt-P can do that. Thus, you can type along and change character types without worrying about the effect this might have on the paragraph shape. At the end of the paragraph, press the Enter key.

For the next part of the text, we don't want the indent created by Alt-N. So once again, press Alt-P. This will give us the plain-paragraph look that we want for "As your letter . . . ." Type the sentence and press the Enter key at the end.

Your plain-paragraph format is still in effect. Now we want to change back to the first-line indented shape. Press Alt-F to reinstate the first-line indent. Continue typing the letter until you reach "$E = mc^2$."

SUPERSCRIPT AND SUBSCRIPT

The "2" in the equation "$E = mc^2$" should be a superscripted exponent sign. In addition, the "2" requires special attention as a single-character alteration. (A *superscript* is a character that's raised slightly above the base line. Characters that are lowered slightly, as in H_2O, are called *subscripts*.)

As in our earlier examples, creating a single-character alteration when initially typing in the text involves three steps. First you must tell Word to turn the format on, then you type the character that you want in the altered state, and finally you press Alt-Spacebar to turn the format off. Let's try this with "$E = mc^2$."

1. Type the text

    E = mc

. 2. Press the Alt- + key combination, using the plus key to turn on the superscript feature. You must use the plus/equal key on the top row of the keyboard; the plus key on the keypad doesn't work here. Also, do not press the Shift key to type the plus sign—only use the Alt key.

3. Type the text for alteration:

    2

4. Press Alt-Spacebar to turn off the superscript feature.

The monitor and display mode will determine whether you see the superscript. Now you can finish typing the rest of the example as it appears in Figure 5.5. When you have completed it, save the document under the name ESPRIT.

A CLOSER LOOK AT FORMATTING PREVIOUSLY TYPED TEXT

Formatting does not end once material is typed into the computer. As we have learned, you can also use Word to format after the fact. If you're fortunate enough to know in advance exactly how you want your text to look, you can format as you type. Even so, after you've printed your document, you might review it and decide that there are other formatting choices you wish to include.

To make character and paragraph changes after you have entered your text, there are two specific pieces of information you must provide. First, you must designate the material you want to have specially altered by highlighting it. Second, you must let Word know the nature of the alteration.

ALTERING PREVIOUSLY TYPED PARAGRAPHS

Word provides two ways you can make paragraph changes to text previously typed in. The easier way is with the Alt codes. Just bring the cursor to any spot in the selected paragraph and type the appropriate code. For more exacting specifications, you'll have to use the second method: the Format Paragraph command.

Let's assume that you want to give a more official look to the third paragraph by *justifying* it—that is, by creating even margins on both sides of the paragraph.

1. Scroll up (using the ↑ or Page Up key) and place the cursor anywhere within the third paragraph.

2. Press Alt-J to justify the paragraph on both the left and right sides. Your document should now look like Figure 5.6.

THE FORMAT PARAGRAPH SWITCHBOX   You can use the Format Paragraph command to view the settings for paragraph shapes and change those settings. Let's look at the switchbox for the paragraph we've justified.

1. Position the cursor anywhere within the third paragraph and press Esc to activate Command mode.

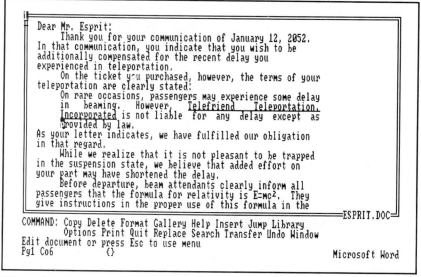

Figure 5.6: Justifying a paragraph

2. Type F for Format and P for Paragraph to run the Format Paragraph command.

You'll see the menu displayed in Figure 5.7. This paragraph now has two Alt codes in effect; they are reflected in the settings. Because Alt-J has been activated, the word

Justified

is highlighted for the alignment setting. Because you also pressed Alt-N (entire paragraph indent), the left indent setting displays

0.5″

TIP

When you change the numeric settings, you don't have to enter the inch symbol. Typing the number is sufficient when Word displays inches in the fields.

instead of the normal 0″. This is because Alt-N indented the entire paragraph ½ inch from the left. Because this paragraph does not contain an additional first-line indent, the first line setting displays

0″

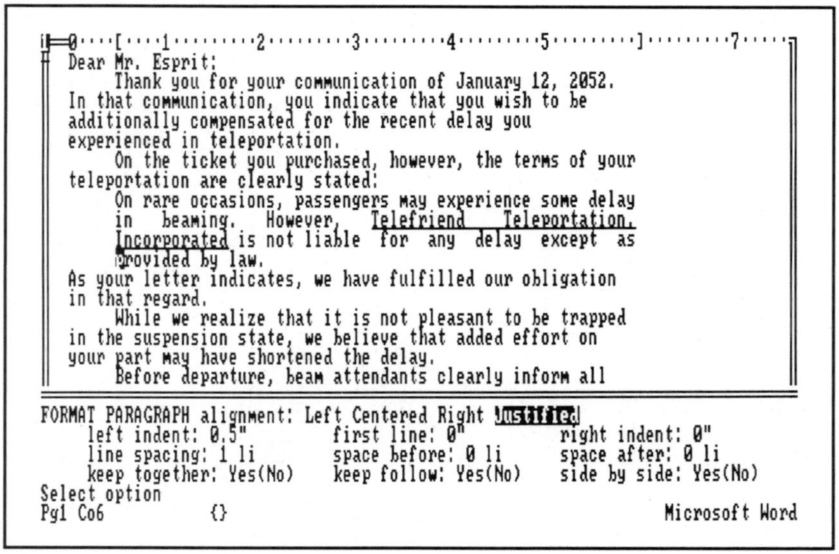

```
 ‖ 0····[····1·········2·········3·········4·········5·········]·········7····
 ‖ Dear Mr. Esprit:
 ‖     Thank you for your communication of January 12, 2052.
 ‖ In that communication, you indicate that you wish to be
 ‖ additionally compensated for the recent delay you
 ‖ experienced in teleportation.
 ‖     On the ticket you purchased, however, the terms of your
 ‖ teleportation are clearly stated:
 ‖         On rare occasions, passengers may experience some delay
 ‖     in  beaming.  However,  Telefriend  Teleportation,
 ‖     Incorporated is not liable for any delay except as
 ‖     provided by law.
 ‖ As your letter indicates, we have fulfilled our obligation
 ‖ in that regard.
 ‖         While we realize that it is not pleasant to be trapped
 ‖ in the suspension state, we believe that added effort on
 ‖ your part may have shortened the delay.
 ‖         Before departure, beam attendants clearly inform all

 FORMAT PARAGRAPH alignment: Left Centered Right Justified
      left indent: 0.5"         first line: 0"         right indent: 0"
      line spacing: 1 li        space before: 0 li     space after: 0 li
      keep together: Yes(No)    keep follow: Yes(No)   side by side: Yes(No)
 Select option
 Pg1 Co6              {}                              Microsoft Word
```

Figure 5.7: The Format Paragraph menu

You can modify these settings by using the same keyboard and mouse techniques we employed with the Format Character command. That is, move (or point) to the format option and change it. Some of the menu options don't require much additional discussion. For instance, the choices for the alignment setting simply mean left flush, centered, right flush, and justified left and right. They correspond to their respective Alt equivalents (Alt-L, Alt-C, Alt-R, and Alt-J). The side by side option places paragraphs next to one another. (We'll study that feature in Chapter 11 when we look at tables.) We will be discussing the other Format Paragraph settings later in the chapter.

THE RULER LINE You probably noticed the line at the top of the window border, called the *ruler line*. The numbers on this line indicate the measurements of the paragraph in inches when the text is printed. The brackets

[   ]

indicate the left and right margin settings for the paragraph containing the cursor. When the first line of the paragraph is indented to a position different from that of the rest of the paragraph, a vertical bar

indicates the location of the indent.

You can use the mouse to change the paragraph margin settings that appear on the ruler line. Doing so will change the corresponding settings in the Format Paragraph menu.

1. Click left on Format and click left on Paragraph to display the Format Paragraph menu.

2. Point to the symbol on the ruler line you wish to change.

3. Using the mouse's right button, drag the symbol to a new ruler location. As you do, notice that the numeric settings adjust to reflect changes in the ruler line.

T IP

The ruler line that is displayed corresponds to the paragraph that holds the highlight. Even though there may be more paragraphs displayed on the screen, changes in the ruler line will affect only this paragraph.

5 New in
Word 5

MORE INDENTS AND PARAGRAPH ALT CODES   Now suppose you decide that this same paragraph could use some additional
indenting, to set it off even more. To achieve this, return to Document mode and simply press Alt-N: the entire paragraph is indented
even further.

Notice that the effect of the Alt codes is cumulative. Since you
didn't use Alt-P to turn off your last Alt code, the paragraph is now
both justified and twice indented. Each time you press Alt-N, the
paragraph is indented from the left an additional 1/2 inch on the
printed page.

You might now feel that the indent is too great. By pressing Alt-M,
you can decrease the paragraph indent. Each Alt-M decreases the left
indent by 1/2 inch.

You can use a Word 5 Alt code to indent text from the left and
right margins simultaneously. Each time you press Alt-Q, Word
indents the paragraph containing the cursor an additional 1/2 inch
each from the left and right margins. As with Alt-N, the effect is
cumulative; Alt-M undoes the left indent only.

There are a variety of paragraph shapes that the Alt codes will
allow you to assign to your documents; these are listed in Table 5.2.
All the paragraph shapes can be formed simply by placing the cursor
anywhere in the selected paragraph and specifying an Alt code. The
Alt-P (plain-paragraph) code turns off these paragraph formats.

You can center text with the Alt-C code. This code is handy when
you want to center a multiline heading. Of course, you can use it to
center a single line as well: the single line is considered a paragraph
when it ends with a paragraph mark.

One of the more unusual paragraph shapes is the hanging indent,
created with Alt-T. In this format the first line of the paragraph is
even with the left margin, but the remaining lines are indented 1/2
inch with each Alt-T. You can also decrease this indent by
using Alt-M.

Figure 5.8 contains a highlighted hanging paragraph. Make the
same paragraph in your document hang by selecting it and pressing
Alt-T. After you create this format, you can see that it doesn't match
the rest of the document. If the last line of the hanging paragraph was
longer, it would be difficult to tell where this paragraph ended and
the next began. Because of this, change it back by invoking the Undo
command.

Table 5.2: Paragraph Alt Codes

PARAGRAPH SHAPE	ALT CODE
Centered	Alt-C
First line indented	Alt-F
Justified left and right	Alt-J
Left flush	Alt-L
Decrease left paragraph indent	Alt-M
Indent paragraph left	Alt-N
Open up paragraphs	Alt-O
Plain paragraphs	Alt-P
Indent paragraph left and right	Alt-Q
Right flush	Alt-R
Hanging indent	Alt-T
Double-spaced	Alt-2

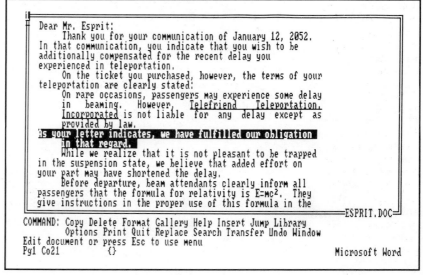

Figure 5.8: A hanging paragraph

ALTERING PREVIOUSLY TYPED WORDS AND SENTENCES

As with reformatting previously typed paragraphs, to reformat characters you first have to highlight the text to be altered. Highlighting individual words or sentences is trickier than highlighting paragraphs, though. Once you have selected the text, you press the appropriate Alt key combination or use the Format Character command to change its format.

The cursor is the key to highlighting in Word. The cursor starts out the size of one character, but you can increase its size, making it expand in any one direction. As the cursor expands, it overtakes letters, words, sentences, and whole paragraphs, highlighting them as it goes. You can even expand the cursor to highlight the entire document.

There are two basic methods you can use to expand the cursor. The first method, *highlight tagging,* uses the function keys to highlight discrete chunks of text. The second method, *anchoring and stretching,* consists quite simply of anchoring the cursor in one location and stretching it until it highlights the text you want to change.

HIGHLIGHT TAGGING   Four function keys are used in highlight tagging: F7 through F10. Each of these keys has two functions, depending on whether the key is pressed alone or with the Shift key. Use them to highlight as follows:

KEY	HIGHLIGHTS
F7	Previous word
F8	Next word
F9	Previous paragraph
F10	Next paragraph
Shift-F7	Previous sentence
Shift-F8	Next sentence
Shift-F9	Current line
Shift-F10	Whole document

For highlight tagging, the cursor must be in (or sometimes right next to) the text you wish to tag. When you press the function key, the text becomes highlighted, and you can use one of the Alt codes for character alterations.

To use the mouse for highlight tagging, point to the appropriate text to highlight a letter, a word, or a sentence. To highlight a line, a paragraph, or the entire document with the mouse, you must position the pointer to the left of the text, just inside the window border. This area is called the *selection bar*.

Here's how you perform highlight tagging with the mouse:

- To highlight a character, click left on it.

- To highlight a word, click right on any character in the word.

- To highlight an entire sentence, click both buttons on any part of it.

- To highlight a line, click left on the selection bar.

- To highlight a paragraph, click right on the selection bar.

- To highlight the entire document, click both buttons on the selection bar.

T I P

To check which method you need to use to highlight with the mouse, click either button on the Help command or on the mouse's question mark and then click either button on the Mouse command. You will then see a listing like that shown in Figure 5.9.

```
                                    Help
   MOUSE    Screen 1 of 9

   To select:      Do this:
   Character       Point to character and click left button.
   Word            Point to word and click right button.
   Sentence        Point to sentence and click both buttons at once.
   Line            Point in selection bar to left of line and click
                   left button.
   Paragraph       Point in selection bar to left of paragraph and click
                   right button.
   Document        Point anywhere in selection bar and click both buttons.
   Text block      Point to first character and hold down left button;
                   drag to last character and release button.
   Column          Point to one corner and click left button; press,
                   SHIFT+F6; then point to opposite corner and click
                   left button.

                        Tutorial: Selecting Text
                        Using: Ch. 4, "Scrolling, Selecting Text, ..."

   HELP: Exit Next Previous Basics
         Index Tutorial Keyboard Mouse
   Provides help on using the mouse with Word
   Pg1 Co16          {}           ?                      ESPRIT.DOC
```

Figure 5.9: Help for highlighting with the mouse

CH. 5

As you can see in Figure 5.10, I clicked right on the selection bar to select the paragraph that we formatted and unformatted as hanging.

Note that you have different commands for a line and a sentence. When you click both buttons on a sentence, Word knows to highlight the text until it reaches the sentence's ending period or question mark, even if the sentence carries over to the next line.

To practice highlight tagging, let's italicize the last sentence in the letter.

M O U S E

Click right on the left window border, about halfway down, to move to the sentence. Click both buttons on it to select it. Then click right on Format and click right on Yes for the italic option to italicize the sentence.

1. Move the cursor to the sentence by pressing the Page Down key and using the arrow keys if necessary.

2. Press Shift-F7 or Shift-F8 to highlight the sentence. (These key combinations both highlight the sentence containing the cursor the first time you press them. Pressing Shift-F7 or Shift-F8 a second time highlights the previous or next sentence, respectively.)

3. Italicize the sentence by pressing Alt-I.

You may need to move the highlight off the sentence to see that its format has changed.

```
  Dear Mr. Esprit:
       Thank you for your communication of January 12, 2052.
  In that communication, you indicate that you wish to be
  additionally compensated for the recent delay you
  experienced in teleportation.
       On the ticket you purchased, however, the terms of your
  teleportation are clearly stated:
       On rare occasions, passengers may experience some delay
       in  beaming.  However,  Telefriend  Teleportation,
       Incorporated is not liable  for  any  delay  except  as
       provided by law.
  As your letter indicates, we have fulfilled our obligation
  in that regard.
       While we realize that it is not pleasant to be trapped
  in the suspension state, we believe that added effort on
  your part may have shortened the delay.
       Before departure, beam attendants clearly inform all
  passengers that the formula for relativity is E=mc². They
  give instructions in the proper use of this formula in the
                                                    ═ESPRIT.DOC═
COMMAND: Copy Delete Format Gallery Help Insert Jump Library
         Options Print Quit Replace Search Transfer Undo Window
Edit document or press Esc to use menu
Pg1 Co16            {}              ?                Microsoft Word
```

Figure 5.10: Clicking right on the selection bar to highlight a paragraph

Now for stronger emphasis, use these techniques to boldface the same sentence. If you cannot see boldfacing after you remove the sentence highlight, try adjusting the controls on your monitor. Notice that the formatting is once again cumulative, resulting in boldface italics. You could, of course, turn off one formatting feature before activating another by using Alt-Spacebar or the Format Character command. These same techniques work for all the character alterations.

ANCHORING AND STRETCHING WITH THE KEYBOARD

Anchoring and stretching the cursor is the second method of expanding the highlight. Like highlight tagging, you can also accomplish it using the keyboard or the mouse.

With the keyboard, there are two methods for stretching the cursor. The first method uses the Extend key (F6) as a catalyst. After placing the cursor at a given spot, covering any amount of material, you anchor it in position by pressing F6. The letters

      EX

will then appear in the lock area of the screen.

Once the cursor is anchored, you can use the directional keys to stretch the cursor on the screen. You can also extend the highlight with the four function keys that you use for highlight tagging. Once the cursor is expanded to include your desired text, use one or more of the Alt codes to specify your formatting choice. Performing an action like this automatically turns Extend off. When you move the cursor away from the highlighted material, the cursor shrinks to normal size.

Another way you can use the keyboard to stretch the cursor is to use the Shift key with the keys on the directional keypad. For instance, by pressing Shift-→, you can extend the cursor to the right by one character. By pressing Shift-↓, you can extend it down to the next line. You don't use the Extend key (F6) with this method, but the highlight stretches as if you did. The possible key combinations and their functions are listed on the pages inside the back cover.

Regardless of the method you use to extend the cursor, be aware that the cursor expands in only one direction at a time. You cannot place the cursor in the middle of the text you want to highlight and stretch it in both directions.

ANCHORING AND STRETCHING WITH THE MOUSE

To anchor and stretch with the mouse, you drag it. Dragging with the left button highlights text a character at a time; dragging with the right button highlights text a word at a time; using both buttons highlights the text sentence by sentence. Drag the mouse to your destination and release the button(s). The text between the starting and ending positions of the drag will be highlighted. Be sure not to release the button(s) until you have reached your true destination.

Let's use these anchor-and-stretch methods to italicize the words ''may experience some delay in beaming,'' which appear in the third paragraph of our sample letter.

MOUSE

Using the right button, drag the pointer from the word ''may'' to the period after the word ''beaming.'' To italicize this selected text, click right on Format and then click right on Yes for the italic option.

1. To highlight that portion of the sentence, move the cursor up to the ''m'' in ''may'' and press Shift-End to stretch the cursor to the end of the line. Next, press the Extend key (F6) to anchor the cursor, and press the Next Word key (F8) to stretch the cursor to the next line. Continue to press it until you reach the period (Figure 5.11).

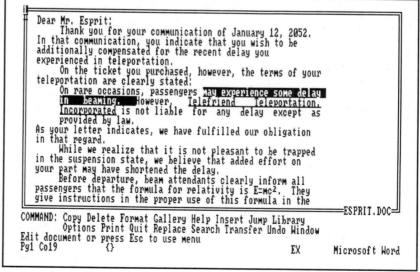

Figure 5.11: Highlighting part of a sentence

2. Now italicize this text by pressing Alt-I. Watch the lock area as you italicize the highlighted words. Word turns off Extend when the Alt code is activated.

Notice how we used the Shift-End to stretch an anchored highlight. Similarly, you can use Shift-Home to stretch it to the beginning of a line. Likewise, you can use Shift-Page Up or Shift-Page Down to stretch up or down by windows of text. Now, let's practice stretching all the way to the beginning or end of a document.

CHANGING THE SPACING OF AN ENTIRE DOCUMENT

Although we've been working with a lot of detail up to this point, it is important to look at your documents as a whole as well. You change the format of an entire document by first highlighting it and then specifying the change. You can change both characters and paragraphs in this fashion. Only the settings that you modify will be affected.

To practice designating whole documents as the text to be altered, let's open up one blank line between each paragraph in the document. When you alter entire documents, the cursor can initially be located anywhere within the document.

M O U S E

Click both buttons on the selection bar to highlight the document. Then click left on Format, click either button on Paragraph, click left on space before, type 1, and click either button on Format Paragraph to register your command.

1. Highlight the entire document by pressing Shift-F10.

2. Press Alt-O, which adds one blank line in front of selected paragraphs.

By highlighting the entire document, you designated all the paragraphs, so all of them received that additional blank line. The result is that the paragraphs moved apart. If you now look at the Format Paragraph menu for any one paragraph, you'll see that the space before option is set to 1.

You can also use the Format Paragraph command's space after option to add blank lines after each paragraph in your document. The total amount of space between any two given paragraphs is the value specified for space after the first paragraph plus the value for space before the second paragraph plus the number specified for the paragraphs' line spacing when it is greater than 1.

Since Alt-O changes the space before setting in a paragraph, I recommend that, at least until you're comfortable with these options, you change only that setting. If you avoid changing space after, you won't need to be concerned about the cumulative effect.

You can highlight the entire document for a variety of formatting reasons. You might want to work with single-spaced text on the screen, since you can see more of it at a time, and then change it to double-spaced, with Alt-2, before you print it. You could also justify the entire document with Alt-J. You could even change it to all capital letters by changing the uppercase setting in the Format Character command. With Alt-I you could italicize the entire document, should that strike your fancy.

It is possible to change the left and right margins of a document by changing the indent settings in the Format Paragraph command with the entire document highlighted. However, changing margins is generally accomplished with the Format Division command, which we'll study in Chapter 9. The indent settings in the Paragraph command are designed for indentations of isolated paragraphs, not entire documents.

FORMAT COPYING

You can alter your document by copying character or paragraph formatting from one spot to another throughout it. Let's demonstrate how by showing a way you can boldface the initial letters of "Telefriend Teleportation, Incorporated" quickly. You can use this method to avoid repeating the entire format procedure for each letter. First, let's format the first letter in the normal fashion:

1. Move the cursor to the "T" in "Telefriend."

2. Press Alt-B-B to boldface the selected letter.

Before doing anything else, follow these steps to copy the boldface format to the "T" in "Teleportation" and the "I" in "Incorporated":

1. Highlight the "T" in "Teleportation."

2. Press the Repeat Edit key (F4). The selected "T" becomes boldfaced.

M_O U S E_ _____

Highlight the letter
you wish to format
and then point to the
formatted "T." Press
Alt-Left (hold down
the Alt key and click
the left button) to copy
the boldface format to
the highlighted char-
acter. Repeat this
procedure for the
third letter.

M_O U S E_ _____

Place the cursor some-
where within the
paragraph you want to
format. Move the
pointer to the selection
bar (the far-left edge
of the window, just
within the border),
adjacent to the para-
graph with formatting
you want to copy.
Press Alt-right to copy
its formatting to the
paragraph containing
the cursor.

3. To copy the same format to the "I," highlight it and press F4 again.

You can repeat this technique for any number of characters. You can also copy formatting from one paragraph to another, in a similar fashion:

1. Move the cursor to anywhere in the paragraph with the for-matting you want to copy.

2. Press Esc, type F for Format, type P for Paragraph, and press Enter to execute the Format Paragraph command. (This tech-nique can also be used with the Format Character command.)

3. Move to the paragraph you wish to format and press the Repeat Edit key (F4).

As with character formatting, you can copy the formatting to more than one paragraph. Just highlight each additional paragraph in turn and repeat the procedure. Note, however, that if you have consecu-tive paragraphs to reformat, it's quicker to highlight them and use the Format command or an Alt code.

FORMATTING AN INSIDE ADDRESS AS ONE PARAGRAPH

Now let's give the letter an inside address and a closing. We'll start with the address. To move to the beginning of the document, you can press Ctrl-Page Up or click left near the top of the left window bor-der. (Don't use the very top corner, which is for changing windows.)

To allow flexibility in formatting these parts of the letter, we will use Word's new-line code in place of the Enter key. The _new-line_ code is useful when you wish to treat similar short lines of text as a single paragraph. The inside address is an example of such a situation. We want to make sure that Alt-O doesn't open up space between each line of the heading.

To enter the inside address, it looks as though you would have to press the Enter key at the end of each line. Pressing the Enter key, however, creates a paragraph mark. Typed in this manner, each line of the inside address—that is, the line containing the name, the line containing the street address, and the line containing the city, state, and zip code—would become a separate paragraph. You can use the new-line code, however, to tell Word that these lines are not paragraphs in themselves.

To create a new-line mark, you press Shift-Enter instead of Enter. The cursor moves to the next line as if you inserted a hard return, but Word considers the new line to be part of the same paragraph. After the line containing the zip code, press the Enter key. This makes Word register the end of the paragraph at that point. Using Shift-Enter, type the inside address at the top of the letter, as shown in Figure 5.12.

You can see the new-line mark by changing show non-printing symbols in the Options command to Partial. Remember, the Partial setting displays some of the normally invisible characters, including paragraph and new-line marks. When displayed, the new-line mark looks like a downward-pointing arrow (↓).

Now we want to get to the bottom of the letter, where we will place the closing. To do that quickly, you can use Word's end-of-document command, Ctrl-Page Down. (You can also click both buttons on the bottom of the left window border. Don't forget to click on some text or the end mark [◆] after scrolling to move the cursor down as well.)

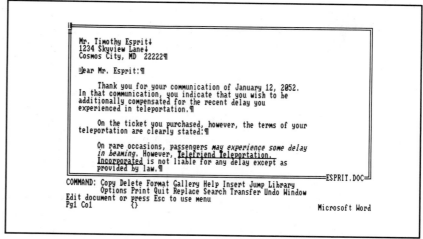

Figure 5.12: Adding the inside address

You can also use the Extend key with these cursor-movement keys. In other words, you can anchor the cursor at a given point by pressing F6 and then stretch the cursor to the beginning or end of the document by pressing Ctrl-Page Up or Ctrl-Page Down. In addition, you can achieve the same effect by using the Shift key instead of the Extend key. Press Shift-Ctrl-Page Up to stretch to the beginning and Shift-Ctrl-Page Down to stretch to the end. In either case, everything between the anchor point and the other point will be highlighted, ready to be formatted.

Go ahead and write the closing of the letter now, supplying a closing of your own choosing ("Yours truly," "Sincerely," or whatever) and typing your own name. Press Shift-Enter to create new-line marks for each line. Since Shift-Enter makes the block look like one paragraph to Word, you can indent the closing lines from the left edge with a series of Alt-N codes, if you wish.

Return to the beginning of the document and add an appropriate date. Again, you can indent the line if you wish.

FORMATTING LINE BREAKS

Word provides you with special codes that control the words that fall at the end of a line. Normally, the word-wrap feature moves entire words from line to line. If two words are connected with a hyphen, it will break the words after the hyphen if necessary.

But sometimes word wrap can cause awkward gaps at the end of a line. To avoid such gaps, you may wish to run Word's automatic hyphenation program on all or part of your document (see Chapter 13). On the other hand, you may choose to do the hyphenating yourself. If so, use an *optional hyphen* on long words, so that they are hyphenated where you indicate if they fall at the end of a line, rather than pushed down to the next line. The optional hyphen prints like a regular hyphen at the end of the line. However, if the word containing the optional hyphen ends up in the middle of a line, the hyphen does not appear in print. You create an optional hyphen by typing Ctrl-hyphen. An optional hyphen won't appear on the screen if you set show non-printing symbols in the Options command to None, unless the hyphen is at the end of a line.

Sometimes there are hyphenated words containing elements that you want kept together on the same line. Examples would include

T-square, −1.25'', 1-2-3. To keep the hyphen plus the characters to the right of it on the same line, press Ctrl-Shift-hyphen instead of hyphen. The resulting character is called a *non-breaking hyphen.*

Occasionally you will have two words (separated by a blank space) that you always want to keep together on the same line. Some examples are numbers and titles, such as March 1, Dr. Dunn, Chapter 4. You can keep both elements together by typing a *non-break space* instead of a regular space. You create a non-break space by pressing Ctrl-Spacebar. Thus to keep March 1 on the same line, you'd type March, press Ctrl-Spacebar, and then type 1.

Remember, the breaking points for the screen lines will not necessarily match your printouts if Word is in the wrong display mode. For more on Word displays, refer to Chapter 8.

FINE-TUNING YOUR FORMATS

The Alt codes we have studied cover most of the character and paragraph alterations you will want to make. They are easy to learn and to remember, and they give you a lot of flexibility in formatting documents.

There are some character and paragraph formats available in Word, however, for which there are no Alt equivalents. For these, you must use the Format command. In addition, the Format Paragraph command provides options that enable you to fine-tune some of the measurements available with the Alt codes. Below, we examine some special formats and discuss their use.

FORMATTING AS UPPERCASE

One way you can change highlighted text to all uppercase is by invoking the Format Character command and setting uppercase to Yes. When you use this method, you can later return the letters to their original state, because the uppercase attribute is treated as a formatting characteristic of the actual characters (which are still intact). Should you decide that you don't want capital letters, simply change the uppercase setting to No. Letters originally typed in lowercase will be lowercased again; letters originally typed as capitals will remain capitals.

New in Word 5

T IP

When only one letter is highlighted, pressing Ctrl-F4 reverses its case. Thus, if you entered a lowercase letter that should be uppercase, simply move to it and press Ctrl-F4 to capitalize it.

T IP

You can use the Format Paragraph's right indent option to create a margin release. To extend a line beyond the normal right margin, change its right indent setting to a negative number. Since Word usually has margins of 1¼ inches on either side, changing the right indent setting to − 1.25'' would use the entire right margin of the paper (assuming your printer will allow this).

Ctrl-F4 is a new function-key shortcut that changes the case of the highlighted text in stages. If you press it once, it changes the text to all uppercase; press it again and it changes text to initial caps; press it a third time and the text changes to all lowercase. With the next press, the cycle starts over. This shortcut actually changes the highlighted text, not just its formatting. So be careful if you use it—you may not be able to get back the initial case of all letters exactly, except by immediately using the Undo command or by retyping. Of course, the three formats are always available, but they may not be appropriate: initial caps capitalizes the first letter of every word, and lowercase doesn't capitalize any letters, not even those that begin sentences.

LEFT INDENT, FIRST-LINE INDENT, RIGHT INDENT

With the left indent, first line, and right indent settings, you can fine-tune the Alt codes. While the Alt code is capable of measuring in increments of ½ inch only, the Format Paragraph menu allows you to specify the indent with more precision. (Your printer, of course, will determine just how precise you can really get.) Note that there is no Alt equivalent for right indentation alone, although in Word 5 you can set both the left and right with Alt-Q. However, you can use the Format Paragraph command to set just a right indent. Alternatively, you could create your own customized Alt code by using the style sheet feature (see Chapter 17).

The system of measurement Word uses for display on the Format Paragraph menu is the one you established with the Options command. Measurement is usually in inches. Using other systems of measurement is discussed in Chapter 9, where you'll learn to use Word's advanced formatting features.

Hanging indents (Alt-T), in which the first line protrudes to the left of the paragraph, are created with a positive value for the left indent for the paragraph's main body and a negative value for the first line setting. When creating a hanging indent, you usually match these positive and negative values for the left and first-line indent. This extends the first line to the left margin. If you do choose to make hanging paragraphs, you will want to change the spacing between them to make them easier to read. Remember, you can set the space before or space after option to separate the paragraphs. Let's examine other spacing techniques now.

LINE SPACING

If you are proofreading or editing a document, extra space between the lines makes it easier to read. To set a paragraph to double-spacing, you can press Alt-2 while the cursor is within the paragraph. This is the only Alt code for line spacing.

If you wish to have your document printed in anything besides single- or double-spacing, you must specify the spacing in the line spacing setting of the Format Paragraph command. Specify triple-spacing by entering 3 in this field: to Word this means three lines (3 li), and a line is 1/6 inch. Similarly, spacing your text one and a half lines apart can be specified by entering 1.5. You can go back to single-spacing by entering 1.

Keep in mind, however, that increasing the line spacing above 1 will affect the amount of space between paragraphs if you have also set the space before and space after settings. For example, if you set line spacing to 2 and space before to 1, you will have two lines of text between any two paragraphs.

If you type the word

Auto

in the line spacing field, Word will automatically set the line spacing to the size of the largest size of type in the line. (You can also press F1 or click right on line spacing to select Auto.) We'll look at other ways to correct line spacing for varying fonts when we examine fonts in Chapter 7. Once again, the end result may be constrained by the capabilities of your printer.

KEEP TOGETHER, KEEP FOLLOW

You can use the keep together and keep follow options to control the way text breaks into pages. Normally, if an entire paragraph cannot fit at the bottom of a page, Word will split it between pages. There may, however, be instances in which you want to be sure that certain material is always kept together on a page.

By setting the keep together option to Yes for a given paragraph, you specify that the paragraph will never be broken between pages. If your editing should happen to place it toward the bottom of the page and all its lines can't fit there, Word will move the whole paragraph to the next page, rather than split it. It would be wise to assign this status to a table of numerical data, for instance. (We'll study tables, a specialized form of paragraph, in Chapter 11.)

In a similar way, you can use the keep follow option to keep a particular paragraph with the paragraph that follows it. Suppose you have an explanatory paragraph preceding and referencing the table we just discussed. You might decide that it's important to keep this paragraph with the table. By changing the keep follow setting to Yes for that paragraph, you ensure that the two will always be kept together.

In this chapter, we've concentrated on formatting characters and paragraphs. Knowledge in these areas allows you to communicate your ideas visually as well as textually. The format techniques you've learned here will serve in many circumstances. As you can see in the Format command menu, there are several other Format subcommands. We'll study the remaining formatting commands in Chapters 9, 11, and 17, where you'll examine features, such as footnotes, tables, and wider margins, for longer and more specialized documents. When you become comfortable with these formatting features, you will be ready to use Word's glossary to store your customized formats, including ones you have discovered in this chapter. In the meantime, we'll work with features you might need sooner. In the next chapter, we'll see how to move parts of your document from place to place.

PART II

Enhancing Your Word Processing Skills

6

**Editing
Techniques
to Refine
Your
Document**

Fast Track

BY NOW YOU'VE PICKED UP QUITE A BIT ABOUT WORD processing with Word. You've learned how to get Word going and how to type your documents. You know how to move documents back and forth from the hard disk to the computer's memory. You can also print your documents and use the various formatting commands to achieve special printed effects. In sum, you now possess a good working knowledge of Microsoft Word.

Now imagine this: what if a document you had to prepare demanded many duplicate passages of text? With Word, a task like this is a simple chore. Say you changed your mind about where to present a particular idea in your document. With Word, it's no problem.

Suppose that you want to keep track of the changes you're making, which is often important when you're working with contracts, for example. If so, you can have Word mark the revisions as you proceed. We'll see how that's done toward the end of this chapter.

A unit of material that you delete, move, or copy is called a *block* of text. A block is simply a chunk of text any size you choose. It can be a character, word, sentence, paragraph, or any combination of these units of text. Text blocks can differ vastly in size, composition, and purpose. Indeed, one entire document could be treated as a block.

You designate the block in your document. As with formatting, there are two ways to define blocks of text for deleting, moving, or copying. Both procedures involve expanding the cursor. In either case you enlarge the highlight, thereby designating the text you want to affect. You can use the highlight tagging method or the anchor-and-stretch method. You'll recall that with highlight tagging, you highlight a single word, line, sentence, paragraph, or an entire document with the function keys or by clicking the mouse. With the anchor-and-stretch method, you set the highlight at one end of the block and stretch it to the other end.

PERFORMING BLOCK OPERATIONS

Once you have defined your block, Word can work wonders. You can play with it just about any way you'd like. You can delete it, move it around, or copy it over and over. Deleting, moving, and copying chunks of text are commonly referred to as block operations. They are also called *cut-and-paste* procedures.

Special formatting of characters and paragraphs is often done so that the reader pays special attention to significant material. Block operations, on the other hand, should go unnoticed by the reader. For instance, once Word has completed a move, the reader should not be able to detect the previous location of the material. You accomplish this by paying attention to the context of the material and by checking spacing before and after the block.

Anything you type can be moved. You can even move invisible characters such as tab characters, spaces, paragraph marks (carriage returns), and new-line marks.

Using the scrap area, there are two ways to perform each of the block operations. The first method involves the Insert and Delete keys. The second method makes use of three commands that appear on the command menu—the Copy, Delete, and Insert commands. These commands are primarily for use with the mouse and the glossary (a handy feature of Word that we'll be discussing in detail in Chapter 15). With the keyboard, you can accomplish normal block operations with fewer keystrokes by using the Delete and Insert keys. If you have a mouse, you can click on these commands to perform the block operations quickly. The mouse also provides another way of performing some of these commands, without using the scrap area. We'll study these methods for performing each block operation one at a time, beginning with deleting. But first we should take a look at the role of the scrap area in block operations.

As you'll recall, the scrap area is located in the bottom-left corner of the screen, indicated by the curly braces. This area provides a sort of layaway location for text that you delete. It can hold any amount of material; oversized text is abbreviated with ellipses (. . .).

Don't think that because it's called scrap, this area is only for unwanted material. It could contain textual scraps of gold as well: anything that you've set aside for the moment.

In the next few sections we'll be working with the document shown in Figure 6.1 to perform some simple deleting, moving, and copying operations. At this point you should type in this document, which concerns the departure procedures used by Telefriend Teleportation, Inc.

As you're typing it, remember the formatting commands we learned in Chapter 5. To center the title, first press Alt-C: the cursor will move to the center and automatically center your material as you type.

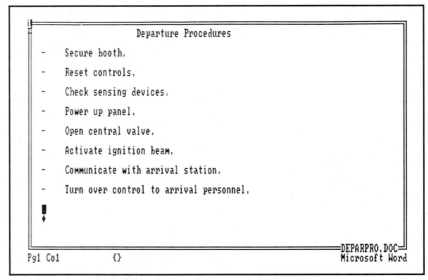

Figure 6.1: The DEPARPRO document

When you're finished with the title, press Enter and turn off the centering format by pressing Alt-P (for plain paragraph); the cursor will move to the far left. If you want your material to be double-spaced, as in the sample, just press Alt-2—remember to use the 2 key on the top row.

As you're typing the list, type a hyphen, press the Tab key, and then type the instruction for each line. Press Enter at the end of each line. When you're finished, save the document on disk under the name DEPARPRO.

DELETING TEXT

Now that you have typed in your document and reviewed it, let's say you realize that advances in technology have eliminated one of the steps in the list. It's no longer necessary to reset the controls, so you need to delete the second step. There are two ways you can do this. The first method uses the Delete key.

allow you to save and restore up to three sets of deletions (see Appendix C).

M O U S E

Click left on the selection bar to the left of the text to select it. (Using the mouse to select text can speed up keyboard operations.)

DELETING WITH THE DELETE KEY

In Word, you must first highlight your chosen text before you can actually delete it. To highlight with the mouse, you use the selection bar. Follow these steps to delete the line

– **Reset Controls.**

1. Move the cursor to the line and highlight it by pressing Shift-F9.

2. Press the Delete key.

Presto: the entire line is removed from the screen and placed in the scrap area, as shown in Figure 6.2. Two things are important to notice here.

First, we had to highlight the line. Highlighting the sentence (using Shift-F7 or Shift-F8) would not have worked: the hyphen preceding the list and the invisible paragraph mark at the end wouldn't have been included in the deletion, because Word does not consider them part of the sentence.

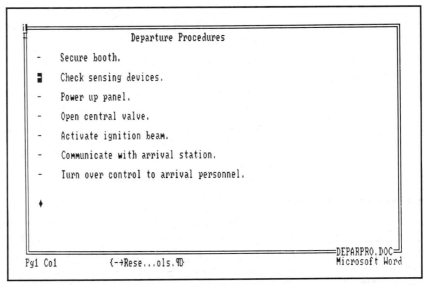

Figure 6.2: Deleting an item in the DEPARPRO document

Second, notice that your deleted text now appears in the scrap area, along with some strange symbols. First, there's the hyphen. Next to it is a right arrow, which indicates the tab. After the tab mark you see

Rese...ols

followed by a paragraph mark (¶). This is the invisible character created by pressing the Enter key. Table 6.1 lists the characters that you might find displayed in the scrap area, along with their meanings.

The material that appears in the scrap area always replaces whatever was there before. Scrap does not build up in Word.

DELETING WITH THE DELETE COMMAND

You can also use the Delete command to delete text. Besides deleting to the scrap area, you can use it to send material to the glossary. (We'll see how in Chapter 15.)

Table 6.1: Symbols in the Scrap Area

Symbol	Meaning
§	Column break or division mark
▯	Dateprint
▮	End of a row (Column Selection on)
♟	Footnote number
↓	New-line mark
▯	Page number
¶	Paragraph mark (carriage return)
•	Space character (suspended dot)
→	Tab or nextpage number
♥	Timeprint

T *I P*

If you are using the keyboard and not the mouse, you will probably want to use the Delete key rather than the Delete command, as it involves fewer keystrokes. If you have a mouse, use it to select text and then use either the Delete key or the mouse with the Delete command.

Let's try the Delete command using the same example we used with the Delete key. To practice, restore the material you just deleted by simply pressing the Insert key: the "Reset controls" line will return to its original position in the DEPARPRO document. (Notice that it remains in the scrap area as well.) Here are the steps for deleting this line with the Delete command:

1. Check that the line

   – Reset controls.

   is highlighted. Reselect it if it isn't.

2. Press the Esc key to activate Command mode.

3. Type D for Delete. The message area now suggests deleting your text to the scrap area (as opposed to the glossary) by displaying

   DELETE to: { }

4. Accept the suggestion by pressing the Enter key. Your text is removed to the scrap area, just as it was in Figure 6.2.

There is no change in the scrap area when you delete or copy the same text to it that was already there.

BYPASSING SCRAP WHEN YOU DELETE

Occasionally, you might encounter a situation where you want to delete something on the screen but retain whatever text is already in the scrap area. Let's say you have a paragraph of important text that you set aside in the scrap area to use momentarily. Unexpectedly, you notice that some text in the window has a typo, say an extra "o" in "boooth." How to get rid of one without disturbing the important text in scrap? Neither the Delete key nor the Delete command enables you to do this.

There are two ways you could handle this situation. You could use the Backspace key to take care of the typo: material that you erase with this key is not sent to the scrap area. The other way is to press Shift-Delete. Shift-Delete operates exactly like the Delete key, except the text disappears without going to the scrap area. If necessary, you

M O U S E

With the line highlighted, click right on the Delete command. By using the right button, you immediately delete the text to the scrap area. There is no suggestion pause, as there would be with the left button.

could reclaim the text with the powerful Undo command, provided you had no intervening edits.

MOVING TEXT

Now that you've learned how to delete text, you're ready to use the delete operation to move a block. For the time being we'll be working with small blocks of text, but the block operations that we perform here can be used just as easily on larger blocks.

Let's swap the positions of two of the lines in DEPARPRO because, in fact, the "Communicate with arrival station" step must come before the "Activate ignition beam" step. To make the switch, we'll perform a block move, shifting the "Communicate with arrival station" step to the spot now occupied by the other step, as shown in Figure 6.3.

To move the "Communicate with arrival station" step, we must first delete it to the scrap area. Then we will move the cursor to the new location: the spot presently occupied by the "Activate ignition beam" line. Lastly, we will insert the "Communicate with arrival station" line from scrap, placing it at the new location.

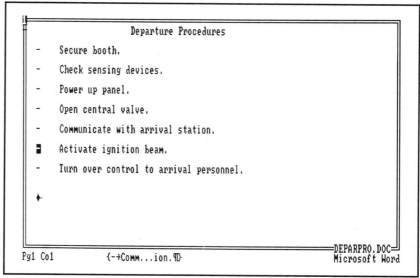

Figure 6.3: Moving an item in the DEPARPRO document

You can move blocks of text in two ways: with the Delete and Insert keys or with the Delete and Insert commands.

MOVING WITH THE DELETE AND INSERT KEYS

To move the ''Communicate with arrival station'' line using the Delete and Insert keys, do the following:

M O U S E

To highlight the line quickly, click left on the selection bar next to the line.

1. Highlight the line of text by pressing Shift-F9.

2. Press the Delete key. Doing so removes the line from the screen and places it in the scrap area.

3. Move the cursor to your new location; that is, position it on the hyphen that begins the ''Activate ignition beam'' line.

4. Press the Insert key.

The line in the scrap area is inserted in the new location.

When you insert text, always use the first character in the scrap area as your guide. Position the cursor on the spot where you want that character to go. The rest of the text will follow along and fall into place.

Now look at the scrap area. The text that you inserted is still there. When you insert from scrap, Word inserts an identical copy of the scrap: the text remains in scrap even after the move.

T I P

Word supplies the macro, **move_text-.mac**, which prompts you to select the text to be moved and indicate the destination; then it inserts the text there (see Appendix C).

MOVING WITH THE DELETE AND INSERT COMMANDS

When you use the Delete and Insert commands to move, the resulting action is the same as if you used the Delete and Insert keys. First you issue the Delete command to delete the text to scrap; then you invoke the Insert command to copy the scrap text to the new location.

M O U S E

Click left on the selection bar next to the line to highlight it. Then click right on Delete to delete it.

1. Highlight the line of text to be moved.

2. Press Esc and type D for Delete. Word proposes deleting to scrap.

Click left on the hyphen before "Activate" to move the cursor there and click right on Insert to insert the scrap material at the cursor position.

3. Press the Enter key. Word deletes the material and places it in scrap.

4. Move the cursor to the new location (the hyphen before "Activate").

5. To run the Insert command, press Esc and type I for Insert. Like the Delete command, the Insert command proposes to use the text that's in the scrap area. It displays

    INSERT from: {}

6. Press the Enter key to accept the proposition. Word then inserts the scrap text to the cursor position.

BYPASSING SCRAP TO MOVE WITH THE MOUSE

Using the mouse to move text as I just described involves switching back and forth between the text area and the command panel frequently. To simplify move operations with the mouse, Word provides another method that bypasses the scrap area. These are the steps you perform:

1. Highlight the material you want to move.

2. Move the pointer to the new location.

3. Hold down the Ctrl key and click either or both of the mouse buttons.

Once you've got the pointer on the correct line of text, the way you complete the command will determine the precise location of the moved material. The highlighted text will be placed in front of the letter you're indicating if you press Ctrl-left button. If you press Ctrl-right button, Word moves the text in front of the word you're pointing to. If you press Ctrl-both buttons, it goes in front of the sentence. (The pointer can be on the second line if the sentence straddles two lines.)

With the pointer on the selection bar, pressing Ctrl-left button moves the material to the beginning of the line; Ctrl-right button moves the material to the beginning of the paragraph; and

Ctrl-both buttons moves the material to the beginning of the document. With this technique, you can first highlight the passage that you want to move and then look for the new location by scouting with the mouse on the left window border. Once you've found the spot, you can move the text directly to it.

Thus, we could accomplish our sample move using this method:

1. Highlight the "Communicate with arrival station" line by clicking left on the selection bar next to it.

2. Move the pointer to the selection bar before the "Activate ignition beam" line (Figure 6.4).

3. Press Ctrl-left to move the material to that line.

You can use this method to move the highlighted text anywhere in the document except, of course, within the highlighted text itself. If you attempt to do this, you'll get the message

Cannot move text into itself

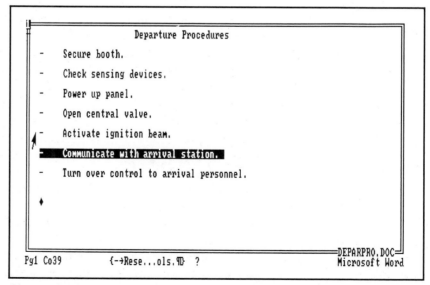

Figure 6.4: Moving with the mouse without using scrap

MOVING AND DELETING ALL AT ONCE

Now that you know the mouse shortcuts for moving, let's exam- ine a keyboard shortcut for moving and deleting, Shift-Insert. You use it when you want to delete highlighted material permanently and at the same time replace it with a copy of the text that's in the scrap area. Thus, Shift-Insert has the same effect as if you pressed Shift-Delete and then pressed the Insert key.

Assume that you have the word ''good'' highlighted on the screen, as in ''the good doctor.'' If the word ''excellent'' is in the scrap area, pressing Shift-Insert will change the screen's text to ''the excellent doctor.'' The word ''excellent'' will still be in scrap as well, and the word ''good'' will be gone for good. (Of course, Undo could get it back if you use it right away.)

COPYING TEXT

Although you have already seen a Word copying operation—it copied from scrap to text when you pressed Insert—there is more to it. Copying differs from moving in that copying keeps the material in the original location and also places an exact copy of it in a new spot. The result is that you have identical copies of the same mate- rial in two locations.

To copy, you can use the Delete and Insert keys, or you can use the Copy and Insert commands. These two methods employ quite different strategies to accomplish the same thing. You can also copy by using the Copy key (Alt-F3).

COPYING WITH THE DELETE AND INSERT KEYS

Using the Delete and Insert keys to perform a copy operation actually constitutes pulling a fast maneuver. Here's how we'll go about it. First, we want to keep the text where it is and place a copy of it in the scrap area. To do this, we highlight the text, delete it to the scrap area, and immediately reinsert it at the same spot. Then we move the cursor to the new location and insert a copy of it there as well.

To practice copying, let's assume that we must make another change in our sample document, DEPARPRO. Suppose you realize that there should be another instruction between "Check sensing devices" and "Power up panel." There are two control valves, and one valve needs to be opened between checking the sensing devices and powering up the panel, while the second needs to be opened after the panel is powered up. You could just type the new step, but this is an ideal job for a copy procedure. Let's try this now.

1. Highlight the line to be copied, "Open central valve," by pressing Shift-F9.

2. Press the Delete key to delete the highlighted text to scrap.

    Shortcut:

    Alt-F3

3. Press the Insert key without moving the cursor to reinsert the text at its original location, leaving an identical copy in the scrap area.

4. Move the cursor to the spot where you want the first character in the scrap area to go—namely, to the hyphen before "Power up panel."

5. Press the Insert key again. This copies the text in the scrap area to the new location, as shown in Figure 6.5.

6. For the finishing touch, add the letters A and B to steps 3 and 5 to identify the two valves to be opened (see Figure 6.6).

COPYING WITH THE COPY AND INSERT COMMANDS

M O U S E

Click left on the selection bar next to the line to be copied to highlight it. Then click right on Copy to copy it. After clicking either button on the location for the copy, click right on Insert to complete the operation.

You can achieve the same end by invoking the Copy and Insert commands. If you use the Copy and Insert commands, you can use either the keyboard or the mouse.

1. Highlight the text for copying by pressing Shift-F9.

2. Copy the highlighted text to scrap by pressing Esc and typing C for Copy. Word proposes copying the text to scrap.

    Shortcut:

    Alt-F3

3. Press Enter to accept the proposal. The text remains at the original location, and Word places a copy of it in the scrap area.

4. Move the cursor to the new location.

5. To insert the text from scrap to the cursor, press Esc and type I for Insert. Word proposes inserting from scrap.

6. Press the Enter key to register the command. Word then inserts the text from scrap at the new location.

Since the Insert command makes a copy of the scrap material at the cursor position, it's easy to confuse it with the Copy command. Remember, you copy *to* the scrap area and insert *from* the scrap area.

BYPASSING SCRAP TO COPY WITH THE MOUSE

Just as with moving, there's a way to bypass the scrap area when you perform a copy operation using the mouse. The methods are almost identical. The only difference is that you use the Shift key rather than the Ctrl key:

1. Highlight the material to be copied.

2. Move the pointer to the new location.

3. Hold down the Shift key and click either or both of the mouse buttons.

Locate the pointer in step 2 and click in step 3 according to the same ground rules we established with moving. For example, to copy the "Open central valve" line, proceed as follows:

1. Highlight the line by clicking left on the selection bar next to it.

2. Move the pointer to the selection bar next to "Power up panel."

3. Copy the "Open central valve" line to the cursor position by pressing Shift-left.

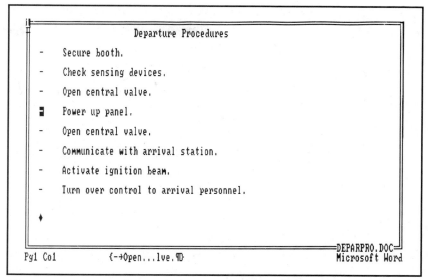

Figure 6.5: Copying an item in the DEPARPRO document

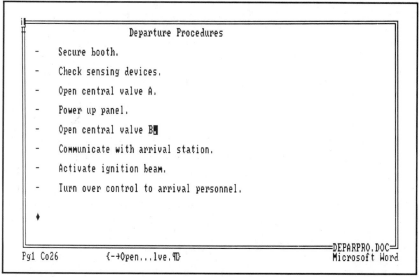

Figure 6.6: Adding the finishing touch after the copy operation

Now that we've examined the various ways of changing the contents of your documents, let's learn how you can keep track of those revisions using Word's revision-mark system.

TRACKING REVISIONS

Word can track the changes you make to your documents, allowing you to reconsider them before they are permanently incorporated. To appreciate this feature, consider how we used to revise typed documents before the days of word processing. First, we examined a rough draft of the document, marking the copy with the desired changes. We then deleted unwanted passages by crossing them out and inserted new material as needed. As a red pencil was often used to cross out deletions, the process became known as *red-lining*. Before retyping, we had the opportunity to reconsider all the revisions (or red-lined material) by reading through the document again.

This ability to evaluate revisions before putting them into place is the advantage that Word's revision-mark (or red-lining) system restores. Previously, changes you made in a word processed document would be final. With the revision-mark system, you can now reconsider the revisions, one by one, before accepting them.

Here's how the revision-mark feature works. First, you turn it on with the Format revision-Marks Options command. Then you make your revisions, using the same deleting and inserting techniques that we've examined in this chapter. As you go, however, Word makes revision marks throughout the document instead of putting the revisions immediately into effect. That is, rather than actually deleting material, Word just crosses it out with strike-through type. Word also underlines new inserted material so that it can be distinguished from the previous text. (You can change underlining as the method that Word uses to demarcate inserted material.)

USING REVISION MARKS

Figure 6.7 shows how the document we've been working with would appear with the revision marks in place, using double underline to flag

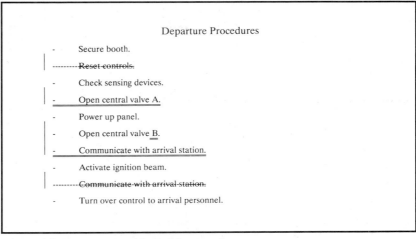

Figure 6.7: Document with revision marks

new text. (I formatted the heading with Times Roman size 14 and the rest of the document with Times Roman size 12. More on fonts in Chapter 7.) Go ahead and set up the revision-mark system following these steps:

M O U S E

Click left on Format and click right on revision-Marks to select the Format revision-Marks Options command. (Using the left button would only select revision-Marks.) Turn on the revision-marks system by clicking right on Yes for the add revision marks option.

1. Press the Esc key and type F for Format.

2. Type M. This stands for the capital M in the Format revision-Marks command. (The R is used by the Format Running-head command.) To remember that Word uses the M, you may wish to think of it as the Format Marks command instead. In any case, this command displays the menu shown in Figure 6.8.

3. Type O for Options. This displays the Format revision-Marks Options menu shown in Figure 6.9.

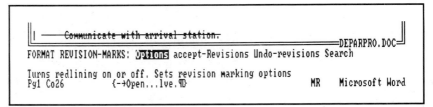

Figure 6.8: The Format revision-Marks command

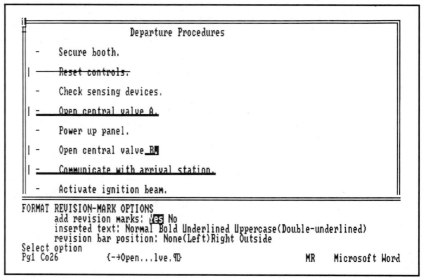

Figure 6.9: The Format revision-Marks Options command

4. To turn on the revision-mark system, set add revision marks to Yes by typing Y and register the command by pressing Enter. The letters

   MR

   then appear in the lock area at the bottom of the screen, as shown in Figure 6.9. MR, which stands for *marking revisions,* reminds you that you are using the revision-mark system. This code remains until you turn the system off by changing add revision marks back to No.

While the revision-mark system is operating, you cannot run Word in Overtype mode (which you set with the F5 key). You also can't use the Backspace key to erase old text; you have to use the Delete key or the Delete command to remove such material instead. (However, the Backspace key does work on new material.)

Let's look at the other settings in the Format revision-Marks Options command menu. Use the inserted text option to specify the manner in which you wish Word to display newly inserted text. Underline is the default setting, but you can choose any of the formats listed. For consistency, Word applies the method you select to the entire document. If you select Normal, Word will not mark newly inserted text; the text will look just like old, existing text.

The revision bar position option governs the use and placement of revision bars. A revision bar is an optional vertical line that Word inserts alongside material that has been revised, acting as a flag to alert you to changes. It appears wherever you deleted material or inserted new text. When you set this option to None, revision bars will not appear in your document. By choosing the Left or Right setting, you can make the bars appear on the left or right side of the page. Choosing Outside makes the bar appear in the document's outer margins (on the left of even-numbered pages and on the right of odd-numbered pages).

Once you have finished editing the document, you can print it with the revision marks in place. That way, you or others can examine your proposed changes to the document.

INCORPORATING REVISIONS

Once your revisions are in place, you have a choice. You can either incorporate all the revisions into your document, or you can review them and selectively incorporate them on a case-by-case basis.

To incorporate all the revisions, follow these steps:

M<u>O U S E</u>

Click both buttons on the selection bar to highlight the entire document. Incorporate all of its revisions by clicking left on Format, clicking left on revision-Marks, and clicking either button on accept-Revisions.

1. Highlight the text containing the revisions. Assuming this is the entire document, press Shift-F10 to do this.

2. To issue the Format revision-Marks accept-Revisions command, press Esc, type F, type M, and then type R. (In Word 4 this was the Format revision-Marks Remove-marks command.)

This will add the new text and the strike-through text will be deleted. The special formatting, if any, that you used to flag the new text will be removed, but the new text's other formatting will be left intact. Word will also remove the revision bars if you turned on that feature.

To decide whether to accept or reject individual revisions, you search for your changes by running the Format revision-Marks Search command and then act on them one by one. Word searches forward in the document and when it finds some revised material, it highlights it. You can then either remove the revision marks, incorporating the revision into the document, or you can undo the revision, restoring the material to its original condition. To incorporate your revisions individually, proceed as follows:

M<u>*O U S E*</u>

Click left on the selection bar near the top of the document to move the cursor before your first revision. To search for a revision, click left on Format, click left on revision-Marks, and click either button on Search. To accept the revision found, click either button on accept-Revisions. To reject the revision, click either button on Undo-revisions. To continue searching for revisions, click either button on Search again and repeat the procedure. When you are done, click both buttons in the command area to return to the main command level.

1. Bring the cursor to the beginning of the document by pressing Ctrl-Page Up or use the directional keys to move it to some point before the first revision that you wish to consider.

2. Press Esc, type F, type M, and type S to invoke the Format revision-Marks Search command. Word heads toward the end of the document, looking for revised text. It highlights the first occurrence of revised text that it finds.

3. Word then presents the highlighted material, continuing to display the Format revision-Marks command menu. Use this menu's accept-Revisions command to incorporate the revised material or use the Undo-revisions command to restore the material to its original condition.

4. After you have made your choice, the Format revision-Marks menu remains on the screen. Run this menu's Search command to locate the next instance of revised text.

5. Repeat steps 2 through 4 for the rest of your document. When you've acted on the last revision, press the Esc key to end the procedure. Attempting to search again after the last revision will display the message

   Revised text not found

   which also ends the procedure.

You can also use the Format revision-Marks Search command simply to locate revisions—you aren't obligated to take any action on them once Word has located them. You might want to do this with a contract, for instance, to check special conditions you've put in place for one party that differ from the norm. By searching for those changes, you can check them before printing the marked version.

Finally, before putting any revisions into effect, you can undo all of them simultaneously by highlighting the entire document and using the Format revision-Marks Undo-revisions command. You could do

T I P

If you mistakenly
delete text and catch
your mistake immedi-
ately, you can simply
issue the Undo com-
mand to fix it.

this to get a copy of the original contract, for instance, should someone request that of you. Be careful though, since you lose your revisions using this command. If you just want to print a copy of
the original and keep the revisions, save the document before you run
the Undo-revisions command. You can then quit Word without saving your changes, which restores all the revisions, or you can save the
document under a new name to keep both the original and revised
versions.

At this point, you are familar with deleting, moving, and copying
blocks of text and keeping track of these maneuvers. In the next chapter, you'll learn how to change the appearance of blocks of text, as
well as the entire document, with fonts.

7

Varying Fonts for Successful Documents

Fast Track

insert a disk containing the fonts. Also, the printer must have enough memory to accommodate all the fonts that you specify.

To create a custom driver for your printer's setup, **186**
you use the MergePRD program provided with Word. First, choose the drivers that have the fonts you want. Then run MergePRD. From this program's Main Menu, specify the drivers that have your fonts. From the Select Fonts and Font Sizes menu, specify the fonts you want. Then save your collection of fonts under a new driver name.

A *FONT* IS A SET OF ALPHANUMERIC CHARACTERS IN a distinctive style and size. Microsoft Word was a pioneer in supporting varied fonts, which is a hallmark of desktop publishing. While other word processors have been sitting on the sidelines, Word has also been exploiting the LaserJet printer to its fullest.

Release 5 adds new font support, including support for color fonts. In this chapter, we'll see how you can apply different fonts to your text. To practice, we'll use the ESPRIT document we created in Chapter 5. We'll also examine the use of fonts on state-of-the-art equipment by studying the way Word works with the LaserJet and PostScript printers.

SELECTING FONTS

T I P

If you plan to use one particular font for most of your documents, you may wish to make it the default font by using the NORMAL.STY style sheet (see Chapter 17). Its settings will become the default settings for documents in its directory. (The initial default font varies from printer to printer.)

T I P

You can use the Print preView command, which accurately displays fonts and spacing on the screen, to examine the effect of fonts before you print. We'll study this command in the next chapter.

The Format Character menu allows you to display the font names and sizes that are available for your printer. The printer driver you choose with the Print Options command determines the choices that appear on the Format Character menu. The Setup program determines the printer drivers that are available with Print Options (see Appendix A).

In measuring font sizes, there are some terms you'll want to become familiar with. The *baseline* is the invisible line that the letters sit on. All capital letters sit on the baseline. Some lowercase letters (g, j, p, q, y) descend below the baseline; the part that extends below the baseline is called the *descender*.

A font's size is measured from top to bottom, from the highest point of a capital letter to the lowest point of a letter's descender. A *point* is simply a unit of measure: there are about 72 points to an inch. Therefore, a 12-point font is 1/72'' × 12, or 1/6'' in height. For the main body of text, generally 10-point and 12-point fonts are used.

The *pitch* of a font can be either *proportional* or *fixed*. (Fixed is also called nonproportional or monospaced.) With proportional fonts, the width of a character varies from character to character; for example, the space allotted for a W is wider than that for an I. This is done to make the text easier to read and enhances its appearance. Characters in a fixed-pitch font are provided with the same amount of space: an I takes up as much room as a W. The characters for the LaserJet Series II's default font (Courier 12) are fixed pitch.

You vary the font sizes in your document to reflect its structure. For example, an important heading should have a larger font (say, 18 points) than its subheads (perhaps 14 points). Headings equal in importance should have the same font size.

Fonts with *serifs,* the thin lines that finish off the main body of a letter or other character, are best used with smaller sizes. Larger type (especially headlines) is generally more readable in *sans-serif* fonts (fonts without serifs).

The font's appearance should be compatible with the subject matter and the image you want to convey. If the subject is staid and formal, generally the font should be, too. On the other hand, if the subject matter is whimsical, you can choose a more informal font.

Selecting a font is a fairly subjective process. Once you have learned how to use the fonts you have, experiment with them to find the font or font combinations you like best.

CHANGING YOUR DOCUMENT'S FONT

Suppose you decide to change the font for your document after you have finished revising it. To do this, proceed as follows:

1. Press Shift-F10 to highlight all the text.

2. Issue the Format Character command by pressing Esc, typing F for Format, and typing C for Character. Then move to the font name field by pressing ↓ three times.

   Shortcut:

   Alt-F8

3. To display the list of font names, press F1 in the font name field. Figure 7.1 presents a sample listing of font names that you could see.

4. Use the arrow keys to highlight the name you want. For example, say you want to choose TMSRMN (Times Roman) from your list, which resembles the list shown in Figure 7.1. Simply press → once and ↓ four times to select it.

5. To display the available sizes for TMSRMN, press the Tab key to move to font size and press F1.

T *IP*

Avoid combining too many fonts on the same page. Most typesetters recommend no more than four.

M *OUSE*

Click both buttons on the selection bar to highlight the entire document. Click right on Format to display the Format Character menu. To display the list of available fonts, click right on the font name option. Click left on the font name you want. To change the size for the font you just selected, click right on the font size field and click right on the size you want. This registers your choices, and you can print the document.

```
┌─────────────────────────────────────────────────────────────────────┐
│                                                                       │
│  Courier (modern a)                   CourierLegal (modern b)         │
│  Prestige (modern c)                  PrestigeLegal (modern d)        │
│  LetterGothic (modern e)              LinePrinter (modern h)          │
│  HELV (modern i)                      OCR-A (modern o)                │
│  OCR-B (modern p)                     TMSRMN (roman a)                │
│  Danish/Norwegian (foreign a)         UnitedKingdom (foreign b)       │
│  French (foreign c)                   German (foreign d)             │
│  Italian (foreign e)                  Swedish/Finnish (foreign f)     │
│  Spanish (foreign g)                  PiFont (symbol a)               │
│  LineDraw (symbol b)                  Math7 (symbol c)                │
│  Math8 (symbol d)                     Bar3of9 (symbol e)              │
│  EAN/UPC (symbol f)                                                   │
│                                                                       │
│                                                                       │
│                                                                       │
│  FORMAT CHARACTER bold: Yes(No)     italic: Yes(No)     underline: Yes(No)│
│           strikethrough: Yes(No)    uppercase: Yes(No)  small caps: Yes(No)│
│           double underline: Yes(No) position:(Normal)Superscript Subscript│
│           font name: Courier        font size: 12      font color: Black│
│           hidden: Yes(No)                                             │
│  Enter font name or press F1 to select from list                     │
│  Pg1 Col              {}                               Microsoft Word │
│                                                                       │
└─────────────────────────────────────────────────────────────────────┘
```

Figure 7.1: Sample font names

6. Use the arrow keys to select the size you want. Since you want the entire letter to fit on one page and be easily read, I recommend you choose 12-point size. Register your choice of font name and size by pressing the Enter key.

When you are selecting either font names or font sizes, always display a list and select from among those available. This way, you'll see which fonts are available for the .PRD file and which font sizes are available for the font you selected. (Word doesn't adjust the size automatically.)

New in
Word 5

If you have a color printer, you can also use the Format Character menu to display and select from the colors that you can assign to the highlighted text. As with the other options, you go to the font color field and press F1 (or click right) to display its list.

Which font colors are available depend on your printer. If you have a color monitor and have chosen the appropriate display mode, you can have Word display text in the correct color on the screen by applying colors to your fonts (more on display modes in Chapter 8).

With color, as with font sizes, restraint is the key to a successful document. Most typographers use only one color (in addition to black) for text within a document. Generally blue and red are the preferred choices.

When you change the font for an entire document, take care to examine the document afterwards. A larger font size, for example, may be available only in boldface, according to the current driver. Should you increase text that isn't bold to that larger font size and then change the text back to the smaller size, you may find the text is still bold, even in the smaller size. Until you have practiced using fonts, it's a good idea to save your document before you change its fonts radically. If you then obtain undesirable effects, you can clear the displayed document, indicating that you wish to lose changes, and retrieve the saved version of the document by reloading it.

5 New in Word 5

You may also find the Alt-Spacebar and Alt-Z codes of use when you are revising your document's fonts and formats. If you decide some text needs to be reformatted, for example, highlight it and press Alt-Spacebar to delete its formatting, including its assigned font name and size. Word then substitutes the default font for the text. Pressing Alt-Z (new in Word 5) turns off all formatting except the assigned font name and size.

For many printers, you can obtain information on the listed font names and sizes by referring to your printer's manual. You can also try them out by formatting and printing some text. You probably want to print the sample document now to see how your new font looks.

ADJUSTING THE LINE SPACING FOR THE FONT

When you use different-sized fonts, you may have to adjust your line spacing to accommodate them. To do this, you use the Format Paragraph's line spacing option. Normally, it is set to 1 line, which means 12 points, regardless of the font size you're using. Thus, if you select an 18-point font, you'll find that your lines of text overlap.

To have Word automatically provide the appropriate line spacing for the font's size, set line spacing to Auto. Using Auto gives the appearance of single-spacing. You can achieve the same printed effect by entering the point value yourself. Thus, entering 18 pt for line spacing with an 18-point font prints the same results as using Auto.

If you want double-spacing, something between single and double, or something even greater than double, you must enter the appropriate value yourself. For instance, to double-space an 18-point font, provide a spacing of 36 pt. For spacing of a line and a half, use 27 pt, and so on.

If you have an 18-point font, practice selecting it for a small document. Then, see if you can print the document single-spaced by using Auto, double-spaced by using 36 pt, and spaced with 1½ lines by using 27 pt.

FORMATTING WITH LASER PRINTERS

Choosing fonts for sophisticated printers like the LaserJet and PostScript printers requires some preparatory work—you have to install the fonts before you can experiment with them.

Word does not provide you with fonts, as some desktop publishing packages do. It simply allows you to use the fonts that you have or can obtain, independently of Word. Therefore, the fonts listed for the driver may not match the fonts that you actually have. In this section, we'll see how to overcome this possible setback.

USING THE LASERJET

LaserJet fonts come in three forms: internal, cartridge, and downloadable. *Internal* fonts are built into the printer itself; they are always available when you use the printer. *Cartridge* fonts are bought separately and plugged into the printer, while *downloadable* fonts are installed into the computer. Cartridge and downloadable fonts both require a printer driver (.PRD) file; however, downloadable fonts also need a .DAT file to be used. Many printer drivers come with Word, and you can obtain additional drivers from Microsoft.

Internal fonts for the LaserJet Series II are Courier 12, Courier Bold 12, and Line Printer 8.5. Each is fixed pitch and available in *portrait* (standard vertical) and *landscape* (horizontal or sideways) orientation. For example, if you're using Courier 12 and you format some text as boldface (with Alt-B), Word will print Courier Bold 12 automatically. You needn't change the font to create boldfacing. Note that italic type is not built into the LaserJet. To print italics, you must add its character set as a separate font, either as a cartridge or downloadable font.

Since the internal fonts offer you a limited variety—two fixed-pitch typefaces and boldfacing—you will definitely want to acquire more fonts. Most fonts for the LaserJet are available either on cartridges or as downloadable fonts. Hewlett-Packard provides a multitude of fonts on cartridges labeled A through Z; for example, Helvetica (HELV) and Times Roman (TMSRM) are on the B cartridge. Each cartridge contains up to eight typefaces and you can plug two cartridges into the Series II at a time. Each time you print a file that has been formatted with cartridge fonts, you need to verify that the correct cartridges are inserted into the printer and use the appropriate printer driver (.PRD) file. Check Table 7.1 for the .PRD file to use with your cartridge.

Downloadable fonts, which are sometimes called soft fonts, come to you on disk, just like documents or programs. Generally, you copy them to your hard disk. When you print a document, Word locates the font files on the disk and sends a copy of them to the printer. The printer stores the font specifications in its memory and then uses them for printing with one of those fonts.

USING POSTSCRIPT PRINTERS

To use PostScript printers, issue the Print Options command and specify POSTSCRP as the printer driver (.PRD) file. You can also download fonts with the PSDOWN file as the printer driver.

PostScript printers provide you with the ability to closely simulate typeset material, just as the LaserJet Series II does. For the highest quality printing, you can set up your file for a PostScript printer (which we won't go into here), preview it by printing it, and take the finalized document to a typesetter. This way, you'll be certain how the document will turn out.

Table 7.1: Word 5 Driver Files for HP LaserJet Cartridges

FONT NAMES	FONT SIZES		
HPLASER.PRD on Printers 2 disk **(Internal fonts only)**			
Courier	10	12	
CourierPC	10	12	
LinePrinter	8.5		
LinePrinterPC	8.5		
HPLASER1.PRD on Printers 2 disk **Cartridges: A B C D E G H J L M N Q W X**			
Courier	12		
CourierLegal	12		
CourierPC	12		
Prestige	7	10	
PrestigeLegal	7	10	
LetterGothic	9.5	10	14
LinePrinter	8.5		
HELV	14		
OCR-A	12		
OCR-B	12		
TMSRMN	8	10	
Danish/Norwegian	12		
UnitedKingdom	12		
French	12		
German	12		
Italian	12		
Swedish/Finnish	12		

Table 7.1: Word 5 Driver Files for HP LaserJet Cartridges (continued)

FONT NAMES	FONT SIZES					
Spanish	12					
PiFont	10					
LineDraw	10	12				
Math7	10					
Math8	7	10				
Bar3of9	12	13				
EAN/UPC	12					
HPLASER2.PRD on Printers 2 disk **Cartridges: F K P R U**						
Courier	12					
CourierPC	12					
LetterGothic	8	14				
LetterGothicLegal	14					
LinePrinter	8.5					
HELV	6	8	10	12	14	15
Presentation	14	16	18			
PresentationLegal	14	16	18			
TMSRMN	8	10				
PiFont	10					
LineDraw	12	14				
Math7	10					
Math8	8	10				
PCLine	14					

Table 7.1: Word 5 Driver Files for HP LaserJet Cartridges (continued)

FONT NAMES	FONT SIZES			
HPLASER3.PRD on Printers 2 disk **Cartridges: J R Z**				
Courier	12			
CourierPC	12			
Prestige	7	10		
LetterGothic	14			
LetterGothicLegal	14			
LinePrinter	8.5			
HELV	8	10	12	14
Presentation	14	16	18	
PresentationLegal	14	16	18	
TMSRMN	8	10	12	14
PiFont	10			
LineDraw	14			
Math7	10			
Math8	7	10		
PCLine	14			
HPLASLAN.PRD on Printers 2 disk **Cartridges: A B C G H L M N P Q R U V (landscape)**				
Courier	12			
CourierPC	12			
Prestige	7	10		
LetterGothic	8	10	14	
LetterGothicLegal	14			
LinePrinter	8.5			
LinePrinterPC	8.5			

Table 7.1: Word 5 Driver Files for HP LaserJet Cartridges (continued)

FONT NAMES	FONT SIZES				
HELV	6	8	10	12	14
Presentation	14	16	18		
PresentationLegal	14	16	18		
TMSRMN	10				
LineDraw	12	14			
PCLine	14				
HPLASMS.PRD on Printers 2 disk **Cartridges: Z Z1A**					
Courier	12				
CourierPC	12				
LinePrinter	8.5				
HELV	8	10	12	14	
TMSRMN	8	10	12	14	
HPLASMS2.PRD on Printers 2 disk **Cartridges: Z 1A**					
Courier	12				
CourierPC	12				
LinePrinter	8.5				
LinePrinterPC	8.5				
HELV	8	10	12	14	
TMSRMN	8	10	12	14	

Table 7.1: Word 5 Driver Files for HP LaserJet Cartridges (continued)

FONT NAMES	FONT SIZES
HPLASMSL.PRD on Printers 2 disk Cartridge: Z (landscape)	
Courier	12
CourierPC	12
LinePrinter	8.5
HPLASPS.PRD on Printers 2 disk Cartridge: B	
Courier	12
CourierPC	12
LinePrinter	8.5
HELV	14
TMSRMN	8 10
HPLASRMN.PRD on Printers 2 disk Cartridge: F	
Courier	12
CourierPC	12
LinePrinter	8.5
LinePrinterPC	8.5
HELV	14
TMSRMN	8 10

Table 7.1: Word 5 Driver Files for HP LaserJet Cartridges (continued)

FONT NAMES	FONT SIZES
HPLASTAX.PRD on Printers 2 disk **Cartridge: T**	
Courier	12
CourierPC	12
LinePrinter	8.5
HELV	6 8 10 12 14
LineDraw	12
HPLAS2S1.PRD on Printers 2 disk **Cartridge: S1**	
Courier	10 12
LinePrinter	8.5
HPLAS2S2.PRD on Printers 2 disk **Cartridge: S2**	
Courier	12
LinePrinter	8.5
HELV	14
TMSRMN	8 12
HPPCCOUR.PRD on Printers 2 disk **Cartridge: Y**	
Courier	12
CourierPC	12
LinePrinter	8.5

Table 7.1: Word 5 Driver Files for HP LaserJet Cartridges (continued)

FONT NAMES	FONT SIZES			
HPPRO.PRD on Utilities/Printers disk				
Courier	10	12		
CourierPC	12			
CourierLegal	10	12		
Prestige	7	10		
PrestigeLegal	7	10		
LetterGothic	3.5	6	9.5	12
LinePrinter	8.5			
HELV	8	10	12	14
HelvLegal	14			
TMSRMN	8	10	12	
TmsRmnLegal	8	10	12	
HPPROL.PRD on Utilities/Printers disk				
Courier	10	12		
CourierPC	12			
Prestige	7	10		
LetterGothic	3.5	6	9.5	12
LinePrinter	8.5			

USING DOWNLOADABLE FONTS

Because the procedures for downloading files are somewhat complicated, let's examine the use of downloadable fonts and printer drivers with the LaserJet. To use any downloadable font with the LaserJet, you have to have two corresponding .PRD and .DAT files in the same hard disk directory—these files were copied to your Word directory when you used the Setup program to install Word (Appendix A). If you are using another directory to store fonts and drivers, invoke the Print Options command and specify the driver in the printer field, providing the complete path, such as

C:\FONTS\HPDWNACP.PRD

New in
Word 5

If you are not sure of the driver's name or directory location, you can press F1 or click right on the printer field to list the possible drivers. To change to another directory, highlight it and press F1 or click right again to see its .PRD files.

To check whether you have the right files for a particular font, you can consult Table 7.2. Note that you need one pair of files to use a downloadable font in portrait orientation and a different pair for landscape orientation.

When you use downloadable fonts, the printer must have enough memory to accommodate all the fonts needed to print a given document. If you have chosen more fonts for your document than the printer's memory can handle, Word will substitute a standard Courier font in place of any font it cannot download. If you don't like the results, you can either reformat your document so that it uses fewer

Table 7.2: Word 5 .PRD and .DAT Files for HP LaserJet Downloadable Fonts

FONT NAMES	FONT SIZES							
HPDWNACP.PRD and HPDWNACP.DAT **on Printers 2 disk** **Downloadable Set: AC**								
Courier	12							
CourierPC	12							
LinePrinter	8.5							
HELV	6	8	10	12	14	18	24	30
TMSRMN	6	8	10	12	14	18	24	30

Table 7.2: Word 5 .PRD and .DAT Files for HP LaserJet Downloadable Fonts (continued)

FONT NAMES	FONT SIZES							
HPDWNACL.PRD and HPDWNACL.DAT **on Utilities/Printers disk** **Downloadable Set: AC (landscape)**								
Courier	12							
CourierPC	12							
LinePrinter	8.5							
HELV	6	8	10	12	14	18	24	30
TMSRMN	6	8	10	12	14	18	24	30
HPDWNADP.PRD and HPDWNADP.DAT **on Printers 2 disk** **Downloadable Set: AD**								
Courier	12							
CourierPC	12							
LinePrinter	8.5							
HELV	6	8	10	12	14	18	24	30
TMSRMN	6	8	10	12	14	18	24	30
HPDWNADL.PRD and HPDWNADL.DAT **on Printers 2 disk** **Downloadable Set: AD (landscape)**								
Courier	12							
CourierPC	12							
LinePrinter	8.5							
HELV	6	8	10	12	14	18	24	30
TMSRMN	6	8	10	12	14	18	24	30

fonts or you can substitute cartridge fonts. Or, of course, you can purchase more memory for your printer. To provide additional memory for the Series II, you can plug in a memory board of 1, 2, or 4 megabytes.

When Word 5 is printing and encounters a font that it must download to the printer, it displays the message

Enter Y to download New Fonts, A to download All Fonts, N to skip

If you press Y, Word downloads only the new fonts it encounters; the printer checks the font specifications it has in memory for the fonts that were previously downloaded. Pressing A tells Word to download all fonts, which would be necessary if you had just turned the printer on. Press N if you want Word to skip the downloading operation. You can do this if you have already downloaded the font to the printer (by previously printing the same document without turning the printer off afterward, for instance). Pressing N in this case allows you to save the time necessary for downloading. You can also press Esc here to cancel the printing.

Try printing the sample document with which we've been working by following these steps:

1. Issue the Print Options command to specify the appropriate .PRD file for your downloadable fonts.

2. Invoke the Print Printer command to print the document. When prompted, respond with Y to download the fonts. Insert a disk with the fonts if prompted to do so.

3. Compare your document to Figure 7.2, which shows a printed "before-and-after" shot of the sample document. The entire letter has been formatted with 12-point Times Roman (TMSRMN) font.

 New in Word 5

If Word 5 cannot find the downloadable font that you specified, you'll see a message that begins with

Download file not found. Enter Y to read A:

followed by the name of the file for the font. This would happen if you had not copied the font to the hard disk. This message gives you the

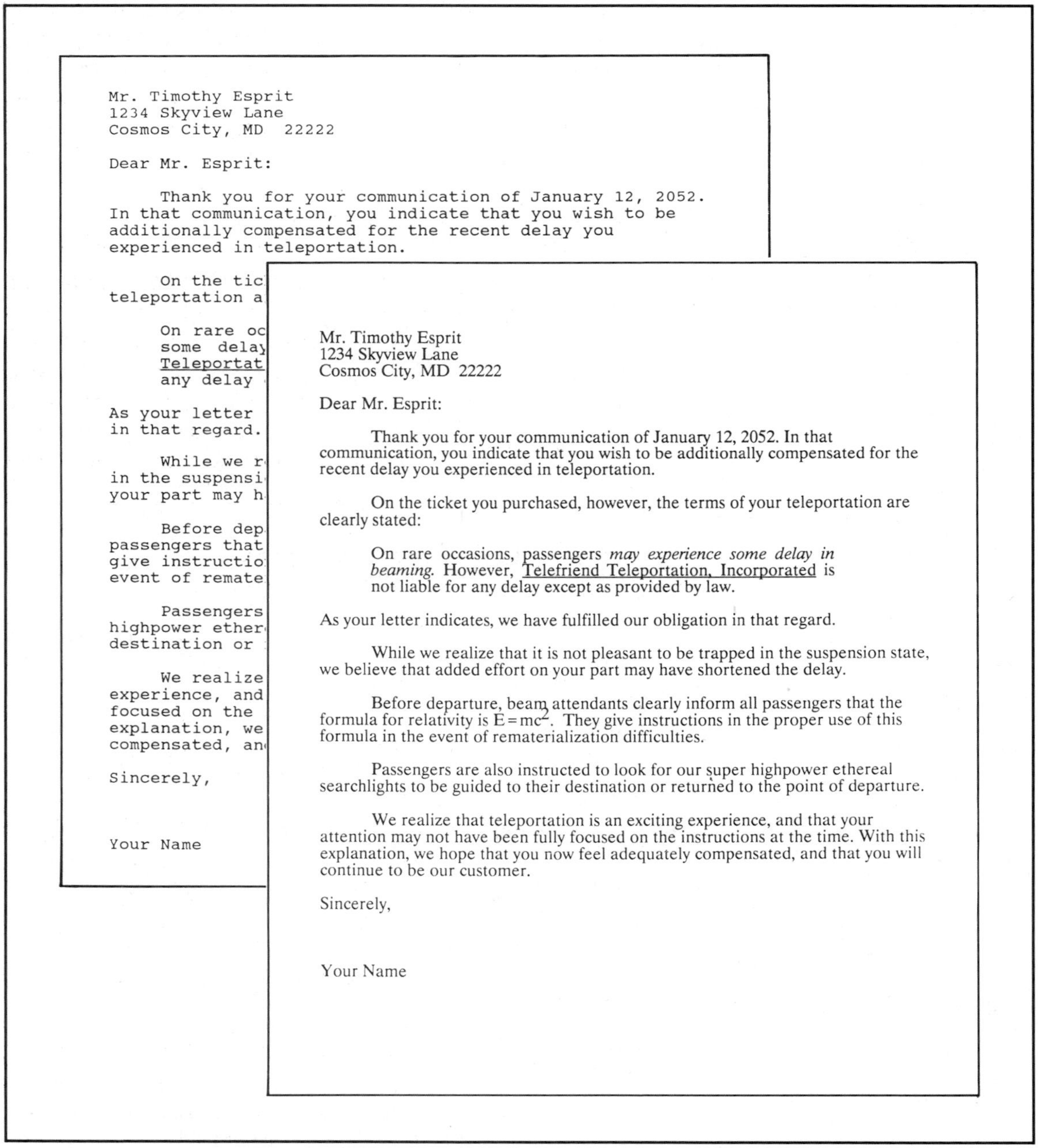

```
Mr. Timothy Esprit
1234 Skyview Lane
Cosmos City, MD  22222

Dear Mr. Esprit:

     Thank you for your communication of January 12, 2052.
In that communication, you indicate that you wish to be
additionally compensated for the recent delay you
experienced in teleportation.

          On the tic
teleportation a

          On rare oc
          some delay
          Teleportat
          any delay

As your letter
in that regard.

          While we r
in the suspensi
your part may h

          Before dep
passengers that
give instructio
event of remate

          Passengers
highpower ether
destination or

          We realize
experience, and
focused on the
explanation, we
compensated, an

Sincerely,


Your Name
```

Mr. Timothy Esprit
1234 Skyview Lane
Cosmos City, MD 22222

Dear Mr. Esprit:

    Thank you for your communication of January 12, 2052. In that communication, you indicate that you wish to be additionally compensated for the recent delay you experienced in teleportation.

    On the ticket you purchased, however, the terms of your teleportation are clearly stated:

    On rare occasions, passengers *may experience some delay in beaming*. However, <u>Telefriend Teleportation, Incorporated</u> is not liable for any delay except as provided by law.

As your letter indicates, we have fulfilled our obligation in that regard.

    While we realize that it is not pleasant to be trapped in the suspension state, we believe that added effort on your part may have shortened the delay.

    Before departure, beam attendants clearly inform all passengers that the formula for relativity is $E = mc^2$. They give instructions in the proper use of this formula in the event of rematerialization difficulties.

    Passengers are also instructed to look for our super highpower ethereal searchlights to be guided to their destination or returned to the point of departure.

    We realize that teleportation is an exciting experience, and that your attention may not have been fully focused on the instructions at the time. With this explanation, we hope that you now feel adequately compensated, and that you will continue to be our customer.

Sincerely,

Your Name

Figure 7.2: Printing the FEEDBACK document

opportunity to insert a disk containing the font in drive A, which means you can keep your fonts on floppy disks and insert them as necessary, rather than keep them on the hard disk. For example, if you use three or four downloadable fonts regularly and need to conserve space on your hard disk, just install them on the hard disk and store all your other downloadable fonts on floppies.

USING SEVERAL FONTS IN YOUR DOCUMENT

Using more than one font in the same document is not difficult. For example, suppose you want to add a letterhead at the top of the page and increase the size of the company name that appears within it. First, enter the letterhead text as it appears in Figure 7.3. Because the company name will be set in large type, you decide to use a sans-serif font for it. Helvetica (HELV) is a nice sans-serif font that goes well with Times Roman. Assuming you have this font, here's how

---

Telefriend Teleportation, Incorporated
9876 Beacon Boulevard
Das Universe, California 99999

Mr. Timothy Esprit
1234 Skyview Lane
Cosmos City, MD 22222

Dear Mr. Esprit:

Thank you for your communication of January 12, 2052. In that communication, you indicate that you wish to be additionally compensated for the recent delay you experienced in teleportation.

On the ticket you purchased, however, the terms of your teleportation are clearly stated:

On rare occasions, passengers *may experience some delay in beaming*. However, <u>Telefriend Teleportation, Incorporated</u> is not liable for any delay except as provided by law.

As your letter indicates, we have fulfilled our obligation in that regard.

While we realize that it is not pleasant to be trapped in the suspension state, we believe that added effort on your part may have shortened the delay.

Before departure, beam attendants clearly inform all passengers that the formula for relativity is $E=mc^2$. They give instructions in the proper use of this formula in the event of rematerialization difficulties.

Figure 7.3: Announcing your letter with a large letterhead

you'd select it in 18-point size for the letterhead:

1. Highlight the company name, "Telefriend Teleportation, Incorporated" using the F6 key.

2. Press Esc, type F, and type C to invoke the Format Character command and move to its font name field.

3. Press F1 to list the available fonts and select HELV.

4. Tab to the font size field and press F1 to list the sizes available for HELV.

5. Highlight 18 and press Enter to register the command.

Although you could also type in the size that you want, displaying a list and highlighting a size helps assure that the size you specify is available.

Repeat the previous steps to select fonts for the sample document as shown in Figure 7.4. If you don't have these fonts, substitute others, but try to keep the sizes proportional to one another as they are in the example.

MERGING FONTS TO CREATE A NEW PRINTER DRIVER

If none of the drivers that Word provides contain the right combination of fonts that you have for your printer, you can build your own driver. This could happen, for instance, if you are using two cartridges, or one or two cartridges and downloadable fonts, or several sets of downloadable fonts.

It's wise to have the fonts on your driver correctly reflect the fonts that are available for your printer's setup. This way, the fonts you select with the Format Character command are accurately depicted and usable. If your driver does not have all the fonts in it that are available, you won't be able to use some of the fonts that you have (unless you switch drivers, which in turn can make other fonts unavailable). If your driver lists fonts that you don't have, you could end up choosing them from the Format Character menu only to get an error message when you print.

The MergePRD program is your key to creating a proper driver for your printer setup. With it, you can pick and choose fonts from

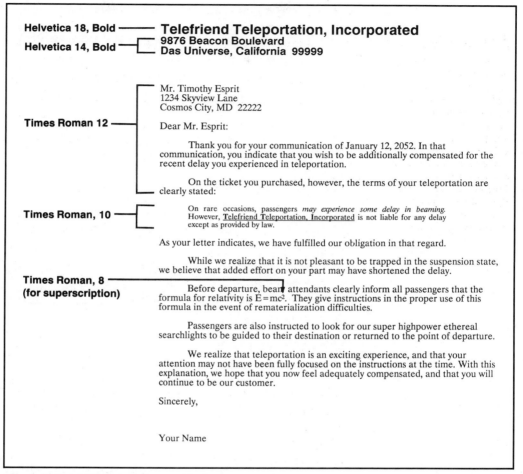

Figure 7.4: Adding more fonts to the letter

among existing drivers, and then save the fonts as a new driver under a name that you provide.

To select from the drivers that are already installed, first invoke Word's Print Options command. Move to the printer field and press F1 to display the list of drivers. Then jot down what appears so you can specify the drivers you want when you run MergePRD. Consult Table 7.2 to determine which files you need for the LaserJet. If you're using some other printer, you can see what's available by using the MergePRD program itself; I'll explain how shortly.

When you set up Word, a copy of the MergePRD program was placed in the directory you specified. You can now run the program by entering its path and name, for example,

C:\WORD\MERGEPRD

at the system prompt. This displays the MergePRD opening screen (see Figure 7.5). Enter 1, 2, or 3 to indicate the type of printer you are working with.

When you make your selection, the Main Menu appears (Figure 7.6). Begin by selecting 1 to specify the .PRD files (drivers) that you wish to use. Enter the drivers one at a time, providing the complete path and pressing Enter after each driver. You don't need to give the .PRD extension.

After you're done, the Main Menu appears again. If you want to check on the fonts that you can use, enter 2. The fonts are then listed on the screen (see Figure 7.7). Each font's .PRD file is indicated, as well as the names that the font goes by and the sizes in which it is available. Pressing any key returns you to the Main Menu.

```
MergePRD 2.00 - Microsoft Word Printer Description (.PRD) Merging Utility

Copyright (c) James E. Walsh, 1987, 1988, 1989. All Rights Reserved.
Portions Copyright (c) Intuition Systems Corporation, 1987, 1988, 1989.
All Rights Reserved.


        Welcome to MergePRD. This utility will help you customize your
    printer driver for the fonts you are using with Microsoft Word.


            What type of printer are you using?

    1) A Hewlett-Packard LaserJet Series printer or compatible. (For
          example, HP LaserJet, HP LaserJet+, HP Series II, HP 2000, etc.)
    2) A PostScript printer. (For example, an Apple LaserWriter)
    3) Other. (For example, an Epson Printer)

    Enter selection:
```

Figure 7.5: MergePRD's opening screen

```
              MergePRD - Microsoft Word .PRD Merging Utility


                              Main Menu

        1) Enter input .PRD list
        2) Display the list of available fonts and font sizes
        3) Print the list of available fonts and font sizes
        4) Select fonts and font sizes
        5) Display selected fonts and font size entries
        6) Change bin support
        7) Create the output .PRD file with the fonts you have selected
        8) Quit program

        Enter selection:
```

Figure 7.6: MergePRD's Main Menu

```
                              Main Menu

           1) Enter input .PRD list
           2) Display the list of available fonts and font sizes
           3) Print the list of available fonts and font sizes
           4) Select fonts and font sizes
           5) Display selected fonts and font size entries
           6) Change bin support
           7) Create the output .PRD file with the fonts you have selected
           8) Quit program

           Enter selection: 2


Font  PRD File  Generic     Font Name     Sizes
  #
  0   HPLASER   Modern a    Courier       10 12
  1   HPLASER   Modern b    CourierPC     10 12
  2   HPLASER   Modern h    LinePrinter    8.5
  3   HPDWNACP  Modern a    Courier       12
  4   HPDWNACP  Modern b    CourierPC     12
  5   HPDWNACP  Modern h    LinePrinter    8.5
  6   HPDWNACP  Modern i    HELV           6  8 10 12 14 18 24 30
  7   HPDWNACP  Roman a     TMSRMN         6  8 10 12 14 18 24 30
Press a key to continue...
```

Figure 7.7: Displaying the list of available fonts

To select fonts, press 4. This displays the Select Fonts and Font Sizes menu (see Figure 7.8). After you choose one of its first five menu options and complete the procedure, the menu reappears. When you're done working with it, you must enter 6 to return to the Main Menu. Assuming you have the correct driver files installed on your hard disk and you don't need to make any changes to their font entries, you only need to use the first menu option to build your own driver.

To select this option, press 1. MergePRD then displays the fonts that are available and asks you to enter the number for the font you want (see Figure 7.9). The font numbers are listed in the left-hand column. As you can see in Figure 7.9, I entered 6 for the HELV font. MergePRD displays the sizes that are available for that font name, and as the prompt indicates, you should enter the sizes that you want, separated by spaces. For example, you can enter

10 12 14 18

if you want only these sizes. Be sure to specify only the sizes that you actually have, as indicated in the documentation for your fonts or on

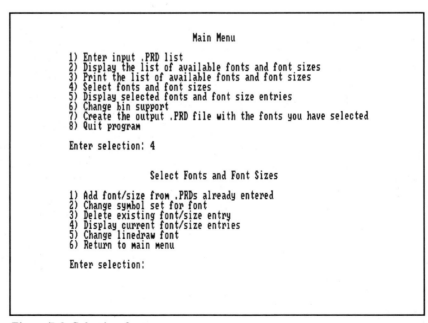

```
                        Main Menu

        1) Enter input .PRD list
        2) Display the list of available fonts and font sizes
        3) Print the list of available fonts and font sizes
        4) Select fonts and font sizes
        5) Display selected fonts and font size entries
        6) Change bin support
        7) Create the output .PRD file with the fonts you have selected
        8) Quit program

     Enter selection: 4


                   Select Fonts and Font Sizes

        1) Add font/size from .PRDs already entered
        2) Change symbol set for font
        3) Delete existing font/size entry
        4) Display current font/size entries
        5) Change linedraw font
        6) Return to main menu

     Enter selection:
```

Figure 7.8: Selecting fonts

```
        Font  PRD File   Font Name      Set
          0   HPLASER    Courier        R8
          1   HPLASER    CourierPC      P8
          2   HPLASER    LinePrinter    R8
          3   HPDWNACP   Courier        R8
          4   HPDWNACP   CourierPC      P8
          5   HPDWNACP   LinePrinter    R8
          6   HPDWNACP   HELV           US
          7   HPDWNACP   TMSRMN         US




        Add - Enter Font # (0-7): 6

          6   HPDWNACP   Modern i    HELV        6  8 10 12 14 18 24 30
        Enter Sizes desired, separated by spaces, then press Enter
        (ALL = All Sizes):
```

Figure 7.9: Selecting font sizes

the label of its disk or cartridge. You can enter ALL if you have all the
sizes for that font name.

Continue working with this screen until you have all the fonts you
need. Press Enter a second time when you're done to redisplay the
Select Fonts and Font Sizes menu. Notice that you can use options 2
to 6 to further customize your .PRD file. The second option allows
you to change the extended character set associated with the font (discussed in Chapter 11); the third option allows you to delete fonts; the
fourth option allows you to see a list of the fonts you have selected;
and the fifth option permits you to change the font with which Word
draws lines (this feature is also discussed in Chapter 11).

Select 6 to return to the Main Menu. From the Main Menu,
choose 7 to combine the fonts you've indicated into a new driver file.
Specify a name, including its complete path; MergePRD then saves
the new driver on the disk. Exit MergePRD from the Main Menu by
choosing 8. You are now ready to use Word's Print Options command to install your custom driver file. Once you do so, the Format
Character command will accurately reflect the fonts that your printer
setup has.

Using the right combination of fonts can enhance the appearance of any document. As we proceed through this book, we'll apply various fonts to the examples we create. Of course, the fonts you have may differ. Nonetheless, you can experiment with your fonts when you format the examples. In the next chapter, you'll learn how Word 5 lets you see those fonts on the screen, as well as in print.

8

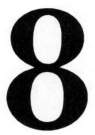

Multiple
Views with
Word's
Windows and
Displays

Fast Track

A WINDOW IS SIMPLY A VIEW OF A FILE THAT YOU ARE editing. As your documents get longer, you may want to split the screen so that you can look at the different parts of your document at one time. Suppose that as you are writing a long proposal, you decide a certain section in the middle of a document should be moved to the end. Using two windows allows you to perform such an operation more easily and assess the impact of a move or copy operation on both parts of your document simultaneously. Windows are thus an important tool for anyone engaged in writing or revising a long piece of text. What is more, you can take something from one document and put it in another by using the Copy, Delete, and Insert commands with windows.

When you choose to work with several windows, you can split the window horizontally or vertically. You can also create a special window for footnotes, as we'll see in Chapter 9. *You* determine the size of the windows, doing so when the window is created or anytime after it has been opened.

To create, change, or close windows, you can use either the Window commands or the mouse pointer on the right or upper window border. The mouse offers a real advantage when you are working with windows: it is much easier and quicker to create, change, or close a window with the mouse than with the Window commands. If you prefer using the keyboard, however, you can improve window performance by using macros (see Chapter 15).

While you can open as many as eight different windows on your screen at once, you will generally need to open at most three windows, since you work in the *activated* window, and only one window can be activated at a time. Opening more than three windows takes up a lot of room with a normal-sized screen and, except with macros, would probably become more confusing than helpful. Because of such screen limitations, you might find it helpful to remove the command menu so you can see more text when you are working with more than one window. You can do this by setting show menu in the Options command to No.

Let's create a sample text with which to practice using windows. If you have a document on the screen, save it. Then perform the Transfer Clear Window command, so you can type the material shown in Figure 8.1 on a clear screen. I formatted the first two lines with Times

To: Staff

From: **Jess January, Telefriend New York Division Head**

Feedback indicates that there seems to be some misunderstanding in regard to certain areas of the recent quarterly report. The purpose of this memo is to clarify the information presented and to act as a springboard for further discussion.

We hope that this memo will aid in clearing up questions and uncertainties. I will be glad to provide further clarification if necessary.

(1) Efficiency of Service

Overall efficiency was definitely improved. Even though there have been problems in some areas, the programs that were instituted in the previous quarter have made a positive impact. For example, incidents of lost luggage have declined drastically, and there is every indication that this trend will continue. (Table 1.)

(2) Sales

Sales have dropped slightly, but only to the degree expected for this time of year. Undoubtedly, considerable improvement will be seen during the holidays, although it may not be as much as originally projected. (Table 2.)

We did consider the introduction of a discount travel arrangement, but we decided to table this idea until next year at the earliest.

(3) Commissary Furniture

The commissary has made arrangements to deal with the problem furniture that was installed. Tables that have proved to be too low will definitely be removed and replaced. However, the cost of the entire project is still expected to come in under budget. (Table 3.)

Figure 8.1: The FEEDBACK document

Roman 14 to enhance the printout, but doing so is not necessary for the purpose of demonstration.

Let's go over the formatting commands you'll use to prepare this sample document. Use the Alt codes to set the formatting as you type. Since it will be double-spaced, press Alt-2 before you begin. Remember to use the 2 on the top row of the keyboard. Use the Tab key after you type the "To:" and "From:". After you reach "Division Head," press the Enter key twice.

Activate the first-line indent shape with Alt-F for the appropriate paragraphs. You'll see the cursor jump in when you do. Turn off this format by pressing Alt-P before you type the headings. After you enter the number and parentheses that begin each section, use the Tab key before you type the headings ("Efficiency of Service," and so on).

When you've finished typing this material, save it under the name FEEDBACK. When your document is complete, we can use it to see how you can look at the top and bottom of the document at the same time.

SPLITTING THE SCREEN INTO MORE THAN ONE WINDOW

While you can split your screen either vertically or horizontally, I normally recommend splitting horizontally, because that way you can see complete lines of text. Splitting vertically may require that you scroll the window from side to side, as Figure 8.2 illustrates. Nonetheless, vertical windows do have their uses, as we'll see later in the chapter.

Word will not accept some window splits for a variety of reasons. For instance, the split you propose must be far enough away from an existing window border so that the resulting new window will be large enough to accommodate at least one line of text. Also, you are permitted to make only two vertical splits on the screen (which, side by side, create three windows). Other limitations arise in the use of footnote windows, which will be studied in Chapter 9. If you get the message

Not a valid window split

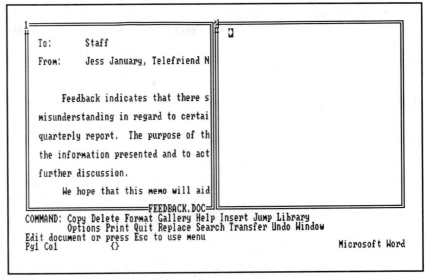

Figure 8.2: Text lines cut off in vertical windows

just try to split again at a different spot so that these restrictions are accommodated.

SPLITTING THE SCREEN HORIZONTALLY

Let's split the screen in half horizontally. Begin with your cursor at the beginning of the document. To get there, press Ctrl-Page Up or click both buttons on the top-left corner of the window border.

M O U S E

Point to where you want the split on the right border of the window and click left on it to split the window.

1. Move the cursor to one of the lines in the center of the screen. This spot will be the location of the split.

2. Press Esc to activate Command mode.

3. Type W for Window. This displays the Window menu (see Figure 8.3).

4. Type S for Split and H for Horizontal.

5. The line number that is then displayed in the command area is the line of the window that your cursor is on (see Figure 8.4). Accept this line number by pressing the Enter key. The window

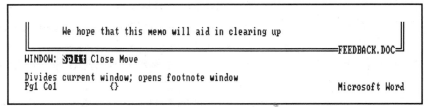

Figure 8.3: The Window command

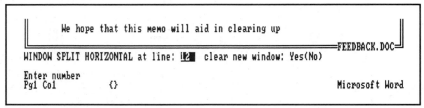

Figure 8.4: The Window Split Horizontal command

splits into two and the second window is activated. You screen should now look similar to the one shown in Figure 8.5.

In this example you chose the position for the split and then invoked the Window Split Horizontal command. You can also specify where you want the screen to be split, however, by changing the line number that the invoked command displays or by using the F1 key. To change the displayed line number, you simply type a new number and then press Enter or click right on the words WINDOW SPLIT HORIZONTAL to register your choice. When you press the F1 key, a *slide marker,* a rectangular highlight, appears on the left edge of the window. By using the directional keys, you can position it. When the slide marker is where you want the split, press the Enter key and the window will split at that position.

Although these methods of splitting the window with the Window command are fairly easy, they are time-consuming compared to the mouse's window-splitting method. Let's look at two speed-up techniques you can use with the Window Split Horizontal command.

QUICK STROKES FOR OPENING A SECOND WINDOW ON YOUR DOCUMENT
To split the window in the middle of your document (as you did in the step instructions), all you have to do is position

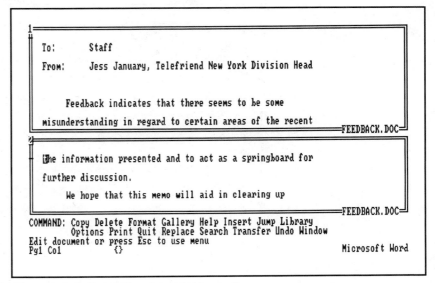

Figure 8.5: Splitting the screen horizontally

the cursor, press Esc, type W, and press Enter three times. The Esc key activates Command mode, and W chooses the Window command. The first Enter is the same as typing S for Split at the next command level, since Split is already highlighted. Pressing the next Enter chooses Horizontal for the same reason. Then, since the correct location is proposed for

WINDOW SPLIT HORIZONTAL at line:

you accept the proposal with the third Enter.

To provide more room on the screen for the two windows on your document, change the Options command's show menu setting to No. Your screen should now resemble Figure 8.6. You can redisplay the menu by simply pressing the Esc key.

Suppose, however, that you don't want to view the same document in both windows. Since you have both windows open, you can clear one of them by invoking the Transfer Clear window command in it. You could then load another document if you wished. A quicker way to clear the second window would have been to open a clear window with the Window Split Horizontal command. Let's see how you could have done that.

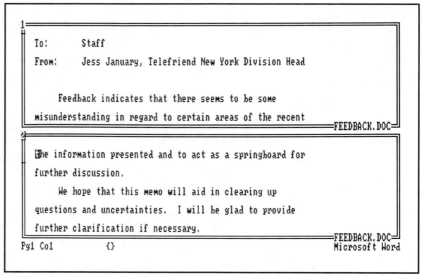

Figure 8.6: Removing the command menu to view more text

OPENING AND CLEARING A WINDOW SIMULTANEOUSLY

When you invoke the Window Split Horizontal command, you'll see the option

    clear new window: Yes(No)

*M*OUSE

To open a clear window, click right on the right border (where you want the split to occur).

on the right side of the command area. Use the Tab key, the → key, or the mouse to move over to it. If you set it to Yes, Word will create a clear window when you press the Enter key or click right on Yes. This new window then represents a clean slate to write on; the two windows no longer have any connection. The effect is the same as if you split the window without this setting and then used the Transfer Clear Window command on the newly opened window.

This window-splitting technique is particularly useful when you are working with one file and want to copy some of its text to another file, or move some text from another file to it—in short, open a clear window whenever you know you need to work with two files.

For the moment, let's continue working with just our FEEDBACK document to practice working with multiple windows. (If you did open a clear window, go ahead and load the FEEDBACK document in it by using the Transfer Load command.)

*T*IP

Word provides the macro **save-selection.-mac**, which opens a clear window, copies the highlighted text to it, and saves, allowing you to provide a file name for the text (see Appendix C).

VIEWING ONE DOCUMENT IN TWO WINDOWS Now that window 2 is open, it's the activated window: everything you do is directed at it. You can tell it's the activated window because the 2 in the top-left corner is highlighted. In addition, the cursor is in window 2, and the cursor can appear only in the activated window. When you need to change the activated window, press the F1 key or click the mouse once in the window you want. (You can also click either button on the window number to select the window.)

As you edit text in one of the windows, your revisions affect the text in the other (unless you clear the other window). That's because they're both windows on the same document, like two cameras focused on the same subject. You can see this effect in action by moving the cursor to the top of the document in window 2: both windows now display the beginning of the document, as shown in Figure 8.7.

Now try typing some gibberish. You'll see how it mystically appears in the other window as well, as if a ghost writer were typing without a cursor in the first window.

Though interesting at the moment, having two views of the same portion of text is really only of practical value if you're working with hidden text (see Chapter 18). Erase the gibberish so we can practice

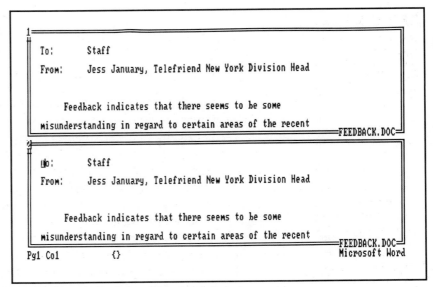

Figure 8.7: Two windows, one view

the techniques involved in doing something more useful: namely, looking at the beginning and the end of a document simultaneously.

VIEWING THE BEGINNING AND END OF A DOCUMENT

With window 2 activated, you can position it at the end of the document while leaving the first window at the beginning. To do this, press Ctrl-Page Down or click both buttons on the bottom-left corner of the window.

Once you reach the end of the document, use the Page Up key or click left on the bottom-left corner of the window border to bring the last paragraph into view. Since window 1 is not affected by these movements in window 2, you can view both parts of the document, the beginning and the end, as shown in Figure 8.8.

USING WINDOWS TO MOVE TEXT IN A FILE

Suppose we decide that the second paragraph, ''We hope that . . .,'' should be the last paragraph in our FEEDBACK document. Let's try moving it there using the windows.

M O U S E

Highlight the paragraph by clicking right on the selection bar next to it. (This automatically activates the window it's in.) Move the highlighted paragraph to the end of the document in the second window by pointing to its new location and pressing Ctrl-left button.

1. Activate the first window by pressing F1.

2. Highlight the paragraph by moving the cursor to it and pressing the F10 key.

3. Delete the paragraph to the scrap area with the Delete key.

4. Activate window 2 by pressing F1.

5. Place the cursor at the end of the document and press the Insert key to copy the paragraph from scrap to the end of the document. You can use the Page Up key to move the window up so you can view the results (see Figure 8.9).

To insert a blank line between the last two paragraphs, as is shown in the figure, move the cursor to the beginning of the last paragraph and press Enter.

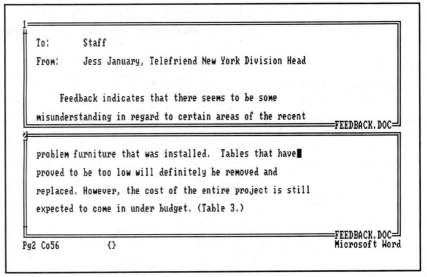

Figure 8.8: The beginning and end of a document

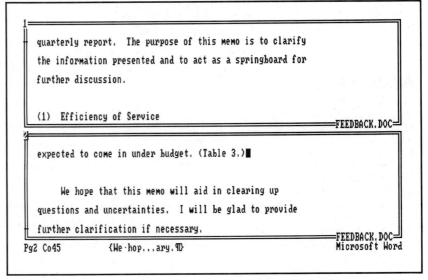

Figure 8.9: Moving the second paragraph to the end of the document

As you can see, scrap works the same way between windows as it does within a single window. You could accomplish the move by using the Delete and Insert keys, the Delete and Insert commands, or the mouse's method of bypassing the scrap area. You can also copy text between windows with the Copy command or its function-key shortcut, Alt-F3.

You can now save this new version of the document with either window activated. Invoke the Transfer Save command and save the document under the same name, FEEDBACK.

USING WINDOWS TO MOVE OR COPY TEXT BETWEEN FILES

You can also move or copy text between documents by using the two windows. Let's suppose (very hypothetically) that one of the paragraphs in FEEDBACK makes some reference to steps in our other document, DEPARPRO, and you want to duplicate the steps in FEEDBACK. (We won't save this version of the document.)

To incorporate material from DEPARPRO into FEEDBACK, follow these steps:

M O U S E

If window 2 is not activated, activate it by clicking either button in it. Click right on Transfer to invoke the Transfer Load command. To display the list of files, click right on filename. Then select the DEPARPRO file by clicking right on it. Drag the mouse over the first three steps to highlight them, point to the new location in window 2, and press Shift-left button to copy the text.

1. Use the F1 key to activate window 2 if necessary.

2. Press Esc to activate Command mode; then type T for Transfer and L for Load.

3. Type the file name, DEPARPRO, and press Enter. The file should appear in window 2 (see Figure 8.10).

4. Highlight the first three steps in DEPARPRO and copy them as a block to scrap. You can use the Extend key (F6) to highlight the steps and press Alt-F3 to copy them to scrap.

5. Activate the first window by pressing F1 and move the cursor to the correct location in the FEEDBACK document.

7. To insert the steps from scrap to the cursor in window 1, press Insert.

Once you have moved or copied text to a file, you usually want to review and edit the file. Although you can do this on your split screen as it is now, Word offers other alternatives as well.

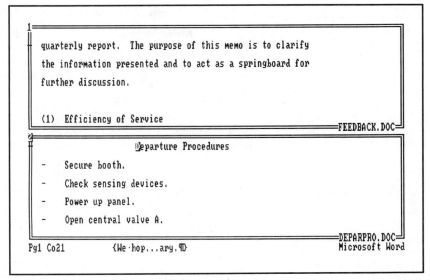

Figure 8.10: Displaying two files at once

REDUCING AND ENLARGING WINDOWS

Suppose that you have two documents loaded but want to concentrate on one of them for the moment. There are two ways you can devote more or all of the screen to the window in which that document appears while keeping the secondary document available in a different window.

ZOOMING A WINDOW

First, you can *zoom* a window. This window then fills the screen area as if no other windows were open. All other windows disappear for the time being. Once you zoom a window, you can change to another window, which Word will display full-sized as well. Later, to see both windows simultaneously, you can turn off the zoom. Follow these steps to turn the zoom on and off:

1. Use the F1 key to activate the window that you wish to zoom, say window 2 if it isn't already activated.

M *O U S E*

To zoom a window, click right on its number in the top-left corner.

M *O U S E*

To zoom the next window, click left on the zoomed window's number. To zoom the previous window, press Shift-left instead. Click right on the zoomed window's number to turn off the zoom and redisplay the split screen.

M *O U S E*

Point at the lower-right corner of the window you wish to resize. When the pointer is correctly positioned, its arrow changes to a four-way arrow in Graphics mode and to a set of intersecting lines in Text mode. Now drag the mouse to the new location for the borders.

2. Press Ctrl-F1 to zoom the activated window. It enlarges to full size and the letters

   ZM

   appear in the lock area on the bottom line of the screen.

At this point, you would normally revise your document. Since we are just practicing zooming and have no interest in keeping the displayed version of the FEEDBACK document, go ahead and zoom the first window:

3. Press F1 to activate and zoom the next window. As there are only two windows, window 1 is then zoomed. Press F1 again to switch among full-sized windows as often as you wish.

4. Press Ctrl-F1 to turn off the zoom.

When you turn off the zoom, the screen is split just the way it was before you zoomed.

RESIZING A WINDOW

You can also keep both windows on the screen while changing the amount of area that they respectively occupy. To do this, you move the window borders with the Window Move command or with the mouse.

To resize the windows, you always use the *lower-right corner* of one of the windows. The adjoining border of the other window adjusts with it. In this case, to make window 1 larger, we will move its lower-right corner, and the upper border of window 2 will be adjusted at the same time.

1. Activate the window whose border you wish to move (in this case, window 1).

2. Press Esc, type W for Window, and type M for Move. The Window Move command will appear (see Figure 8.11). It proposes moving window 1, the activated window. (If you forgot to activate the appropriate window before beginning the command, you could type another window number here before performing the next step.)

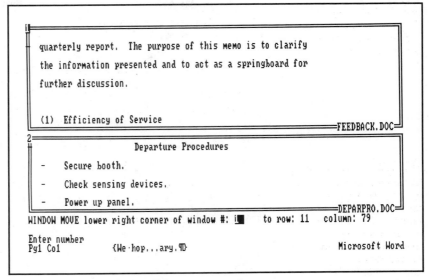

Figure 8.11: The Window Move command

3. Move to the to row option with the → or Tab key. Its setting indicates the current position of the lower-right corner. (The column option is used only when the window has been split vertically.)

4. Press the F1 key and you will see the slide marker (a rectangular highlight) appear in the lower-right corner of window 1. Tap the ↓ key until you reach the border position that you want, about four-fifths of the way down the screen.

5. Press the Enter key, and the borders of the window are moved (see Figure 8.12).

A small window such as our window 2 can be useful in a variety of situations: when referencing a short file, for instance. You could also use one as a place holder. When you are working in one part of a document and want to see the text in another part, mark your position by opening a small window. Use the large window to move around the document and edit. When you're done with your tasks, close the large window. The small window will reoccupy the full screen, and your pinpointed text will appear again.

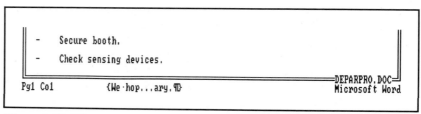

Figure 8.12: The resized windows

You could even use a small window to work with a file that you know well. For example, you might want to do this if you're editing a large, unfamiliar file in the other window. You might find it surprisingly easy to work your way around a familiar file when only one line is displayed.

Finally, you could use a small cleared window as a kind of scratch pad for notes. We'll look at using a small vertical window for this purpose in a moment.

═══════════════   ## *CLOSING A WINDOW* ═══════════════

At this point we've completed our work with window 2, so let's go ahead and close it.

1. Activate the window to be closed (in this case, window 2).

2. Press Esc, type W for Window, and type C for Close. Word proposes closing the activated window (see Figure 8.13).

3. Press the Enter key to accept the proposal.

If you made any changes in the window's document that haven't been saved, you'll get the message

> Enter Y to save changes to document, N to lose changes, or Esc to cancel

If you want to save the changes, type Y. You won't get this message if the same document is displayed in another window.

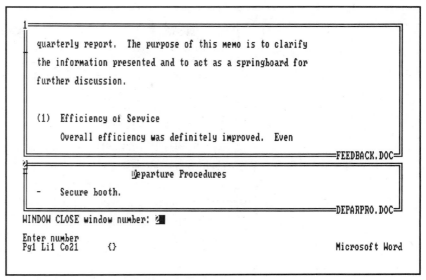

Figure 8.13: The Window Close command

USING A VERTICAL WINDOW AS A SCRATCH PAD

T I P

You can also use glossary entries for scratch pad notes. See Chapter 15.

Unless you are working with wide material or a twelve-pitch setting (specifying measure: P12 with the Options command), the area on the right of the screen is generally unused. One way to make use of this space is to place a vertical scratch pad in it and use the scratch pad for notes to yourself as you write (see Figure 8.14). You can then move and copy notes between the document and the scratch-pad window. Rather than relying on the scrap area, you can also use this scratch pad as a temporary holding zone for material. This frees the scrap area for other deleting, moving, and copying operations.

Let's create a scratch pad by opening a vertical window. Since we closed window 2, we have only one window on the screen. We'll split this window vertically to create a new window 2. Because the mouse requires the top border to do this, make sure that the ruler is not displayed if you are using a mouse. (To turn off the ruler display, change the Options command's show ruler setting to No.)

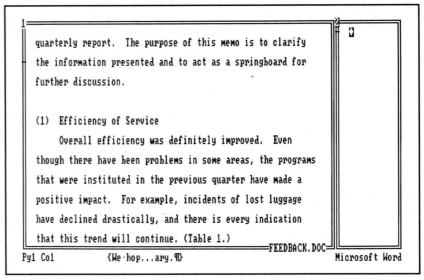

Figure 8.14: A vertical scratch pad

*M**O U S E*

Point to the spot on
the top border where
you want the split and
click right to open a
clear window.

1. Press Esc and type W for Window, S for Split, and V for Vertical. As you can see in Figure 8.15, you then specify where you want the screen to split. (Column refers to the number of spaces across the screen from left to right.)

2. For a scratch pad that doesn't interfere with the rest of the document, enter the number 63 and press Tab or → to move to the clear new window option.

3. Set clear new window to Yes by typing Y and press Enter to create the vertical window.

Another handy use for a narrow window is as a memory aid. For instance, you could use it to display the instructions for a particular type of document, or you might find it helpful to list the Alt codes there (see Figure 8.16).

When you use the narrow window as a scratch pad, normal typing will cause the text to move past its border and out of sight. Here are

```
   positive impact.  For example, incidents of lost luggage
                                                       =FEEDBACK.DOC=
WINDOW SPLIT VERTICAL at column: 63█  clear new window: Yes(No)

Enter number
Pg1 Li12 Co1         {}                              Microsoft Word
```

Figure 8.15: The Window Split Vertical command

some ways to handle the situation:

- Don't type anything wider than the vertical window. Make only short notes and press the Enter key when you reach the border.
- Change the margins of window 2 by using the Format Division Margins command, which is discussed in Chapter 9.
- Type normally and enlarge the window by zooming or using the Window Move command when you wish to view the entire window.
- Scroll horizontally to view text as necessary.

SCROLLING SIDE TO SIDE

If you work with a vertical window or a document that's wider than usual, you may find that you need to scroll the window from left to right to view the entire document. This action is called *horizontal scrolling*. Scrolling with the keyboard differs quite a bit from scrolling with the mouse, so we'll treat them separately. Let's examine the keyboard method first.

SCROLLING WITH THE KEYBOARD

Perhaps the simplest way to scroll is with the directional keys in the normal fashion. When you use them to move the cursor, more text will come into view as you reach the window border.

You can also use the Scroll Lock key to scroll. When you press the Scroll Lock key,

SL

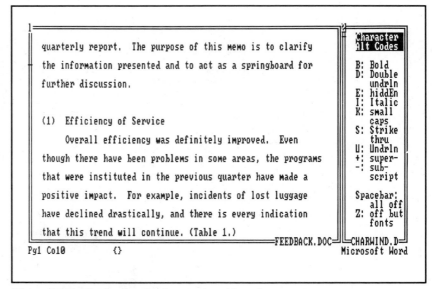

Figure 8.16: Displaying the formatting Alt codes

will appear in the lock area. Now the ← and → keys will scroll the text by one-third of a window. Let's say that we load our ANNOUNCE document into window 2. Initially, it would appear as seen in Figure 8.17. If we turn on the Scroll Lock and use the → key, we would scroll to the position shown in Figure 8.18. You can only scroll the window like this if the text extends beyond its border.

SCROLLING WITH THE MOUSE

To use the mouse for horizontal scrolling, position the pointer on the vertical window's bottom border, as shown in Figure 8.19. To scroll to the right, click right on the border; to scroll left, click left.

Just as with vertical scrolling, the amount of scrolling you do will be determined by the pointer's position on the border. In the case of horizontal scrolling, the farther right, the greater the scroll; the farther left, the less the scroll. When you point far to the right (close to the corner), you scroll about a windowful. Conversely, when the

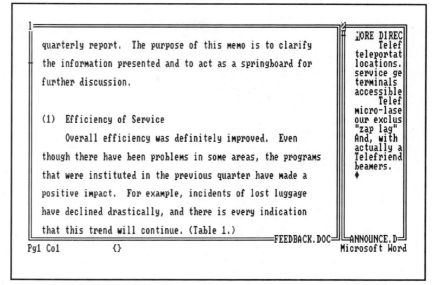

Figure 8.17: Loading the ANNOUNCE document in the vertical window

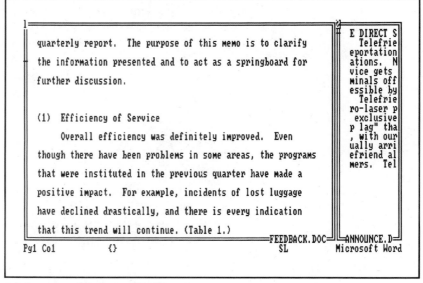

Figure 8.18: Using the Scroll Lock key

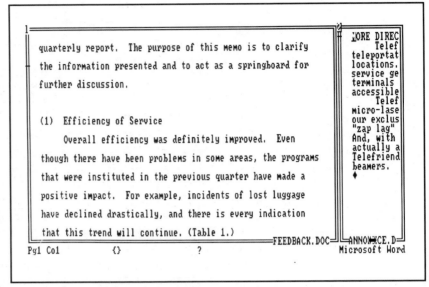

Figure 8.19: Using the mouse to scroll horizontally

pointer is next to the lower-left corner, you scroll only one character at a time. Do not use the corners of the border. With the pointer as it is in Figure 8.19, clicking right would scroll to the position shown in Figure 8.18.

Now that you are familiar with Word's windows, let's see how you can change their look.

CHANGING WORD'S DISPLAY

Word provides you with several types of displays for its screen. The general rule of thumb is that the more closely the screen display matches the printed copy, the slower or less flexible your word processing is. Here are the types of displays, in increasing order of accuracy, and the means by which you set them:

5 New in Word 5

Text mode	Options command's display mode option
Graphics mode	Options command's display mode option

Show line breaks	Options command's show line breaks option
Show layout	Options command's show layout option
Print preView	Print command's preView subcommand

Let's examine each type of display. Be aware, though, that not all of these displays are mutually exclusive. For example, you can show line breaks in either Text or Graphics mode. Note, too, that these modes and Print preView affect the entire screen, while show line breaks and show layout affect only the current window. Both of these displays are grouped under the Options command's Window Options in Word 5, and the Window Options' for window field indicates which window is current (see Figure 8.20). In Word 4, you use the Window Options command to access these displays.

To demonstrate the various displays, we'll use the sample ESPRIT letter from Chapter 7. So that you can see the entire letter at once, I used a full-page display. With smaller screens, you may need to scroll to see all the material.

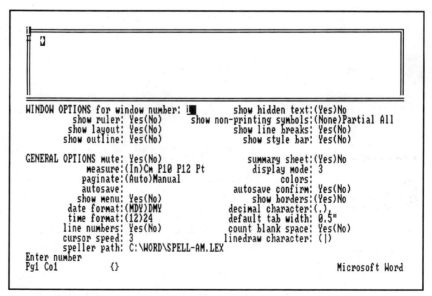

Figure 8.20: Reviewing Word's Options command

TEXT MODE AND GRAPHICS MODE

With some setups, using Text mode (Figure 8.21) pays off significantly in terms of processing speed. However, depending on how extensive your formats are, its appearance on the screen may bear little resemblance to the printed version of the document.

Graphics mode (Figure 8.22) improves the text's appearance greatly but often slows down operations. With Graphics mode, you can see typographic features such as italics and superscript. Graphics mode does not, however, depict font sizes accurately.

Depending on your monitor, you may have several types of Text or Graphics modes. If you have a CGA monitor and board, for example, both modes display 25 lines, and you can set Text mode to show in either monochrome or 16 colors. For other monitors, the number of lines you can display on the screen varies.

Word 5's Options command allows you to choose from whatever display modes are available for your monitor. (The display option in earlier versions provided only two settings: Text and Graphics.) To display and choose from the modes you can use, follow these steps:

5 New in Word 5

MOUSE

Click right on Options and click right on display mode to list your mode choices. To select a mode and leave the Options menu, click right on the mode you want.

1. Issue the Options command by pressing Esc and typing O.

2. Move to the display mode option and press F1 to display your possible choices.

3. Select the mode you want with the arrow keys and press Enter to register your choice.

Shortcut:

Alt-F9 toggles between the last two modes you used.

For example, the list that appears for a CGA monitor would be:

1   Text, 25 Lines, Monochrome
2   Text, 25 Lines, 16 colors
3   Graphics, 25 Lines, 2 colors

You can use the arrow keys or the mouse to select the mode you want, or you can enter the number on the left (in this example, 1, 2, or 3) that corresponds to the mode you want and press Enter.

```
1
 ═══════════════════════════════════════════════════
  Telefriend Teleportation, Incorporated
  9876 Beacon Boulevard
  Das Universe, California  99999


  Mr. Timothy Esprit
  1234 Skyview Lane
  Cosmos City, MD  22222

  Dear Mr. Esprit:

       Thank you for your communication of January 12, 2052.
  In that communication, you indicate that you wish to be
  additionally compensated for the recent delay you
  experienced in teleportation.

       On the ticket you purchased, however, the terms of your
  teleportation are clearly stated:

            On rare occasions, passengers may  experience
            some delay in beaming.  However,  Telefriend
            Teleportation, Incorporated is not liable for
            any delay except as provided by law.
  As your letter indicates, we have fulfilled our obligation
  in that regard.

       While we realize that it is not pleasant to be trapped
  in the suspension state, we believe that added effort on
  your part may have shortened the delay.

       Before departure, beam attendants clearly inform all
  passengers that the formula for relativity is E=mc2.  They
  give instructions in the proper use of this formula in the
  event of rematerialization difficulties.

       Passengers are also instructed to look for our super
  highpower ethereal searchlights to be guided to their
  destination or returned to the point of departure.

       We realize that teleportation is an exciting
  experience, and that your attention may not have been fully
  focused on the instructions at the time. With this
  explanation, we hope that you now feel adequately
  compensated, and that you will continue to be our customer.

  Sincerely,


  Your Name

      ♦


 ═══════════════════════════════════════════ESPRIT.DOC═
 Pg1 Co6        ()                              Microsoft Word
```

Figure 8.21: Viewing your document in Text mode

SHOWING LINE BREAKS

Neither Text nor Graphics mode necessarily shows the correct line breaks; that is, where one line of text ends and the next begins. To have the line breaks displayed accurately on the screen, invoke the Options command and set show line breaks to Yes. (In Word 4, this option is called printer display.) To see the difference between this

T IP

When you display the accurate line breaks for text that is formatted in a small-sized font, you may have to scroll the screen from left to right to see all the text. Because Word doesn't portray the size of fonts on the screen, more text may fit on a line and not in the window than when the correct line breaks don't show.

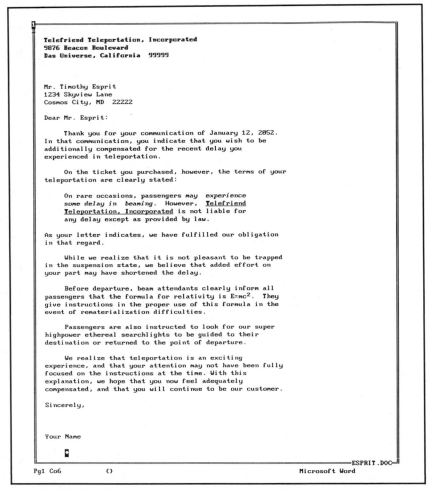

Figure 8.22: Viewing your document in Graphics mode

display and the regular display, compare Figure 8.23's line endings to those in Figure 8.22. You can also compare these figures to Figure 7.3, which contains the printed document.

You can display the correct line breaks in either Text or Graphics mode, and edit text as usual. Again, depending on your setup, you may notice a slowdown in Word's operation when you set show line breaks to Yes.

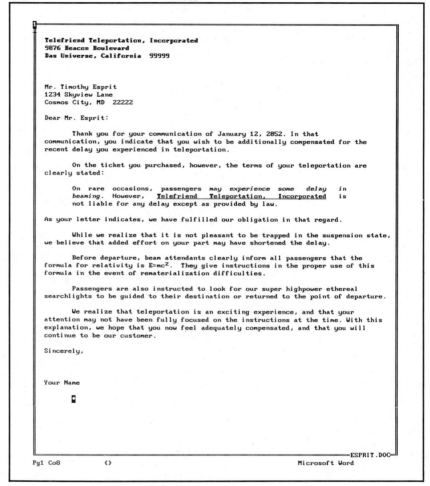

Figure 8.23: Showing accurate line breaks in Graphics mode

SHOWING LAYOUT

New in
Word 5

Until Word 5, it was not possible to display two types of layouts accurately, next to each other. This included newspaper-style columns and side-by-side paragraphs (features we'll examine in Chapter 11). With Word 5, however, you can use show layout to see and work with these layouts, though it too may slow down Word's operations.

T I P

When you use show layout with an empty window, Word automatically inserts a paragraph mark in the window that you cannot delete.

To display these elements' layout accurately, do this:

1. Activate the window where you want to see the layouts (by pressing F1 or clicking on the window).

2. Invoke the Options command.

3. Set show layout to Yes and register the command. LY then appears in the lock area to indicate that show layout is on.

Shortcut:

Alt-F4 toggles show layout on and off.

Since our example does not have these features, show layout will not reposition its text. However, when we work with these layouts, you'll be able to display them more accurately.

PREVIEWING PRINTOUTS

 New in Word 5

The new Print preView command allows you to review your documents on the screen before you print them. This ability can save rounds of printing out and then readjusting your format based on the printed copy.

To use this feature, you simply invoke the command:

M O U S E

Click left on Print and click right on preView to see how your document will look printed.

1. Press Esc and type P for Print to access the Print command's subcommands.

2. Type V to invoke the preView command.

Shortcut:

Ctrl-F9 toggles Print preView on and off.

Word then displays the current page of your document in Print preView (see Figure 8.24).

Print preView places all of Word's elements correctly on the page, in a page mock-up of sorts. You cannot edit the text in Print preView. Use the Page Down and Page Up keys, respectively, to display the next and previous page.

Print preView also enables you to work with imported graphics more easily. As we'll see in Chapter 18, you can add graphics from

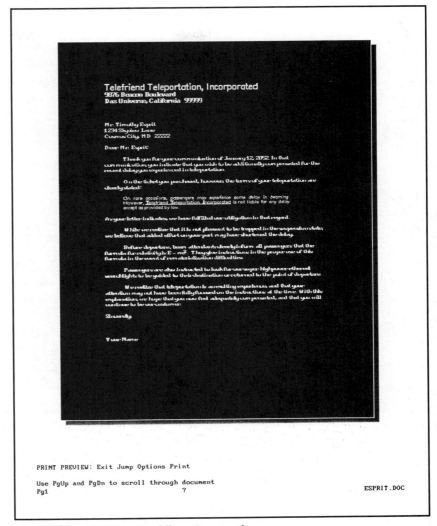

Figure 8.24: The Print preView command

other programs, such as AutoCAD, to Word documents by inserting a code in the Word documents. With Print preView, you can see most imported graphics on the screen before you print. You can then return to the document to adjust their placement on the screen and avoid unnecessary trial printouts.

When you're finished checking your document, type E for Exit or click on Exit to return to Document mode. In addition to Exit, Print preView has three other subcommands. You can use Print pre-View's Options command (Figure 8.25) to display a single page (as in the example), two consecutive pages, or two facing pages. When you choose the Facing-pages setting, the even-numbered page is on the left, and the odd-numbered page follows it.

```
OPTIONS display: 1-page 2-page Facing-pages
Select option
Pg1                                            Microsoft Word
```

Figure 8.25: The Print preView Options command

Print preView's Jump command allows you to immediately display a particular page by providing the page number or the name of a placemarker you've inserted with the Format bookmarK command (see Chapter 12).

When you select Print preView's Print command (Figure 8.26), you can use its subcommands to print without going back to the main menu. Use Options to set up Print Options, Printer to start printing, or File to store the document formatted for printing in a file.

```
PRINT: Printer File Options
Prints document in the active window
Pg1                                            Microsoft Word
```

Figure 8.26: The Print preView Print command

CHANGING THE DISPLAY'S COLORS

5 New in Word 5

If you have a color monitor, you might be interested in the Options command's colors option. You can use it to see and select the colors for many of Word's display elements. This includes parts of the screen, font sizes, and character formats, alone or in combination. By using colors to indicate character formats, you may be able to edit more quickly in Text mode, while still keeping an eye on your formats.

Press F1 or click right on colors, and a display like that shown in Figure 8.27 appears (only yours will be in color). Samples of the colors you can use are at the top, marked with letters of the alphabet. To the right of these letters, you can see

* (ignore)

this indicates that you can type an asterisk in a display element's field to instruct Word not to assign a color to it.

The character format elements are listed in order of priority. The font 8.5 or less display has the highest priority, followed by the rest of the left column; the uppercase display comes after double underline in priority, and the italic and underline display has the lowest priority. If you have assigned more than one of the listed formats to the same text, Word will select the color associated with the highest-priority format, unless you set its display to ignore on this screen.

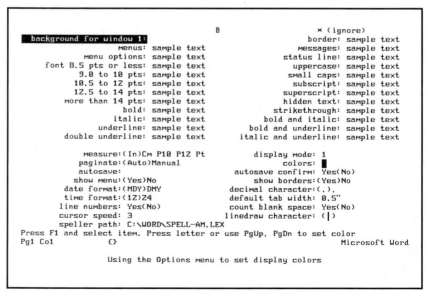

```
                                                B              × (ignore)
  background for window 1:                          border: sample text
                  menus: sample text              messages: sample text
           menu options: sample text           status line: sample text
     font 8.5 pts or less: sample text            uppercase: sample text
             9.0 to 10 pts: sample text          small caps: sample text
            10.5 to 12 pts: sample text           subscript: sample text
            12.5 to 14 pts: sample text         superscript: sample text
           more than 14 pts: sample text        hidden text: sample text
                   bold: sample text          strikethrough: sample text
                 italic: sample text        bold and italic: sample text
              underline: sample text      bold and underline: sample text
       double underline: sample text    italic and underline: sample text

           measure:(In)Cm P10 P12 Pt          display mode: 1
        paginate:(Auto)Manual                       colors: █
        autosave:                         autosave confirm: Yes(No)
        show menu:(Yes)No                  show borders:(Yes)No
        date format:(MDY)DMY              decimal character:(.),
        time format:(12)24                default tab width: 0.5"
        line numbers: Yes(No)             count blank space: Yes(No)
        cursor speed: 3                   linedraw character: (|)
        speller path: C:\WORD\SPELL-AM.LEX
 Press F1 and select item. Press letter or use PgUp, PgDn to set color
 Pg1 Co1            {}                                     Microsoft Word


                Using the Options menu to set display colors
```

Figure 8.27: Using the Options menu to set display colors

To change the color assigned to an element's display, move to the element and press the letter corresponding to the color you want. You can also use the Page Up and Page Down keys to rotate colors for the sample text that appears in the display element's field. Except for the background for window option, these settings are not confined to a particular window.

USING OTHER PROGRAMS IN WINDOWS

The windowing procedures we've discussed up to now fall under the context of windowing within Word. However, Microsoft also sells another program related to windowing that may be of interest to you: Microsoft Windows.

Microsoft Windows allows you to operate other programs independently within separate windows. Thus, with enough computing power, you could use Microsoft Windows to run Word and other application programs, such as Lotus 1-2-3, simultaneously. Because each program operates in a window of its own, switching between programs is quicker and simpler than having to quit one program to use another. As Windows becomes more and more popular, it is replacing the DOS prompt as the way to go from one program to another.

Another advantage of Windows is that it allows you to communicate with Word through a set of intuitive, visual elements, such as pull-down menus and symbolic icons—all greatly influenced by the Macintosh style of screen display.

There are two versions of Microsoft Windows currently available. They're designed to exploit the capabilities of the processor chip that the computer uses. Their requirements are the following:

Windows/286	Windows/386
80286-based computer	80386-based computer
512K of memory	2Mb of memory
DOS 3.0 or later	DOS 3.1 or later
1.2Mb (5¼'') floppy disk drive	1.2Mb (5¼'') or 1.4Mb (3½'') floppy disk drive

hard disk   hard disk with at least 2Mb free

graphics card   graphics card

A mouse is optional but highly recommended for any of these Micro-soft Windows programs.

In this chapter, you learned how to use windows to view text and move chunks of text from one remote location to another, within the same document or between different documents. Efficiency is the payoff.

In the next chapter, you'll learn techinques for formatting your documents consistently; once you've acquired these techniques, you'll be able to streamline the creation process for a document even further.

9

Formatting Pages for a Professional Look

Fast Track

IN CHAPTER 5 WE LEARNED HOW TO ALTER THE
appearance of characters and paragraphs with Alt codes and the Format Character and Format Paragraph commands. In this chapter,
we will look at formatting elements that compose the page as a whole.
For page composition, we'll use other Format subcommands: Format Division, Format Running-head, Format Footnote, and Format
Annotation.

ELEMENTS OF PAGE COMPOSITION

T I P

Running heads at the
bottom of pages are
also called *footers*.
Running heads at the
top of pages are also
called *headers*.

In Word, running heads (material repeated at the top or bottom of
pages) and footnotes are both special kinds of paragraphs. You can
format them as you do other paragraphs, but they require separate
Format commands to deal with their special characteristics—the
exact placement on the page, for example. You use the Format Division command alone (for margins and simple page numbers, for
example) or with these other Format commands to assign compositional elements to the page.

In Word's vocabulary, a *division* is a page or cluster of contiguous
pages in which you want certain format elements, such as margins,
page numbers, text, running heads, footnotes, and so on, to be consistent. You can think of a division as simply a section of the document that is formatted the same.

In most of your documents, the page format will probably be the
same for the entire document. If so, although it may seem contradictory, you will have only one division in the document.

But there are also situations that will require the use of multiple
divisions. For example, suppose you are preparing a report that must
include explanatory text with standard margins on 8½-by-11-inch
paper; an organizational chart, which is printed with the paper
turned sideways; and several financial statements with no margins.
Because of the differing page formats, each of these elements would
constitute a separate division in the document.

By using the Format Division command and other Format subcommands in this chapter, you will learn how to give your documents
the professional polish that comes from a consistent and functional
presentation of page elements, such as page numbering, running
heads, footnotes, and placement of your text on a particular size of

paper. We will also see how to set up multiple page formats within a single document.

Before we plunge into our work with these various characteristics of page format, let's examine the Format Division command and how to use it.

THE FORMAT DIVISION COMMAND

When you invoke the Format Division command, you will see that it has four subcommands: Margins, Page-numbers, Layout, and line-Numbers. The settings in each subcommand apply to page features that we'll be studying individually in this chapter and later in this book. If you are satisfied with the settings that Word automatically provides, you don't have to use the Format Division command at all.

When you issue one of the Format Division commands to adjust its settings and then register the command (by pressing Enter or clicking right on it), Word creates a row of colons at the end of your document, like so:

: :

T I P

Because the division mark affects the text that precedes it, you must keep your text to be governed by this mark's settings *above* the mark as you work.

This row is called the *division mark,* and Word considers it a single character even though it extends across the screen. Just as the paragraph mark stores settings for paragraph format, so the division mark stores settings for page composition. Also like the paragraph mark, it formats the material that *precedes* it.

You can also create a division mark by typing Ctrl-Enter. Whenever you wish, you can see the current settings by positioning the cursor *on* or *before* the mark and issuing the Format Division command. Like any character, you can highlight the division mark and delete, copy, insert it, and so on.

Although many of your applications will probably require only one page format (one division) for the entire document, you may often find it useful to vary the format within the document. For example, if you normally provide a title page for your documents, you can set up one format for that page, enter a division mark, and set up another format for the rest of your document. The same goes for documents accompanied by a cover letter. Before we discuss the nitty-gritty details of page formatting, let's explore how divisions work.

USING MULTIPLE PAGE FORMATS WITHIN A DOCUMENT

As you're printing, Word will use the settings of the new division to determine what action it should take when moving into that division. The division break option in the Format Division Layout command dictates the action:

division break: (Page) Continuous Column Even Odd

This command is usually set for Page, which means that when Word encounters a new division, it will advance the paper and begin a new page. This setting would be used in applications such as chapters, large charts, tables, and so on: any formatted text that you want to make sure begins on a page of its own.

New in
Word 5

When you select the Continuous setting, Word 5 will combine the division with the previous one without starting a new page. Because of this, you could get different formats on the same page. For example, if the division mark falls in the middle of a page, the left and right margins for the first paragraphs and the top margin will be determined by the first division's format, while the margins for paragraphs after the mark and the bottom margin will be established by the second division. Always preview your documents when you use this setting to make sure your two page compositions aren't conflicting.

The Even and Odd settings will cause Word to move to the next such respective page number. Column, used with a multicolumn format, will print text in a new column on the page. (We'll study columns in Chapter 11.)

For an application that has letterhead paper for its first page and plain paper for the rest of the document, you would use two divisions. Assuming you have already entered the text for the first page and established its page composition (we'll learn how later in this chapter), here are the steps for creating a new division:

1. Place the cursor at the beginning of the second page's text and press Ctrl-Enter to create a division mark.

T I P

Word's supplied macro **print_letter.mac** prompts you to provide margins for the first page that differ from the rest of the document's margins, and then it prints the letter (see Appendix C).

2. With the cursor after this mark but before the end mark, use the various Format Division commands to create its page composition. Their settings will reflect your layout from the second page on (in other words, for the second division).

Once the document is formatted, should you add text to or delete text from the first page, you will need to move the division mark to keep it between the first and second pages.

With multidivision documents, Word indicates which division the cursor is in. It's displayed in the bottom-left corner, along with the page and column numbers. Thus

P1 D2 Co1

indicates page 1 of division 2, column 1.

Since you have already decided how many divisions your document will have, you are ready to format each division. As you read through the subsequent sections, you can consider which settings would be appropriate for your document's divisions. The examples with which we will practice give instructions for changing just one division. If you have created a multidivision document on the screen, you can practice some commands on one division and issue other commands for another division, or you can repeat the instructions again, varying the settings as you like.

Table 9.1 breaks down the Format Division command into its component parts. As the table suggests, Word normally specifies its measurements in terms of inches. Note that the *default* (or standard) settings are in parentheses. If you are more comfortable with a different system of measurement, however, you can change this display.

Table 9.1: Subdivisions of the Format Division Command

Format Division Margins
top: 1"
bottom: 1"
left: 1.25"
right: 1.25"

Table 9.1: Subdivisions of the Format Division Command (continued)

Format Division Margins
page length: 11''
width: 8.5''
gutter margin: 0''
running head position from top: 0.5''
running head position from bottom: 0.5''
mirror margins: Yes (No)
use as default: Yes (No)
Format Division Page-numbers Yes (No)
from top: 0.5''
from left: 7.25''
numbering: (Continuous) Start at:
number format: (1) I i A a
Format Division Layout
footnotes: (Same-page) End
number of columns: 1
space between columns: 0.5''
division break: (Page) Continuous Column Even Odd
Format Division line-Numbers Yes (No)
from text: 0.4''
restart at: (Page) Division Continuous
increments: 1

T I P

Although you can usually select a setting by typing its initial letter, you can't do this for the choices that begin with P (the two pitch settings and the point setting). To choose one of these systems of measurement, use the Space-bar to rotate the highlight among the choices or use the mouse.

SPECIFYING THE SYSTEM OF MEASUREMENT

You change the system of measurement that Word uses for display in all its menus by changing the measure setting in the Options command. The measure option (in Word 5, it's grouped under the General Options) looks like this:

measure: (In) Cm P10 P12 Pt

Each of these settings represents a system of measurement. Table 9.2 explains what each abbreviation means and gives the equivalent of one inch in that system. The choice you specify will be recorded in the MW.INI file and will remain in place when you quit Word.

Figure 9.1 presents the normal Format Division Margins menu. Figure 9.2 demonstrates how the menu would appear if you changed the measure setting in the Options command to cm (centimeters).

Table 9.2: WORD's Systems of Measurement

ABBREVIATION	SYSTEM OF MEASUREMENT	UNITS CORRESPONDING TO ONE INCH
In or "	Inches	1 in
Cm	Centimeters	2.54 cm
P10	10-pitch or pica	10 p10
P12	12-pitch or elite	12 p12
Pt	Points	72 pt
Li	Lines (vertical measurements only)	6 li

Notes: The space after a number is optional: **1 in** and **1in** are both acceptable.
Use decimals for fractions: **1.25 in** is acceptable, but **1-¼ in** is not.

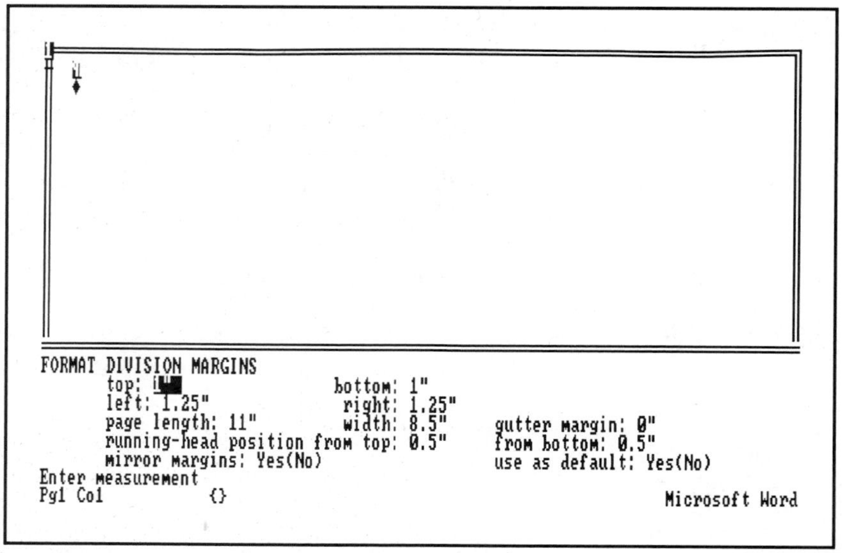

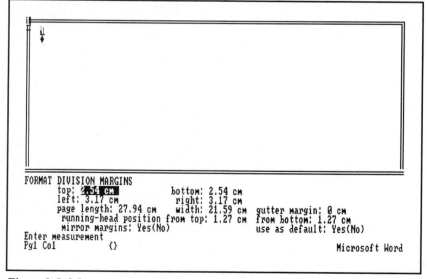

Figure 9.1: Measurements displayed in inches

Figure 9.2: Measurements displayed in centimeters

Figure 9.3 shows what would happen if you specified 10-pitch (pica) characters as the system of measurement.

Remember that your measure setting only dictates the way Word communicates to you. Regardless of which setting you choose, you can always communicate with Word by typing in any system of measurement you want. For instance, even if you set Word so it displays in points, you could still specify a measure as one inch, as long as you designate it as such by typing

        1 in

or

        1in

or

        1″

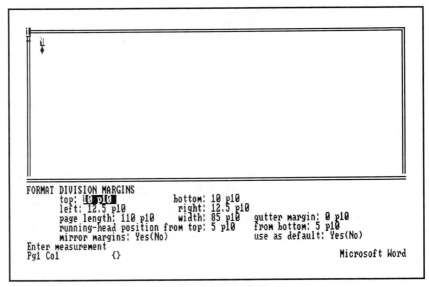

Figure 9.3: Measurements displayed in 10 pitch

However, if the Options measure is set to inches, you can simply enter 1: you don't need the inch mark since inches are being displayed. (The same holds true for other systems of measurement when they are displayed.)

You'll have to specify measurements to place your page's compositional elements. Let's look at page margins first.

ADJUSTING PAGE MARGINS

One of the first aspects of page composition you'll probably want to consider is how best to place your text on the page. Settings in Format Division Margins govern a number of the factors that affect the size of the printed text page. The default settings for Word are for the standard 8½-by-11-inch sheet of paper, with margins set for 1 inch at the top and bottom and 1¼ inches on the left and right. This leaves room for text that is 6 inches by 9 inches. When you work with standard pica (10-pitch) characters, you can have textual material 60 characters wide and 54 lines long.

All situations are not the same, however. On occasion, you may find it necessary to work with legal-sized (8½-by-14-inch) paper. Alternatively, your organization might require standard margins that differ from Word's defaults. You may even need to set up two margin formats on the same page (using two divisions and setting the Division Layout's division break option to Continuous); for instance, you could establish margins for wide body text in one division and create narrower margins in the other division to align several columns below the regular text.

These kinds of applications require that you change the default size specifications. Word 5 uses the first three rows of options in the Format Division Margins command to indicate the size of your paper and the width of your margins (see Figure 9.1).

Figure 9.4 illustrates the areas determined by these options; most require no further explanation, but gutter margin may be unfamiliar to you. To provide room for binding a double-sided document, this is an additional margin on the inside edges of the pages. Word adds the gutter margin you specify to the right margin setting for even pages

T I P

Remember, margins are regulated by the division mark that appears after the text you want affected. Keep the division mark below the text to control its margins.

T I P

If you plan to bind a document that's printed on one side only, you'll want to increase the width of the left margin, not the gutter margin.

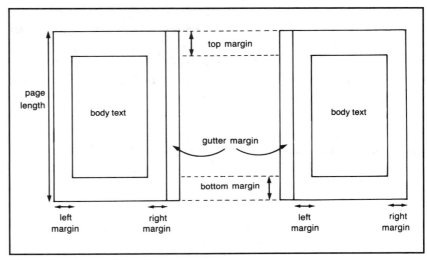

Figure 9.4: Areas of the page

(which by convention are the pages on the left for bound documents since the numbering starts on a right-hand page) and to the left margin for odd-numbered pages (the pages on the right).

You can set page length, or the length of the paper you're using, to a maximum of 22 inches and a minimum of 1 inch. Word also allows the same values for the width, but it is more than likely that your printer will only accept paper that is at most 14 inches wide. To change to legal-sized paper (inserted in the normal lengthwise fashion), all you have to do is change the page length setting to 14.

It's important to realize that you cannot directly specify measurements for the text area with these options' settings. Instead, Word calculates the area available for text by subtracting the size of the margins from the size of the paper. What's left is allocated to the text. For example, if you wanted the text in your printed document to be 5 inches wide on paper that is 8½ inches wide, you'd get this by allotting a total of 3½ inches to the side margins. Thus you would set the left margin to 1.75 inches and the right margin to 1.75 inches.

Once again, remember that you can type the setting using any system of measure you desire, regardless of which system is displayed. Be sure to specify the unit of measurement when it differs from that of the display setting.

CH. 9

For the vertical measurement settings—page length and top and bottom—you are free to specify lines (abbreviated li). For instance, if you normally begin typing on the thirteenth line from the top edge of the paper, you could set the top margin as

12 li

to achieve this effect. (Notice that no periods are used after abbreviations in Word.) If you specify lines, however, Word will not display the setting in terms of lines. Thus, because there are six lines to the inch, the next time you looked at the Format Division Margins settings, you'd see the top margin setting displayed as

2″

which is the same as 12 lines.

MIRRORING MARGINS AND CHANGING DEFAULT MARGINS

When you are working with a document that will be double-sided and bound, you might want to take advantage of Word's new margin options in the Format Division Margins command: mirror margins and use as default. The mirror margins option lets you create one consistent format for all the even-numbered pages and another for all the odd-numbered pages. The use as default option enables you to set the margin formats you prefer to new documents automatically, ensuring a consistent appearance for all your documents.

If you set mirror margins to Yes, you only need to establish the margin formats for the first page. Word will then recreate those settings on all odd-numbered pages and reflect them on even-numbered pages (it will apply the right margin settings to the left margin and vice versa).

After you have established page margins that you like, you can save them for other documents by setting the use as default option to Yes. Once Word has stored all your settings on the Format Division Margins menu as the default, any documents you then create will be initially formatted with them. If you later change your default margins, Word will only add them to new documents; you will have to

5 New in Word 5

5 New in Word 5

reformat existing documents individually. Unless you are positive you are not going to revise your documents' margins, you may prefer to use a style sheet to establish your default margins for a given directory's document since Word will reformat documents attached to the style sheet automatically (see Chapter 17).

NUMBERING PAGES AUTOMATICALLY

You use the Format Division Page-numbers command to determine how your pages should be numbered (see Figure 9.5). The settings that are initially displayed indicate the default status of the command. Because Word does not normally number the pages when it prints a document (although it does usually display the page numbers in the command area), the first option reads No. To have page numbers appear in your document when you preview it or print it, simply change this setting to Yes. (Word can also number pages as part of a running head, in which case you would leave the first setting in Format Division Page-numbers as No. We'll see how to number pages in this way when we study running heads in the next section.)

If you indicate that you want page numbers with the first option, Word will normally place them in the upper-right corner of the page, as indicated by the from top and from left settings. To specify a different position for the page number, reset these two options. Word 5 allows you to place the page number anywhere on the page, so you should preview your document after providing measurements to make sure the page number doesn't overlap existing text. (Word 4 only allows you to place the page number within the top or bottom margin.)

5 New in Word 5

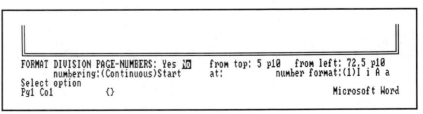

Figure 9.5: The Format Division Page-numbers command

To specify the vertical measurement from top, Word allows you to type the number of lines rather than inches if you prefer. So, you could specify that the page number be placed one-half inch from the top of the page by typing one of the following measurements:

```
.5 in
.5″
3 li
```

Each places the page numbers in the same spot in the top margin.

To place the page numbers in the bottom margin, type a number that results in enough distance from the top of the page to position it within the bottom margin. For example, to have the number appear one-half inch from the bottom of an 11-inch sheet, you would set the from top option to 10.33″ (10.33 in) or 62 li. This would place the page number on line 63, leaving three lines (one-half inch) below the page number.

Usually, once you set up numbering to occur, the first page of your document will be page 1, the next page 2, and so on *continuously* throughout the document. This is indicated by the default number-ing setting:

numbering: (Continuous) Start

If you planned to add this document to another document that, say, ended on page 70, you could have Word begin the numbering with page 71. To do this, you would need to change two settings to specify that numbering *starts* at 71, like so:

numbering: Continuous (Start)   at: 71

Perhaps you would rather have your page numbers printed as Roman numerals or as letters of the alphabet. Word provides you with a choice of five numbering formats, indicated for the number format option by the first character of each numbering system:

1	Arabic numerals	1 2 3 4 5
I	capital Roman numerals	I II III IV V
i	lowercase Roman numerals	i ii iii iv v

T I P

The line numbers Word displays in the command area are for the text only. The line numbers you can enter here refer to the paper and include blank space.

T I P

Word's supplied macro **chainprint-.mac** prints one docu-ment after another according to a list you provide, numbering the documents sequentially (see Appendix C).

A	capital letters	A B C D E
a	lowercase letters	a b c d e

You might wish to use lowercase Roman numerals, for example, in the preface to a long report. If your numbering format changes from one part of the document to another (say the numbers in the preface differ from the rest of the document), you must set up multiple divisions to accommodate the change.

CREATING HEADINGS THAT APPEAR ON EACH PAGE

If you want to include running heads in your document, you should include the page number in it, since both features compete for space in the margins. A *running head* is a group of words that are repeated at the top or bottom of a series of pages, used to identify the pages' contents for anyone quickly glancing through the document. Running heads at the top are also called *headers*. Running heads at the bottom are also called *footers*.

A running head can be a title, a chapter name, a corporate division, a description of the subject matter, or a warning that the text on that page is confidential. It can be repeated throughout a particular division (section) of a document or throughout the entire document (one division). Word even allows you to have two different running heads on a page; one at the top and one at the bottom. If the document will be double-sided and bound, you could even have one set of running heads for the odd pages and another set for the even pages. Thus on two facing pages you can have a total of four different running heads (see Figure 9.6). Running heads can be as long as several paragraphs or as short as one line.

As far as Word is concerned, a running head is a kind of paragraph even if it's just one line long. This is because you press the Enter key at the end of the line.

There are three commands that you use when working with running heads:

Format Running-head

Takes a normal paragraph and turns it into a running head (or vice versa). You also use this command

Telefriend Corporation

Annual Report

Figure 9.6: Running Heads on Facing Pages

to indicate the general area in which you want the running head to appear (that is, at the top or bottom of the page, on odd or even pages, and whether it should appear on the first page of the document).

Figure 9.6: Running Heads on Facing Pages (continued)

Format Paragraph

Formats the running head. For example, you can make the running head left- or right-aligned, or you can provide values to indent it from the left and right. You can also use the paragraph Alt codes to format the running head.

Format Division Margins

> Allows you to specify the exact placement of a running head from the top and bottom edges of the paper.

We will use these three commands as we create and modify running heads in the next few pages.

CREATING A RUNNING HEAD

To create a running head, you begin by typing the text you want for a running head, just as you would type a normal paragraph at the beginning of the document. You end the paragraph as usual by pressing the Enter key.

For practice, type the text that appears in Figure 9.7 on a clear screen (use Transfer Clear if necessary). Press Enter at the end to make it a paragraph. I set the Options command's show nonprinting symbols setting to Partial for the figure so you can see the

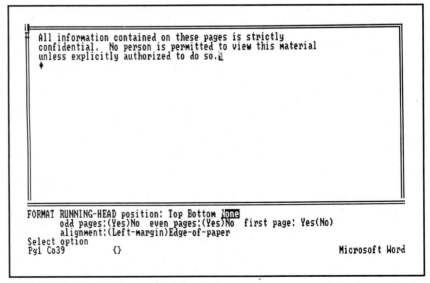

Figure 9.7: Creating a running head

paragraph mark. This paragraph will be used as a running head in a document about a top-secret formula, so we'll call the file TSFORMU. Running heads are often just one line; however, this long example allows you to see the alignment properties of running heads.

Always keep the Options command's show layout option set to No as you work with running heads. Although show layout illustrates the placement of newspaper-style columns and side-by-side paragraphs on the page, it makes the running heads in the text disappear. If you need to see the page's layout for other elements in your document, you can set show layout to Yes and preview the placement of your running heads by using the Print preView command.

Place the cursor somewhere within the paragraph and make it a running head as follows:

1. Press the Esc key and type F for Format.

2. Type R for Running-head. This displays the Format Running-head menu (see Figure 9.7).

3. To make the paragraph a header, type T for Top and press Enter. If you want to create a footer instead, type B for Bottom and then press Enter.

Shortcuts:

Ctrl-F2 creates a header. Alt-F2 creates a footer.

5 New in Word 5

M O U S E

Click left on Format and click either button on Running-head to issue this subcommand. Click right on Top to make the paragraph a header or click right on Bottom to make it a footer.

Note that with release 4, you can just press Enter to create a header since Top is the default setting. (Word 5's default is None for the position option.) Once you've completed the command, a caret (^) will appear on the far left, next to the first line of the running-head paragraph in the window. The caret indicates that the paragraph to its right is a running head.

When used on the first paragraph in the document, these techniques create a header or a footer that appears on every page except the first one. Let's examine the Format Running-head menu's default settings, shown in Figure 9.7, and consider each setting.

POSITIONING THE RUNNING HEAD ROUGHLY

The first option in the menu is position:

position: Top Bottom (None)

With the first two choices, you indicate the running head's general position on the page: in the top or bottom margin. However, you don't issue the Format Running-head command to specify the exact placement from the top or bottom edges of the paper; you use the Format Division Margins command to accomplish that.

As you'll see when you preview or print your document, the running head's position on the page has little relation to its position on the screen. In other words, even though text for the running head is displayed at the beginning of the document (which is where people usually put it), the running head will be printed at the bottom of the page if you so specify with the position option.

Also note that its setting affects only the running head that you are working on at the moment. Thus, you could create two running heads, one after another on the screen, and format them separately to print at the top and bottom of the page.

5 New in
Word 5

If you later decide that you don't want a certain running head and you want to change its text back into a regular paragraph, you can do so by changing position to None. (In Word 4 you have to change all the Yes/No settings in the Format Running-head menu to No.) You can also change a running head into a standard paragraph by pressing the plain-paragraph Alt code (Alt-P) in it. However, this turns off all formatting you may have established as well.

The next two options in the Format Running-head command are for documents that will be printed double-sided:

odd pages: (Yes) No   even pages: (Yes) No

Normally, Word prints your running head on all pages in the document, so both odd pages and even pages are initially set to Yes. However, you might want different running heads on each side for your double-sided documents. To do this, you would create two running heads, setting the odd pages option to No for the even pages' running head and setting the even pages option to No for the odd pages' running head.

Because the odd-numbered pages are conventionally on the right and the even-numbered pages are on the left in double-sided, bound documents, you can create a balanced look in your double-sided document by making the running head on the right-hand (odd) pages flush right with the Alt-R code. Leaving the running head on the left pages flush left, which is the default for all paragraphs—including running heads—the text of the running heads will thus always appear at the outer edge of the document. This setup would make it easy for readers to see running heads as they leaf through your document.

Now look at the next Format Running-head option:

first page: Yes (No)

Unlike the other Format Running-head options, this is usually set to No. Unless you change this setting, Word will not print a running head on the first page. Since the first page of a document is often a title page or has a letterhead, you will probably leave first page set to No.

If you do want a running head to appear on the first page, you must do two things. First, of course, you change the first page setting to Yes. Second, you place the running head before anything else in the document. (If your running head isn't to be printed until the second page, it can be located anywhere on the first page of the document. Normally, however, it's a good idea to place it at the beginning, if only for the sake of clarity and consistency.)

Supposing you add another running head, it will not take effect until the page after the one on which it appears. A running head set to appear in the same position (top or bottom) and on the same pages (odd or even) replaces any similarly formatted running head that appears earlier in the document. Therefore, to change a running head in the document, insert the new running-head paragraph on the page before the one on which it should appear and assign it the same position and page settings as the one it is replacing.

New in
Word 5

You can set the last option, alignment, to Left-margin or Edge-of-paper, which determines the alignment of the running head with the text. This new feature gives you the flexibility of having Word calculate running-head indents from the margin or from the edge of the paper. By using Edge-of-paper, you create a *hanging* running head for the document. If you just want to align the running head with the body text, select the Left-margin setting and Word 5 does it automatically for you. In Word 4 you have to indent the running head from the edge of the paper to line it up with the margins. Note that Word 5's Left-margin setting is misnamed; it should simply be "margin" since right-aligned running heads (formatted with Alt-R) will line up with the right margin when you assign Left-margin to them.

INDENTING
AND FORMATTING A RUNNING HEAD

For the purposes of printing our sample running head, we'll have to display it on the first page. Let's also see how Word can spill the running head into the margins. To do this, issue the Format Running-head command and set first page to Yes and alignment to Edge-of-paper.

When you specify edge-of-paper for the running head, the paragraph suddenly extends farther across the screen than it did previously (compare Figures 9.7 and 9.8). The result is a hanging running head. Normally, with paper 8½ inches wide, Word allows only 6 inches for text because the left and right margins are each initially

***T** I P*

Remember that the LaserJet cannot print clear to the edge of the paper. Even with the Edge-of-paper setting, you cannot get any closer than ¼ inch from the edge.

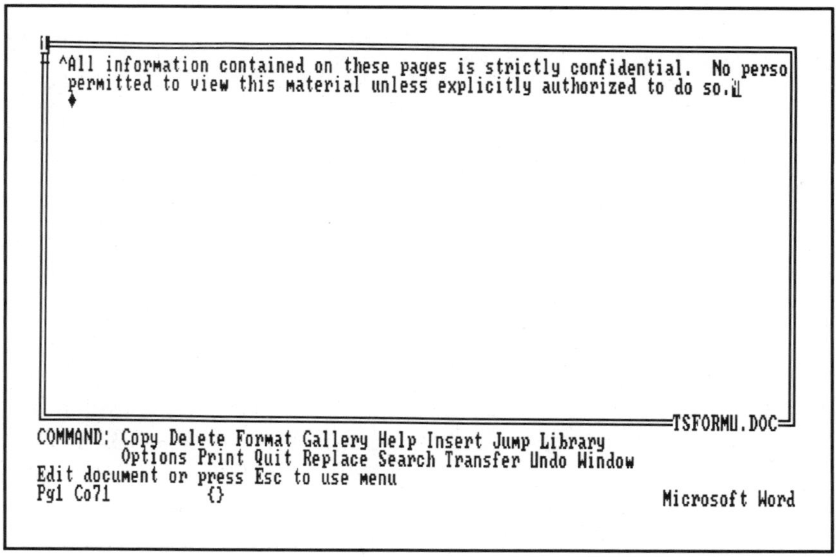

```
 ^All information contained on these pages is strictly confidential.  No perso
 permitted to view this material unless explicitly authorized to do so.







                                                              =TSFORMU.DOC=
COMMAND: Copy Delete Format Gallery Help Insert Jump Library
                  Options Print Quit Replace Search Transfer Undo Window
Edit document or press Esc to use menu
Pg1 Co71              {}                              Microsoft Word
```

Figure 9.8: Creating a hanging running head

1¼ inches wide. With hanging running heads, however, the sample paragraph spreads out to 8½ inches because Word uses the full width of the paper.

Even with a hanging running head, you'll probably want to indent it a bit from the left and right. Issue the Format Paragraph command and set both left indent and right indent to 0.5'', as I've done in Figure 9.9.

A hanging running head will not align with the text on the screen exactly as it does when printed. To demonstrate this, type the text that's been added below our running head in Figure 9.10. Format the regular text as justified (Alt-J) with a blank line before each paragraph (Alt-O). Center the title with Alt-C and underline it with Alt-U. Also, justify the running head, again using Alt-J. When you then preview the document (with Print preView) or print it, it will look like the document shown in Figure 9.11.

USING THE RULER LINE

As you work with running heads, you may find it helpful to turn on the *ruler line* at the top of the window (see Figure 9.10). When the cursor is in the hanging running head, the ruler line indicates

```
┃═0····[····1·········2·········3·········4·········5·········6·········7····┓
┃┃ ^      All information contained on these pages is strictly confidential.  No
┃┃        person is permitted to view this material unless explicitly authorized
┃┃        do so.▌
┃  ♦




FORMAT PARAGRAPH alignment: Left Centered Right Justified
     left indent: 0.5"          first line: 0"          right indent: 0.5"
     line spacing: 1 li         space before: 0 li      space after: 0 li
     keep together: Yes(No)     keep follow: Yes(No)    side by side: Yes(No)
Select option
Pg1 Col2          {}                                          Microsoft Word
```

Figure 9.9: An indented, hanging running head

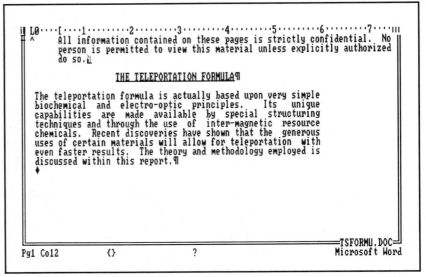

Figure 9.10: Screen alignment of an indented, hanging running head with the text

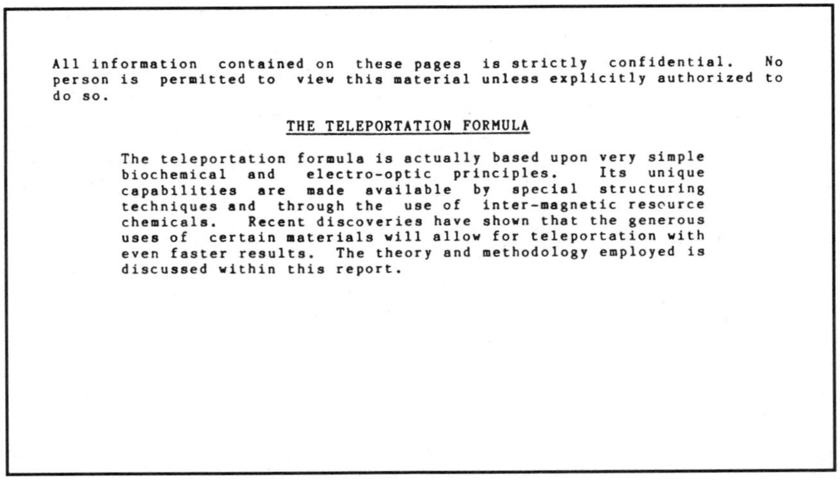

Figure 9.11: Printout of the same document

the position of the running head on the printed page. The ruler line is always turned on when you're using the Format Paragraph command, but you can turn it on at other times as well. This way, you will know where the running head will be printed as you edit it.

M*OUSE*

Click either button on the upper-right corner of the window border to display the ruler. Notice that the mouse pointer changes shape when you move it to this corner (see Figure 9.10). By dragging the margin ([ ]) and first-line (¦) indicators with the right mouse button, you can adjust their settings for the paragraph. To turn the ruler off, click both buttons on the upper-right corner.

Follow these steps to turn on the ruler line:

1. Press the Esc key and type O for Options.

2. Move to the show ruler option (using the Tab or → key) and type Y for Yes.

3. Press the Enter key to register the command.

If you have the ruler on when you quit Word, Word will remember this and turn it on the next time you start up.

INCLUDING PAGE NUMBERS IN YOUR RUNNING HEAD

If you want your running head to display page numbers, first type the word

page

in the running head text, in the spot where you want the page number to appear. Then, with the cursor right after the word "page," press the Glossary key (F3). You'll see Word surround "page" with parentheses, like so:

(page)

As we'll see in Chapter 15, this designation is a special use of Word's glossary feature. When you preview or print the document, Word will automatically replace this designation in the running head with the current page number. To choose the format for the page numbers, issue the Format Division Page-numbers command and specify the setting you want for the number format option. Make sure the Page-numbers command is set to No, however, so that the page numbers aren't placed on the page with this command in addition to being placed in the running head.

In Word 5 you can also have your running heads display the page number of the next page of the document. This ability is useful for some legal applications. The procedure is similar to that for page. Simply type

nextpage

5 New in Word 5

T *I P*

Word's supplied macro
stop_last_footer.mac
works with the new
nextpage feature to
suppress the printing of
any footer on the last
page of a document
(see Appendix C).

and press F3. Word will replace the resulting (nextpage) designation with the appropriate number when you print or use Print preView.

SPECIFYING THE EXACT VERTICAL PLACEMENT OF RUNNING HEADS

To specify the exact placement of the running head from the top or bottom of the page, you must use the Format Division Margins command. This time, we want to focus our attention on the command's following options:

running-head position from top: 0.5″   from bottom: 0.5″

Notice that Word normally sets running heads ½ inch from the edge of the page, whether it appears at the top or bottom of the page. To place it somewhere else in the respective margin, simply highlight the option that corresponds to your running head (from top or from bottom) and type the measurement you want. You can use any system of measurement here, including lines, as these settings are vertical measurements.

Now that we've learned how to create, format, and position running heads on a page and throughout a division, we can turn our attention to another special kind of paragraph in Word—footnotes.

FORMATTING FOOTNOTES AND ANNOTATIONS AUTOMATICALLY

Like running heads, Word treats footnotes as another type of paragraph. In addition, Word 5 allows you to create annotations, which are simply a special kind of footnote.

There are four commands involved in the use of footnotes:

Format Footnote	Creates and inserts the footnote's *reference mark* (such as a number or the asterisk) within your document at the appropriate spot.
Jump Footnote	Allows you to move from one reference mark to another and to

and from the reference mark and the actual footnote, which is called the *footnote paragraph*.

Window Split Footnote	Allows you to open a footnote window so that you can view footnote paragraphs along with their corresponding reference marks.
Format Division Layout	Establishes the placement of your footnote paragraph: at the bottom of the page or at the end of the division.

CREATING FOOTNOTES

Let's create a footnote for our top-secret document. We'll put one after the sentence that ends with "even faster results."

The procedure for creating a footnote is quite simple. When you are working on regular text and you find a spot that calls for a footnote, invoke the Format Footnote command (see Figure 9.12). Although Word automatically assigns numbers to designate footnotes by default, you can specify an alternative reference mark, such as an asterisk, before you register the Format Footnote command. If you do want to use numbers, just press the Enter key. Word automatically provides the correct sequence of numbers.

Once you register the command, Word repositions your cursor at the end of your document. It lands next to a newly created duplicate of the number or other reference mark, in a special area that's just for footnote paragraphs (see Figure 9.13). Footnote paragraphs are always recorded here at the end of the document, regardless of the position you specify for them when printed.

Your two choices in this matter are to have the footnote paragraph printed on the same page as the reference mark or to have it printed as an endnote at the end of a division. In either case, as far as the document on the disk and on the screen is concerned, the footnote paragraph is always at the end. The special area for the footnote paragraphs is set off by end marks (the small diamond-shaped characters) at the top and bottom.

T IP

To open a footnote window automatically, press Alt-F4 to turn show layout on before you invoke the Format Footnote command. You then enter the footnote paragraph in this window.

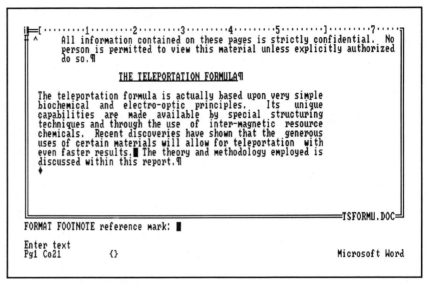

Figure 9.12: The Format Footnote command

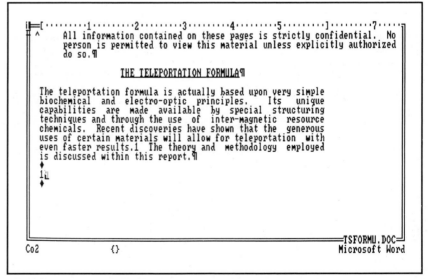

Figure 9.13: Word's placement of your footnote paragraph on the screen

Once you type the footnote paragraph next to the number or other reference mark (add a space between the paragraph and the number), you can return to your document to continue writing or editing. To get back to where you were, you can use normal scrolling techniques (for example, using the Page Up key), or you can use Word's Jump Footnote command (Figure 9.14), which will bring you back to the reference mark in the regular text.

Here is a summary of the procedure for creating footnotes. (First, of course, you must have the cursor positioned where you want the footnote reference mark to appear.)

1. Press the Esc key, type F for Format, and type F for Footnote.

2. Press the Enter key to use an automatically assigned number for the reference mark. If you want to use another symbol, such as *, type it and then press Enter. Word moves the cursor to the special area for footnote paragraphs at the end of the document, next to a duplicate of your reference mark.

3. Press the Spacebar and type your footnote paragraph.

M O U S E

Click left on Format. To create a footnote using a number for the reference mark, click right on Footnote. To use another symbol instead, click left on Footnote, type the symbol, and then click either button on FORMAT FOOTNOTE. You can then type your footnote paragraph. To return to the footnote reference mark, click left on Jump and then click either button on Footnote.

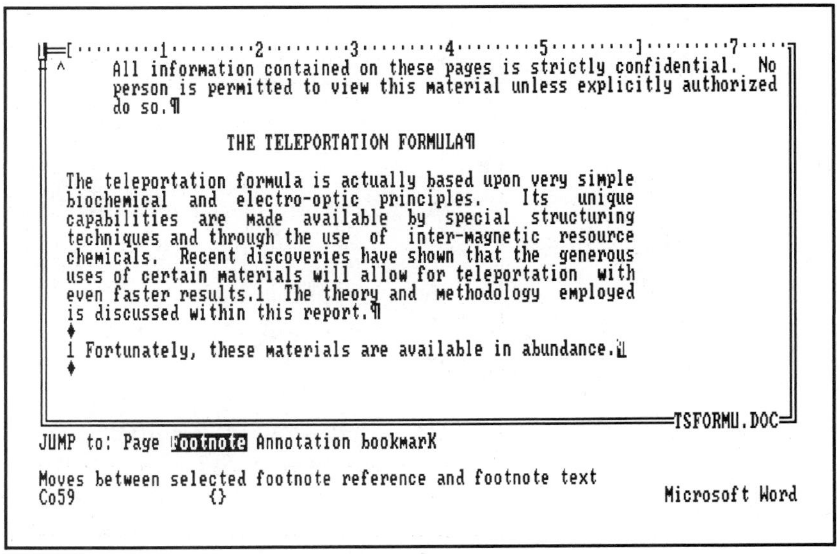

Figure 9.14: The Jump Footnote command

4. Issue the Jump Footnote command to return to the spot where you placed your footnote reference mark; that is, press Esc, type J, and type F. (The command operates automatically—do not press the Enter key.)

To insert new footnotes, simply execute the Format Footnote command in the document wherever you desire. Word automatically renumbers the footnotes that follow.

DELETING FOOTNOTES

Within the footnote paragraph area, there are certain operations, such as deleting the entire text, that are not permitted. If you attempt to perform an action that Word does not allow, you'll get the message

Not a valid action for footnotes

To delete a footnote, you must delete the reference mark. When you do, Word automatically renumbers the remaining footnotes as necessary. By using the Delete key (or the Delete command), you can send a reference mark and its corresponding footnote paragraph to the scrap area. You can then insert them elsewhere in the document with the Insert key or the Insert command. Word will automatically renumber all affected footnotes.

USING JUMP FOOTNOTE

Let's examine the Jump Footnote command more closely. You can use this command in three ways. As we just learned, you can use it to send the cursor from the footnote paragraph back to the corresponding reference mark.

Second, it can operate as the equivalent of the Search command (which we'll examine in Chapter 10) for the next footnote. That is, when the cursor is in the main body of the text, issuing Jump Footnote heads it toward the end of the document and finds the next reference mark. If you invoke the command when the cursor is after the last reference mark in the text, you'll get the message

No more footnote references

The third way to use Jump Footnote is the reverse of the first way: if the cursor is on the reference mark when you invoke the command, the cursor will jump to the footnote paragraph at the end of the document. The action is similar to the jumping that occurs when you use the Format Footnote command, but you use it with footnotes that already exist.

USING FOOTNOTE WINDOWS

Jumping back and forth between text and footnotes is quick, but if you have a number of footnotes, you might want to have Word display them on the screen, together with the matching reference mark in text. Word provides a special type of window for footnotes. It's available only in the horizontal window format.

When a footnote window is pressed into service, a dotted line appears between the text window and the footnote window (see Figure 9.15). The footnote window will automatically display only footnote paragraphs that correspond to reference marks appearing in the text window above it.

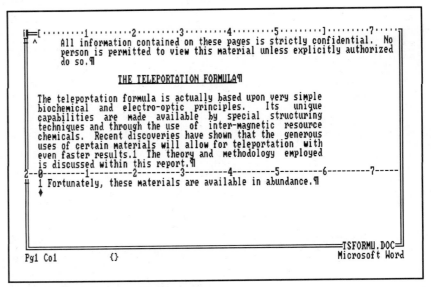

Figure 9.15: A footnote window

New in
Word 5

You can have Word open this window automatically whenever you issue the format Footnote or Jump Footnote command by turning the Options command's show layout option on first. (Remember, you can toggle show layout on quickly by pressing Alt-F4.) If you forget to turn on show layout before you start working with footnotes, you can open a footnote window with the Window Split footnote command.

As with normal window splits, I recommend you position the cursor at the spot you want before you split the window using the keyboard. If you do not, however, you can use the slide marker with the directional keys to adjust the size of your window. You'll probably want the footnote window to be smaller than the window that holds the main text.

Here's how to create a footnote window (when show layout is off):

1. Press the Esc key and type W for Window, S for Split, and F for Footnote. Word suggests the current cursor position for the window split.

2. Split the screen at the designated position by pressing Enter, or use the slide marker (press F1 and move it with the directional keys) to select a new location and then press Enter. If multiple windows are already open, the activated window is the one that will contain the footnote window.

As with other windows, you can activate the footnote window by pressing F1 or clicking in it. Doing so allows you to edit footnote paragraphs and it's usually quicker than using the Jump Footnote command. To close the footnote window, issue the Window Close command for it or click both buttons on its right window border.

M O U S E

Point to the right window border where you want to split the window and press Shift-left or Shift-right to create a footnote window. If you already have several windows open, the window whose border you're pointing at will become the activated window and acquire a footnote window.

USING FORMAT DIVISION
TO POSITION FOOTNOTES

There's one final footnote decision you must make: where do you want your footnotes to be placed when the document is printed? The usual spot is at the bottom of the page that contains the reference mark. If this is where you want them, you need do nothing; Word will place them there for you automatically.

T *I P*

To see how your foot-
notes will appear when
you print the docu-
ment, issue the Print
preView command.

The alternative is to have footnotes placed at the end of the division. If you wish to place them there, you must indicate this to Word
with the Format Division Layout command. (If you just have one
division, they will be placed at the end of the document.)

Display the Format Division Layout menu and you'll see that the
first setting in the menu applies to footnotes.

footnotes: (Same-page) End

If you want, change this setting to End and register your choice either
by pressing Enter or by using the mouse. To have endnotes appear
on a new page, separate from the rest of the document, press
Ctrl-Shift-Enter to enter a page break at the end of the standard text.

Figure 9.16 shows a printed version of the sample document with a
footnote at the bottom of the page. The separator line appears automatically. Notice how I've superscripted the footnote number in the
text and set it in a smaller font (with the Format Character command). Style sheets allow you to automate this kind of formatting
(see Chapter 17).

Compare Figure 9.16's footnote with Figure 9.17, which shows a
printed endnote page. I centered and italicized the running head and

*All information contained on these pages is strictly confidential. No person is permitted to view this material
unless explicitly authorized to do so.*

THE TELEPORTATION FORMULA

The teleportation formula is actually based upon very simple biochemical and
electro-optic principles. Its unique capabilities are made available by special
structuring techniques and through the use of inter-magnetic resource chemicals.
Recent discoveries have shown that the generous uses of certain materials will
allow for teleportation with even faster results.[1] The theory and methodology
employed is discussed within this report.

1 Fortunately, these materials are available in abundance.

Figure 9.16: A printed footnote

All information contained on these pages is strictly confidential. No person is permitted to view this material unless explicitly authorized to do so.

Notes

1. Fortunately, these materials are available in abundance.

2. Triangularism, hexigonism, and sphericism are among the shaping sciences involved.

3. Newly revised and updated figures appear here.

4. This fact stands in sharp contrast to the original theories expounded by G. I. Emanerd. Though founded on sound principles at the time, those ideas have rightly fallen into disfavor.

5. Video transcription of this report is available.

Figure 9.17: A printed endnote page

set it in a smaller font. The endnote paragraphs are formatted as hanging indents (Alt-T) with a tab after each number. They are also formatted as open-spaced paragraphs (Alt-O).

CREATING ANNOTATIONS

Annotations are a type of footnotes; they are referenced in the text and numbered as part of your document's footnotes. Typically, people that are reviewing a document use them to insert their comments. However, they differ from standard footnotes in that they provide a convenient way to create an identifying mark, such as the reviewer's initials, right after the footnote reference number and after the footnote number before the footnote paragraph at the bottom of the page. Word remembers the identifying mark, allowing you to conveniently reinsert it as you work with a document.

To create an annotation, place the cursor where the reference mark will go and issue the Format Annotation command. You'll see the display shown in Figure 9.18. After mark, provide some identifying text if you want. To have Word enter the current date or time, change the appropriate setting to Yes.

New in Word 5

T I P

The supplied macros **annot_collect.mac**, **annot_remove.mac**, and **annot_merge-.mac** respectively compile annotations in a document, remove annotations, and compile annotations from several documents (see Appendix C).

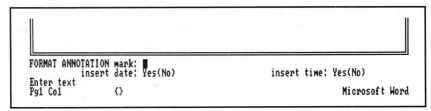

Figure 9.18: The Format Annotation command

When you register the command, Word enters the footnote number into the document, followed by the identifying mark, and displays the number and identifying mark in the footnote area at the end of the document. The date and time will also be displayed if you set their options to Yes.

Thus, if you were to use the initials MH as your identifying mark, along with the date and time, in place of our sample footnote, you would see the following display in text:

> even faster results.1MH   The theory and methodology employed

Word would also insert something like

> 1MH, 4/1/90, 2:36 PM

in the footnote area to provide the operating system date and time. The cursor would appear at the end of this line so you could type your comment.

The Jump Annotation command operates like the Jump Footnote command, allowing you to get back to your text, find the next annotation, and so on. As annotations are a type of footnote, the Jump Footnote command operates on both footnotes and annotations. However, the Jump Annotation command operates only on annotations, not standard footnotes.

T *I P*

You can also use hidden text (Alt-E) to add editing notes directly in the document. According to your settings in the Options and Print Options commands, Word will show the notes or keep them hidden, on screen as well as in the printed document. You may wish to enter hidden text instead of adding comments with the Format Annotation command—for example, when you don't want comments to be combined with existing footnotes. See Chapter 18 for more on hidden text.

PREPARING DOCUMENT TEMPLATES

Once you've formatted a document, you might find that you need to perform the same process all over again for a similar document. In fact, you might even want all your letters to be formatted exactly the same for consistency. To avoid having to format each letter individually, you can create a *template file*.

A template file (sometimes called a *shell*) is the skeleton for a completed document. It could have all the formatting in place, and some of the text as well. Once created and saved, you can use it by starting with a clear screen and issuing a Transfer Merge command for the template document.

Transfer Merge displays an exact copy of the template file on the screen. You can then tailor it to fit a particular need and save the new document under its own name. The template file on the disk will be untouched and you can reuse it as often as you like.

Let's see how this would be accomplished with, say, an office memo. Assume that you're responsible for producing memos for Anna Babcock Carrington, and that your initials are efg. First, we'll prepare the template document that you see in Figure 9.19. Then we'll use the template to create an actual memo.

Start with a clear screen. Continue as follows:

1. Type the title

   MEMORANDUM

   centering it with Alt-C, and press Enter.

2. Turn off the centering format with Alt-P. The cursor moves to the left.

3. For the "TO" paragraph, first issue the Format Paragraph command and match the settings to those shown in the figure. That is, change left indent to 1 inch, first line to −1 inch, and space before to 1 line. We create this unusual indent so that if you have several names to include, you could line them up by simply pressing Shift-Enter (which creates a new-line mark) between each name. You'll see how this works shortly. Register the new settings.

4. Type 5 spaces, "TO:", 2 spaces, and press Enter.

5. Type 3 spaces, "FROM:", 2 spaces, and the sender's name, "Anna Babcock Carrington." Press Enter. This paragraph will automatically have the same format as the previous one.

T I P

Word supplies the **memo_header.mac** macro that prompts you for the creation of a memo (see Appendix C). The use of macros and other glossary entries provides another way to handle repeatedly typed material (see Chapter 15).

```
|=!········[········2·····3····4·······5·······]······7····|
                        MEMORANDUM¶
        TO:  ¶
      FROM:  Anna Babcock Carrington¶
      DATE:  ¶
   SUBJECT:  ¶

   ¶
                        ABC¶

   efg¶
   ◆
FORMAT PARAGRAPH alignment: Left Centered Right Justified
        left indent: 1"           first line: -1"        right indent: 0"
        line spacing: 1 li        space before: 1 li     space after: 0 li
        keep together: Yes(No)    keep follow: Yes(No)   side by side: Yes(No)
Select option
Pg1 Col1            {}                                   Microsoft Word
```

Figure 9.19: A template file

6. Type 3 spaces, "DATE:", 2 spaces, and press Enter.

7. Type "SUBJECT:" and then 2 spaces. Don't press Enter just yet.

8. Let's assume that we always want the subject to be underlined. To accomplish this, press Alt-U twice. The paragraph mark will then contain the character formatting. Don't press Enter yet.

9. We'd also like to have an extra blank line between the subject and the body of the memo. Issue the Format Paragraph command and change space after to 1 line. You can just type the number 1: Word will know you mean line here. Register the new paragraph settings.

10. Press the Enter key to move to the area for the body text.

11. Turn off all existing character and paragraph formats for the body area by pressing Alt-Spacebar and Alt-P.

12. Type Alt-O so that the body text will be open-spaced; there will be a blank line before each paragraph. Press Enter.

13. Press Alt-C and type

    ABC

    to center the initials and press Enter.
14. To align the small initials on the left, press Alt-L and type them.
15. Format the page as desired by using the Format Division commands.
16. Save the template under the name TPMEMO (for template memo).

Now clear the screen so you can use the template to create the document you see in Figure 9.20. Proceed as follows:

1. With the screen clear, perform a Transfer Merge of the file TPMEMO. The memo template will appear with the cursor at the end of the document.

MEMORANDUM

TO: New Employees
Visitors

FROM: Anna Babcock Carrington

DATE: August 25, 2050

SUBJECT: Nonsmoking Policy

Following is the nonsmoking policy for **Telefriend Teleportation** facilities.

Smoking is prohibited throughout company facilities except in designated smoking areas identified by smoking permitted signs. Smoking permitted areas will be designated only upon request. Employees who are interested in having such areas designated should discuss the matter with their supervisors.

ABC

efg

Figure 9.20: Creating a document from the template file

2. Press Ctrl-Page Up to move to the word "MEMORAN-
   DUM" and press the ↓ key to move the cursor to the "TO"
   paragraph. Type

   New Employees

   and press Shift-Enter.

3. Type

   Visitors

   and press the ↓ key (not Enter). The cursor moves to the
   "FROM" paragraph.

4. Press the ↓ key again to move to the "DATE" paragraph.

5. Type the date and press ↓ to move to the "SUBJECT"
   paragraph.

6. Type the subject without typing Alt-U. Notice that it gets
   underlined automatically. Press the ↓ key to move to the area
   for the body of the memo.

7. Type the first paragraph of the body. Press Enter and then
   type the second paragraph.

8. Save the finished document under the name NOSMOKE.
   Because you loaded TPMEMO with Transfer Merge and
   saved your changes to a new file, it will remain intact on the
   disk and can be used to create a similarly formatted memo at
   a later point.

Notice that we used Coronet font for the title and author's initials.
We had to use Courier 12, the LaserJet's built-in fixed-pitch font, for
the heading text because of the spaces before "TO:", "FROM:",
and so on. (To line up colons like this with a proportional font, you
must set a right-aligned tab at the colon position and insert tab characters instead of spaces. We'll see how to set tabs in Chapter 11.)

You can see how template files lend themselves to many situations.
For example, you could create one for internal memos and another for
letters, including a division for the envelope at the end. Just leave the
Format Division Layout's division break option set to Page for the envelope so that the envelope text will begin on a new page.

T IP

Word's supplied macro
envelope.mac assists
you in creating an
envelope with an
address in your docu-
ment (see Appendix C).

As you can tell, Word affords you a great deal of flexibility in creating page formats. In fact, you may find that it provides more possibilities than you'll ever need. However, it's good to know that should you need to customize a page's composition, Word will accommodate you.

As you work with larger and longer documents, you'll find it increasingly difficult to remember where material you need to review or revise is. In the next chapter, we'll examine the tools Word provides for finding text, formats, and files easily.

10

Locating Text, Formats, and Files

Fast Track

SEARCH OPERATIONS ARE ONE OF THE MOST USEFUL word processing tools for dealing with large documents, and Word's search capabilities are particularly extensive. In this chapter, you will learn how to use the various tools Word provides for finding and amending particular words or phrases in a document, for displaying a specific page, for locating text in different documents at the same time, and even for locating files in a list of files. In addition, you can use the Search command to highlight portions of text quickly. Thus, when you search for text for another word processing procedure, such as formatting and copying, you save time.

While most of what we will be learning in this chapter will center around the Search command, we will also practice with several related commands:

Replace command	Locates text and substitutes a new word or phrase for the original.
Jump Page command	Allows you to go directly to a given page in order to zero in on its contents.
Format sEarch and Format repLace	Allow you to search for and replace formatting.
Library Document-retrieval	Expedites locating, retrieving, and other handling of document files.

Before we get acquainted with these commands, let's examine the Search command.

SEARCHING FOR TEXT

The Search command serves a function similar to that of a book's index. By using the Search command, you can instruct Word to look for a particular piece of text or some kind of pattern within the file. The name commonly given to the piece of text or pattern—that is, to the input you provide for the search—is string. A *string* is simply any sequence of typed characters. In Word, a search string can be up to 255 characters in length.

You can use the Search command to look for any string of text. For instance, you could use it to check the usage of a term throughout a document. While writing, you could use it to refer back to the last time a concept was discussed, to avoid repeating material or to make sure the concept was fully developed at that point. You could also use the Search command to find the beginning of a section by searching for the title of the section.

Another handy use for the Search command is in checking table or figure numbers in a document after you have added, rearranged, or deleted tables or figures. When you're done, you would want to double-check that the numbers are sequential and that they match the actual tables or figures. This is the operation we'll perform with our example.

Besides text, the Search command can also look for special character codes, such as paragraph marks, new-line marks, and tabs. It will also seek out specified patterns of text when you include wild cards in the string.

To demonstrate how Word's Search command operates, we'll use the FEEDBACK document we created in Chapter 8. Go ahead and load it with the Transfer Load command. We'll use this short document so you don't have to do a lot of typing just to practice searching. Realize, however, that search operations are generally of benefit on longer documents. On short documents, it's often simpler and quicker just to scroll through the document and scan the text.

INITIATING A SEARCH

As a rule, Word begins its search at the cursor location and heads toward the end of the document, examining everything in its path to see how the material compares with the string you specified.

For this reason, to search the entire document, you need to have your cursor at the beginning of the document and no larger than a single character before you begin the search. It should be in place if you've just loaded the document. If it isn't, you can bring it to the beginning by pressing Ctrl-Page Up, or by clicking both buttons on the left window border just below the corner and then clicking on the

T IP

Because of the way the wild-card feature operates, special care must be taken if you wish to search for a question mark (?) or for the caret (^). If you need to search for these, be sure to see the latter part of this chapter.

first character in the document. With the cursor in place, issue the Search command.

1. Press the Esc key and type S for Search. Word then displays the words

   SEARCH text:

   on the screen. This is where you type in your string.

2. In this case, type the word

   Table

   as shown in Figure 10.1.

3. Press the Enter key to initiate the search.

For the moment, ignore the other settings that appear on the Search menu. Word is constructed in such a way that you can use many of its features without fine-tuning them. Just typing the text and pressing Enter, without concerning yourself about the rest of the menu, will work in most circumstances. We will look at how these settings can be useful later in the chapter.

Just after you initiated the Search command, the note

   Searching . . .

appeared in the message area. It appeared only momentarily because, in this case, Word found the string we were searching for quickly.

The cursor stops at the first occurrence of the string (see Figure 10.2). This action completes the search for the moment. The cursor highlights the word "Table" because it's the string you specified.

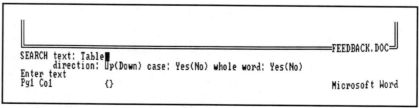

```
                                                                 =FEEDBACK.DOC=
SEARCH text: Table█
        direction: Up(Down) case: Yes(No) whole word: Yes(No)
Enter text
Pg1 Col            {}                                    Microsoft Word
```

Figure 10.1: Entering the text to be searched for

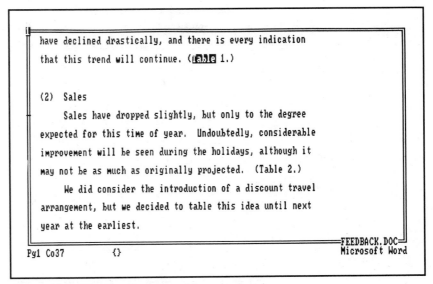

Figure 10.2: The first instance of the search string

The first table reference number is 1, which is correct, so you can now search for the next reference. If there were any problem with this number, or with any of the surrounding text, you could simply edit at this point.

USING THE REPEAT SEARCH KEY (SHIFT-F4)

Word provides a handy method for continuing the search throughout the file or even in other files. When you press the Repeat Search key (Shift-F4), Word repeats the search procedure, using the same search string you specified earlier. Word begins at the current cursor location and heads toward the end of the file. (There is no mouse equivalent for this key.)

Press Shift-F4 and you'll see the cursor jump to the next occurrence of "Table" in our document (see Figure 10.3). Once again, if the table number were not correct here, you could edit it.

Repeat the search for the next occurrence of "Table" by using Shift-F4 again. This time, we find ourselves at the phrase "table this idea" (see Figure 10.4), even though our search text was "Table" with a capital T. Unless you instruct otherwise (as we'll see shortly),

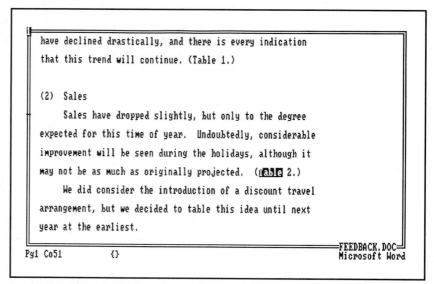

Figure 10.3: Using Shift-F4 to find the second instance of the search string

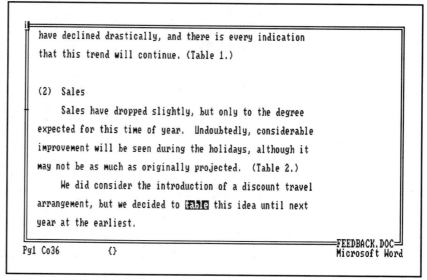

Figure 10.4: The third instance of the search string

Word will ignore the case (capitals or lowercase) when it searches. Because we're not interested in changing the located material right now, simply press the Repeat Search key again. When your search involves relatively few occurrences, it may be easiest to let the Search command present each one to you and quickly move on to the next, without specifying a more precise search string.

Having pressed the Repeat Search key again, we find that the cursor stops at the word "Tables" (see Figure 10.5). Notice how the "s" in "Tables" is not highlighted. Unless you tell it otherwise, Word will find the string you've indicated even when it's part of another word. Thus, it would find "no" in "know" and "love" in "glove."

Press Shift-F4 again, and this time you reach the text "Table 3." This entry is correct as is, so proceed with the search.

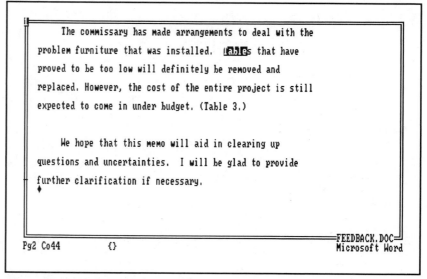

Figure 10.5: The fourth instance of the search string

COMING TO THE END OF A SEARCH

Pressing the Repeat Search key (Shift-F4) once again causes the computer to beep (unless you've silenced the beep with the mute option in the Options command). In the message area you now see

Search text not found

This indicates that you have come to the end of the search—that is, there are no more instances of the string in the document. The cursor will stay where it is (at the last occurrence of the search string) until you move it.

REPLACING TEXT AUTOMATICALLY —

Suppose you decide that you want to change the references. Instead of "Table" and the number, you want the reference to read "See Table . . ." To do this, you use Word's Replace command.

Like the Search command, the Replace command also searches for strings of text. The difference between Search and Replace is that when Replace finds the string in question, it substitutes another string of text for the found string.

To replace the word "Table" with the phrase "See Table," bring your cursor to the beginning of the document. Like Search, Replace begins at the cursor's position and heads toward the end of the document.

*M**OUSE***

Click either button on Replace to display its menu. Then click either button on with text and type the substitution text. Click either button on REPLACE to initiate the search.

1. Press the Esc key and type R for Replace. The Replace menu will appear (see Figure 10.6). Notice that the menu already lists the text to be searched for:

   REPLACE text: Table

   As you can see, the Search and Replace commands work closely with one another: what you enter in one is automatically registered in the other. You could change what is entered as the text you will be replacing by simply typing in the new text at this point. You can also use the four function keys F7 to F10 to edit the entry. Otherwise, the text will disappear as soon as you start to type.

2. Press the → or Tab key to move to the with text field. Now type the substitution string:

   See Table

3. Press the Enter key to initiate the search and replace operation.

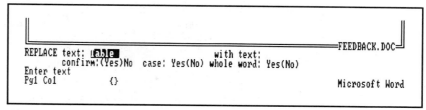

Figure 10.6: The Replace command

TIP

Word supplies you with two macros, **repl_w_scrap.mac** and **repl_w_gloss-.mac**, that allow you to replace the search string with scrap or glossary text. Using these macros enables you to provide long replacement strings (see Appendix C).

The cursor will move to the first occurrence of your search string and stop there. Word displays the confirmation message

Enter Y to replace, N to skip and continue, or Esc to cancel

With the Replace command, the cursor stops at each occurrence of the search string, just as it did with the Search command. This time, however, you are asked if you wish a substitution to be made. To make the substitution, type Y. If the substitution is not appropriate at that point, type N. After either of these responses, the search automatically proceeds. Continue to substitute the replacement strings throughout, responding with Y or N as appropriate. (Pressing the Esc key halts the replace operation.)

When you have finished replacing text, you will see this note in the message area:

3 replacements made

The cursor then returns to the point where the search began.

NARROWING YOUR SEARCH

During the search and replace operations we have performed so far, the cursor made several unnecessary stops. If you were searching a file of great length, stopping like this would be inefficient and annoying. To avoid such unnecessary stops, we can place certain constraints on the way we want Word to search. Doing so will cause the cursor to stop only at places we really want, making for a more efficient search. Be careful, though, that you don't spend an inordinate amount of time coming up with constraints. You may find that it's quicker to conduct simple, plain-vanilla searches and just make the system move on if it displays an inappropriate string.

In the next several sections, we will practice using the Search and Replace command options to see how each setting modifies the performance of the command. While in most instances the settings for the Search and Replace command options are quite similar, in some cases Replace behaves differently than Search, and in one instance Replace has an option for which there is no equivalent in Search. We'll look at each option's use in Search first and then in Replace.

SPECIFYING CAPITALS OR LOWERCASE

The first command option we will examine is called case on both the Search and the Replace menus. Case specifies whether capital and lowercase distinctions should be taken into consideration. Normally, case is set to No, meaning that when Word is searching, it stops at any occurrence of a word, regardless of whether the capital and lowercase letters match. When you specify Yes for case, Word will look for only those occurrences that exactly match your search string, in case as well as content.

Let's change the case setting in our example and observe how this affects the search. First, check that your cursor is at the beginning of the file.

M O U S E

To set the case and initiate the search, click either button on Search and click right on Yes for the case option. (If you clicked left on Yes, you could also initiate the search by clicking either button on SEARCH.)

1. Press the Esc key and type S for Search. Note that the word "Table" is still listed as the search text.

2. Use the directional arrows or the Tab key to reach the case option and type Y for Yes.

3. Press the Enter key to initiate the search.

After changing the case in the Search command, use the Repeat Search key (Shift-F4) and proceed to search throughout the document. Notice that this time you do not stop at the phrase "to table this idea," since the case of "table" does not match that of your search string, "Table." Changing the case in the Search command automatically changes it in the Replace command as well.

Like the Search command, the Replace command's default setting for case is No. Thus, when case is set to No, Replace will find any occurrence of the string, regardless of case. When the string is located, however, Replace goes on to examine the letters of the string it finds in order to match the replacement string's lowercase letters to the case of the string being replaced. For instance, if you asked the Replace command to substitute the word "love" for the word "hate," it would replace "hate" with "love," "HATE" with "LOVE," and "Hate" with "Love." If you want Replace to substitute a word using the existing case in each context, type the replacement string in all lowercase letters; otherwise, Replace would assume that the word's case was an error and correct it. For instance, if you replace "hate" with "Love," all occurrences of "hate," regardless of case, will become "Love."

However, if you set Replace's case option to Yes (which changes case to Yes in the Search command as well), Replace will locate only instances in which capital and lowercase letters match the replacement text exactly. In other words, you can keep Replace from stopping at any string that doesn't match the case of the string you asked it to search for. The strings Replace finds will be replaced with the replacement string exactly as you typed it.

CHANGING DIRECTION

Now let's suppose that as you were checking the table numbers, you couldn't recall something about the previous number. How can you go back to check material you've already passed? You can search backward by changing the direction setting in the Search menu.

The direction of a search operation can be either up or down. Although a search is usually conducted down the document (heading toward the end), it's easy to have the search conducted up—that is, heading toward the beginning of the document.

When you change the direction setting, notice that case remains set to Yes. Changes in Search and Replace settings remain the same until you quit the program. They even remain the same when you issue a Transfer Clear All command, although the text strings are cleared and in Word 4 the confirm setting in the Replace command reverts back to Yes if you changed it.

MOUSE

Click either button on Search and click right on Up to set the direction and initiate the search.

1. Press Esc and type S for Search.

2. Move to the direction option and type U for Up.

3. Press Enter to register your choices and initiate the search.

Use the Repeat Search key (Shift-F4) to proceed backward through the document. Notice that you don't stop at "table this idea . . . " because case is still set to Yes.

When you use the Replace command, there is no setting available for direction. With Replace, Word always starts at the cursor location and heads toward the end of the document. Thus, you will usually want to place the cursor at the beginning of the document before you initiate the Replace command.

Now let's look at another way we can narrow our search.

STOPPING ONLY AT WHOLE WORDS

For both the Search and the Replace command, the whole word setting is No by default. This means that Word finds any occurrence of a string, whether it appears as a word by itself or as part of another string.

If you set whole word to Yes, however, you are asking Word to search for only instances in which your string is a word unto itself rather than part of a longer word. (A *word* is defined as a string surrounded by either punctuation or blank spaces.)

Let's demonstrate a whole word search. Start with your cursor at the beginning of the file.

MOUSE

Click either button on Search and click left on Down to reverse the direction. To change the whole word setting and initiate the search, click right on Yes.

1. Press the Esc key and type S for Search. "Table" is still listed as the search text.

2. Move to the direction option and type D for Down. The previous search brought the cursor back to the beginning, so we need to change directions for this search.

3. Move to the whole word option and type Y for Yes.

4. Press the Enter key to register the new settings and initiate the search.

Continue through the text and complete the search. This time, you'll stop only at occurrences of "Table," not "Tables."

The whole word option in the Replace command operates in the same fashion and is a valuable tool when you are replacing text. By setting whole word to Yes, you can ensure that some incorrect replacements are not made. For example, if you left whole word set to No and wanted to replace "table" with "figure," you might accidentally end up with "vegefigure," especially if you had set confirm to No. Although you can also guard against this type of error by leaving confirm set to No, you may sometimes deem it necessary to change it. Let's examine this option next.

CONFIRMING REPLACEMENT

Normally, when Word replaces text, it stops at each string it finds and asks if you wish to make the substitution. There may be times, however, when you wish to perform massive substitutions in a file—for example, when a proper name has been spelled incorrectly throughout a document. In such a situation, it would be inefficient to stop at each occurrence of the string in the text. Instead, you can change the confirm setting in the Replace command to No.

Replacing text without confirmation is a powerful procedure. For this reason, it is potentially disastrous. Because Word will make the replacements without your approval, you must verify that you typed your text correctly and that the search string you specified is precise—that it will not be located in the incorrect context. In addition, you should double-check that your case and whole word settings are correct.

I recommend you save the document before making such massive substitutions. If something goes wrong with the replace operation, you can simply load the original version of the document from the disk, specifying N to lose changes. Alternatively, you can use the Undo command if you catch the problem before making any further edits.

Let's say that now you want the table references to read "Refer to Table" rather than "See Table." To perform this operation automatically, let's change the Replace confirm setting to No.

1. First save the document and bring the cursor to the beginning of the document.

2. Press the Esc key and type R for Replace.

3. Type the string

   (See Table

   as the text you will be replacing. Although "See Table" would probably work just fine, especially in a small document like this, the opening parenthesis makes its context more precise. It's doubtful that this string could appear in the wrong location.

4. Press the → or Tab key to move to the with text option and type the replacement text

   (Refer to Table

5. Move to the confirm option and type N for No.

6. After making sure you've done everything correctly, press the Enter key to register the settings and initiate the automatic search and replace operation.

The note

   Searching . . .

appears briefly in the message area. Soon it's replaced with

   3 replacements made

indicating that your substitution has been successful. Once the replace operation is complete, the cursor returns to the location it occupied prior to the search.

HIGHLIGHTING WITH THE SEARCH AND REPLACE COMMANDS

When used with the Extend key (F6), the Search command has another important function: it can expedite the highlighting process.

Once your designated text is highlighted, it can be altered with the Alt codes or Format commands, or moved, copied, or deleted.

Let's say, for example, that you had decided to set the main body of this memo in another font to differentiate it from the opening and closing portions.

Start by bringing your cursor up to the first topic listed:

(1)   **Efficiency of Service**

You might try, by the way, to use your newly acquired skill with the Search command to get the cursor there.

Now let's practice highlighting with Search:

1. Press the Extend key (F6).

2. Press the Esc key and type S for Search.

3. Type the last phrase that you want in the new font:

    (Refer to Table 3.)

4. Press the Enter key. Notice that all the material from the first topic heading, "Efficiency of Service," through the reference to Table 3 is highlighted.

5. Use the Format Character menu (or Alt-F8) to change the font.

Highlighting serves a different purpose when used with Replace. Although you can't use Replace to highlight text, you can highlight text to restrict a replace operation to strings that appear within the highlighted text.

Suppose, for example, that in a series of invoices contained in one file, certain terms had been typed the same throughout the file. The terms were correct for the last half of the invoices in the file but incorrect for the first half. With a lot of invoices being changed, you might want to replace automatically by changing the confirm setting to No. To have the Replace operation stop at the middle and avoid searching through the correct terms in the last half of the document, you could expand the cursor to highlight the first half of the file. The Replace command would work exclusively in the highlighted portion of the file, and the second half would remain unchanged.

M O U S E

Press F6 and click either button on Search. Type the last phrase to be set in the new font and click either button on SEARCH. Click right on Format to display the Format Character menu and choose the font (both name and size) you want.

SEARCHING WITH INVISIBLE AND WILD-CARD CHARACTERS

At this point, we have seen that Word is capable of conducting some pretty sophisticated searches. There are times, however, when the techniques we've used so far are insufficient. You may, for example, remember only one portion of a string that you wish Word to search for. Or you may need to find a particular word that is preceded or followed by an invisible or non-printing character, such as a tab. In such situations, you can ask Word to search for special invisible or wild-card characters.

Invisible characters are defined as the characters that do not normally appear on the screen but are nonetheless an integral part of the text. The tab character (created with the Tab key) and the paragraph mark (created with the Enter key) are examples of invisible characters.

Wild-card characters function like wild cards in a game of poker. When you use these characters in your search text, any character or characters will be accepted in place of them. They can be used, in effect, to complete a string.

Table 10.1 lists the special characters that Word uses to conduct searches. Notice that most of these characters begin with

^

This character is called a *caret*. It appears on the 6 key located on the top row of your keyboard and you create it by pressing Shift-6. (Note that Word does not use the caret to represent the Ctrl key as some software packages do.)

The wild-card codes are the question mark (without a caret preceding it) and ^w (pronounced "caret w"), which we'll discuss in a moment. You use the question mark to allow any single character to complete the string. What's more, you can combine a wild card like the question mark with the other codes. Suppose, for example, you wanted to look at each topic heading in this memo. You could search for them, one after another, by searching for the string

SEARCH text: (?)

Table 10.1: Special Characters Word Uses for Searches

CHARACTER	USE TO FIND	HOW CREATED
^c	Column break	Ctrl-Alt-Enter
^d	Division mark	Ctrl-Enter or Format Division command
^d	Page break	Ctrl-Shift-Enter or pagination
^n	New-line mark	Shift-Enter
^p	Paragraph mark	Enter key
^s	Non-breaking space	Ctrl-Spacebar
^t	Tab character	Tab key
^w	White space	Spacebar, Tab key, Enter key or anything else creating non-printing characters
^-	Optional hyphen	Ctrl-hyphen or the Library Hyphenate Command
?	Single character	Any key creating a single character
^?	Question mark	Question mark key
^^	Caret	Caret key (Shift-6)

With this string you are telling the computer to highlight an open parenthesis, followed by a single character, followed by a closing parenthesis. Thus, you would find

(1)
(2)
(3)

and so on using the Repeat Search key (Shift-F4). It would not find

(10)

however, since 10 is made up of two characters.

There are two other ways to perform the same search by using invisible characters. The first would be to tell the computer to find instances where there's a closing parenthesis followed by a tab. For the search text, you would specify

)^t

The second way is to tell the computer to search for a paragraph mark followed by an opening parenthesis. You'd specify this with

^p(

You could combine invisible characters with the wild-card code to make your search extremely narrow:

^p(?)^t

This tells Word to look for a paragraph mark, followed by an open parenthesis, which is in turn followed by any single character, a closing parenthesis, and a tab character. Try this search on the sample document.

Because the question mark has a special use, if you wish to search for an actual question mark, you must type

^?

Likewise, to search for a caret you must type two carets (^^).

The ^w code is a wild card that will match "white" space in a document, regardless of the way that space was created. In the previous example, for instance, you might not know whether the space following the parenthesis was created by the Tab key or whether the typist created it by pressing the Spacebar several times. For the search, you could use ^w instead of ^t to be sure of finding the space in either case.

Finally, Table 10.1 lists several other special characters you can search for. These include the new-line character, division mark, page break, and so on.

When you use the Replace command, you can include any of the special characters in the string to be replaced. In the substitution string, however, the wild cards (the question mark or ^w) will not function as wild cards—Word will not know what you want to replace them with and will look for the actual characters. However, you can include invisible characters (paragraph mark, tab, and so on) in the replacement text.

You can also use the wild-card characters to search for files whose names you only partly remember. You can even set up your file names so that you can use wild cards to select groups of files. We will learn about this in the "Searching for Files with Wild Cards" section later in this chapter.

SEARCHING FOR AND REPLACING FORMATS

Although we have already searched for invisible symbols, such as the paragraph mark, that keep track of a text's format, there may also be times when you need to search for the formatting characteristics themselves. To do this, you search for text that contains specific character or paragraph formatting. You could, for instance, search for boldface text or a paragraph with the open format (one line of space before the paragraph). You can also search for combinations of character or paragraph formatting. Thus, you could have Word look for text that is set in boldface italics or open-spaced paragraphs that are indented ½ inch. All the Format Character and Format Paragraph menu options are available for use with searching.

Searching for formats is quite similar to searching for strings of text, even though you use a different command. When you search for formats, Word usually searches down the document, although you can have it search up instead. It looks for formatted text matching the criteria you specify and highlights the first instance of such text. Thus, if you search for boldface characters, Word highlights the first set of characters that are boldfaced. If you search for centered paragraphs, Word highlights the first paragraph that's formatted as centered.

CONDUCTING A SEARCH BY FORMAT

You could locate the headings in our example by having Word search for their format. Their distinguishing characteristic is that the first line is not indented. Here's how you would proceed. First move the cursor to a position where you want Word to begin the search. (You can move to the beginning of the document with Ctrl-Page Up.) Then follow these steps:

MOUSE

Click left on Format and then click left on sEarch. (If you click right on sEarch, you'll get the Format sEarch Character command.) Click left on Paragraph and specify which format Word should search for. To initiate this search, click either button on FORMAT SEARCH PARAGRAPH.

1. Press Esc, then type F for Format and E for sEarch. You'll see the Format sEarch menu, as shown in Figure 10.7.

2. Choose the format you wish to search for; in this case, type P for Paragraph. (The Style format is for use with style sheets, which we'll examine in Chapter 17.) The Format sEarch Paragraph menu will then appear (see Figure 10.8).

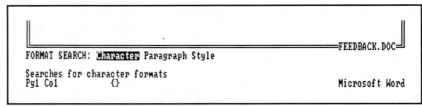

Figure 10.7: The Format sEarch command

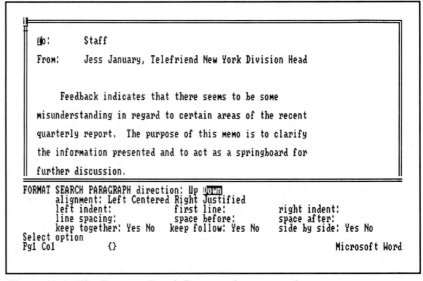

Figure 10.8: The Format sEarch Paragraph command

3. Since the cursor is at the beginning of the document, leave direction set to Down.

4. To search for the headings, type 0 in the first line field.

5. Press Enter to initiate Word's search for the format that you indicated.

After Word finds the first instance of text that matches your formatting criteria, you can continue the search by using the Repeat Search key (Shift-F4).

REPLACING ONE FORMAT WITH ANOTHER

Because you'll often want to replace a format once you have found it, just as with with text strings, Word also provides this capability with its Format repLace command. Let's say that you get a new printer that can print italics. Previously, you've only underlined text because your printer couldn't print italics. With Word you can replace all the underlining in your existing documents with italics.

To replace formatting, issue the Format repLace command. Again, you can specify Character, Paragraph, or Style. Once you make your choice (in this case, Character), the appropriate menu will appear, as it did with the search procedure (Figure 10.9). You can

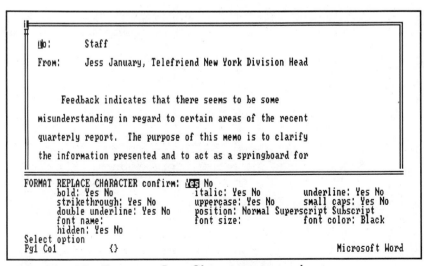

Figure 10.9: The Format repLace Character command

then indicate the original formatting that Word should search for (underline) and whether Word should replace automatically or ask you to confirm each replacement.

Once you specify the format to search for, a similar formatting menu appears. Now you indicate the format that Word should substitute for the existing format. In our example, you would indicate italic in this second formatting menu.

After you execute this command on the document you are currently working on, you may want to repeat it for other documents. Let's examine an efficient way to do this now.

SEARCHING DIFFERENT DOCUMENTS SIDE BY SIDE

So far we have only practiced our newly acquired search and replace techniques on one document file, although the techniques that we've discussed can be utilized when additional windows are open.

The excellent windowing capabilities of Microsoft Word afford you the opportunity to conduct quick searches among multiple documents. The entries that you make in search and replace operations remain there as you activate different windows. This means that you can search for (and replace) a string in one document and then perform the same operation in another. For instance, if you were working on a report, you might use the Search command to locate another document's material that you want to copy. Similarly, you could open a window to use the Replace command as well. Imagine that you are working on a document and you need to change the name of your department throughout the displayed document and in several other documents as well. Assuming that you'd be returning to the first document to continue working, you could open a window to make replacements in the others.

To search for the same string in a second document on the screen, follow these steps:

M O U S E

You can split a window by clicking either button on the right window border.

1. Split the window horizontally by issuing the Window Split Horizontal command.

2. As the new window is the activated one, issue the Transfer Load command to load the second document into it.

3. Use the Search or Replace command in the second window to search for or replace a string of your choice (see Figure 10.10). The option settings (direction, case, and so on) remain intact. Because they do, the Repeat Search key (Shift-F4) will function in the newly activated window, just as it did in the first window. Similarly, you could use the Format sEarch and Format repLace commands with windows to change underlining to italics in numerous documents, for example.

4. Save the document if you made any changes, load another document into the second window, and repeat the search procedure.

When you are finished working with the documents, you can close the second window.

Whether you are working with one document or several, there are often times when you want to move to a specific page rather than to a phrase or format; you need to see the larger context.

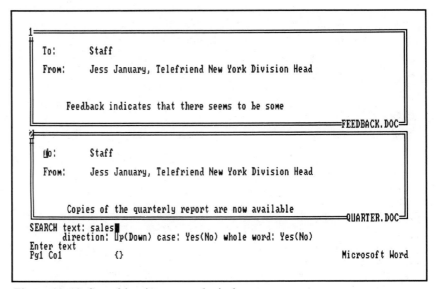

Figure 10.10: Searching in a second window

SEARCHING FOR PAGES

Word provides a quick way to get to a specific page of the document. When you need to review an entire page, jumping to it is usually quicker than using the Search command, especially with large documents. The Jump Page command will bring you to the beginning of the page that you specify. It will only work, however, if you have left the Options command's paginate option set to Auto or if you have printed or repaginated the document (Chapter 3).

This command is extremely useful for making changes in a document that you've already printed. For any page that contains corrections, just look at the page number on the printed document and issue Jump Page, specifying that number. Generally, it works faster than the Search command. If you use Jump Page to edit your printed document, set the Options command's paginate option to Manual and do not issue the Print Repaginate command after printing. Otherwise, Word will assign new page numbers as you edit and the numbers might no longer agree with the document's printed version.

If you are revising your document's pages without automatic pagination, be careful not to delete whatever character happens to be at the end of the line before the page break. If you do, Word will delete the page break symbol as well, and you won't be able to use Jump Page to find that page. If you try to use Jump Page under these circumstances, you'll get the message

No such page

Here, then, are the steps for performing the Jump Page command:

1. Press Esc and type J for Jump.

2. Press P for Page or press the Enter key.

3. When you see the display

JUMP PAGE number:

type the page number you want.

4. Press the Enter key to register the command and move to that page.

Shortcut:

Alt-F5

T I P

Word supplies you with two macros, **next_page.mac** and **prev_page.mac**, that display the next and previous pages of a document. More on these macros in Appendix C.

M O U S E

Click right on Jump to display the Jump Page menu. Type the page number you want and click either button on JUMP PAGE to move to that page.

Now that you have explored all the techniques of searching within displayed files and have accumulated many files on your hard disk, you are ready to acquire the techniques that enable you to search for files to display.

SEARCHING FOR FILES WITH WILD CARDS

As you know, when you are using the Transfer Load command, you can simply type the name of the file you want, or you can use the F1 key to display a list and choose from it if you can't remember the exact name. As your word processing skills grow and the number of documents on your disk increases, however, you may find it difficult to spot the document name you're trying to recall. One technique you can employ to make it easier is to use directories (see Appendix B). Two other ways are with wild cards and Word's document-retrieval system. Let's begin with wild cards.

As with the Search command, the question mark (?) acts as a wild card for any single character. In addition, you can include the asterisk (*) in a file name to match any group of characters. By using the question mark and the asterisk, you can load a file whose full name you can't remember, or you can display fewer file names so that it is easier to find the file you want.

To use wild cards effectively, you need to name your files in a consistent fashion. Whenever you write letters to business associates, let's say that you decide always to use LE as the first two of the possible eight characters in the file name, letting Word add its standard .DOC extension. The LE will signify that the document is a letter. Then if you wish to look for a letter whose file name you can't remember exactly, you could have the Transfer Load command display only files that are letters. Here's how you would go about doing this:

1. Press Ctrl-F7 to initiate the Transfer Load command.

2. When the screen shows

    TRANSFER LOAD filename:

    type

    LE

    and press F1 or click right on filename.

Word will then list only those document names that begin with "LE."

Now suppose that you set aside the remaining character spaces in the file name for the person's name. Thus, the file name for a letter to a Ms. Oshiro would be LEOSHIRO.

To demonstrate the usefulness of wild cards for selecting groups of files, let's suppose you have written a variety of documents to Ms. Oshiro, a letter (whose file name begins in LE), a memo (whose file name begins in ME), and a report (whose file name begins in RE). Now you wish to call up everything you've addressed to Ms. Oshiro. How can all the Oshiro files be displayed without showing other documents?

Using the question mark wild card, it's simple to do. Type

>   ??OSHIRO

in the filename field and press F1 or click right to display all of Ms. Oshiro's files.

As you know, Word will usually display only files that end with .DOC when you're using the Transfer Load command. You could have Word display the .BAK files instead (and only the .BAK files) by typing

>   *.BAK

To display file names that do not have the optional extension, type an asterisk followed by a period. (You can save file names without an extension in a similar fashion: type the file name and end it with a period.)

As our final example, let's have Word display all files in the current directory, regardless of their extension. Do so by typing

>   *.*

As before, press F1 or click right to display the files. Files with any extension and files without an extension will be listed. Whenever you can list the files in a directory, such as with the Transfer Delete command, you can limit the display as well. Just use the same methods we've used with Transfer Load.

LOCATING FILES WITH SUMMARY SHEETS AND THE DOCUMENT-RETRIEVAL SYSTEM

Another way to retrieve documents easily is to use summary sheets. By providing a title, the author's name, the name of the person who entered the document, the date the document was created or revised, and important words or categories when you save the document, you will later be able to identify it easily.

Using summary sheets is entirely optional, however. If you don't wish to use summary sheets, you can issue the Options command and change the summary sheet setting to No. Then, of course, you can skip the rest of this section.

SAVING AND SUMMARY SHEETS

When the Options command's summary sheet option is set to Yes, Word presents you with a summary sheet when you first save a document. You can then provide the information that the sheet calls for. If you don't want to bother with the summary sheet for a particular document, simply press Enter or Esc.

Figure 10.11 shows a possible summary sheet for the FEEDBACK document that we created earlier. Let's examine the information that appears in it.

The title field allows you to give the document a more complete title than the eight characters allowed for a file's name. You can enter

```
filename: C:\WORD\FEEDBACK.DOC
title: Quarterly Report Feedback Memo
author: January
operator: May
keywords: Memo Efficiency Sales Commissary Furniture
comments: This memo was well received and serves as a good
     model.
version number: 1
creation date: 03/06/88
revision date: 04/02/89
char count: 1504
```

Figure 10.11: A summary sheet for our sample document

up to 40 characters for the title, which you will be able to see when you go to retrieve the document (more on retrieving like this later in this section). You can also enter up to 40 characters in the author or operator fields. Use author for the name of the person or persons who wrote the original text. Separate multiple names with commas or spaces. Use operator for the person or persons who entered or edited the text and saved the file. Unlike file names, there's no restriction on the type of characters you can use in these fields.

The version number can be up to 10 characters in length. Many offices have sophisticated version number systems for documents, and you can use these characters to accommodate such systems. More simply, though, you can just number your versions with integers beginning with 1.

Word handles the creation date and revisions date fields automatically. It enters the creation date when the document is first created and saved. The revision date reflects the last time that the file was updated and saved. For both of these, Word uses the date that the operating system provides.

You can use up to 80 characters for keywords. Your keywords should be words that pertain to the subject matter addressed. Word can search for, select, and display documents that are earmarked with keywords. Don't think, however, that the words you provide here are the only ones Word can use to retrieve documents. In fact, Word can use any word or string of words that appears in the document. Nonetheless, searching is quickest when accomplished by keywords.

The comments field is a place for you to leave memos and can hold up to 256 characters. You can use it to describe the document's contents or to remind yourself about work that needs to be done on the file. You can also leave notes or questions here for others who may be working on the file.

Although the summary sheet is originally presented when you save the document, you can also change it later by using the Library Document-retrieval's Update command. Let's examine the document-retrieval system now.

USING WORD'S DOCUMENT-RETRIEVAL SYSTEM

The Library Document-retrieval command is the heart of Word's ability to retrieve documents according to information stored on the summary sheets and within the documents. When you issue this command, you'll see the screen that appears in Figure 10.12. To return to Document mode when you're done with this screen, you use the Exit command.

Originally, Word displays all the documents contained in the current directory or disk. You can load a file for editing from the displayed files, just as with the Transfer Load command. The power of the document-retrieval system, though, lies in your ability to limit which files are displayed. Shortening the list of files makes it easier to locate the file you want.

MARKING FILES FOR OPERATIONS

 New in
Word 5

One way to target the files on which you want to issue Library document-retrieval commands is by marking them. Word will then consider only the marked files as it performs various document-retrieval operations. For example, you can print all the marked files in succession or delete them as a group.

To mark files, first use the arrow keys to highlight a name from the list of files or click left on it. Here are the marking operations you can perform:

M O U S E

You can also click right on an unmarked file name to mark it, or click right on a marked file name to unmark it.

Spacebar or Enter	Marks an unmarked file name or unmarks a marked file name.
Ctrl-Spacebar	Marks all displayed file names.
Shift-Ctrl-Spacebar	Unmarks all marked files.

```
DOCUMENT-RETRIEVAL: Query Exit Load Print Update View Copy Delete
Press Spacebar to mark-unmark file, Ctrl+Spacebar to mark all, or Esc for menu
                                                              Microsoft Word
```

Figure 10.12: The Library Document-retrieval command

When you mark a file, Word places an asterisk (*) before the file's name on the list. For example, if you mark the FEEDBACK file, you'll see

    *C:\WORD\FEEDBACK.DOC

in the displayed list. Unmarking the file removes the asterisk.

Once you've marked the files you want, one procedure you can perform is querying. In the Library document-retrieval's Query menu, set marked files only to Yes. Then, Word will perform your query only on the files you've marked. We'll examine other operations you can perform on marked files shortly.

QUERYING TO SEARCH FOR FILES

Once you choose Query, the query menu appears (see Figure 10.13). You use this menu to specify the search criteria that you want Word to use in locating files. After you've completed your settings and registered your choices (with Enter or the mouse), Word displays

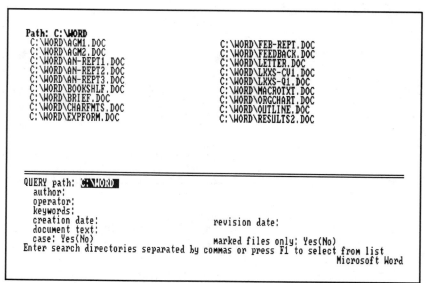

Figure 10.13: The Library Document-retrieval's Query command

the names of files that meet your specifications. You can then choose the document you wish to use from among those listed.

SPECIFYING A PATH The first information you provide is the path. The path is simply a list of directories, separated by commas, that you want Word to check for the documents you indicate. Thus, if you would like Word to check for documents in drive C's WORD directory and root directory, as well as the SMITH and JONES directories on drive D, you'd specify the path as

C:\WORD\,C:\,D:\SMITH\,D:\JONES\

You can even limit the search to particular files in the directories by including them in the path and using wild cards as part of any file names you provide. Thus, if you want Word to search among the .BAK files in the WORD directory on drive C, you'd include the following as part of the path:

C:\WORD*.BAK

When you don't include an extension, Word assumes that you are only interested in .DOC files.

With Word 5 you can display a list of drives and directories and select from them to create a query path. With this method, not only can you see what drives and directories are available, but you don't have to worry about the correct syntax for the path. To choose from the list, follow these steps:

New in
Word 5

1. In the path field, press F1.

2. To change drives or directories, highlight the drive or directory you want and press F1.

3. To add a drive, directory, or file name to the path, highlight it and enter a comma (,).

4. Continue to add to the path by repeating these steps.

USING QUERY EXPRESSIONS You can enter a query expression for most of the other options in the Library Document-retrieval's Query

M O U S E

Click right on path to list the available drives and directories. Then click left on a drive or directory, type a comma, click left on the next selected directory, and type a comma. Continue until all the drives, directories, and files you want are included in the path.

menu. With *query expressions,* you specify the criteria that you want Word to use in its search.

For simple queries, you can use one word. To search by author, operator, keywords, or document text, just type a word in the appropriate field. To search for a date, enter a date in the same format that is set in the Options command.

For multiple entries and other complex searches, you need to make use of *logical operators.* You can enter up to 256 characters for all fields except creation date and revision date, where the limit is 25 characters. Let's examine the use of logical operators in query expressions.

Comma: the OR operator   Use a comma to indicate OR in a query expression. Thus, if you wanted Word to list documents composed by either Johnson or Davis, you'd enter

    Johnson, Davis

in the author field. The space after the comma is optional.

Ampersand and Space: the AND operators   Use an ampersand (&) or a blank space to indicate AND. Thus, if you want Word to display documents that were entered or revised by both Anderson and Brown, you could enter any of the following in the operator field:

    Anderson & Brown
    Anderson Brown
    Anderson&Brown

Tilde: the NOT operator   Use a tilde (˜) to indicate NOT. You'll find this operator helpful for handling embedded words. Normally, Word will display files where the specified word is part of a longer word. Thus, if you ask Word to display files whose keyword is John, Word will normally also display those files containing the keyword Johnson. To repress the display of files that have Johnson as one of their keywords, enter

    John ˜ Johnson

meaning John, not Johnson, in the keywords field. However, documents with other keywords such as Johnstone or Upjohn would still appear.

Date operators   There are two logical operators that you can use with the date fields only. They are the less-than ($<$) and greater-than ($>$) signs. The less-than sign is for dates earlier than the specified date; greater-than is for later dates. For example, to search for all dates before April 2, 1990, enter

> <4/2/90

To search for all dates after April 2, 1990, enter

> >4/2/90

Parentheses for combining   You can use parentheses to combine logical operators. For example, to search for Zachery and either Jones or Smith, enter

> Zachery&(Jones,Smith)

Word will find occurrences of Zachery and Jones as well as of Zachery and Smith.

PRECAUTIONS FOR QUERYING   You must enclose the entire search string in quotes when the entry you are searching for contains one of the logical operators. Thus, if you wish to find the string

> Telefriend Teleportation, Incorporated

you must enter

> "Telefriend Teleportation, Incorporated"

because the comma is a logical operator.

Because the quotation marks are themselves used in this special fashion, you must treat them specially as well. When quotes are part of the search string, double the quotes, and then enclose the entire search string in quotes as well. For instance, to search for

Danny "Duke" Dove

you must enter

"Danny " "Duke" " Dove"

You can also use the wild cards, ? and *, as substitutes for a single character or group of characters, respectively. As with text searches, you must precede a search for an actual question mark, asterisk, or caret with a caret (^?, ^*, and ^^ respectively).

Lastly, when Word searches for document text, it does not normally take the case (capitals or lowercase) into consideration. To have Word find only those files whose text matches the case of your specified text exactly, change the case setting to Yes.

VIEWING DOCUMENT NAMES

T I P

By using the Microsoft Windows program, you could make changes that are not reflected in the list of file names. If this happens, press Ctrl-F4 to update the file listings.

After you mark files, set up your last query expression, and press Enter, Word will display the list of files that fulfill the criteria you've specified. However, it can display the list in one of three layouts or views. You indicate which view you desire with the Library Document-retrieval's View command (see Figure 10.14). When you choose a view, you can also specify the order in which the file names should be listed. Use the sort by option to accomplish this.

Normally, Word displays the Short view (see Figure 10.14). This allows you to see the maximum number of file names possible.

In the Long view (Figure 10.15), Word shows the category that you have sorted the files by. It also provides the directory path and the title of each document.

The Full view (Figure 10.16) is the most comprehensive. With it, you can see a document's complete summary sheet when you highlight its name.

RETRIEVING AND PRINTING DOCUMENTS

Regardless of which view you use, once you have found the document you are searching for, you can retrieve it by issuing the Library

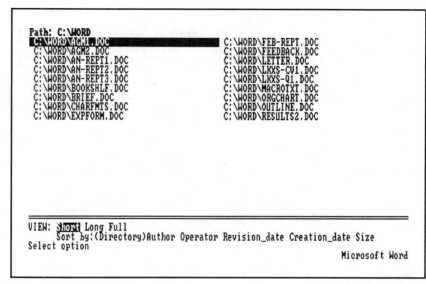

Figure 10.14: The Short view

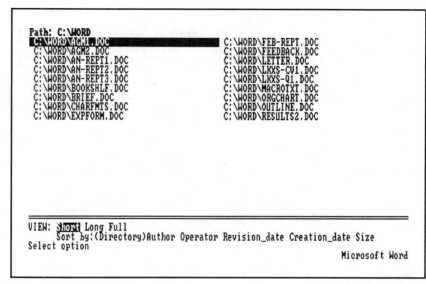

Figure 10.15: The Long view

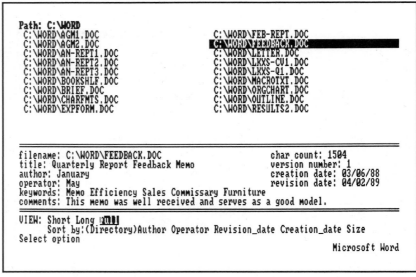

Figure 10.16: The Full view

Use Ctrl-F7 as the shortcut for the Library Document-retrieval's Load command.

Document-retrieval's Load command. You can then edit it just as you would a file retrieved with the Transfer Load command.

If you wish to retrieve a document's summary sheet, invoke the Library Document-retrieval's Update command. You don't need to retrieve the entire document to update its summary sheet.

Likewise, you don't need to load a document to print it or its summary sheet. Simply invoke the Library Document-retrieval's Print command (see Figure 10.17). If you want to print the summary sheets of the marked files, select Summary. Use Document to print just the marked files. Selecting Both prints the marked documents and their summary sheets. Printing is governed by the Print Options command's current settings.

T I P

Press Ctrl-F8 to print a document instead of using the Library Document-retrieval's Print command.

```
PRINT marked files: Summary Document Both
Select option
                                        Microsoft Word
```

Figure 10.17: The Library Document-retrieval's Print command

You can also have Word print the summary sheet when you print with the Print Printer command. To do this, first issue the Print Options command and set summary sheet to Yes. Word will print the summary sheet on a separate piece of paper before printing the document when you invoke Print Printer.

COPYING, MOVING, AND DELETING FILES

5 New in Word 5

Word 5's Library Document-retrieval system also enables you to copy marked files from one drive or directory location to another, move marked files by copying them and then deleting them from their old location, or delete marked files.

Here are the steps for copying or moving files:

1. Mark the files you want by highlighting each one and then pressing Enter or the Spacebar, or by clicking right on them.

2. Issue the Library Document-retrieval's Copy command (Figure 10.18).

3. In the first field, provide the path for the destination directory, either by typing it or by selecting it from the list.

4. If you want to remove the original files once they are copied, set delete files after copy to Yes. If you want Word to copy the selected documents' style sheets (if there are any), set copy style sheets to Yes.

5. Register the command by pressing Enter or clicking right on COPY. Word then starts the copying process.

To delete files from the directory without moving them elsewhere, simply mark the files and issue the Library Document-retrieval's

T I P

Word 5 supplies you with two macros, **archive_author.mac** and **archive_keyword.mac**, that make it easy to copy files associated with an author or a keyword to their respective directory (see Appendix C).

```
COPY marked files to drive/directory: █
       delete files after copy: Yes(No)         copy style sheets: Yes(No)
Enter path or press F1 to select from list
                                                        Microsoft Word
```

Figure 10.18: The Library Document-retrieval's Copy command

Delete command. Word will display the message

Enter Y to confirm deletion of marked files

Double-check that the correct files are marked with the asterisk (*) and type Y to remove them.

We've seen how searching can be useful in a variety of circumstances, although they have all been in standard documents. In the next chapter, we'll see how you can create other types of layouts, in particular, tables, multicolumns, and organizational charts.

PART III

Using Word's Specialized Features

11

Tables, Multiple Columns, and Other Sophisticated Layouts

Fast Track

SO FAR, THE MATERIAL WE HAVE WORKED WITH HAS been *linear* in nature. That is, the text starts at one point, flows in a continuous fashion until it reaches the end, and then stops. For instance, when you read a paragraph, you consider words in sequence, one after another.

Sometimes, however, your ideas might be better served when presented in a nonlinear format. Tables, multicolumn text, lines, and boxes allow you to communicate information in a more relational fashion. Note that in this context, the word *column* refers to textual columns, not isolated character positions, as it does for the column numbers displayed in the lower-left corner of the screen.

AN OVERVIEW OF WORD'S MULTICOLUMN LAYOUTS

Tables allow you to organize material so that it can be read from top to bottom as well as from left to right. To make a table that is composed of discrete units of text that are no longer than one line, you use tabs. A schedule with routes, fares, and destinations is a good example of this (see Figure 11.1). On the screen, a table created with tabs looks similar to its printed version (see Figure 11.2).

Other times, you may want your textual material to appear in a multicolumn format. To accommodate this, Word can create two kinds of textual columns: *newspaper-style* (or *snaking*) columns and *side-by-side* columns. With newspaper columns, the text is continuous, flowing sequentially down one column to the bottom of the page and then jumping to the top of the next column. The result is the kind of snaking effect you see in a newspaper. In Word, with the Options menu's show layout option set to No, the text flows sequentially in one narrow column as shown in Figure 11.3; you don't see multiple columns on the screen. Nonetheless, the printed result is newspaper-style columns (see Figure 11.4). This arrangement may seem disadvantageous at first, but actually it works quite well. At the computer, you can read the material in order, and you don't have to worry about jumping around the screen to follow the columns.

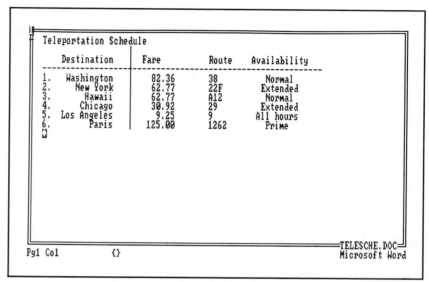

Figure 11.1: Displaying a table created with tabs

Teleportation Schedule

	Destination	Fare	Route	Availability
1.	Washington	82.36	38	Normal
2.	New York	62.77	22F	Extended
3.	Hawaii	62.77	A12	Normal
4.	Chicago	30.92	29	Extended
5.	Los Angeles	9.25	9	All hours
6.	Paris	125.00	1262	Prime

Figure 11.2: A printout of a table created with tabs

 New in Word 5

When you initiate the Options command and set show layout to Yes, you can see snaking columns on the screen and revise your text. By doing so, you will know exactly how the text will align, and you can adjust any column breaks that you don't like by adding or deleting text and column breaks. Bear in mind, though, that operations may be slower with show layout on than with it off, depending on your computer system.

With side-by-side columns, you can align lines and paragraphs horizontally. You can, in fact, think of them as another way of creating tables (when each item is too long to use tabs). When you set show layout to No, the paragraphs are displayed one after another,

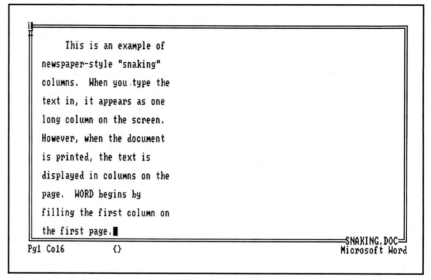

This is an example of
newspaper-style "snaking"
columns. When you type the
text in, it appears as one
long column on the screen.
However, when the document
is printed, the text is
displayed in columns on the
page. WORD begins by
filling the first column on
the first page.█

Pg1 Co16   {}

═SNAKING.DOC═
Microsoft Word

Figure 11.3: A newspaper-style column on the screen

but they jump from left to right (see Figure 11.5). Set show layout to Yes if you want to work with the properly aligned paragraphs; this way, you can easily see where the effect begins and ends. If you find that doing so slows down Word's questions and you prefer working quicker, leave it set to No. You can then print or use Print preView to see how the side-by-side paragraphs align with each other (Figure 11.6).

Finally, another kind of structured format you can create with Word is boxes. This feature is especially handy for creating organizational charts.

Let's begin with these layouts by studying tabs and tables.

USING TABS TO CREATE TABLES

A table consists of information lined up in columns and separated by tabs. As we'll see, Word gives you a lot of flexibility in how you can line up the columns: they can be left-aligned, right-aligned, centered, or decimal-aligned. You choose the alignment as you set up the tabs.

```
         This is an example of        page, WORD starts at the
newspaper-style "snaking"             top of the new page and
columns.  When you type the           begins by filling the first
text in, it appears as one            column on the left-hand
long column on the screen.            side. Either way, WORD
However, when the document            fills in to the bottom of
is printed, the text is               the page.
displayed in columns on the                  When the text reaches
page.  WORD begins by                 the bottom of the page,
filling the first column on           WORD jumps to the top of
the first page.                       the next column. The next
         When the text reaches        column can be on the same
the bottom of the page,               page or on a new page (when
WORD jumps to the top of              the current page is filled
the next column. The next             with text). If the new
column can be on the same             column is on the same page,
page or on a new page (when           WORD begins at the top of
the current page is filled            the page and, picking up
with text). If the new                where the text left off,
column is on the same page,           places the new text in a
WORD begins at the top of             column to the right of the
the page and, picking up              previous column. When the
where the text left off,              next column is on a new
places the new text in a              page, WORD starts at the
column to the right of the            top of the new page and
previous column. When the             begins by filling the first
next column is on a new               column on the left-hand
```

Figure 11.4: Printed newspaper-style columns

First we'll create a table, and then we'll see how Word allows you to manipulate columns. For instance, you can perform cut-and-paste operations, such as deleting, moving, and copying. You can also perform math calculations without resorting to a calculator. Word can alphabetize the items in your table or order them numerically. If you want, you can have Word renumber items as you add and delete material.

```
     This is a standard paragraph.  It uses the full width
of the area available for text.  Most documents will use the
full text area like this.¶

     You may want paragraphs that relate to be printed next
to one another.  To do that, use side-by-side paragraphs.  ¶

This is the first
of three side-by-
side paragraphs.¶
                    This second para-
                    graph relates to the
                    first.  It appears
                    to the right of the
                    first one when the
                    document is printed.¶
                                           This is the last
                                           of the side-by-
                                           side paragraphs.¶

     This is a standard paragraph again.  WORD will print it
below the longest of the side-by-side paragraphs above.
                                                     SIDESIDE.DOC
Pg1 Co58          {}                               Microsoft Word
```

Figure 11.5: Side-by-side paragraphs on the screen

```
     This is a standard paragraph.  It uses the full width
of the area available for text.  Most documents will use the
full text area like this.

     You may want paragraphs that relate to be printed next
to one another.  To do that, use side-by-side paragraphs.

This is the first   This second para-      This is the last
of three side-by-   graph relates to the   of the side-by-
side paragraphs.    first.  It appears     side paragraphs.
                    to the right of the
                    first one when the
                    document is printed.

     This is a standard paragraph again.  WORD will print it
below the longest of the side-by-side paragraphs above.
```

Figure 11.6: Printed side-by-side paragraphs

Producing a table requires that you first use the Format Tab commands to create the necessary tab stops. Once the tabs are set, you can enter the text for the table, using the Tab key to move from one column to the next. If you find you need to adjust the tabs after you have typed the table text, you can do so with the Format Tab command: the text will automatically adjust to the new tab settings.

The Format Tab command includes three subcommands, as shown in Figure 11.7. Most of your tabular work can be accomplished with the first of these subcommands, the Format Tab Set command. Its menu appears in Figure 11.8.

SETTING TABS

The Format Tab Set command allows you to set, move, and clear your tabs one by one. In a moment, we'll examine the settings on its

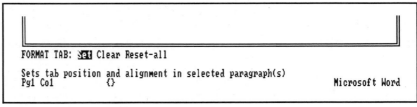

Figure 11.7: The Format Tab command

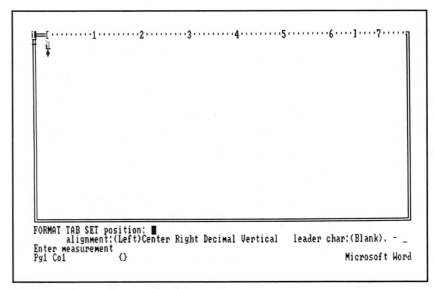

Figure 11.8: The Format Tab Set command

menu, but first let's discuss some general information about this command.

Whenever you activate the Format Tab Set menu, the ruler line automatically appears in place of the top window border (see Figure 11.8). It can contain many symbols, which are presented in Table 11.1.

These symbols initially reflect the settings registered in the Format Paragraph command for the paragraph the cursor is in. The left bracket, vertical bar, and right bracket represent, respectively, the left indent, first-line indent, and right indent currently established for that paragraph. Symbols for the tab stops are added to the ruler line as you set them.

Initially, Word has tab stops preset for you every five spaces. These preset tab stops do not appear on the ruler line. You can change this default distance (1/2 inch) with the Options command. Display the Options menu and move to default tab width. Type the distance that you want and press Enter to register the change.

Table 11.1: Ruler Symbols in the Format Tab Set Menu

RULER SYMBOL	MEANING
1, 2, 3, etc.	Measurement in tens of characters
[	Left margin
¦	First-line indent
|	Vertical alignment
]	Right margin
L	Left-aligned tab
R	Right-aligned tab
C	Center-aligned tab
D	Decimal-aligned tab
—.—	Period leader
—-—	Hyphen leader
—_—	Underline leader
—·—	Other positions

T I P

Word provides you
with four macros to
make setting tabs
easier: **table.mac**,
tabs.mac, tabs2.mac,
and **tab3.mac**. For
more on the use of
these macros, see
Appendix C.

When you set a tab for a particular paragraph in your document, Word automatically clears its preset tabs that are to the left of the newly set tab. Word assumes that preset tabs to the right are ones you may wish to have available, so it leaves them in place. Only Word's preset tabs will be affected; the tabs you set will remain in place.

Now let's examine the menu options for the Format Tab Set command. We'll use them to create the tabular format we saw earlier in Figure 11.1.

With the position option, you indicate where you want the tab set. You can choose the spot by typing a measurement to indicate its distance from the left margin, or by using F1 and the → or ← key. Pressing F1 displays a slide marker (a small highlighted box) on the ruler line that you move with the arrow keys. Pressing F1 again deactivates the slide marker; you can then type a tab measurement.

T I P

When you gain access
to the Format Tab Set
menu by pressing
Alt-F1, Word auto-
matically activates the
slide marker.

Once you've specified a tab stop position, press the Tab key to move to the alignment option. Tabs can have the following alignment:

(Left)   Center   Right   Decimal   Vertical

Tabs are normally left-aligned, which means that the left edge of the column is flush with the tab's position. You can change this setting for different effects. The columns in our sample table in Figure 11.1 demonstrate the results of various alignment settings. The "Destination" column is right-aligned, and I created the vertical line by setting alignment to Vertical for the second tab stop. The "Fare" column is decimal-aligned, the "Route" column is left-aligned, and the "Availability" column is center-aligned.

Decimal alignment usually means that the decimal points in a column of numbers line up. However, Word can also use a comma instead of a decimal point, as some forms of currency do. To use this format, change the decimal character setting in the Options command.

Leading characters fill in the tab area that precedes tabbed items. When you use leading characters, each line in the table will be affected. Normally, the leader char option is set to Blank, which means that no leading characters will be displayed. The other possible leader char settings are the period, the hyphen, and the underline character. For example, you can instruct Word to fill the area between columns with periods automatically, which produces the following effect:

Teleportation Technology............................17

Specifying hyphens, on the other hand, produces this result:

Gary James--------Teleporter First Class--------0103

You can use the underline characters for a leader as well. This format is handy for creating fill-in-the-blank forms such as

First name: _____   Last name: _____

Once you've specified the position, alignment, and leader character, you create the tab by pressing the Insert key. Keep in mind that the tabs you set here will affect only the paragraph (in this case, the table) you are working with, not paragraphs that you already typed. The settings remain with that paragraph and are not changed when you change the settings for other paragraphs.

If you press Enter at the end of the table (on or before its paragraph mark) to create a new paragraph, it will initially have the same tab settings. So long as you don't press Alt-P to turn off the format or change the settings, all the subsequent paragraphs will have the same paragraph formatting and the same tab settings.

You can also move or copy tab settings and paragraph formatting by moving or copying the paragraph mark that stores them. With the keyboard, just copy the mark to the scrap area and then insert the copy in its new location. With the mouse, copy paragraph formatting and tab settings by moving the cursor to the paragraph you want to change. Then press Alt-right button on the selection bar to the left of the paragraph that has the desired format.

In addition, you can set and clear tabs in adjacent paragraphs simultaneously, as well as change their format. Just expand the cursor to highlight at least part of each paragraph that you wish to affect and then reposition the tabs with the Format Tab Set command. (Other formatting can be changed in the same manner as well.)

Now let's set each tab for the sample table in Figure 11.1. After setting all the tabs, we'll register the command and then type the text. Start with the "Destination" column.

1. Set the position for the "Destination" column either by typing

   1.5

   or by pressing the F1 key, which displays a slide marker that you can move with the arrow keys along the ruler line. The marker's position is automatically reflected as a measurement.

2. When the measurement is correct, press the Tab key to move to the alignment option and set it to Right, since we want the "Destination" column to be right-aligned. There are no leader characters in this table, so we don't need to adjust that setting.

3. Create the tab stop by pressing the Insert key. This action adds the appropriate tab symbol to the ruler line (R for right-aligned in this case).

4. Repeat the procedure for the other columns, setting each column's position and alignment. Estimate the positions of the subsequent columns—you can adjust the positions if necessary after you've typed in the text. On the last tab stop you set, you don't need to press the Insert key before proceeding to step 5.

5. Once you have set all the tabs, register your choices by pressing the Enter key.

You can also use the mouse to set left-aligned tabs without issuing the Format Tab Set command. To do this, display the ruler by setting the Options menu's show ruler option to Yes. To set a tab, you can then click left on the ruler, in the location for the new tab stop.

Now that you've set the tab stops, you can enter the text for the table, as shown in Figure 11.1. (You can leave the ruler turned on while you are working.) As you type, press the Tab key between each column entry. The vertical line appears automatically when you land on its stop. At the end of each line, press Shift-Enter. (By doing so, you group all the text of the table as one paragraph.)

T I P

You can automatically import spreadsheet tables, from Lotus 1-2-3, for instance, to your documents. Word automatically inserts tab characters between the spreadsheet columns. The procedure uses hidden text and is discussed in Chapter 18.

If you need to work with a lengthy table, you might find it helpful to keep an eye on the table's headings. You can do this by splitting the screen into two windows. Start by placing the headings at the top of the screen. (Positioning may be more easily achieved with Scroll Lock on.) Then move the cursor to a spot just below the headings and split the screen horizontally. With this setup, you can use the lower window to scroll and edit the table, while leaving the upper window focused on the headings.

CLEARING TABS

As you work with tables, occasionally you may need to clear all or some of the tabs you've set. For example, when your table comprises several paragraphs and you pressed Enter on or before a paragraph mark to create another paragraph, Word formatted the new paragraph to match the paragraph preceding it, which may not be what you want. There are several ways you can change the formatted tabs for a paragraph born out of another such as this.

CLEARING ALL TABS   To clear all tabs for a paragraph at once, place the cursor in the paragraph and issue the Format Tab Reset-all command. When you use this command, you restore Word's default tab settings to the paragraph. (To restore these settings to several paragraphs, highlight them before issuing the command.) All the other tab stops—those you have previously specified—are cleared. This command has no options. Choosing Reset-all automatically completes the command and reactivates Document mode. If you realize that clearing the tabs was a mistake, use the Undo command right away to reverse the effects.

If you want, you can clear a paragraph's formatting as well as its tabs by placing the cursor somewhere in the paragraph and pressing Alt-P. You might use this if you decided to keep the contents of a table but present it with Word's standard tabs and flush-left paragraph format.

CLEARING SELECTED TABS   Rather than clearing all the tab stops, you may want to keep some and clear the rest. There are two ways to clear tab stops selectively. The first way is with the Format

Tab Set command. After highlighting the position option, you use the directional keys or type a measurement to select the tab to be deleted. Then press the Delete key to clear the tab. Using F1 and the ← and → keys will display and move the slide marker along the ruler, one character at a time. The ↓ and ↑ keys will move the slide marker to the right and left, respectively, one tab setting at a time.

You can also clear tabs by using the Format Tab Clear command (see Figure 11.9). Using the keyboard, you indicate the tab you wish to clear by typing that tab's measurement or by using the directional keys. Each time you press F1 and then the ← or → key, Word displays the slide marker and then moves it to the next tab setting in the arrow's direction. If you wish to delete additional tabs simultaneously, type a comma and, without typing a space after the comma, enter the next stop you want to clear by typing its measurement or moving the slide marker to it. When you are through designating the tabs to be cleared, press the Enter key.

CLEARING TABS WITH THE MOUSE To clear tabs with the mouse, display the ruler line with the Options command's show ruler option and click both buttons on the tab stop you want to delete. To use the Format Tab Clear command, click either button on a tab stop in the ruler line. To clear additional tab stops, alternate pressing the comma key with clicking on tab stops. When you've indicated all the tabs you wish to clear, click either button on FORMAT TAB CLEAR.

If you work with tables a lot, you may find that using the mouse is a more efficient way to clear and set tabs. The mouse can also move tabs in a way not available with the keyboard.

MOVING TABS

With the keyboard, you can move a tab stop by issuing the Format Tab Set command. After you delete a tab stop in one location with the Delete key, you can use the Insert key to insert it in another location. The appropriate position, alignment, and leader char settings will be reset automatically.

With the mouse, you can move tabs by dragging the tab stop to its new position. The settings for alignment and leader char will remain with that tab when it is repositioned. You can drag the tab stop on the ruler line using either mouse button.

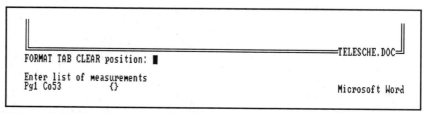

Figure 11.9: The Format Tab Clear command

MOVING, DELETING, AND COPYING COLUMNS

Word gives you the ability to manipulate blocks of text in columns, in a way similar to the standard paragraph operations covered in Chapter 6. The catalyst for this feature is the lock key for Column Selection (Shift-F6).

Start by imagining the block you wish to highlight as a rectangle on the screen. The first step is to bring the cursor to the top left or the bottom right of that imaginary rectangle. Then press Shift-F6 to turn on Column Selection. This will anchor a special column highlight in that spot, and CS will appear in the lock area. Next, use the directional keys to highlight the area you wish to designate as a block. You can use the entire directional keypad, including the four arrow keys, Page Up, Page Down, and the Home and End keys, for this purpose. However, the F7 to F10 keys do not extend the column highlight as they do the regular highlight. Once you've highlighted the block, perform the delete, move, or copy procedure as usual. When Word has completed the operation, Column Selection turns off automatically, and the abbreviation disappears from the screen.

Let's say that you wish to delete the "Fare" column from the sample table in Figure 11.2. When you perform a block operation with columns, you must consider tabs carefully. So it is usually wise to make the tabs visible before proceeding. Here are the steps for deleting the "Fare" column:

1. If you haven't already done so, activate the Options command and set show non-printing symbols to All. Tab characters appear on the screen as small right arrows.

2. Bring the cursor to the "F" in "Fare."

3. Turn on Column Selection by pressing Shift-F6.

4. Use the → and ↓ keys or the mouse to highlight the "Fare" column. Include the tab characters that follow the fares (see Figure 11.10).

5. Use the Delete key or the Delete command to remove the column. When you turn Column Selection on, the Delete and Copy commands will only work with the scrap area, not the glossary. Thus, Word doesn't suggest the scrap braces as it usually does with these commands.

The "Fare" column now appears in the scrap area. The small block in scrap indicates the spot where one row in the column highlight ends and the next begins. (For a review of the symbols in the scrap area, refer back to Table 6.1.)

Once you have deleted the column, you can move it to another location. Let's say that you wish to move it to the position occupied by the "Availability" column, pushing that column to the right.

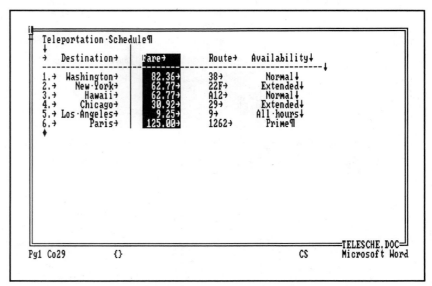

Figure 11.10: Highlighting a column

1. Move the cursor to the "A" in "Availability."

2. Press the Insert key or issue the Insert command to copy the "Fare" column from scrap to its new position.

Notice what has happened to the alignment of the "Route" and "Fare" columns (see Figure 11.11). The "Route" column is now decimal-aligned, and the "Fare" column is now left-aligned (its decimals no longer line up). This occurs because the tab stops determine which settings are active, not the column text. Moving the column does not move its tab settings. To line up the decimals in the "Fare" column once again, initiate the Format Tab Set command and then use the mouse or the F1 and ↓ keys to reach the current tab stop for the "Fare" column. Change the alignment setting to Decimal and register the command with Enter or the mouse.

Always double-check your column alignments after a move. Be especially careful when you work with the last column; that is, the one farthest to the right. Generally, the rows of your tables will have no tab characters at their right-hand ends. Thus, it may be necessary to insert tab characters before you move material to the far right. You

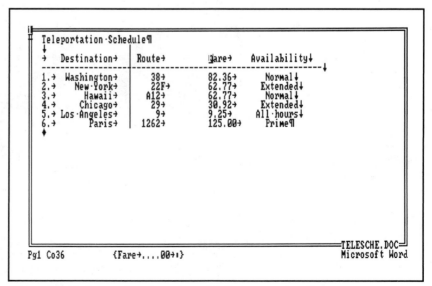

Figure 11.11: Correcting the column's alignment after the move

can use the Replace command, described in Chapter 10, to assist you in doing this. Highlight the table in the standard fashion (that is, non-column format) or move the cursor to the beginning of the table so that Replace will operate on the entire table. Then, assuming that each line ends with a new-line character (created with Shift-Enter), replace each new-line character (^n) with a tab and a new-line character (^t^n). If each line ends with a paragraph mark, replace ^p with ^t^p.

Word has one final trick that you can use to move columns to the right. You can insert a new set of tab characters before each item in a column, moving the entire column one tab setting to the right. To do this, turn on Column Selection by pressing Shift-F6 and highlight the column you want moved. Then just press the Tab key, and Word puts in a tab character before each highlighted item, moving the whole column to the right.

ESTABLISHING NEWSPAPER-STYLE COLUMNS

So far, we've been looking at the kind of column formatting used with tables. However, Word can also treat longer text as columns; we will first examine newspaper-like multicolumn formats and then look at side-by-side paragraphs.

Newspaper or snaking columns (Figures 11.3 and 11.4) are created by the following options in the Format Division Layout command:

number of columns: 1   space between columns: 0.5″

Notice that number of columns is usually set to 1—that is, Word normally treats all documents as having one column, albeit a large one, between the left and right margins. You can give your text a multicolumn format by highlighting it and specifying the number of columns you want with this option. Use space between columns to indicate how much room you want between each column. Changing it affects the width of the columns, as Word will allocate what's left for text. Space between columns is usually set for $1/2$ inch, but this setting is meaningless until you've increased the setting for the number of columns.

T I P

Alt-F4 is a shortcut for the show layout option, and Ctrl-F9 is a shortcut for the Print preView command.

As mentioned earlier, when you have the Options menu's show layout set to No, Word does not display the columns next to each other on the screen, but rather one after another, narrowing the displayed text to the width of one column. When you set show layout to Yes, print the document, or use Print preView, you see the multicolumn format (see Figure 11.4).

If you prefer, you can work on the document with show layout set to Yes. You can move between the columns with this option turned on by holding down the Ctrl key and then pressing 5 (using the keypad number) and pressing the arrow key that corresponds to the direction of the column. For example, to move the cursor from its current column to the previous column, press Ctrl-5-←. To move to the next column, press Ctrl-5-→. With the mouse, you can move to another column simply by clicking on it.

Assuming you've left the Options command's paginate option set to Auto (or reset it), you can review the column breaks as Word paginates. With pagination set to Manual, you can preview column breaks by issuing the Print Repaginate command or by pressing Alt-F4 to toggle the Options menu's show layout option on. If you want to prevent a paragraph from being split between columns, set the Format Paragraph menu's keep together option to Yes for the paragraph.

5 New in Word 5

You can enter column breaks yourself by pressing Alt-Ctrl-Enter. Word indicates a column break by a row of dotted lines on the screen. Text following the column break goes to the top of the next column, even if this leaves blank space at the bottom of the previous column.

5 New in Word 5

Remember that newspaper-style columns are a division format. Thus, you can combine different column formats in a document by setting up additional divisions. In fact, Word 5 even lets you combine different column formats on the same page. To do this, follow these steps:

1. Issue the Format Division Layout command and provide settings for the number of columns and space between columns options.

2. Press Ctrl-Enter after this formatted multicolumn group to create a division break.

3. Below the division break, issue the Format Division Layout command and provide the settings for the next group of

columns. Set the division break option to Continuous to allow text from the second division to continue on the same page as the first division.

You can use multiple columns for most types of sequential text. When you want the columns to relate from left to right, create a table, either with tabs or with side-by-side paragraphs. Let's now look at side-by-side paragraphs.

ARRANGING PARAGRAPHS SIDE BY SIDE

Word gives you another method of arranging text across the page by allowing you to set paragraphs side by side. Use side-by-side paragraphs to create a table with text that needs to flow down within a column.

5 New in Word 5

With Word 5 you can see side-by-side paragraphs displayed accurately on the screen. To do this, toggle the Options menu's show layout option on by pressing Alt-F4. Remember, this may slow down Word's processing speed.

With show layout set to No, the paragraphs will appear to follow one another down the screen, though offset (see Figure 11.12). When you print or use Print preView (Ctrl-F9), however, the first paragraph will appear on the left, and the next paragraph will be to its right (see Figure 11.13). You can arrange up to six paragraphs in this side-by-side fashion at a time.

T I P

Word provides the **sidebyside.mac** macro to make side-by-side paragraphs easier to create (see Appendix C). There is also a style sheet for side-by-side paragraphs, **sideby.sty** (see Chapter 17).

To create side-by-side formatting for two paragraphs, format the left paragraph so that its *right* indent is set wide enough to accommodate the right paragraph. Similarly, you format the right paragraph so that its *left* indent is wide enough to hold the left paragraph. In addition, change the Format Paragraph menu's side-by-side setting for both paragraphs to Yes.

Let's see how to do this using the text in Figure 11.13. Remember, Word usually allows 6 inches of width for your text. To change the width, use the Format Division Margins command. Here are the steps for creating the first set of side-by-side paragraphs:

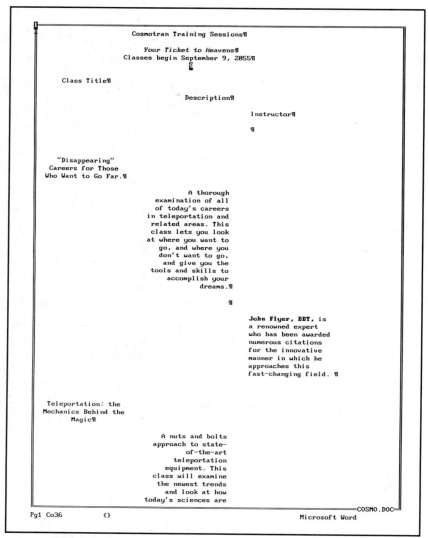

Figure 11.12: Creating sample side-by-side paragraphs

steps for creating the first set of side-by-side paragraphs:

1. Enter the text for the first paragraph, leave the cursor in the paragraph, and issue the Format Paragraph command.

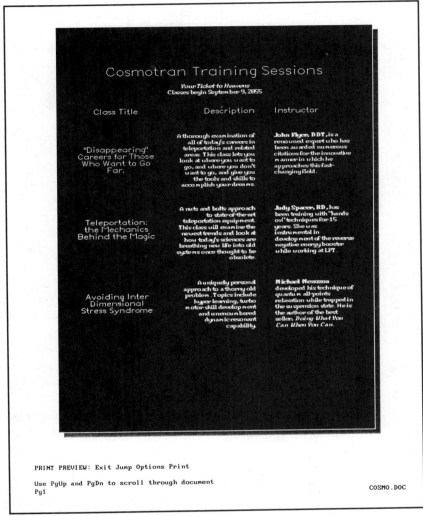

Figure 11.13: Previewing the side-by-side paragraphs

2. Set right indent to 5 inches. Change the side by side setting to Yes, and select Centered for the alignment option. For additional readability, set space before to 3 lines for this first-column paragraph.

3. Type and format the second (center) paragraph. After reissuing the Format Paragraph command, set left indent to 2.5

inches, which allows enough room for the preceding paragraph to fit. Then set right indent to 2.5 inches. Change side by side to Yes and alignment to Right.

4. Type and format the third (right) paragraph. Set left indent to 5 inches, right indent to 0 inches, side by side to Yes, and alignment to Left.

Remember, you don't need to repeat all the formatting steps for subsequent paragraphs. You can copy the formatting in one of several ways. You can use the Repeat key (F4) or the Alt-mouse combination, or you can copy the paragraph mark by using the scrap area or the glossary.

Word is smart in its handling of side-by-side paragraphs. For instance, it won't split a group of such paragraphs between pages. If there's not enough room at the bottom of one page, it will move the whole row of paragraphs to the next page. Also, text, or even another set of side-by-side paragraphs, that follows the group will always start below the last line of the longest paragraph in the previous set, so there's never any overlapping, and related material stays together.

You can even place more than one paragraph in one column, aligning the paragraphs with the rest of the paragraph columns. For instance, if you have set up two columns of paragraphs side by side, you can have the first two paragraphs go in the first column by formatting them the same. To place the subsequent paragraph in the second column, simply format it for that position and Word will align it with the first paragraph in the first column.

ADDING BORDER NOTES AND BANNER HEADLINES TO YOUR DOCUMENT

5 New in Word 5

Word now allows you to position paragraphs more precisely on the page. This feature is especially handy for inserting graphics (Chapter 18), but you can also use it to position text in unusual locations. For example, you can create *border notes,* such as the one that appears in Figure 11.14. Notice how the border note straddles the margin and the column of text, displacing text in the column.

To: **Staff**

From: **Jess January,**

             Telefriend New York Division Head

Feedback indicates that there seems to be some misunderstanding in regard to certain areas of the recent quarterly report. The purpose of this memo is to clarify the information presented and to act as a springboard for further discussion.

(1)   Efficiency of Service

Overall efficiency was definitely improved. Even though there have been problems in some areas, the programs that were instituted in the previous quarter have made a positive impact. For example, incidents of lost luggage have declined drastically, and there is every indication that this trend will continue. *(Table 1.)*

(2)   Sales

Sales have dropped slightly, but only to the degree expected for this time of year. Undoubtedly, considerable improvement will be seen during the holidays, although it may not be as much as originally projected. *(Table 2.)*

We did consider the introduction of a discount travel arrangement, but we decided to table this idea until next year at the earliest.

> This is a margin note. You can create it by inserting its text anywhere on this page. The Format pOsition command has significant settings for this paragraph as follows: horizontal frame position: Right, relative to: Page; vertical frame position: Bottom; relative to: Margins; frame width: 1.25"; distance from text: 24 pt. This paragraph also has five line-break characters (Shift-Enter) at its end, to create the white space that appears below.

(3)   Commissary Furniture

The commissary has made arrangements to deal with the problem furniture that was installed. Tables that have proved to be too low will definitely be removed and replaced. However, the cost of the entire project is still expected to come in under budget. *(Table 3.)*

Figure 11.14: A border note in the right margin

To position a paragraph, imagine that it has a frame around it. The Format pOsition command dictates the placement of the invisible frame that holds the paragraph. The paragraph text usually fills this frame. However, you can shrink the size of the paragraph within the frame by adjusting the indent and spacing settings stored with the paragraph's

MOUSE

Click left on Format
and then click either
button on pOsition to
issue this subcommand.

Format Paragraph command. You might want to do this to create more space around the paragraph, which makes it easier to read.

Display the Format pOsition command now by pressing Esc, typing F for Format, and typing O for pOsition (see Figure 11.15). You use the first two options, horizontal frame position and relative to, with each other. If you have indented the paragraph using the Format Paragraph menu, the paragraph's placement will also reflect this. Likewise, you use vertical frame position and relative to together, and any spacing you provide with the Format Paragraph menu will affect the paragraph's vertical placement. You can adjust the Format pOsition settings to achieve the effects listed in Tables 11.2 and 11.3. The Inside and Outside settings refer to the binding's location for double-sided, bound documents. (The binding is on the right for even-numbered pages and on the left for odd-numbered pages.) The Inside setting is for the side of the paper with the binding, and the Outside setting is for the opposite side of the paper.

When you first display the Format pOsition menu, the highlight is on the horizontal frame position field and you are prompted to

Enter measurement or press F1 to select from list

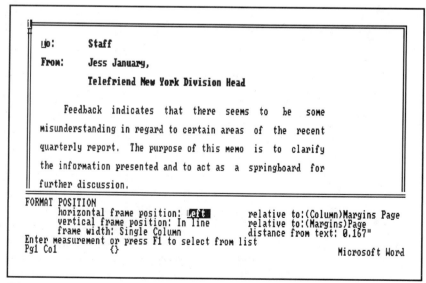

Figure 11.15: The Format pOsition command

Table 11.2: Horizontal Formats for Frame Positions

HORIZONTAL FRAME POSITION	RELATIVE TO	EFFECT ON THE FRAME (PARAGRAPH)
Left	Column	Aligns its left edge with the left edge of the column.
Left	Margins	Aligns its left edge with the left margin on the page.
Left	Page	Aligns its left edge with the left edge of the page (as close as the printer allows).
Centered	Column	Centers it within the column.
Centered	Margins	Centers it between the left and right margins.
Centered	Page	Centers it between the left and right edges of the page.
Right	Column	Aligns its right edge with the right edge of the column.
Right	Margins	Aligns its right edge with the right margin.
Right	Page	Aligns its right edge with the right edge of the page (as close as the printer allows).
Inside	Column	Aligns it with the inner edge of the column.
Inside	Margins	Aligns it with the inner margins.

You can enter a value in the field, or you can press F1 or click right on the field to display a list and select from it. Even after you list the possible values, you can enter a value if you wish. This prompt also appears for vertical frame position and frame width.

Table 11.2: Horizontal Formats for Frame Positions (continued)

HORIZONTAL FRAME POSITION	RELATIVE TO	EFFECT ON THE FRAME (PARAGRAPH)
Inside	Page	Aligns it with the inner edge of the page.
Outside	Column	Aligns it with the outer edge of the column.
Outside	Margins	Aligns it with the outer margins.
Outside	Page	Aligns it with the outer edge of the page.
(value)	Column	Displaces it from the left edge of the column by the value you provide.
(value)	Margins	Displaces it from the left margin by the value you provide.
(value)	Page	Displaces it from the left edge of the page by the value you provide.

Table 11.3: Vertical Formats for Frame Positions

VERTICAL FRAME POSITION	RELATIVE TO	EFFECT ON THE FRAME (PARAGRAPH)
In line	Margins	Leaves the top line of text where it would appear if you didn't use this command.

When you select a paragraph's position with this command, it takes priority over other text on the page. The other text then flows around the specially positioned paragraph, as it does around the border note in Figure 11.14.

Table 11.3: Vertical Formats for Frame Positions (continued)

VERTICAL FRAME POSITION	RELATIVE TO	EFFECT ON THE FRAME (PARAGRAPH)
In Line	Page	Leaves the top line of text in its standard position (with In Line, both Margins and Page have the same effect).
Top	Margins	Aligns its top edge with the top margin.
Top	Page	Aligns its top edge with the top edge of the page (as close as the printer allows).
Centered	Margins	Centers it between the top and bottom margins.
Centered	Page	Centers it between the top and bottom edges of the page.
Bottom	Margins	Aligns its bottom edge with the bottom margin.
Bottom	Page	Aligns its bottom edge with the bottom of the page.
(*value*)	Margins	Displaces its top edge from the top margin by the value you provide.
(*value*)	Page	Displaces its bottom edge from the bottom edge of the page by the value you provide.

You determine the width of the paragraph with the Format pOsition's frame width option. You can enter a value yourself (the border note is 1.25''), or you can select a value from the list. Settings include Single Column and Width of Graphic. With Single Column, you give the paragraph the width of the column it is in; with Width of

Graphic, no extra space is added between the graphic and its frame. If your document is set up for two or more columns, you can also choose Double Column, which gives your paragraph the width of two columns, or Between Margins, which centers the paragraph between the left and right margins.

The final Format pOsition option is distance from text. The value you provide here regulates the distance that Word keeps outside text away from the paragraph's invisible frame. Initially, it is set for .167 inches or ¹⁄₆ inches. Try to create the border note in Figure 11.14 if the printer you are working with can print different font sizes. The important information for creating it appears in the note itself.

Another use for the Format pOsition command is in creating *banner headlines*, text that extends across multiple columns (see Figure 11.16). If you like, you can create this example as well. Again, the germane settings are listed in the example.

CREATING ORGANIZATIONAL CHARTS

As we've seen, you can organize your text in tabular formats or in columns. You can even insert paragraphs that interrupt the flow of text. Sometimes, however, you want to emphasize the structured format that presents the text, rather than just the text itself. In this case, you can create an organizational chart. Readers easily grasp the relations presented for the text since their attention is focused on the structure of lines and boxes that connect the text.

There are several ways you can create charts composed of lines and boxes. The method you use often depends on your printer's capabilities. A couple of methods rely on the Format Tab Set menu; let's examine these methods now.

Creating Lines with Leader Characters   You can use the hyphen (-) and the underline character (_) as leader characters to create a line before a tab stop. For this type of line to appear, you set the tab for the paragraph you are working with and press the Tab key to move to the

This is a banner headline. The Format pOsition command has significant settings for this paragraph as follows: horizontal frame position: Centered, relative to: Page; vertical frame position: Top, relative to: Margins; frame width: Between Margins; distance from text: .75"

To: **Staff**
From: **Jess January,**
           Telefriend New
           York Division Head

Feedback indicates that there seems to be some misunderstanding in regard to certain areas of the recent quarterly report. The purpose of this memo is to clarify the information presented and to act as a springboard for further discussion.

(1)   **Efficiency of Service**

Overall efficiency was definitely improved. Even though there have been problems in some areas, the programs that were instituted in the previous quarter have made a positive impact. For example, incidents of lost luggage have declined drastically, and there is every indication that this trend will continue. *(Table 1.)*

(2)   **Sales**

Sales have dropped slightly, but only to the degree expected for this time of year. Undoubtedly, considerable improvement will be seen during the holidays, although it may not be as much as originally projected. *(Table 2.)*

We did consider the introduction of a discount travel arrangement, but we decided to table this idea until next year at the earliest.

(3)   **Commissary Furniture**

The commissary has made arrangements to deal with the problem furniture that was installed. Tables that have proved to be too low will definitely be removed and replaced. However, the cost of the entire project is still expected to come in under budget. *(Table 3.)*

Figure 11.16: A banner headline

tab stop you've set. Word then replaces the tab character you entered with the selected leader characters.

Creating Vertical Lines with Tabs   As you learned earlier, setting alignment to Vertical in the Format Tab Set menu automatically draws a vertical line at the specified tab stop. The line appears throughout the paragraph formatted with this tab setting.

Creating Lines with Standard Keyboard Characters In addition to these menu features, you can simply enter the characters directly as you type the text. To draw horizontal lines, you can use the hyphen, equal sign, or underline character. For vertical lines, use the vertical bar: you type it by pressing Shift-backslash (/). You can create corners with the plus sign, or you can just leave them blank. You can create simple lines with these standard characters, but for more sophisticated figures you'll probably want to use another method.

Word has three other methods you can choose from: drawing with the directional keypad, border formatting, and using numeric Alt codes. First, let's learn how to draw using the directional keys.

DRAWING LINES
WITH THE DIRECTIONAL KEYS

Once you activate Line-Draw mode with Ctrl-F5, the letters LD appear in the bottom right of the screen. You can then use the directional arrows to draw horizontal and vertical lines on the screen. You can also use the Home key to draw a line from the cursor's position to the left edge of the paragraph and the End key to draw a line from the cursor to the right edge of the paragraph.

No other keys will operate while you're drawing lines with the directional keys. To edit or use commands, you must exit Line-Draw mode by pressing Ctrl-F5 again, which activates Document mode, or by pressing the Esc key, which activates Command mode.

You can change the type of line that Line-Draw mode uses by invoking the Options command and moving to linedraw character. Normally Word uses a single line, as the default setting indicates, but you can display and select from other settings by pressing F1 (see Figure 11.17).

Figure 11.18 presents a chart I created with the single- and double-line sets. The third choice in the list uses the hyphen, the vertical bar,

```
( ) Single Set        ( ) Double Set       ( ) Hyphen/Bar Set  ▮




WINDOW OPTIONS for window number: 1          show hidden text: Yes(No)
              show ruler: Yes(No)    show non-printing symbols: None Partial(All)
             show layout: Yes(No)            show line breaks: Yes(No)
            show outline: Yes(No)             show style bar: Yes(No)

GENERAL OPTIONS mute: Yes(No)                 summary sheet: Yes(No)
             measure:(In)Cm P10 P12 Pt        display mode: 3
            paginate:(Auto)Manual                  colors:
            autosave:                     autosave confirm: Yes(No)
           show menu: Yes(No)                show borders:(Yes)No
         date format:(MDY)DMY             decimal character:(.),
         time format:(12)24              default tab width: 0.5"
        line numbers: Yes(No)             count blank space: Yes(No)
        cursor speed: 3                   linedraw character: ( )
        speller path: C:\WORD\SPELL-AM.LEX
Enter line draw character or press F1 to select from list
Pg1 Co1          {}                                      Microsoft Word
```

Figure 11.17: Listing choices for the linedraw character option

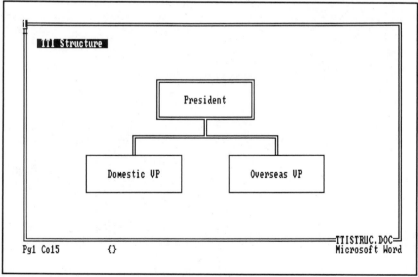

Figure 11.18: An organizational chart using single and double lines

and the plus sign, to draw lines in much the same fashion as you do by entering these characters directly. You may need to use the third choice if your printer is not capable of printing lines otherwise.

When you specify the character for Line-Draw, you can select one of the listed choices or you can enter your own character to use. For instance, if you want to draw with a set of asterisks, you can simply type * in the linedraw character field. Once you press Ctrl-F5, the directional keys will then draw asterisks as you move around the screen.

After drawing your lines, you can type text between and around the lines. Before you add text, turn on Overtype mode (by pressing the F5 key) so that your lines are not moved. Keep things simple around your drawings. Don't use indent formatting, especially first-line indents, on the paragraphs, as this can distort the vertical lines. Don't select proportional fonts because they will be spaced differently when printed than they look on the screen; it is impossible to align the lines. Don't press Enter to move to the next line, as that will also move any lines to the right of the cursor and distort the next line as well; use the ↓ key instead. Also, it's best not to draw lines around text that you've already entered, as this may cause distortion problems as well. For example, you can't draw in indented areas and Word substitutes one line-draw character for each tab character.

ADDING BORDERS TO PARAGRAPHS

You can also create lines with paragraph borders. Borders can be a box that surrounds its paragraph entirely, or they can be lines that partially surround the paragraph. Boxes created with this method adjust in size as you add or remove text in the paragraph.

Move the cursor to the paragraph you want to add a border to—highlight several paragraphs if you like. Then issue the Format Border command to display the menu shown in Figure 11.19.

Figure 11.20 shows the sample memo with border lines above and below the memo heading. There are also border boxes around each of the numbered headings.

You must first choose the type of border you want. By default, the type option is set to None, so paragraphs have no borders. Choose

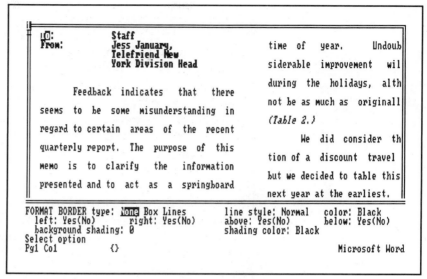

Figure 11.19: The Format Border command

Box if you want to enclose your paragraph in a box. Choose Lines if you only want one or more borders to appear next to the paragraph.

If you choose Lines, use left, right, above, and below to specify which lines you want. Setting all four to Yes and type to Lines is the same as choosing Box for type.

Use the Format Border's line style option to specify Normal (which creates a standard line with no emphasis), Bold (which creates a boldface line), or Double (for a double line). You can also choose Thick if your printer can produce a thick line.

5 New in Word 5

With Word 5, you can also set the color of the border and its background shading, assuming your printer has these capabilities. To specify the color of the border lines, press F1 or click right in the color field to choose from a list of colors for your printer. You can set background shading by providing a value of 0 (no shading) to 100 (solid). Without paragraph lines or boxes, this feature shades the area in which the paragraph appears. With lines or boxes, it shades the area within the lines or box (which is a larger area, because Word allocates additional space to accommodate the lines or box). You can also specify the color for shading by using the shading color field.

T I P

For best results when adding color or shading to your borders, set the Format Paragraph's line spacing option to a whole number only. (When you specify a fractional number, the shading or color characters may not align well.)

Figure 11.20 shows the sample memo with border lines above and below the memo heading. There are also border boxes around each of the numbered headings.

To: Staff
From: Jess January,
        Telefriend New
        York Division Head

Feedback indicates that there seems to be some misunderstanding in regard to certain areas of the recent quarterly report. The purpose of this memo is to clarify the information presented and to act as a springboard for further discussion.

(1)   Efficiency of Service

Overall efficiency was definitely improved. Even though there have been problems in some areas, the programs that were instituted in the previous quarter have made a positive impact. For example, incidents of lost luggage have declined drastically, and there is every indication that this trend will continue. *(Table 1.)*

(2)   Sales

Sales have dropped slightly, but only to the degree expected for this time of year. Undoubtedly, considerable improvement will be seen during the holidays, although it may not be as much as originally projected. *(Table 2.)*

We did consider the introduction of a discount travel arrangement, but we decided to table this idea until next year at the earliest.

(3)   Commissary Furniture

The commissary has made arrangements to deal with the problem furniture that was installed. Tables that have proved to be too low will definitely be removed and replaced. However, the cost of the entire project is still expected to come in under budget. *(Table 3.)*

We hope that this memo will aid in clearing up questions and uncertainties. I will be glad to provide further clarification if necessary.

Figure 11.20: Border lines and boxes

Normally, paragraphs that are adjacent to one another will share one line if they're formatted with compatible line formats (for instance, if the top paragraph has a below line while the bottom paragraph has a box). This won't happen, however, if the paragraphs' line style settings are contradictory or if the other paragraph formats, such as their indents, differ. In these cases, each paragraph receives a distinct line.

If a paragraph is formatted with a box around it, Word keeps all the text in that paragraph together on the same page. This does not normally apply to paragraphs formatted only with lines; however, you can set the Format Paragraph command's keep together option to Yes, if necessary.

You can also build a single box around a sequence of paragraphs. First, format lines on the left and right of all the paragraphs involved. (You can do this in one step by highlighting at least part of each paragraph before setting the lines with the Format Border command.) Then establish an above line for the first selected paragraph and a below line for the last paragraph. Once you have created the box like this, you can type in additional paragraphs and the sequential paragraph will remain boxed.

DRAWING WITH THE NUMERIC ALT CODES

T IP

Word 5 provides the **character_text.mac** macro to check which characters a font uses for drawing lines with the IBM character set. For more on this macro, see Appendix C.

The final way to enter line characters is with the numeric Alt codes. To do this, you use the numeric keypad for the character's code, not the numbers on the top row of the keyboard. Figure 11.21 shows some characters used to create boxes, along with their Alt codes. For a complete listing of the IBM character set, see Appendix D.

When you draw with the codes, make liberal use of Word's copying capabilities. You might find it useful to assign glossary codes and retrieve the symbols that way (see Chapter 15), or load a file like Figure 11.21 into a window and copy from it as needed.

A few ASCII characters produce some interesting and useful effects on some printers. Pressing Alt-8 produces a diamond in a box on the screen. However, when you print, this code causes some printers to backspace. You can use this trick to make characters print on top of each other. For instance, you can make a cents sign with the letter c and a slash. Type c, press Alt-8, and type the slash. For flow

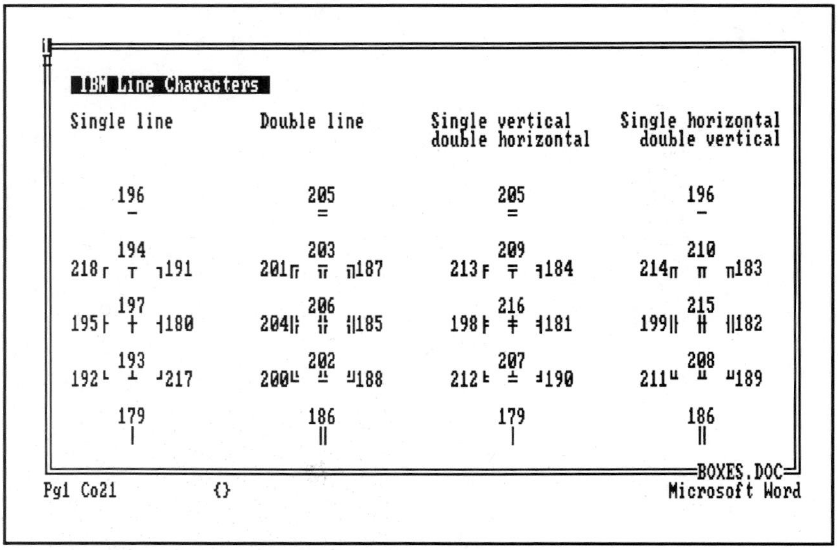

Figure 11.21: IBM line characters

charts, you can create horizontal arrows by combining the hyphen with the greater-than or less-than signs. For vertical arrows, combine the vertical bar with the letter V or the caret (Shift-6 on the upper row of the keyboard).

When some printers encounter Alt-7, they buzz. If you were printing queued documents, you might want to know when a certain document was finished. Enter the Alt-7 code at the end of the document and, just like a good typist, the printer will let you know when it's done.

Graphics like this can add a finishing touch to many kinds of charts and tables. In the next chapter, we'll continue to examine specialized applications with Word; in particular, calculations, alphabetizing, numbering, and cross-references.

12

**Numbering,
Calculating,
Alphabetizing, and
Cross-Referencing**

Fast Track

To print line numbers, 354

issue the Format Division line-Numbers command. When you print or preview the document, Word will place numbers to the left of the lines containing text or a paragraph mark.

To perform math operations, 356

highlight the numbers and operators. Press the Calculate key (F2) and Word will pop the calculation into the scrap area. You can then insert the answer wherever you wish.

To alphabetize items in a column, 361

highlight the column you wish to sort by pressing Shift-F6 and issue the Library Autosort command.

To sort paragraphs, 363

highlight the paragraphs with F6 (not Shift-F6) and issue the Library Autosort command.

To renumber items, 363

highlight the paragraphs with F6 or Shift-F10 (not Shift-F6) and then use the Library Number command. Each item must be in a separate paragraph, and the paragraph must begin with a number (or opening parenthesis), followed by a period (or a closing parenthesis), and then a space or tab character.

To number with a code name, 366

type the code name and a colon. Then press the Glossary key (F3). Repeat or copy the designation to number items sequentially. Numbering will appear when you print or preview the document.

To create cross-references, 369

issue the Format bookmarK command and assign a bookmark name to the text that you want to refer your readers to. Then provide the cross-referencing text in the document by typing the type of cross-reference (page, footnote, para-num, or some custom code name with which you're numbering items), a colon, and the bookmark name. Then press the Glossary key (F3). Cross-references appear when you print or use Print preView.

To move quickly to a bookmark, 374

use the Jump bookmarK command. It lets you display a list of bookmark names and select from among them.

JUST A FEW YEARS AGO, USING A WORD PROCESSOR meant working with a program devoted almost strictly to words. Numbering was usually limited to page numbering, and you had to make calculations or number text on your own.

With Microsoft Word, you can now perform calculations on numbers that appear in your text. Although Word is not a spreadsheet program, it does give you some of a spreadsheet's features. Word can also sort and number material, similar to the way in which a database program can. Finally, Word 5 provides you with the ability to cross-reference material throughout your document. Such cross-references adjust automatically as you edit your text.

Let's start with the simplest numbering feature: line numbering.

PRINTING LINE NUMBERS

When you just want to number each line of text, you can have Word do this automatically with its Format Divisions line-Numbers command. The numbers will appear only when you use Print preView or print the document. They are helpful when you are working with complex text; for example, people in the legal profession normally refer to their documents' text by line number. You may also want to number the lines of a computer program listing or a macro you need to check.

Line numbers are printed to the left of the text and do not appear in top and bottom margins, running heads, or footnotes. In a double-spaced document only the lines with text are numbered; the blank lines (unless created with a paragraph mark) are not.

Consider, for example, the memo we were working with in the last chapter. If it were to be the subject of a discussion, you may wish to number its lines. To add printed line numbers, begin by pressing Esc and then typing F for Format, D for Division, and N for line-Numbers. The Format Division line-Numbers menu then appears (see Figure 12.1).

Next, set the command to Yes. The default setting for the from text option is $^4/_{10}$ of an inch. Change it when you want the numbers

M O U S E

Click left on Format, click left on Division, and click either button on line-Numbers to display the Format Division line-Numbers menu.

spaced closer to the text or further from it. (The example uses $^2/_{10}$ inch.) Of course, you must provide a value less than the width of the left margin; otherwise, the line numbers are pushed off the edge of the page. In addition, you mustn't force the numbers into an area in which your printer cannot print. If Word can fit some of the number but not all of it in the left margin, it will *truncate* (trim off part of) the number. The number's units column is the last to go.

With the increment option, you indicate how often you want Word to print a number. For instance, if you enter a 3, Word will only number lines 3, 6, 9, 12, and so on.

Restart at has three settings: Page, Division, and Continuous. The default is Page, which makes Word number the lines starting with 1 on each new page. Set it to Division if you only want line numbering to restart when it crosses a division mark. (This only occurs if you have a document with multiple divisions.) When you choose the Continuous setting, Word numbers the entire document without resetting at all, not even for a new division.

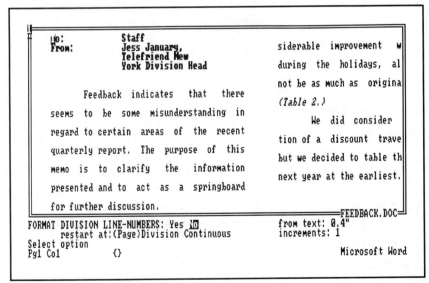

Figure 12.1: The Format Division line-Numbers command

Since our document only has one division and is a page long, leave the default settings in place after you specify Yes. Register your settings and Word inserts a division mark, as indicated by the row of colons at the end of the document. Since printing the line numbers is a division format, take care to keep all the text you want numbered above this mark.

Print the example and the line numbers will appear on the printed document (see Figure 12.2). Notice Word numbers each line containing text or a paragraph mark. It will not number blank lines that appear as a result of the page's formatting. For example, you could delete the paragraph marks that create the blank lines above each heading and then create similar blank lines in their place by issuing the Format Paragraph command to provide the headings with a space above value. When you print, Word would not number those blank lines.

To remove line numbers, you can delete the division mark or, with the cursor on or above the division mark, change the Format Division line-Numbers command to No.

As you can see, Word's line-numbering feature is easy to learn and use. Before getting into complex situations for numbering lines, let's examine Word's math feature, another easy-to-use feature that enables you to include numbers in your documents.

MATH CALCULATIONS

Word's math ability is simple and straightforward. Although you'll mostly use math operations on a highlighted column, be aware that Word will also perform math operations on text highlighted in the regular fashion.

Math operations use the Calculate key (F2). First, you highlight the text that contains the numbers and math symbols to be calculated, and then you press the Calculate key (F2). Word will ignore any nonmathematical text that you highlight, considering only numbers and the special math symbols. As with decimal-alignment,

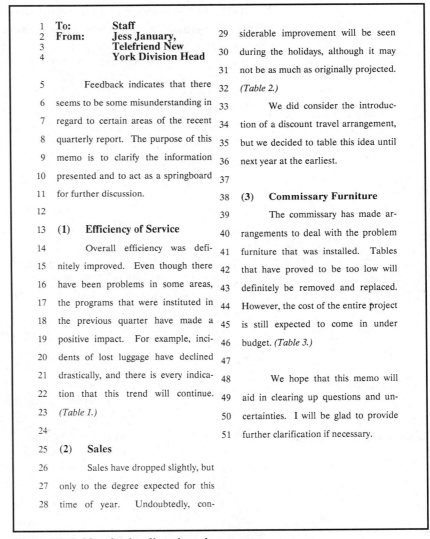

1 To: **Staff**
2 From: **Jess January,**
3   **Telefriend New**
4   **York Division Head**

5   Feedback indicates that there
6 seems to be some misunderstanding in
7 regard to certain areas of the recent
8 quarterly report. The purpose of this
9 memo is to clarify the information
10 presented and to act as a springboard
11 for further discussion.
12
13 **(1)   Efficiency of Service**
14   Overall efficiency was defi-
15 nitely improved. Even though there
16 have been problems in some areas,
17 the programs that were instituted in
18 the previous quarter have made a
19 positive impact. For example, inci-
20 dents of lost luggage have declined
21 drastically, and there is every indica-
22 tion that this trend will continue.
23 *(Table 1.)*
24
25 **(2)   Sales**
26   Sales have dropped slightly, but
27 only to the degree expected for this
28 time of year. Undoubtedly, con-

29 siderable improvement will be seen
30 during the holidays, although it may
31 not be as much as originally projected.
32 *(Table 2.)*
33   We did consider the introduc-
34 tion of a discount travel arrangement,
35 but we decided to table this idea until
36 next year at the earliest.
37
38 **(3)   Commissary Furniture**
39   The commissary has made ar-
40 rangements to deal with the problem
41 furniture that was installed. Tables
42 that have proved to be too low will
43 definitely be removed and replaced.
44 However, the cost of the entire project
45 is still expected to come in under
46 budget. *(Table 3.)*
47
48   We hope that this memo will
49 aid in clearing up questions and un-
50 certainties. I will be glad to provide
51 further clarification if necessary.

Figure 12.2: Numbering lines in a document

Word usually treats a period as the decimal indicator. Results of the calculation appear in the scrap area. You can then insert the calculated value anywhere in the document by using the Insert key or the Insert command.

Let's try addition on our "Fare" column from the example in Chapter 11 by following these steps:

1. To highlight the column as shown in Figure 12.3, start with the cursor on the bottom-right corner of the column of figures. If you started on the "8" in the first row of the column ("82.36"), the "1" in "125.00" on the bottom row would be left out, as it protrudes beyond the tens column where the "8" is located. (You could also highlight from top-right to bottom-left.)

2. Turn on Column Selection by pressing Shift-F6. CS appears in the lock area.

3. Move the cursor up and to the left, with either the directional arrows or the mouse, until you highlight all the fares.

4. Press the Calculate key (F2). Word adds up the numbers, and the answer appears in the scrap area. The highlight shrinks so that it highlights only the first character (in this case, the tab character), and Column selection is turned off.

5. With the cursor on the paragraph mark, press Enter three times, press Tab twice, type "Total," press Tab again, and insert the answer from scrap (see Figure 12.4).

If any number in the highlighted area is preceded by a minus sign or enclosed in parentheses, Word subtracts it from the total. Table 12.1 shows the other symbols that determine which math operations are performed. Word follows the standard algebraic methods of calculation. That is, percentages are calculated first, then multiplication and division, and then addition and subtraction. You can use parentheses to prioritize operations.

You can easily check and, if necessary, correct totals that are already typed into a document. For example, if after calculating a total, you went back and revised figures in the column, you would need to recalculate the total. First, highlight and use the Calculate key (F2) as described. Then, with the correct total in the scrap area, highlight the incorrect value in the document and press Shift-Insert. This action will replace the highlighted value with the correct total from scrap in one step.

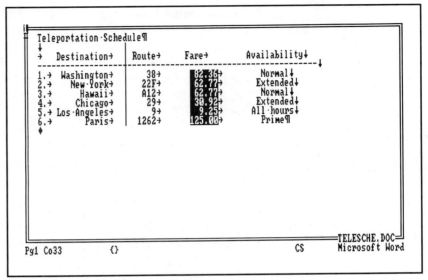

Figure 12.3: Highlighting a column for math

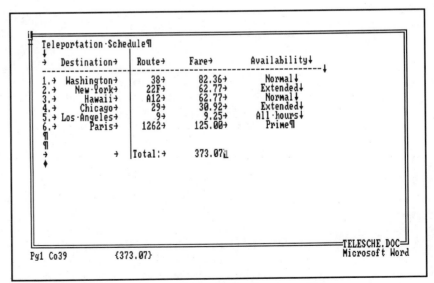

Figure 12.4: Inserting the calculation in the document from scrap

Table 12.1: Symbols Used for Math Operations

OPERATION	SYMBOL
Addition	+ or none
Subtraction	– or parentheses ( )
Multiplication	*
Division	/
Percentages	%

You can also use this technique to perform calculations on the fly as you type. Use it when you don't want the values that go into the calculation to appear in the document, only the results. Say, for instance, you need to make a reference to the number of working hours there are in a month, but you don't know how many hours that is. Just type a formula right where you want the value to appear, like so:

. . .works an average of 40*52/12 hours per month.

Then highlight the math sequence and get the answer by pressing the Calculate key (F2). Next, replace the highlighted sequence with the calculated total in one step by pressing Shift-Insert.

In this case, the actual answer is 173.333. . . . However, Word 5 rounds off its results so that they have no more than two decimal places unless there are decimal places specified by a value in the highlighted formula (in which case, it uses that number of decimal places). Thus, it rounds this value to 173.33.

Word also takes its comma cues from the highlighted values. That is, if any value in the highlight has a comma (for instance, 100,000), the answer will also contain commas if they're needed.

In addition, Word can only calculate answers having up to 14 digits on either side of the decimal point. If the answer is longer than that, you'll see the message

Math overflow or underflow

depending on whether the answer is too large or infinitesimal. If you get this message instead of an answer, simplify your calculation and try again.

ALPHABETIZING LISTS

Just as the math feature makes it unnecessary for you to reach for your calculator when using Word, its sorting capability makes it unnecessary for you to use index cards and alphabetize a list before you type it in. Instead, just highlight the material that you want sorted and issue the Library Autosort command. Let's try it on our sample table and sort—that is, alphabetize—it according to destination.

1. To alphabetize the table by destination, press Shift-F6 to turn on Column Selection and highlight the column of cities, starting from the bottom-right corner.

2. Press the Esc key to activate Command mode. Then type L for Library and A for Autosort. The Library Autosort command appears, as shown in Figure 12.5.

3. For standard alphabetizing, leave the settings as they are and press Enter to sort the list.

M O U S E

Press Shift-F6 to turn on Column Selection. Drag the highlight over the destinations and click right on Library to initiate the Library Autosort command. To accept the standard sort settings, click either button on LIBRARY AUTOSORT.

This procedure alphabetizes the list by city. Now, however, the numbers on the left are no longer in order. That is, each number is still paired with the same city as it was before the sort. We'll see how to sort those numbers in a moment.

You can use Library Autosort to perform multiple sorts. Multiple sorts allow you to sort items within other items. Suppose you have a long list of people and addresses, with first names in one column and last names in another. When the list is sorted, you would want to have some kind of order for the people who have the same last name. How can you arrange it so that all the Smiths, for instance, are alphabetized by their first name?

First, you must decide which category is the major one. Then decide the priority of the other categories and sort the list in order of reverse priority. In other words, sort by the least important category first and sort by the most important category last. Thus, to organize a

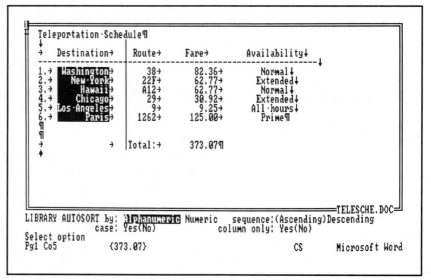

Figure 12.5: The Library Autosort command

list of names properly, you would sort the list by first name and then by last name.

You can apply Word's multiple sort feature to many contexts, and the Library Autosort command's options allow for even more flexibility in the way that you sort. Consider, first, the by option. Usually, you'll want to leave it set to Alphanumeric. Word then compares each item in the list character by character from left to right. Even some numeric items, such as phone numbers and zip codes, can be sorted this way when each item contains the same number of digits. If the numbers to be sorted vary in length, change this setting to Numeric. Otherwise, because characters are considered from left to right, Word would place 1, 10, and 100 before 2, 3, and 4.

Ascending sequence, which is the norm, alphabetizes the items in order from A to Z. Descending sequence, on the other hand, reverses the order: the items are listed from Z to A. Likewise, you can reverse any numbered items' order by setting sequence to Descending (greatest to smallest).

If you mix numbers with letters and sort in ascending sequence, the numbers will come first, followed by the letters. Usually, Word won't consider a letter's case when it sorts; that is, A and a will come before B. However, if you set case to Yes, Word will place all the capital letters before all the lowercase ones.

The column only option allows you to sort items in the column you highlight without sorting their corresponding rows. This is how we can resort the numbers on our sample list. Turn on the Column Selection (Shift-F6), highlight the column with the numbers, and initiate the Library Autosort command. Change the column only setting to Yes. When you complete the command, the numbers will be readjusted without affecting the new order of the cities.

The sorting examples we've considered so far have been accomplished with a list of items in a table. However, Word is not restricted to this setup. Word can also sort paragraphs. To do so, it uses the text that begins each paragraph. Suppose, for instance, that you have a list of course descriptions, with the name of the course at the beginning of each paragraph, followed by its description. You can alphabetize all the course names along with their respective descriptions. To do that for paragraphs you wish to sort, just highlight in the normal manner (do not use column highlighting) and issue the Library Autosort command.

You can also sort database information that you use with Word's Print Merge feature or sort your outline topics. We'll look at Word's capacity to perform these operations when we study Print Merge in Chapter 14 and outlines in Chapter 16.

RENUMBERING PARAGRAPHS

Besides sorting paragraphs, Word can also renumber them. To renumber our list, we can use this feature or the one we'll study next, numbering with variables. Suppose that one of the destinations is deleted; say, Hawaii (unfortunately). Resorting the numbers won't help, because a number is missing. But you can use the Library Number command to renumber the remaining destinations.

The Library Number command is rather fussy, though, so be careful when you use it. The first point to consider is that the material must be in paragraph format. As it is, we couldn't automatically renumber our list. Instead, each line must end with a paragraph mark, rather than a new-line mark. Thus each line becomes a paragraph. We can use the Replace command to help make this substitution.

Next, all items to be renumbered must already have a number at the beginning. Thus, if you add an item, you must put a number—any number—at the beginning of the paragraph/line if you want it to be renumbered later.

Also, each number must be followed immediately by a period or a closing parenthesis. Then there must be a space or a tab character right after that. (If the number is followed by a closing parenthesis, it may be preceded with an opening parenthesis as well.)

Finally, you must highlight with standard highlighting, by pressing F10, for example. Don't use column highlighting (Shift-F6).

Let's see how to renumber our sample schedule after removing one of the items. Before doing so, save the document as a precaution. If something goes wrong, particularly with the Replace command, and you miss the opportunity to use the Undo command, you can still load the saved version, losing the edits. Then follow these steps:

1. Highlight and delete the line with the Hawaii destination.

2. To change each new-line mark at the end of a line to a paragraph mark, highlight the paragraph that makes up the table.

3. Use the Replace command and change the new-line marks to paragraph marks, like so:

   REPLACE text: ^n   **with text:** ^p

   When you do, set confirm to No to expedite the procedure. Also, be sure to use lowercase letters for the codes.

4. To renumber the new paragraphs, highlight the entire document or only one character so that the command affects all the text.

5. Fully execute the Library Number command without changing its settings (see Figure 12.6). Word will then renumber the lines.

Although this feature is called the Library Number command, Word can reorder a variety of characters. You may recognize these, except for legal format, as the characters it can use for page numbering as well (see

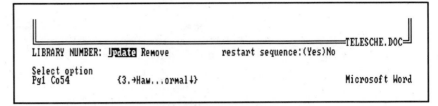

Figure 12.6: The Library Number command

Chapter 9):

> Arabic numerals: 1 2 3 4 5
>
> Capital Roman numerals: I II III IV V
>
> Lowercase Roman numerals: i ii iii iv v
>
> Capital letters: A B C D E
>
> Lowercase letters: a b c d e
>
> Legal format: 1.1 1.2 1.3 1.4 1.5

When it renumbers, Word follows the type of character specified for the first item. Also, the period or parenthesis is made to match that first item.

The Library Number command's options are rather simple. First, you can choose Update or Remove. If you choose Remove, Word will strip the highlighted text of its numbers at the beginning of the paragraphs. For instance, you might want to use this setting for temporary numbers you added to order some paragraphs. After adding the numbers, you could issue the Library Autosort command to rearrange them in the new order. You could then use the Library Number command, set to Remove, to eliminate those temporary numbers.

Library Number also has a restart sequence option, which is usually set to Yes. With this setting, the first paragraph will be renumbered as 1., the next 2., and so on. If you reset it to No, Word will start numbering with the first number that appears within the highlight. Thus, if the first highlighted paragraph begins with

20.

Word will number the following paragraphs as 21., 22., and so on.

Another useful feature of this command involves the renumbering of different levels within a document. Word renumbers according to the formatted indent. That is, items indented ½ inch will be numbered in proper sequence, items indented one inch will be numbered together, and so on. However, Word uses only its formatting schemes to determine if material is indented. It ignores indenting that you've created by pressing the Tab key or the Spacebar. To create formats that Word will renumber hierarchically, use left indent (Alt-N), first-line indent (Alt-F), left and right indent (Alt-Q), or provide your own (consistent) indents with the Format Paragraph command.

Because of Word's ability to renumber indented levels, its Library Number command is especially handy when used with the outline processor. We'll discuss outlining in Chapter 16.

When you use Library Number to renumber paragraphs, the numbers must come first in the paragraphs. Thus, you cannot use Library Number to renumber items like "Figure 1" followed by a caption. However, you can use the next method, numbering with code names, to handle such tasks.

NUMBERING WITH CODE NAMES

New in
Word 5

Word 5 can number material by using code names. This method of numbering has a lot more flexibility than that of the Library Number command: you can insert numbers wherever you wish and you don't have to perform a special operation to update them. The drawback, however, is that you do not see the numbers as you edit. The numbers only appear when you use Print preView or print the document.

The technique for numbering with code names is simple. In each place where you want an ordered number to appear, you insert a code name that you make up. Then you designate the text you provided as a code name. To replace each occurrence of the code with a number that is automatically incremented, print or preview the document.

For practice, let's replace the numbers at the beginning of each line in our sample table with a code name. For each number in turn, first delete the number. Then proceed as follows:

1. Type your code name. For our example, use "Dest_No" as the code name. Code names can be up to 31 characters in length, made up of letters, numbers, underline characters, periods, and hyphens.

2. After the code, type a colon (:). The colon signals Word that this is a code name when you perform the next step.

3. After the colon, press the Glossary key (F3). Word then relegates the text as a code name by surrounding it with parentheses, like so:

(Dest_No:)

Once you provide the code names and use the Glossary key for each destination number in our example, your screen will look like that shown in Figure 12.7. Notice that to accommodate the wider text, Word pushes the columns to the right and some of the text goes off the screen. Since the numbers that will appear in print won't be as wide as the code name that we're using, you can ignore the apparent

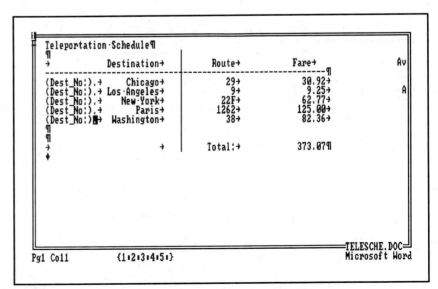

Figure 12.7: Adding the code name to number the rows

alignment problems. When you print the document, the result will be correct, as you can see in Figure 12.8.

Obviously, when you are really using this feature to number items, you won't be replacing existing numbers with the code name. The most effective method would be to enter the code name when you type the text and edit the document as you normally would. Then, when you think the document is in its final form, issue the Print pre-View command to see how the text is aligned and return to Document mode to revise the format for the coded numbers as necessary. (If your document's format is rather complex, you may need to pre-view it again to make sure everything is aligned properly.)

You can also have Word count items without printing the number. To do this, type two colons at the end of the code name before you press the Glossary key (F3). For example, enter

Dest_No::

You might want to use this technique to count a listing of parts, for instance. If you want to include the total count, create a standard code name (with just one colon) for the last item, and the total will be printed.

You can also use double colons to make Word reset the numbering; numbering can begin with any positive number you want. To do this, move the cursor to any point in the document before the first code you want specially numbered. Enter the code name, two colons, and a number one less then the number for the first code. Then press

```
┌─────────────────────────────────────────────────────────────┐
│                                                               │
│     Teleportation Schedule                                    │
│                                                               │
│           Destination │ Route      Fare      Availability     │
│        ---------------┼-----------------------------------    │
│        1.    Chicago  │   29       30.92      Extended         │
│        2. Los Angeles │    9        9.25      All hours         │
│        3.   New York  │  22F       62.77      Extended         │
│        4.     Paris   │ 1262      125.00      Prime            │
│        5. Washington  │   38       82.36      Normal           │
│                       │                                       │
│                       │ Total:    373.07                      │
│                                                               │
└─────────────────────────────────────────────────────────────┘
```

Figure 12.8: Printed numbers created by code names

F3. For example, to start numbering destinations with 101, you'd enter

> **Dest_No::100**

somewhere before the first destination number and press F3. For the subsequent code, simply enter

> **Dest_No:**

and the number 101 will be printed there.

Remember, you can use code-name numbering wherever you want, not just at the beginning of lines or paragraphs as in the example. As you add or delete code names, Word will automatically renumber those that remain when you use print preView or print the document. You can have several numbering systems that operate independently in one document by simply including different code names.

We'll next see how you can use code-name numbering to number the tables in a document. You'll then see how you can automatically cross-reference those numbers as they are discussed in text.

CROSS-REFERENCING WITH BOOKMARKS

New in Word 5

For perhaps the ultimate in numbering capabilities, Word 5 provides you with a comprehensive cross-referencing feature, which allows you to alert readers to related material elsewhere in a document. You cross-reference text by using a *bookmark,* an identifying tag that you assign to the text. You can assign bookmarks to any text, and they are especially handy for cross-referencing numbers created by code names. Because your editing may renumber the codes, cross-referencing them with bookmarks ensures that each cross-reference always reflects the correct numbering.

CREATING BOOKMARKS

For example, let's see how to cross-reference the FEEDBACK document that we last worked with in Chapter 11. Assume that each of the three tables discussed in the document should appear on separate pages following the text. Figure 12.9 contains the printed document, along with labels that show how the code names and cross-references will appear on the screen. Don't just type the codes in, though. You must create them by using the Glossary key (F3) and cross-reference them using bookmarks. In this section, I explain how to code all these elements of Word's new, sophisticated cross-referencing system. Let's begin by using the code name "table_no" as the flag Word should use for inserting table numbers.

To create the captions for these pages, proceed as follows:

1. Go to the end of the document and move the cursor below the division mark. This division mark formats the preceding text in two columns. Entering the captions after the division mark ensures that they do not appear in columns and that the first table is placed on the next page.

2. Type the word "Table," followed by a space, the code name "table_no," and a colon (Word's signal for a code name) like so:

   Table table_no:

   Then press the Glossary key (F3). Word will surround the code name with parentheses.

3. To include a colon with the table number when you print the document, type another colon. Then provide the caption. On the screen, the caption for the first table will be

   Table (table_no:): Less Lost Luggage at Telefriend

   When you print the document, the caption will change to

   Table 1: Less Lost Luggage at Telefriend

4. To provide a bookmark name for the code name (so you can cross-reference it), highlight the code name, and issue the Format bookmarK command (see Figure 12.10). For the first caption, enter "Luggage" as the bookmark name.

5. To place the caption paragraph at the bottom left of the margins, issue the Format pOsition command and provide the following settings:

horizontal frame position: Left	relative to: Margins
vertical frame position: Bottom	relative to: Margins

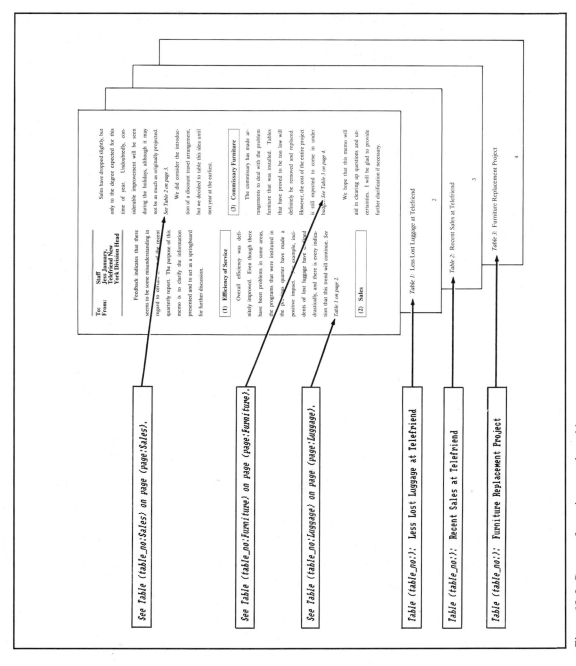

Figure 12.9: Cross-referencing numbered items

(Note that with show layout on, Word will place the caption at the bottom of the page, with lots of white space above. For easiest editing, set show layout to No with the Options command or Alt-F4.)

6. To place the next table on a new page, press Ctrl-Shift-Enter. This creates a page break, as indicated by a row of periods.

7. Repeat steps 2 through 6 for each table caption. For the second caption's bookmark name, use "Sales." For the third, use "Furniture."

8. Add page numbers for the pages containing the tables by issuing the Format Division Page numbers command.

When you use Format bookmarK, you can list the existing bookmark names by pressing F1 in the name field or clicking right on name. By doing so, you can avoid selecting similar bookmark names that you might confuse with each other. You don't have to worry

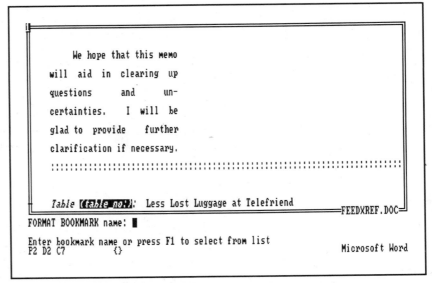

Figure 12.10: The Format bookmarK command

about overwriting a bookmark's name accidentally, since Word will ask you for verification before overwriting it.

PROVIDING PAGE
NUMBERS IN YOUR CROSS-REFERENCES

Now let's see how to cross-reference the three bookmarks that we created. To create cross-references, you provide their cross-reference codes, followed by a colon. Codes you can use include the following:

page:	inserts page number.
footnote:	inserts the footnote number (see Chapter 9).
para-num:	inserts the number at the beginning of the paragraph. You use this referencing code with the Library Number command, discussed in "Renumbering Paragraphs" earlier in this chapter.
code:	inserts the code-name number, where *code* is any code name you created to number material. This same code name must also appear in the bookmarked text.

After the cross-reference code and colon, you provide the bookmark name to which you wish to direct the reader. Then you press the Glossary key (F3), which surrounds the cross-reference and bookmark codes with parentheses. Let's say that for each place in text where we want to refer to a table, we want to provide the table number and the page number that it is on. For the first cross-reference, we want the document to show

See Table 1 on page 2.

In effect, we want Word to find the "Luggage" bookmark and display its table number, which is provided by the "table_no" code. Then we want Word to check Luggage again and display the page number it appears on. Thus, the first cross-reference is actually two cross-references and would end up as

See Table (table_no:Luggage) on page (page:Luggage).

since we used Luggage as the bookmark for the first table's caption.

Let's go ahead and try this for the sample document's tables. Its table references are simply "(Table 1.)," "(Table 2.)," and "(Table 3.)" right now. To change them to the bookmarked references that will list the correct table and page number for each table, use the Replace command, which expedites the process. After you register the command, you should see the following replace each of the three table references in the document:

See Table table_no: on page page:

Move to the first table's new reference and continue with the following steps:

1. Place the cursor after the colon following "table_no," type the bookmark name "Luggage," and press the Glossary key (F3).

2. Then move to the period after "page:", type "Luggage" again, and press F3 again.

3. Move to the second table reference and repeat steps 1 and 2 using the bookmark "Sales." Then repeat them for the third reference using "Furniture" as the bookmark.

4. Issue Print preView or print the document to see the cross-referenced numbers.

JUMPING TO BOOKMARKS

As you cross-reference your text, you can move quickly from one bookmark to another by issuing the Jump bookmarK command. Type the name of the bookmark you want or display the list of bookmark names and chose from among them. When you register the command, Word highlights and displays the text assigned to the bookmark.

You can use Jump bookmarK for two other purposes. First, if you forget which bookmark name you're using for some text, you can issue Jump bookmarK and press F1 or click right to look at the names. Specify the name that seems appropriate and see if it highlights the text that you want. If it doesn't, highlight the correct text and issue Format bookmarK to assign that bookmark name to the highlighted text.

Second, you can create bookmarks as placeholders in your document, even if you have no intention of cross-referencing them. You might want to do this with long documents, leaving placeholders in sections that you know will need to be revised later. Using Jump bookmarK to find such placeholders is usually quicker than using the Search command to locate a string of text.

Word's numbering, calculating, sorting, and cross-referencing features are tools that help you produce and revise your documents' contents. While you may not need them for every single document, you'll want to use Word's speller to complete each document's revision process. We'll explore this feature in the next chapter.

13

Help with Spelling, Hyphenation, and Synonyms

Fast Track

To customize Spell,   390

 use Spell's Options command to require a more complete
 lookup; to have Spell ignore words that are all caps; to have
 Spell only display alternative spelling when you select Spell's
 Correct command; or to have Spell not check punctuation.

To hyphenate your document automatically,   390

 issue the Library Hyphenate command. Word will hyphenate
 the text from the cursor position forward. To hyphenate a section of your document, highlight it before invoking Library
 Hyphenate.

To control the hyphenation process,   391

 set confirm to Yes when you use Library Hyphenate.

To find a synonym for a word,   393

 highlight the word or the punctuation or space after it. Then
 press Ctrl-F6. Highlight a synonym and press Enter to substitute it for the highlighted word in your document.

To find a synonym for a synonym,   394

 highlight the synonym and press Ctrl-F6 again.

WHEN YOU PURCHASE MICROSOFT WORD, YOU ACQUIRE powerful word-oriented features. Two of these features, the spelling checker and automatic hyphenator, can truly put the finishing touches on your documents and make them letter-perfect. In addition, its thesaurus feature can help perk up your writing style by providing you with synonyms as you compose or edit your material. We will focus on these features in this chapter.

You run the spelling checker, Spell, once you've finished editing and your document is complete. When you run Spell, it compares the document, word by word, against an electronic dictionary of 130,000 words (without definitions). Fortunately, Spell performs this comparison with truly astounding speed. When Spell can't find a word that you've typed, it presents the word to you. You can instruct Spell to correct or ignore it (it may be spelled correctly even though it is not in Spell's dictionary).

Even more incredibly, Spell will quickly scrutinize its dictionary and display one or more words similar to the flagged word. You can then choose from among the words displayed, and Spell will move on to the next word it can't find in the dictionary.

Once your document is complete, you may also want to run Word's automatic hyphenator. This feature looks at each line of the document and automatically hyphenates words to fill in the gaps that occur at the ends of lines because word wrap has moved a word to the next line. It automatically places hyphens in the proper spots in the words, saving you the trouble of deciding how to hyphenate. However, Word allows you to retain veto power over the placement of these hyphens if you so desire.

Another feature you'll want to use even before you're done writing is Word Finder. This is a thesaurus that provides you with a listing of words similar in meaning to one that you've indicated in your document. Choose a word from the list, and Word will substitute the synonym for your highlighted word. You can use the thesaurus to find a substitute for an overused word or to provide just the right shade of meaning.

Let's begin to study these word-oriented features by looking at Spell, which you invoke with the Library Spell command.

CHECKING YOUR SPELLING

The electronic dictionary that Spell utilizes is extremely large and comprehensive. Words that are plurals, derivatives, and so on are listed in the dictionary as words separate from their root word. Thus Spell flags only words that are truly suspect. The result is that checking your spelling is actually enjoyable rather than arduous.

SETTING UP FOR THE SPELLING CHECK

Using Spell is easy. There are a few steps you should take, however, before you begin.

First, it's wise to save the edited document. Although Word 5's Spell has an Undo command, it only undoes the previous correction. Having a saved version of the document allows you to retrieve the document as it was before you ran Spell, affording you an extra degree of safety in case you commit a series of Spell errors.

Once you've saved the document, keep it on the screen. The document you want to check must be loaded when you issue the Library Spell command. If you have more than one window open, the document must be in the activated window. You can also check part of a document if you want. Just highlight what you want to check before you issue the Library Spell command. You can even check a single word by highlighting only it.

RUNNING SPELL

Let's create a simple document replete with errors and check it with the Spell program. Type the document that appears in Figure 13.1, leaving your cursor at the end of the document when you've finished. Save the document under the name TELESPEL. Then issue the Library Spell command as follows:

M *O U S E*

Click left on Library and click either button on Spell to run Spell.

1. Press the Esc key.

2. Type L for Library.

3. Type S for Spell.

Shortcut:

Alt-F6

New in
Word 5

At this point, Word 5 displays the message

Checking document. . .

and then the prompt

Enter Y to continue spelling from top of document or Esc to exit

As with the Search command, when you run Spell, Word searches for unknown words from the cursor's initial position to the end of the document. When it reaches the end, Word 5 checks that you want to return to the beginning of the document to continue checking if the cursor was not there initially. When you start Spell with the cursor at the end of the document, as it normally is when you finish entering a new document, Word displays the previous prompt before presenting any words for correction.

Next, Word displays the message

Loading dictionaries . . .

splits the screen into three windows, and presents the Spell menu (see Figure 13.2). Once you issue the Library Spell command, Spell presents you with unknown words one by one; "unknown" means that Spell is unable to locate them in the dictionary. Your role is to ask Spell to correct the misspelled words and to ignore those that are okay.

The first word that Spell couldn't find in the dictionary appears in the bottom window, with the words "Not found" alongside it. The context in which the word appears in the document is displayed in the top window, with the word in question highlighted, while the center window contains a list of possible corrections for the word.

We'll first look at the quickest method of correcting your documents, which may be the only method you'll ever need. Because of this, we won't explain other choices that appear on this initial menu just yet.

Frequently, the word you are looking for will be the first one listed in the center window, and you need only press the Enter key to accept it. You can also choose one of the other words with the arrow keys and press Enter.

If you don't see the word you want among those listed, you can issue the Correct command and type that word, taking your best

T I P

After you issue the Library Spell command in Word 4, you must choose Spell's Proof command to run the spell-checking operation.

T I P

To display Spell's suggested alternatives for an unknown word in Word 4, you must issue Spell's Correct command.

M O U S E

To select one of the suggested words, click right on it.

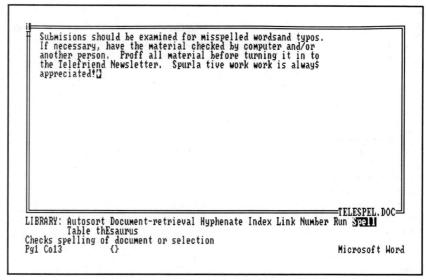

Figure 13.1: The TELESPEL document, complete with errors

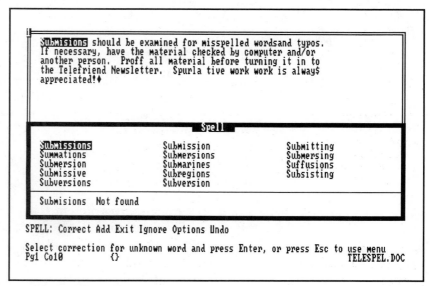

Figure 13.2: The Spell menu

guess at the correct spelling. Once you've typed in a word, Spell will check to see if the typed word is in its dictionary.

Sometimes, Spell will stop at a word when you are sure that you spelled the unknown word correctly. In this case, you can issue the Ignore command to tell Spell to leave the word alone.

CORRECTING THE MISSPELLED WORDS

Let's proof our TELESPEL document's spelling. Spell stops at the words in the same order as they appear in the document. The first unknown word it stops at is

Submisions

In this case, the correct spelling is highlighted in the middle window. Press the Enter key or click right on the highlighted word to accept it. Word immediately substitutes the suggested word for the unknown word in the text.

Next, Spell stops at and highlights two words apparently joined together inadvertently:

wordsand

Spell believes that "wordsand" is intended to be one word. Disregard the suggestions presented and choose the Correct command. Just type the correction, separating the words with a space (see Figure 13.3), and press Enter.

Next, Spell presents the word

Proff

You'll see the alternatives presented in the middle window. Since you want "proof" and it's not the first choice, you must select it from the list by pressing the → key once and pressing Enter or by clicking right on it (see Figure 13.4).

Next, Spell presents the word

Telefriend

T I P

To have Word 5 indicate which words Spell has changed, issue the Format revision-Marks Options command and set add revision marks to Yes before running Spell. For more on using Word's revision-marks system, see Chapter 6.

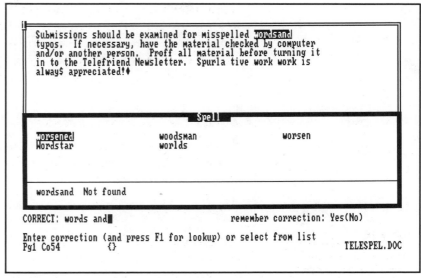

Figure 13.3: Separating two words

Naturally, Spell wouldn't find a company name like this in the dictionary. Have the word left as it is by choosing Ignore. Spell will ignore this word if it encounters it again in the document.

Next, Spell stops at

Spurla

This ''word'' was created as a result of a space ostensibly typed by accident. This situation calls for editing the text to eliminate the space between two parts of the same word.

New in
Word 5

Word 5 allows you to change text easily as you run Spell. Simply issue Spell's Exit command. Word stops Spell, displays a tally of the actions taken, and highlights the word on which you were working. You can then edit the text. In this case, you see the message

32 words checked, 4 unknown

Highlight the space between ''Spurla'' and ''tive'' and delete it.

(In Word 4, you use Spell's Mark command to keep track of the corrections to make in Document mode after you have finished

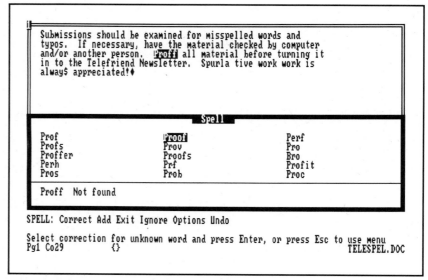

Figure 13.4: Choosing an alternative spelling

checking the document's spelling. You could also quit Spell. The cursor would return to the beginning of the document, and you would have to start Spell all over again; it wouldn't pick up where it left off when you quit.)

Run the Library Spell command again by pressing Alt-F6. In Word 5, Spell picks up correcting at the cursor's location and highlights the newly joined word

Spurlative

However, the message

No alternative words found

appears. Though now one word, the spelling is just too different for Spell to guess which word you had in mind. Choose Correct; Word then displays the following message:

Enter correction (and press F1 for lookup) or select from list

To correct the word, press F9 to move to the "S," press F10 to move a character right, and type "u." Then press F10 again to move to the

T I P

Remember, you use the F7 to F10 keys to edit an entry in a menu field. F7 moves the highlight a word to the left, F8 moves it a word to the right, F9 moves it a character to the left, and F10 moves it a character to the right.

second "u" and press the Delete key to delete it. Then type "e." Once you have corrected the word, press Enter and Word double-checks your correction.

If the spelling was still incorrect—say you forgot to delete the second "u"—and you pressed Enter, Word would display the message

Word not in dictionary. Enter Y to confirm or N to retype.

In this case, you would type N and then press F1 to tell Spell to look up the new spelling. This time Spell would display the correct spelling, "Superlative," as the first alternative. Pressing Enter would accept it and correct the troublesome spelling of this word.

After you correct "Superlative," Spell stops at the word "work" and displays the message

work is repeated.

You typed the word twice, one right after the other. Choose Correct, and Spell deletes the duplicate.

Lastly, Spell displays

alway$ Improper punctuation

New in
Word 5

Word 5 checks for oddball punctuation in your document like this. Choose Correct and you can change the "$" to an "s" by pressing F10 to move to the end of "alway$," pressing Backspace to delete the "$," and typing "s."

As this is the last unknown word, Spell prompts you to

Enter Y to continue spelling from top of document or Esc to exit

Because we already checked from the beginning of the document, you can press the Esc key. (Word forgot that we did since we interrupted Spell to edit "Superlative.")

UNDOING SPELL ACTIONS

While the two commands you'll undoubtedly use most in proofing your documents are Correct and Ignore, let's glance at some of the other commands that you can use.

New in
Word 5

First, Spell's Undo command undoes the previous Spell change you made to the document. As with Undo elsewhere, you can undo the undo. (To reconsider the last Spell change you made in Word 4, use the Previous command.)

Additionally, you can undo all the effects of running Spell. Simply issue the Undo command or press Shift-F1 immediately after you finish running Spell.

ADDING WORDS TO DICTIONARIES

If you use Spell frequently, you may find that it flags too many words, forcing you to use the Ignore command a great deal. This is particularly likely if you often repeat certain proper names, technical terms, and special abbreviations that are naturally missing from Spell's dictionary. To expedite the spell-checking process in this situation, you may consider supplementing the dictionary that Spell consults.

A helpful feature for regular users of Spell is the program's ability to add words to its dictionary. Once you have added these words, Spell will verify their spelling in its check and will not flag them if they are correctly spelled.

In addition to the main dictionary, Spell allows you to establish two other kinds of dictionaries: a *user dictionary* and a *document dictionary*.

Adding entries to Spell's dictionaries is simple. Just use Spell's Add command when reviewing the words Spell has flagged as questionable. Spell will then display three choices:

ADD word to: Standard User Document

TIP

Consider carefully before you add any words to the standard dictionary. If you do decide to add words, make sure that any you add are absolutely correct: once a word is in the dictionary, Spell does not provide a way to remove it.

You add the word to Spell's standard dictionary, which in Word 5 is called SPELL-AM.LEX (UPDATAM.CMP in Word 4), by selecting Standard at this point. Consider carefully whether the word you want to add is likely to be used in a variety of documents because every word you add to Spell's main dictionary slows down the checking process slightly. If it's a word that will show up only in certain types of documents or only in one document, you should establish a user dictionary or a document dictionary and add the word to it. For example, if there are technical terms that appear only in your technical papers, you might create a user dictionary called TERMS. It's called a user dictionary because you, the user, created it for terms you employ often.

TIP

In Word 4 you change user dictionaries by issuing the Dictionary command right after you issue Library Spell.

5 New in Word 5

With Word 5 you specify your user dictionary with Spell's Options command (see Figure 13.5). This must be done while Spell is running; for example, you could have issued the Options command when Spell stopped to check the word "alway$." You can give the user dictionary any name you want, as long as it follows the standard DOS rules. Spell will add the .CMP extension to the name you specify. If you don't provide a name for the user dictionary, Word will assign the default name, SPECIALS.CMP.

You add words to the user dictionary by issuing Spell's Add command and selecting User. After Word has created a user dictionary, Spell will consult both it and the standard dictionary.

You can also add an unknown word to a document dictionary. When you select Add and then Document, Word will create a special dictionary that has the same name as the document you're reviewing but with a .CMP extension. This dictionary is created in the same directory and drive as the document. In addition to the standard dictionary (and the user dictionary, if specified), Spell will automatically consult the document dictionary, but only when checking this document.

Word uses the dictionary indicated by the Options command's speller path option (not Spell's Options command), which is set when

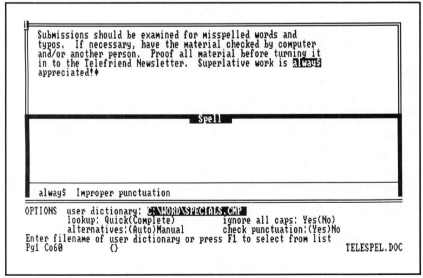

Figure 13.5: Spell's Options command

you set up Word. If you use a different dictionary, such as one you purchased from some third-party vendor, or move your dictionary to a different directory, edit this field.

CUSTOMIZING SPELL WITH ITS OPTIONS COMMAND

Besides customizing your dictionaries, you can also customize the way Spell operates with its Options command.

In Word 5, the lookup option is usually set to Complete. If you change it to Quick, Spell will ignore the first two letters of the unknown words. Doing so speeds the lookup process. (The program assumes that most misspellings occur later in the word.) When set to Complete, Spell will *not* ignore the first two letters, which makes for a more thorough but possibly slower search for alternative spellings.

If you set the ignore all caps option to Yes, Spell will not proof words whose letters are all capitalized. You might want this setting if your document has lots of capitalized initials or acronyms that shouldn't be flagged and presented for review. If you are positive that your capitalized words are correct, you can use this option to speed up Spell's check and avoid setting up a special dictionary.

The alternatives option is usually set to Auto, which displays alternative spellings when Spell presents an unknown word. Change it to Manual if you want the alternative spellings presented only when you select Spell's Correct command.

The check punctuation option is usually set to Yes, allowing the new punctuation feature to operate as we saw earlier. If your document has exotic punctuation that slows down Spell, try setting check punctuation to No to expedite matters.

5 New in Word 5

HYPHENATING AUTOMATICALLY

After checking the spelling in your document, you may want to use Word to hyphenate the document automatically since your final words will then be in place. Long words that were wrapped down a line often create a gap at the end of the previous line. These words will be hyphenated when you use the Library Hyphenate command.

The first part of the word will move to the end of the previous line and will thus fill in the gap. Likewise, hyphenating can also aid in reducing gaps that occur within lines that are justified.

Similar to Spell, the Library Hyphenate command operates from the cursor location toward the end of the document. However, it doesn't automatically recycle to the beginning like Spell does. Therefore, if you wish to hyphenate the entire document, the cursor must be at the beginning of the document. Also, the cursor must not be larger than a single character. If it is expanded, only the highlighted area will be hyphenated.

Initiating automatic hyphenation is simple. Simply issue the Library Hyphenate command:

M O U S E

Click left on Library and click either button on Hyphenate. Click either button on LIBRARY HYPHEN-ATE to initiate automatic hyphenation.

1. Press the Esc key.

2. Type L for Library and H for Hyphenate. The Library Hyphenate menu then appears (see Figure 13.6).

3. Press the Enter key to initiate automatic hyphenating.

Word will hyphenate your document following the correct rules of hyphenation without any further intervention on your part. (To perform the hyphenation, Word consults the file HYPH.DAT, which is in the WORD directory.) The hyphens inserted are called *soft* or *smart hyphens;* that is, they will not be printed if subsequent editing causes them to fall within a line rather than at its end. Likewise, Word won't display them on the screen if they are not at the end of the line and the show non-printing symbols option in the Options command is set to No.

If you want to control how Word hyphenates your document, change the settings in the Library Hyphenate menu before registering the command. If you set the confirm option to Yes, Word will

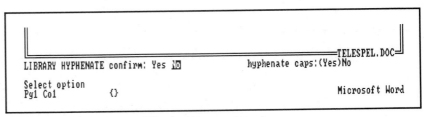

Figure 13.6: The Library Hyphenate command

pause at each word it is considering for hyphenation, highlighting the spot it proposes for hyphenation. When it does, look for the highlight along the left edge of the window since Word restricts itself to words that have been wrapped down to the beginning of lines. Figure 13.7 shows Word attempting to hyphenate the word "appreciate" at the end of the paragraph, along with its prompting message. (To create this hyphenating opportunity, I deleted the words "If necessary" in the second sentence.)

By typing Y, you'll get a hyphen at the spot indicated. By typing N, you will tell Word to leave the word unhyphenated and move on to the next word. You can also use the directional keys to move the highlight to a different spot than the one initially suggested by Word. Use the ↑ and ↓ keys to see other locations Word suggests. Using the ← and → keys moves the highlight to another spot in the word of your own choosing. Finally, you can cancel the hyphenation process altogether by pressing the Esc key.

The other option in the Library Hyphenate menu is hyphenate caps, which is usually set to Yes. Change it to No if you don't want

***T** I P*

If there's a word that you never want to be hyphenated, add what's known as an *optional hyphen* (Ctrl-hyphen) to the *end* of the word. Word never attempts to hyphenate words that already have hyphens, and the optional hyphen at the end of the word will never be printed.

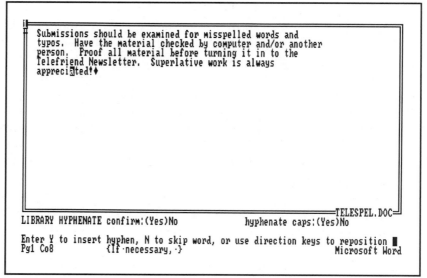

Figure 13.7: Word pausing for confirmation when hyphenating

Word to hyphenate any word that begins with a capital letter. This way, you won't get hyphens in proper names or in the first word of a sentence.

Once the hyphenating process ends, the cursor returns to the position it occupied before you issued the Library Hyphenate command. Word reactivates Document mode and the message area tells you how many words were hyphenated. If you should change your mind at this point about hyphenating the document, you can remove all the hyphenating with the Undo command. You can then undo the Undo to compare the hyphenated and unhyphenated versions of your document.

SUBSTITUTING SYNONYMS FOR OVERUSED WORDS

When you are creating Word documents, a useful feature is the Word Finder thesaurus. At the touch of a button, you can find synonyms for any word in your document. Then, just as easily, you can substitute one of those synonyms for the given word. Additionally, you can find synonyms for one of the synonyms displayed and then substitute one of those instead. To perform these wonders, Word refers to a compilation of some 220,000 words. A floppy disk separate from the Word program holds the thesaurus, and the Setup program copies it to your hard disk (see Appendix A).

DISPLAYING SYNONYMS

To have the thesaurus search for and display synonyms for a given word, you need to indicate the word for the search. You do this by highlighting all or part of the word—highlighting one letter of the word is sufficient. If you highlight the space or other character following a word, the thesaurus uses the word preceding the space for the synonym search. Once you've indicated the word, you activate the thesaurus with the Library thEsaurus command.

Word then displays the synonyms in the Word Finder Thesaurus window. If the selected word is in the top half of the screen, the window opens at the bottom of the screen. Conversely, if the selected

T I P

Column Selection (Shift-F6) must be off before you can use the thesaurus. Otherwise, you'll hear a beep and the operation won't succeed.

word is in the bottom half of the screen, the window will appear at the top. Its location will always allow you to see the highlighted word in context as you consider the synonyms. You use the directional keypad to move the cursor to the synonym that you want. Then you press the Enter key to substitute the synonym for your chosen word in the document.

Let's try this on our sample spelling document, by looking up a synonym for the word "person." Follow these steps:

MOUSE

Click right on the word "person." Click left on Library and click either button on thEsaurus. Click right on the word "associate" to replace the word "person" in your document with "associate."

1. Highlight the word "person."

2. Press Esc, type L for Library, and type E for thEsaurus.

Shortcut:

Ctrl-F6

Word opens the Word Finder Thesaurus window and displays the message

Looking up person . . .

with the word "person" highlighted. Soon the synonyms appear, as shown in Figure 13.8. Let's assume you prefer the word "associate."

3. Use the ↓ key to highlight the word "associate" in the thesaurus window.

4. Press Enter to substitute the word "associate" for the word "person" in your document.

In the thesaurus window, you'll notice that the word you selected in the document is the first word that appears. Below it is the part of speech—noun—that identifies the group of synonyms the thesaurus presents for you. As we'll see shortly, the thesaurus may present more than one part of speech for you. Thus, there can be more than one group of synonyms presented as well.

You can use the Undo command to restore the original word. Issue it now to return the word "person" to the document.

LOOKING UP SYNONYMS OF SYNONYMS

Once you have a listing of synonyms, you may feel that none of them quite hits the spot. However, one synonym may be close. If

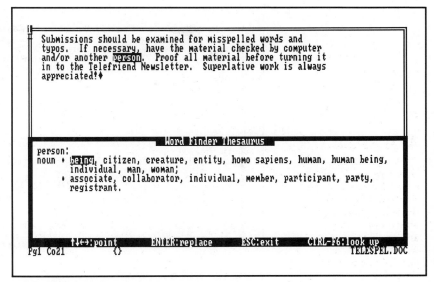

Figure 13.8: Using the thesaurus

that's the case, you can look up the synonyms for that synonym. You do this by selecting it and pressing the Thesaurus key (Ctrl-F6).

To demonstrate this feature, let's again look up synonyms for "person." Start by highlighting this word and continue as follows:

M O U S E

Click left on Library and click either button on thEsaurus to display the thesaurus window. Then click left on "associate" to highlight it. To display synonyms for "associate," click right on the prompt CTRL-F6:look up that appears at the bottom of the window.

1. Press Ctrl-F6 to display the thesaurus window for the word "person." Once the synonyms are displayed, let's assume that you want to see the synonyms for the word "associate."

2. Highlight the word "associate" using the ↓ key.

3. Press Ctrl-F6 to have Word look up synonyms for "associate." Word then lists your possible choices (see Figure 13.9).

As you can see, "associate" has two part-of-speech groupings from which to choose. That's because you can use the word as a noun (an associate) or a verb (to associate with). Notice, too, the message

   MORE: PgDn

in the upper-right corner of the thesaurus window, which means

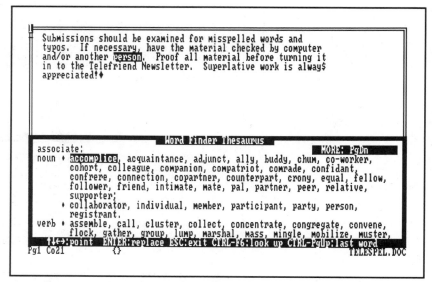

Figure 13.9: Finding synonyms of a synonym

there are more synonyms for the verb grouping. You can see them by using the Page Down key.

The message

Ctl-PgUp: last word

also appears in the bottom-right corner of the screen. Once you look up a synonym for a synonym, you can press Ctrl-Page Up to display the first round of synonyms again. Try pressing Ctrl-Page Up now, and you'll see the set of synonyms for "person." You can look up level after level of synonyms for synonyms. Each time you then use Ctrl-Page Up, you'll see the previous grouping (up to ten groupings back).

You can also have the Word Finder look up a word that you type in directly, even though it doesn't appear in the document or among the listed synonyms. Simply start to type the word. When you type the first letter, the Word Finder will display a box that you can finish typing the word into (see Figure 13.10). Press Enter to initiate the word check.

You can cancel the small look-up window or the thesaurus operation by pressing the Esc key. Try this on our sample document to restore it to its original form.

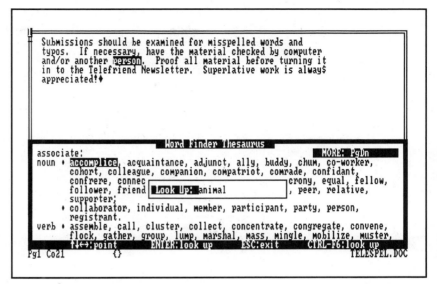

Figure 13.10: Entering a word for synonyms

SPECIFYING WORDS
NOT FOUND IN THE THESAURUS

If the thesaurus can't find your highlighted word, it displays synonyms for your word's *root word.* You can then substitute one of them for the highlighted word. Unfortunately, Word doesn't adjust the word to match the part of speech. You must do that yourself. For instance, if you look up the word "gladly," the Word Finder will display adjectives for the word "glad." Should you choose "happy" from among them, Word will substitute it as is. You'll then have to change it to "happily" in the document.

Word does, however, adjust the case (capitals or lowercase letters) to match that of the word in the document. As with the Replace command (Chapter 10), the thesaurus considers odd case combinations to be an error and ignores them.

If Word cannot find a root word in your highlighted word, it assumes you've misspelled the word and presents you with a listing of 30 suggested words for it. Word also displays the message

The word was not found. Choose another word to look up.

If the word you meant to specify is shown, you can choose it to list its synonyms. If you don't wish to avail yourself of this opportunity, press the Esc key to cancel the thesaurus operation.

Once you have chosen your words carefully, using Word's spelling checker may well be the last thing you do with your document before printing. If you send a letter to an important client, it's vital that the letter be free from spelling errors. If you send the same letter to numerous people, accuracy is all the more important or your error will multiply! Keep this in mind as we study form letters in the next chapter.

14

Creating Personalized Form Letters and Mailing Labels

Fast Track

IN CHAPTER 6, WE LEARNED HOW TO MOVE BLOCKS of text around in a file. We also learned how to take blocks of text, or even whole files, and merge them into other files. In this chapter, we will learn about merging of a different kind: namely, Word's print merge capability.

Print merge is the term Word uses for its ability to automate the production of form letters or mailing labels from a list containing names and addresses. Since most businesses need to produce many form letters and mailing labels, print merge is an indispensable feature for a word processor in the business environment. Word's print merge feature is particularly sophisticated, because it enables you to personalize your form letters to a great extent. As we will see later in this chapter, the Print Merge command allows you to use simple program statements to create form letters that reflect varying circumstances and contexts.

Before we explore such refinements, however, let's take a look at the overall print merge process so that we can produce some sample form letters.

AN OVERVIEW OF THE PRINT MERGE PROCESS

To create form letters with Word's Print Merge command, you usually set up two files. One file is essentially a list of names and addresses; we will call this file the *database*. The database contains the information that will be merged into the form letter. It stores this information in a structured fashion. First, there's a header, which indicates the order in which the information in the database is listed; for instance, it may contain "name," "phone," "address," and so on. This is followed by the actual information in the database, listed for each person in the order indicated by the header ("Jane Jones," "765-4321," "1234 Standard Blvd.," and so on). All the information pertaining to a single person or party is referred to as the *record* for that individual. Ultimately, Word will print the form letters in the same order as the records in your database.

The second file involved in the print merge process is the form letter itself. It contains the text that will be printed in all the letters. This file is called the *master form*. When you issue the Print Merge command, the computer prints the equivalent of photocopies of your master form, addressing each copy according to the information in the database file.

The master form is sometimes called the master document, the matrix, the main document, the primary document, or the invoking document. As these names indicate, the master form really controls the print merge operation. It's the file you display on the screen when you're ready to print. It is also the file that indicates which database Word should use and where the information from the database should be positioned on the printed page. To control the print merge process in these ways, the master form must contain two kinds of information in addition to the actual text of the form letter.

First, the master form must contain placemarkers or *field names* that indicate where each piece of information from the database should go in the letter. These field names ("name," "phone," "address," and so on) are the same ones that are included in the database's header. They are also called *variable names*. They must match the corresponding header exactly for the computer to recognize them in both locations. Also, each field name must be no more than one word long. However, as with file names, you can use the underline character (_) to join two words into one, for example, FIRST_NAME.

Second, the master form must contain a *merging instruction* that tells the Print Merge command which database file to use. (You may have several database files on your hard disk that can be plugged into this master form at various times.) You can also use the merging instructions to personalize the letter, as we'll see later in the chapter.

Note that the master form need not be a form letter. For example, you could also use the master form to set up the layout for printing columns of adhesive mailing labels or for creating an easily updatable name and address directory. Because form letters are by far the most common product of the master form, however, this is the first use to which we will be putting the master form in this chapter.

CREATING THE FORM LETTER

At this point we're almost ready to create the master form that appears in Figure 14.1. This master form, which you will save under

```
 ╔══════════════════════════════════════════════════════════════╗
 ║ «DATA DBBOARD»                                                 ║
 ║                                                                ║
 ║ «FIRSTNAME» «LASTNAME»                                         ║
 ║ «ADDRESS1»                                                     ║
 ║ «ADDRESS2»                                                     ║
 ║ «CITY», «STATE»  «ZIP»                                         ║
 ║                                                                ║
 ║ Dear «SALUTATION»:                                             ║
 ║                                                                ║
 ║       Please be advised that our annual meeting will take place on ║
 ║ November 28, 2054.                                             ║
 ║                                                                ║
 ║       We look forward to the honor of your presence.          ║
 ║                                                                ║
 ║ Sincerely,                                                     ║
 ║                                                                ║
 ║                                                                ║
 ║ Thomas Scrivener                                               ║
 ║                                                                ║
 ║ PS: Hope everything is fine in «CITY».□                        ║
 ║                                              ═MFMEETIN.DOC═    ║
 ║ Pg1 Co39              {}                      Microsoft Word   ║
 ╚══════════════════════════════════════════════════════════════╝
```

Figure 14.1: A master form letter

the name MFMEETIN, contains the main text of a sample form letter. I selected MF as the first two letters to indicate that it's a master form, but this convention is not required by Word. Since the point of the form letter is to inform some fictitious board members of the date of their next board meeting, the phrase MEETIN appears as part of the file name.

The main text of this form letter is quite straightforward: you can simply type it in just as you would type any other document using Word. The codes that appear in capital letters, however, are the merging instructions and the field names, and they are entered differently.

ENTERING THE MERGING INSTRUCTION

The first piece of information in the file is the merging instruction for this master form. It tells Word which data file to merge with the master form. The instruction has two parts: the DATA statement and the name of the database file that should be used—in this case, DBBOARD. The whole instruction indicates that Word should use the *data* that it finds in the DBBOARD.DOC *file* when it print merges the master form. (As usual, Word assumes a .DOC extension unless you indicate otherwise.)

DBBOARD.DOC is the database file that contains the names and addresses of the people we want to receive this mailing. Their particulars will be substituted for the field names in the form letter. In a moment, we'll see how DBBOARD is constructed. (I chose the file name DBBOARD since this file is a database, DB, containing names and addresses of the members of our fictitious board, BOARD. You are not required to follow this convention.)

Always place the DATA merging instruction at the beginning of the master form; otherwise, Word will not know which database file to merge with the master form until it reaches the data statement. In the meantime, you'd get the error message

Unknown field name

and Word would print your first letter with error messages in it.

You can enter a path as part of the DATA instruction. For instance, to specify that drive C's ADDRESS directory contains our sample database, you'd enter

«DATA C:\ADDRESS\DBBOARD»

As you can see, the entire DATA instruction, like the field names that follow it, must be enclosed with the special symbols

« »

called *chevrons*. You create these symbols by pressing Ctrl-[and Ctrl-], which appear on the screen as « and », respectively. Go ahead and type the merging instruction now. If you have trouble displaying the chevrons on your screen, verify that you are using the Ctrl key, not Shift. Note that you cannot use the greater-than or less-than signs to produce these enclosing characters. You must press Ctrl-[and Ctrl-].

I've used capital letters for the DATA instruction, but capitals are not necessary. However, capitals do serve to differentiate the merging instruction and the field names from the text.

T I P

Providing a path lets you specify data in a directory other than the one you are using when you run Print Merge.

ENTERING THE FIELD NAMES

Now type the field names and the rest of the master form, as shown in Figure 14.1. There are eight field names in our master form. Notice that the field name CITY appears in two locations.

When the information in the master form is merged with the data in the database, the resulting letters will look like the examples shown in Figure 14.2. Once you have entered the master form, you are ready for the second phase of setting up the print merge operation: namely, constructing the database file.

CONSTRUCTING YOUR DATABASE

When Word checks the database file for names and addresses during the print merge operation, it works with one name and address at a time. Each name and address make up a paragraph of data called a *record* that contains all the information about each party; each record, in turn, includes specific *field entries* for name, phone number, street address, city, and so on. When you execute the Print Merge command, Word begins with the first record and proceeds through the database, printing one form letter for each record. The print merge operation ends after Word has used the last record.

Because the computer must consult the database, you must construct the database according to certain rules. Let's go over these rules, which are illustrated in the sample database presented in Figure 14.3.

ENTERING THE HEADER RECORD

The first record in the database, shown highlighted and in capital letters in Figure 14.3, is the *header record* or *header paragraph*. This record doesn't contain information that will be printed; rather, it indicates the field names Word should apply to the records that follow. The names that you use for field names here must be identical to their counterparts in the master form.

Looking at Figure 14.3, you will notice that each field name in the header record is separated from the next by a comma. The commas tell Word where one field ends and the next begins. Remember to

Figure 12.2: Form Letters Produced by the Print Merge Operation

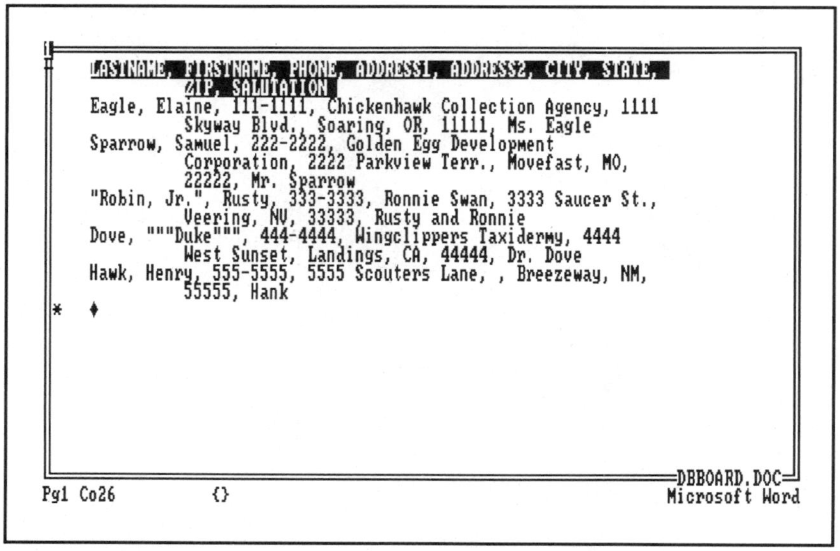

```
LASTNAME, FIRSTNAME, PHONE, ADDRESS1, ADDRESS2, CITY, STATE,
          ZIP, SALUTATION
Eagle, Elaine, 111-1111, Chickenhawk Collection Agency, 1111
          Skyway Blvd., Soaring, OR, 11111, Ms. Eagle
Sparrow, Samuel, 222-2222, Golden Egg Development
          Corporation, 2222 Parkview Terr., Movefast, MO,
          22222, Mr. Sparrow
"Robin, Jr.", Rusty, 333-3333, Ronnie Swan, 3333 Saucer St.,
          Veering, NV, 33333, Rusty and Ronnie
Dove, """Duke""", 444-4444, Wingclippers Taxidermy, 4444
          West Sunset, Landings, CA, 44444, Dr. Dove
Hawk, Henry, 555-5555, 5555 Scouters Lane, , Breezeway, NM,
          55555, Hank
*    ♦
                                                   DBBOARD.DOC
Pg1 Co26          {}                            Microsoft Word
```

Figure 14.3: A sample database

place one comma between each field name when you enter the header record.

Also, notice that there's a blank space after the comma. The space after the comma is optional. Using it, however, makes the information in the database easier to read and understand.

TIP

Make sure that the header record is the first thing in the database. You cannot enter anything before the header record, not even a paragraph mark.

You can see that each record in the database, including the header record, makes up a data paragraph. The paragraph mark (created by pressing the Enter key) indicates where one record ends and another begins. It's important not to press the Enter key until you've typed all the information that applies to a particular individual—that is, until the end of the record. As you type a record, the word-wrap feature will move the cursor to the next line as necessary. Be sure to press Enter once and only once after each paragraph of data. Do not create blank lines between the paragraphs by pressing Enter, or Word will think that you're indicating a separate record in that spot.

As with any paragraph, you can format a data paragraph as you like. Any formatted indent you select won't have any effect on the data or its appearance in the final printed material. However, indenting the paragraph can make it easier for you to read the database on the screen. In Figure 14.3, I created the hanging indent shape (by pressing Alt-T twice). Don't use the Spacebar or the Tab key after typing STATE. Press Alt-T instead. If you want some blank space between the paragraphs, use Alt-O—do not press Enter a second time.

I recommend you open a second window to prepare the database, so you can see the master form at the same time, as shown in Figure 14.4. One advantage of having both files in front of you is that you can check that the field names in both files match: they must be *identical* in spelling. For example, using FIRSTNAME in one file and FIRST_NAME or FIRSTNAMES in the other would cause an error.

Go ahead and enter the header record now, using Figure 14.3 as your guide and following the rules for entering header records I just described. When you have finished typing the header record, you will be ready to enter the data records below it.

ENTERING THE DATA RECORDS

The *data records* contain the actual information that will be printed in the form letters. Like the field names in the header record,

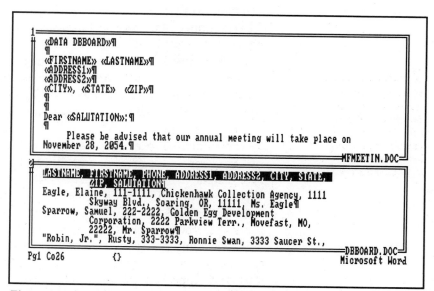

Figure 14.4: Using a second window to prepare the database

information in the data records must be separated by commas. Again, a blank space after the commas is optional.

Each piece of information (field entry) within a record must be listed in the order indicated by the header at the beginning of the database. Notice, however, that the order of the field names in the master form may differ from their order in the header record. For instance, in our sample database the header record determines that last names are listed first in the records and then first names, but in our master form we've used the first name first and then the last name. Thus, the only place you have to be concerned about corresponding order is within the database file.

Remember that information can be used in more than one spot in the master form. Likewise, you aren't required to include all the information in the database on your master form. In this master form, for example, we didn't use the phone number field anywhere, even though phone numbers are listed in the database.

Just as several databases can be plugged into one master form, you can create additional master forms that share the same database. Each master form might utilize the information in the database in a completely different way. For example, we'll later create a master form for a phone directory that uses the database file we are constructing for our form letter. We'll also see how you can use the same database to print mailing labels.

Because commas separate each data field, there must be special procedures for those instances when you need to include a comma as part of the data itself. For example, when the third data record's name is printed, it needs to appear as

Rusty Robin, Jr.

The comma between "Robin" and "Jr." is actually part of the data. Often, such a comma is called an *embedded* comma. The only way to print that comma is to enclose the name in quotation marks, like so:

"Robin, Jr."

In this case, the quotation marks indicate that all the data between them constitutes the last name.

To bring home the importance of the quotation marks, let's suppose you didn't include the quotes but rather typed the record as

Robin, Jr., Rusty, 333-3333 . . .

On encountering this information, Word would follow the field names in the header paragraph—methodically, mindlessly, and erroneously. It would read "Robin" as the last name, "Jr." as the first name, "Rusty" as the phone number, and so on. Word would find that your letter and data don't match and would display the message

Record 3: Too many fields in data or header record

It would also place data in the wrong positions in the printed form letter. The result would be the letter that you see in Figure 14.5. Notice how one simple error can throw the whole letter off.

The fact that Word is oblivious to the kind of information it is inserting into each slot can also be used to your advantage. In the same data record, notice how two names at the same address are handled. The second name is simply typed in the ADDRESS1 field. Word won't care that it's a person's name rather than an address, so it will print the second name at the location we've specified for ADDRESS1—that is, right below the other name—which is just where we want it.

Now look at the fourth data record (Figure 14.3). The name in this record would be printed as

"Duke" Dove

Notice that the first name in this record

""""Duke""""

is surrounded by a triple set of quotation marks. Because you use one set of quotes to mark the beginning and end of a field containing internal punctuation, you need to include two sets of quotes to make one set appear when the field is printed and an additional set to demarcate the field. Thus, if you wanted his actual first name and his nickname to appear as

Danny "Duke" Dove

Jr. Robin
333-3333
Ronnie Swan
3333 Saucer St., Veering NV

Dear 33333:

      Please be advised that our annual meeting will take place on November 28, 2054.

      We look forward to the honor of your presence.

Sincerely,

Thomas Scrivener

PS: Hope everything is fine in 3333 Saucer St..

Figure 14.5: Letter created by a comma error

you'd type

    Dove, "Danny ""Duke"""",

Finally, in the last data record, notice how I handled a board member who doesn't have a second address field: an additional comma marks the position. Always account for nonexisting or *null data* in this fashion. If you don't include the extra comma to mark the absence of a field entry and simply type

Hawk, Henry, 555-5555, 5555 Scouters Lane, Breezeway, NM . . .

Word will read correctly to "5555 Scouters Lane" as ADDRESS1, but will then read "Breezeway" as ADDRESS2, "NM" as the city, "55555" as the state, and "Hank" as the zip (see Figure 14.6). Again, notice how one simple error throws the whole letter off.

Let's suppose, though, that you had the opposite problem. Suppose Henry Hawk had too many address lines—say three lines, not including the city—that you wanted to print like this:

Finance Division
Telefriend International
8924 Mercury Blvd.

To get the address printed properly, enter the data in the database as follows. Type the first four entries:

Hawk, Henry, 555-5555, Finance Division

Then, instead of typing a comma, enter a new-line character by pressing Shift-Enter. The cursor will move to the next line. Continue by typing

Telefriend International, 8924 Mercury Blvd.,

and the rest of the data record. During the print merge operation, Word will consider both "Finance Division" and "Telefriend International" as part of ADDRESS1, since they're not separated from each other by a comma. It will print them on different lines, though, because they're separated by the new-line character. Word will treat "8924 Mercury Blvd." as ADDRESS2.

Though we've been using commas to separate data so far, you could also separate information with a tab instead of a comma. You should use a tab if you plan to alphabetize or otherwise sort the database (see Chapter 12). To separate the data with tabs when you have already used commas, issue the Replace command and replace

T IP

Usually the comma separates data in the database document; however, if you're using the comma as a decimal character (specified with the Options command), you'll have to use a semicolon or a tab character instead.

Henry Hawk
5555 Scouters Lane
Breezeway
NM, 55555 Hank

Dear :

　　　Please be advised that our annual meeting will take
place on November 28, 2054.

　　　We look forward to the honor of your presence.

Sincerely,

Thomas Scrivener

PS: Hope everything is fine in NM.

Figure 14.6: Letter resulting when you don't include a comma for null data

, with ^t. You may also need to use the Format Division Margins
command to make the data file wide enough that each record (paragraph of data) is no more than one line. You can then sort the data
with the Library Autosort command as you like. This way, you could
print a set of form letters in zip-code order, for instance, to take

FOREIGN FILMS [Videos in languages other than English]

Algerian
- Battle of Algiers

Bengali
- Aparajito
- Home and the World
- Pather Panchali
- World of Apu

Chinese
- Chan is Missing
- Dim Sum
- Farewell my Concubine
- Horse Thief
- Ju Dou
- Killer
- Raise the Red Lantern
- Red Sorghum
- Story of Qiu Ju
- Yellow Earth

Czech
- Closely watched Trains
- Fireman's Ball
- Larks on a String
- Loves of a Blonde
- Report on the Party and the Guests
- Shop on Main Street

Danish
- Babette's Feast (Danish & French)
- Emma's Shadow
- Gertrud (Danish & French)

Dutch
- Fourth Man
- Vanishing

French
- A Nous la Liberte
- Age d'Or
- All the Mornings in the World
- Alphaville
- L'Atalante
- Au Revoir les Enfants
- Aventure Malagache
- Babette's Feast (Danish & French) 15459
- Baker's Wife
- Baxter
- Beauty and the beast (#1241)
- La Bete Humaine

- Bizarre Bizarre
- Black and White in Color
- Blood of a Poet
- Bob le Flambeur
- Bon Voyage
- Boudu saved from Drowning
- Breathless
- La Cage aux Folles
- Camille Claudel
- Cesar
- La Chienne
- Children of Paradise
- Chocolat
- Chloe in the Afternoon
- Claire's Knee
- Cleo from 5 to 7
- Conformist
- Confidentially yours
- Contempt (English & French)
- Coup de Torchon
- Cyrano de Bergerac
- Day for Night
- Decline of the American Empire
- Delicatessen
- Diabolique
- The Diary of a Country Priest
- Dirty Dishes
- Discreet Charm of the Bourgeoisie
- Donkey Skin
- Earrings of Madame De
- Elegant Criminel
- Elevator to the Gallows
- Entre la langue et l'ocean
- Entre nous
- Eternal Return
- Fanny
- La Florida
- Forbidden Games
- 400 blows
- La Florida
- French Cancan
- Grand Illusion
- Hairdresser's Husband
- Harvest
- Hiroshima Mon Amour
- L'Homme Qui Plantait des Arbres
- Indochine
- Jacquot
- Jean De Florette
- Jonah who will be 25 in the year 2000

French continued

- Le Jour se leve
- Judex
- Jules and Jim
- King of Hearts
- Lacemaker
- Last Metro
- Last Year in Marienbad
- Leolo
- Life and Nothing But
- Lola Montes
- Love on the Run
- The Lovers
- Madame Bovary [Chabrol]
- Man who Loved Women
- Manon of the Spring
- Maria Chapdelaine
- Marius
- Masculin Feminin
- May Fools
- Mayerling
- Milky Way
- Le Million
- Mr Hulot's Holiday
- Mon Oncle
- Monsieur Hire
- Muriel
- Music Teacher
- My Father's Glory
- My Life to Live
- My Night at Maud's
- A Nous la Liberte
- Olivier Olivier
- Orpheus
- Parade
- Pauline at the Beach
- Pepe Le Moko
- Peppermint Soda
- Phantom of Liberty
- Playtime
- Les Portes Tournantes
- Raven [Le Corneau]
- Red kiss
- Return of Martin Guerre
- Rififi
- Roads to the South
- La Ronde
- Rules of the Game
- Shoot the Piano Player
- Small Change
- Soft skin
- Story of Women
- Summer
- Sundays and Cybele
- Sylvia and the Phantom
- Tall Blond Man with One Shoe
- Tatie Danielle
- Testament of Orpheus
- That Obscure Object of Desire
- 36 fillette
- Three Men and a Cradle
- Tilai
- Too Beautiful for You
- Toto le hero
- Traffic (partially dubbed in English)
- Two English girls
- Vagabond
- Van Gogh
- Vanishing
- Vincent, Francois, Paul and the others
- Wages of Fear
- Wings of Desire
- Woman Next Door
- Wuthering Heights
- Z
- Zero for Conduct

German

- Alice in the Cities
- American Friend
- Aguirre: the Wrath of God
- Blue Angel
- Boat (also known as Das Boot)
- Europa Europa
- Fitzcarraldo
- Germany in Autumn
- Kameradschaft
- M
- Maedchen in Uniform
- Marriage of Maria Braun
- Mephisto
- Nasty Girl
- Stroszek
- Testament of Dr. Mabuse
- Threepenny Opera
- Tin Drum
- Vampyr
- Veronika Voss
- Wannsee Conference
- Westfront 1918
- Zentropa

Greek

- Iphigenia
- Landscape in the Mist
- Never on Sunday

Hindi
- Distant Thunder
- Salaam Bombay
- Spices

Hungarian
- Red and the White

Indian
- Two Daughters

Italian
- Amore
- L'Avventura
- Battle of Algiers
- Before the Revolutionary
- Bicycle Thief
- Big Deal on Madonna Street
- Cinema Paradiso
- La Dolce Vita
- The Family
- Fellini Satyricon
- Fiorile
- Garden of the Finzi-Continis
- Ginger and Fred
- Gospel according to St. Matthew
- Icicle Thief
- Innocent
- Juliet of the Spirits
- Mediterraneo
- Miracle in Milan
- Night of the Shooting Stars
- Nights of Cabiria
- 1900 (Bertolucci)
- Nudo di Donna
- Open City
- Open Doors
- Passion d'Amore
- Red Desert
- Senso
- Seven Beauties
- La Signora di Tutti
- Sleazy Uncle
- Stolen Children
- La Strada
- Stromboli
- Swept Away
- Tree of Wooden Clogs
- Two Women
- Umberto D
- White Sheik

Japanese
- An Autumn Afternoon
- Bad Sleep Well
- Ballad of Narayama
- Burmese Harp
- Dersu Uzala (some dialogue
           in Russian as well)
- Dodes Ka-den
- Eijanaika
- Fires on the Plain
- Floating Weeds
- Gate of Hell
- Golden Demon
- Grave of the Fireflies (animated)
- Hidden Fortress
- High and Low
- Idiot
- Ikiru
- In the Realm of Passion
- Insect Woman
- Kagemusha
- Kwaidan
- Late Spring
- Life of O'Haru
- Lower Depths
- Mishima : a Life in Four Chapters
- Mistress
- Odd Obsession
- Onibaba
- Pornographers
- Ran
- Rashomon
- Red Beard
- Rhapsody in August
- Rikyu
- Samurai Trilogy
- Sanjuro
- Sanshiro Sugata
- Sansho the Bailiff
- Seven Samurai
- Shin Heike Monogatari
- Stray Dog
- Street of Shame
- Tampopo
- Taxing Woman
- Throne of Blood
- Tokyo Story
- Ugetsu
- Woman in the Dunes
- Yojimbo

Norwegian
- Pathfinder

Polish
- Ashes and Diamonds
- Kanal
- Knife in the Water
- Korczak
- Man of Marble

Portuguese
- Black Orpheus
- Dona Flor & her 2 husbands
- Quilombo

Romanian
- Le Chene

Russian
- Alexander Nevsky
- Andrei Roublev
- Ballad of a Soldier
- Come and See
- Commissar
- Dersu Uzala (some dialogue in Japanese as well)
- Europa Europa
- Ivan the Terrible
- King Lear (#2803)
- My Name is Ivan
- Overcoat
- Sea Gull
- Siberiade
- Solaris
- Stalker
- Taxi Blues
- War and Peace

Spanish
- Alsino and the Condor
- Brute
- Camilia
- Carmen (#5712)
- Criminal Life of Archibaldo de la Cruz
- Dracula
- Exterminating Angel
- Final Romance
- Frida
- Garden of Delights
- Illusion travels by Streetcar
- Land without Bread
- Letters from the Park
- Like Water for Chocolate
- Los Olvidados
- Nazarin
- Spirit of the Beehive
- Summer of Miss Forbes
- Tristana
- Viridiana
- Woman without Love
- Women on the Verge of a Nervous Breakdown

Swedish
- Best Intentions
- Cries and Whispers
- Devil's Eye
- Dreams
- Fanny & Alexander
- Hour of the Wolf
- House of Angels
- Intermezzo
- Lesson in Love
- Magician
- Macario
- Miss Julie
- Monika
- Montenegro
- My Life as a Dog
- Pelle the Conqueror
- Port of Call
- Sacrifice
- Sawdust and Tinsel
- Secrets of Women
- Seventh Seal
- Smiles of a Summer Night
- Summer Interlude
- Three Strange Loves
- Through a Glass Darkly
- Torment
- Virgin Spring
- Wild Strawberries
- Winter Light

Turkish
- Journey of Hope
- Yol

Ukrainian
- Shadows of Forgotten Ancestors

Yugoslav
- Time of the Gypsies
- When Father was away on Business

advantage of bulk mailing rates. (Generally, you can't sort tabbed records that contain new-line codes, as the sorted codes realign the tabbed columns incorrectly.)

Go ahead and enter the data records now. Use Figure 14.3 as your guide and follow the rules for entering data records that we have just discussed. Once you've entered the master form and the database, you're ready to print the completed form letters with the Print Merge command.

PRINTING THE LETTERS

When you invoke the Print Merge command, you must have the master form loaded and visible on the screen. If you have more than one window open, activate the window containing the master form. The database may be loaded into a second window, but it doesn't need to be. If it is, Word will use the version of the database on the screen; otherwise, it uses the one on the disk. (The one on the screen may be different if you loaded the database into the window and then made changes in it.)

You may need to adjust the settings in the Print Options menu. For instance, if you use more than one printer with your computer, you'll need to make sure the correct printer driver is specified (see Chapter 3).

Let's run the Print Merge command now.

M O U S E

Click left on Print. Then click right on Merge to select its Printer subcommand and print your form letters.

1. Press the Esc key and then type P for Print. If necessary, adjust the settings in the Print Options menu and return to the Print menu.

2. Type M for Merge and P for Printer. You'll then see

   Merging record 1. . .

   in the message area.

If you need to halt printing, press the Esc key. Printing will pause, and you can continue printing by typing Y. If you want to cancel the print merge operation altogether, press the Esc key a second time.

When you look at the printout of your five form letters, you'll notice that the one for Henry Hawk has a problem: a blank line appears between the address and the city. This occurs because we did not enter information for ADDRESS2. We'll correct the problem later in this chapter by typing a merging instruction for conditional situations such as this.

There may be other problems as well. As each form letter is printed out, different messages may appear on your screen to inform you that something has gone wrong. In addition, there may be messages printed on your letter in the field name positions. For example, the message

Unknown field name

indicates that Word cannot associate one of the field names in your master form with the labels in your database's header record. Check that the spelling is *identical* in both locations, that your labels consist of one word, and that your DATA merging instruction references the correct database.

Also, verify that you've followed all the special procedures for commas and quotation marks; otherwise, you might get the "Unknown field name" message or the message

Missing comma in data record

and Word will print the letter incorrectly.

If the message area says that there are either too few fields in the data record or too many, it means that the data in one of your data paragraphs does not correspond with the header paragraph. Count the commas in the data paragraphs, check the correspondence, and correct them as necessary.

REPRINTING PROBLEM LETTERS

Suppose that after you have finished print merging, you discover some of the letters have been printed incorrectly. How do you get Word to reprint only the incorrect letters?

One way is to specify the records that you want reprinted by number. The method of specifying records is similar to how you specify individual page numbers for printing. Simply follow these steps:

1. Initiate the Print Merge Options command (Figure 14.7).

2. Set range to Record.

3. Move to the record numbers option and specify the records by number, separating numbers with a comma and indicating a range of records by a dash or a colon.

Thus, if you specify

    1,4,7-10

Word will print the first record in the database, then the fourth, and then the seventh through tenth records.

There's another method you can use if you don't know the records by number. Here are the steps:

1. Split the screen if it is not split already, so that the master form is in one window and the database is in the other.

2. Make corrections in the database records as necessary (assuming erroneous data was the cause of the problem). You can use the Search command to locate records quickly.

3. Save the corrected version of the database for future use.

4. In the database window, delete the records that were correctly printed but *do not* save the modified database. You can delete large portions by anchoring the highlight and using the Search command to stretch it.

5. With only those records left that you want reprinted, activate the window with the master form and run Print Merge

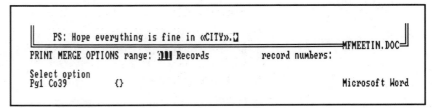

Figure 14.7: The Print Merge Options command

again. Word will use the displayed version of the database for the operation.

6. When Print Merge has finished, activate the database window and issue a Transfer Clear Window or Window Close command. Confirm with N that you want to lose the edited version. The full, corrected database will remain intact on the disk.

ALTERING PARTICULAR DOCUMENTS AS THEY ARE PRINTED

Creating a database is efficient when you have information that you want to keep and use on a regular basis, such as the database for our fictitious board. There may be occasions, however, when you want to personalize a form letter, without storing the letter for future use. For cases such as this, Word provides the special merging instructions ASK and SET.

You can use these instructions to augment information that occurs in a database or as a substitute for a database. The information you input with these instructions will normally appear only in the printed letters; it does not become a permanent part of any file. If you did want to have a record of what you typed with ASK, the only way you could do so would be to issue the Print Merge Document command and send its output to a disk file, rather than to the printer.

USING THE ASK INSTRUCTION

Let's say that you wanted to be able to add comments to the letter. You could add another field name like

«COMMENT»

as a paragraph of its own in the body of the letter. At the top of the master form, under the DATA instruction, you would add the line

«ASK COMMENT»

T I P

The Print Merge Document command is handy for personalizing form letters without using elaborate merging instructions. Using this command creates one long document that consists of one personalized letter after another. You can scroll through the letters, adding or removing material as appropriate to the recipient, and then print the document with the Print Printer command.

When you ran the Print Merge command, you would see

   RESPONSE:

appear in the command area, followed by the message

   Enter text

(see Figure 14.8). This prompt and message would appear for each record, just as Word is about to print its form letter.

When you see the prompt, you could type a comment that would never become part of the database but that would appear only in the letter that's currently being printed. For instance, you could add the following special message in a letter to one of our board members:

   Say hi to your husband and kids.

To another you could add this message:

   The coverup is going great. No one suspects a thing.

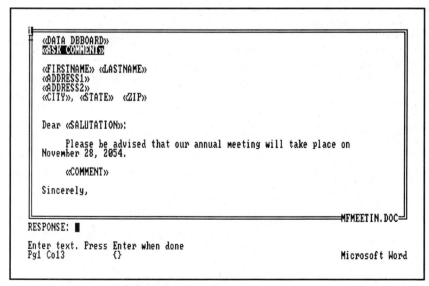

Figure 14.8: Using the ASK instruction

If you didn't have a comment to type for a particular record, you could simply press the Enter key. (To prevent a blank line from appearing in that spot, you could set up the «COMMENT» instruction as shown in the "Printing Text Conditionally" section later in this chapter.)

You can use ASK with any kind of information you want. For instance, you could type the following line into your master form:

To date, you've been responsible for raising $«HOWMUCH».

At the top of the master form you would enter the ASK instruction as

«ASK HOWMUCH»

CUSTOMIZING THE RESPONSE PROMPT   But you may have already noticed that there is a problem with the ASK instruction. Word displays all the ASK questions before printing any part of the corresponding form letter, and as you can see from Figure 14.8, the screen gives you no hint as to which letter your comments are going into. If you have more than one ASK instruction in the master form, it may also become difficult to keep track of which one you're typing during the printing process. To solve this problem, you can customize and even add other field names to the ASK prompt that appears in the message area when you run the Print Merge command. Thus for the comments example, you might want to have the message

Type comments for Elaine Eagle

appear in the message area when the first letter is being prepared. To display this message, you would modify the ASK merging instruction as follows:

«ASK COMMENT = Type comments for «FIRSTNAME» «LASTNAME»»

You simply add an equal sign and a phrase after the field name in the ASK instruction at the top of the master form.

Keep the message short—Word allows you no more than 80 characters for the message and the text substituted for the field names. (In this example, the text is "Elaine Eagle.") When you run Print

Merge, a message will appear in place of the RESPONSE prompt, clearly indicating which letter you are adding text to.

USING ASK WITHOUT A DATABASE By taking the ASK procedure one step further, you can eliminate the database from the merge print operation entirely. Since you are adding the text that varies from letter to letter with the ASK instruction, you can use ASK instructions for all the field entries in the form letter if you don't want to store that information.

Suppose you receive product inquiries every day, but you don't need to keep records on the people you send information to. In this case, you would use ASK merging instructions rather than a database. However, you would want to create a database for entries, such as our list of board members, that you would otherwise have to type again. As you would probably send information to these board members on more than one occasion, you'd want to keep their data permanently on file.

To use ASK rather than a database, you would place a series of ASK instructions for "name," "address," "city," and so on in the master form. When you run Print Merge, this master form would use data that you supply while printing. Anything you type during print merge appears only in the letter, not on disk.

When you use a database, the printing continues until all the names have been used. Without an associated database, however, Word just repeats the ASK-and-print operation over and over. To stop this looping process, you must press the Esc key.

USING THE SET INSTRUCTION

When you print merge, you may have some information that remains the same for the entire print merge operation. Suppose, for instance, you have a standard letter that is sent out by various people in the office. You would probably want to provide the signature name and keep it the same for all the letters printed. To do this, you use the merging instruction SET.

You can use the SET instruction, like ASK, alone or with a custom-tailored message. For example, at the top of the form letter you might type

«SET SIGNER = ?Enter signature name»

Then in the letter, you would add the field name for SIGNER, as I did in Figure 14.9. As soon as you ran Print Merge, you'd see the message

Enter signature name

You'd enter your name at this point, and Word would automatically print it on every letter.

You could also use this technique to print the date; however, you can use the glossary to print the date automatically (see Chapter 15).

You can also include the SET instruction to provide a value to be substituted throughout the document. If you specify

«SET NAME = Jones»

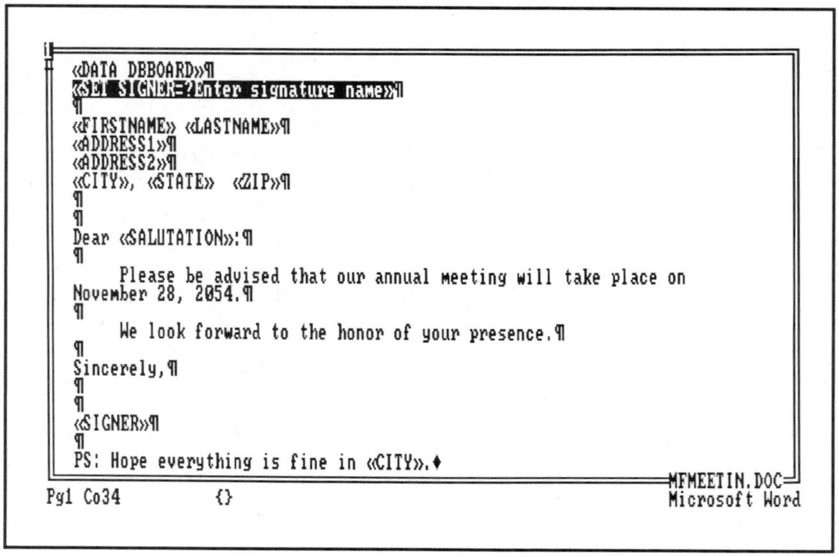

```
«DATA DBBOARD»¶
«SET SIGNER=?Enter signature name»¶
¶
«FIRSTNAME» «LASTNAME»¶
«ADDRESS1»¶
«ADDRESS2»¶
«CITY», «STATE»  «ZIP»¶
¶
¶
Dear «SALUTATION»:¶
¶
        Please be advised that our annual meeting will take place on
November 28, 2054.¶
¶
        We look forward to the honor of your presence.¶
¶
Sincerely,¶
¶
¶
«SIGNER»¶
¶
PS: Hope everything is fine in «CITY».♦
```
Pg1 Co34   {}   MFMEETIN.DOC
                                                        Microsoft Word

Figure 14.9: Using the SET instruction

at the beginning of a document, for example, Jones would replace the «NAME» label throughout the document. Lawyers, in particular, would find this feature useful for changing the name of a party in a document without having to conduct a search and replace operation. To do this, you would simply load the document, change the SET instruction to reflect the new name, and print.

MATH IN MERGING

In addition to changing text in print merge operations, you can change numerical data in your letters quickly by including math calculations. You can perform calculations with values that you store in the database or with those that you input using the ASK or SET instruction.

Suppose, for instance, that each board member in our sample database is responsible for raising $2000 in charitable contributions. You could create a field in the database called RAISED that you use to keep track of the amount the board members have been able to raise so far. In your letters to them, you could then remind them how far they have to go by inserting a line like this:

> So far, you've been responsible for contributions totaling $«RAISED». This means that you are responsible for $«2000 − RAISED» more by December 31.

You can use any of Word's numeric operators in your formulas, as Word's standard calculation methods apply (see Chapter 12).

PRINTING TEXT CONDITIONALLY

Although the SET instruction lets you substitute one piece of information in a form letter easily and the ASK instruction lets you provide varying information for each letter as you print it, you sometimes need a more sophisticated method for these two features' capabilities. That is, you might need to include information for some letters and not for others, and you may need to store all these changes, not add them as Word prints the letters. To do this, you can use the IF, ENDIF, and ELSE merging instructions. These instructions work with each other: IF and ENDIF are always seen together, but the ELSE instruction is optional.

PRINTING IF DATA PRESENT

One way you can use these instructions is to check whether there's any information present for a given field name. If there is, Word prints one thing. If there isn't, Word prints something else, or it doesn't print anything and skips to the next part of the form letter.

To handle the problem we had with ADDRESS2 in the "Henry Hawk" data record (the last record), we could use the IF and ENDIF instructions as shown in Figure 14.10.

The problem is that we want Word to print the line only if there's information for ADDRESS2. If there isn't any, as in Henry Hawk's case, we don't want to print the blank line. To give this instruction to Word, type

«IF ADDRESS2»«ADDRESS2»¶
«ENDIF»

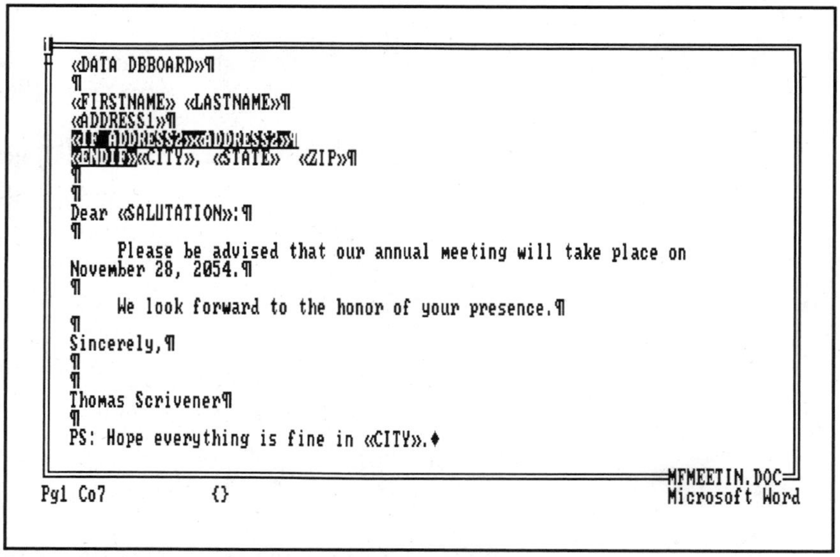

```
«DATA DBBOARD»¶
¶
«FIRSTNAME» «LASTNAME»¶
«ADDRESS1»¶
«IF ADDRESS2»«ADDRESS2»¶
«ENDIF»«CITY», «STATE»  «ZIP»¶
¶
Dear «SALUTATION»:¶
¶
        Please be advised that our annual meeting will take place on
November 28, 2054.¶
¶
        We look forward to the honor of your presence.¶
¶
Sincerely,¶
¶
¶
Thomas Scrivener¶
¶
PS: Hope everything is fine in «CITY».♦
```

Pg1 Co7   {}   MFMEETIN.DOC
                                                       Microsoft Word

Figure 14.10: Using the IF and ENDIF instructions

in place of the field name ADDRESS2 in the master form and immediately follow it with the next field name (CITY), as you see in Figure 14.10. What we're saying to Word is this: "If there's information for ADDRESS2, print that information and create a new paragraph. That's the end of the condition—continue printing the rest of the letter." Notice that the paragraph mark is part of the conditional text: if there's no information for ADDRESS2, there'll be no paragraph mark and hence no blank line (see Figure 14.11).

Now, let's look at an example that requires the ELSE condition. You might construct your database so that rather than having a SALUTATION field, you would have a field for TITLE. Let's say that you enter a title (such as "Mr.," "Ms.," or "Dr.") in the database only if you call the person by that title. For people you greet by their first name, you leave the TITLE field blank.

To do this in your master form, change the salutation line to

Dear «IF TITLE»«TITLE» «LASTNAME»«ELSE»«FIRSTNAME»«ENDIF»:

Look at this example carefully. We're telling Word to print the word "Dear" and a space; if there's a title for this person, Word prints the title followed by a space and the person's last name. Otherwise (ELSE), Word prints the person's first name. In either case, a colon follows the greeting.

COMPARISON PRINTING

Another method of printing text conditionally involves making a comparison to determine if text should be printed. One way we can accomplish this is by comparing strings, similar to how Word compares strings for the Search command.

Suppose, for example, that you want to include a special note for everyone who's from your home state of Georgia. Assuming that you always use two-letter abbreviations for the states in your database, you could type

«IF STATE = "GA"»I'm so happy to have people from my home state participating with me in this endeavor.«ENDIF»

Notice that you must enclose the data string being compared in quotation marks.

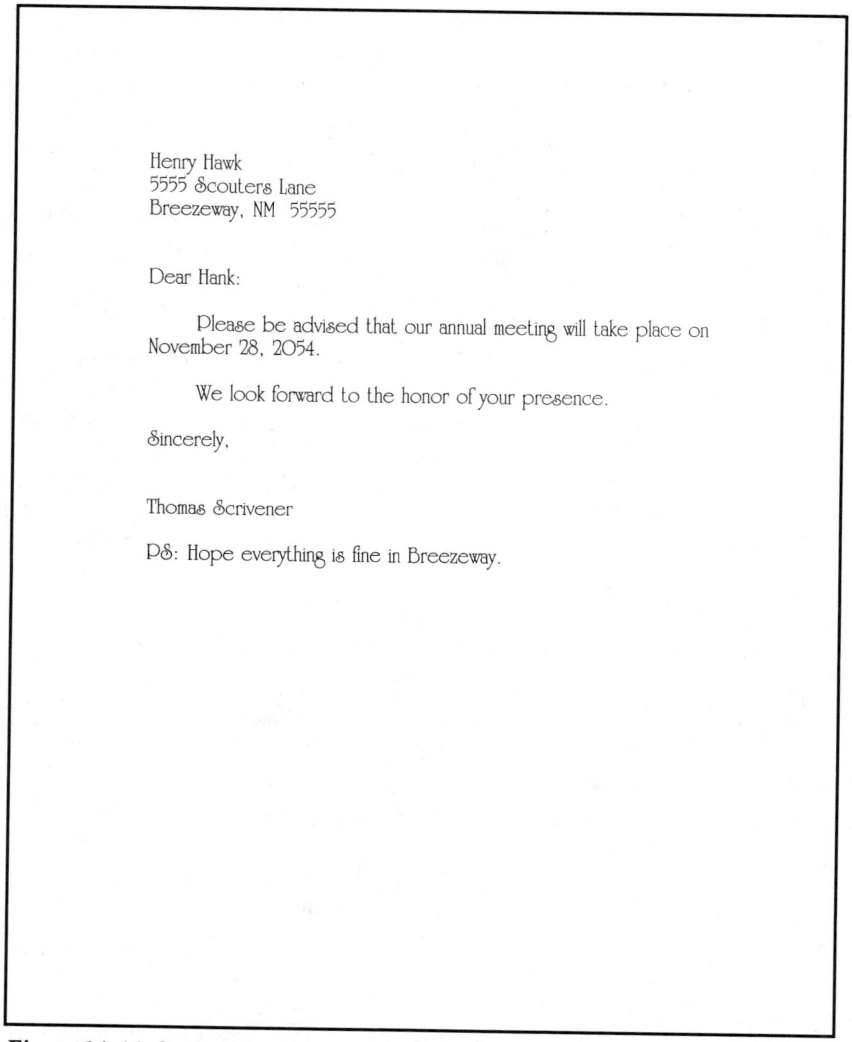

Henry Hawk
5555 Scouters Lane
Breezeway, NM 55555

Dear Hank:

Please be advised that our annual meeting will take place on November 28, 2054.

We look forward to the honor of your presence.

Sincerely,

Thomas Scrivener

PS: Hope everything is fine in Breezeway.

Figure 14.11: Suppressing an undesired blank line

If you wanted to say something along the same lines to everyone, you could use the optional ELSE instruction:

I'm so happy to have people from «IF STATE = "GA"»my home state«ELSE»your neck of the woods«ENDIF» participating with me in this endeavor.

When you use IF, ELSE, and ENDIF, watch your spacing and paragraph marks carefully. As with other characters, Word will print spaces and create new paragraphs according to your instructions. Notice that in this example there is a space after "from" and before "participating." These spaces are part of the regular text because you always want them to appear, regardless of which conditional text is used. Likewise, there are no blank spaces before or after "my home state" or "your neck of the woods." Including spaces there would add a second blank space to the printed material.

Word even allows you to place comparison instructions within comparison instructions. Supposing you wanted to provide special messages for those living in both your home state and your current residential state of Texas, you could do so by typing this instruction:

> I'm so happy to have people from «IF STATE = "GA"»my home state«ELSE»«IF STATE = "TX"»my residential state«ELSE»your neck of the woods«ENDIF»«ENDIF» participating with me in this endeavor.

Notice that you must have two ENDIF statements since you have two sets of conditional instructions (that is, two IFs).

The field name you use for these comparisons does not necessarily have to come from a database. It could be one that gets its information from an ASK statement, for instance.

Word can also make several types of numeric comparisons. Suppose you have a database for members in a club, and it has a field name called YEARINITIATED. Let's say it's now 2056 and you're sending out your annual report. You could include a congratulatory note to those members who were initiated in 2046 by typing

> «IF YEARINITIATED = 2046»Congratulations! This year you get your big tenth anniversary bash.«ENDIF»

Notice that you don't need quotation marks in a numeric comparison. You could also include an ELSE condition as follows:

> «IF YEARINITIATED = 2046»Congratulations! This year you get your big tenth anniversary bash.«ELSE»Every year is special when you belong to the TTI Executive Club.«ENDIF»

Word will also make greater-than comparisons:

«IF YEARINITIATED>2046»Before you know it, you'll be enjoying your big tenth anniversary bash.«ENDIF»

This tells Word to print the text if the year the member was initiated is greater than 2046. For older club members, you could use IF and ENDIF with a less-than comparison:

«IF YEARINITIATED<2046»We know you'll always remember that big tenth anniversary bash.«ENDIF»

If you want, you can specify an ELSE condition with the greater-than and less-than comparisons as well.

Finally, you can combine the comparison symbols to create other evaluations. Use < = for "less than or equal to" and > = for "greater than or equal to." Similarly, you can use < > to specify "not equal to." For example, if you had already sent out invitations to the tenth anniversary bash and had added a field, RSVP, in your database to keep track of who had responded, you could remind people to RSVP with

«IF YEARINITIATED = 2046 and RSVP < > "Yes"» Don't forget to reserve your place in our tenth anniversary bash.«ENDIF»

As you can see, you can include more than one record in the IF condition. To determine which records receive the statement, you can even combine fields in the IF condition with "or" or "not." For instance, you could include "or" to add a statement to letters for people celebrating their tenth anniversary and to those celebrating their twentieth anniversary. You use "not," on the other hand, to eliminate records whose specified field is blank. Thus, for our RSVP example, you could add the same reminder with the IF condition

«IF YEARINITIATED = 2046 and not RSVP»

assuming you had left all the RSVP fields blank if you had not received a reply.

PRINTING SELECTED RECORDS

We've seen how Word can alter the text of a form letter according to information that's in the database. In the examples, we've studied so far, though, everyone in the database gets a letter. But by using the SKIP instruction, you can control whether someone gets a letter at all, depending on some criteria in the database.

One way to do this is to have Word exclude the records of those people who shouldn't get letters. If you wanted to exclude people listed in our DBBOARD database who have the zip code "22222," you'd type the first line of the master form as

«DATA DBBOARD»«IF ZIP = 22222»«SKIP»«ENDIF»

(see Figure 14.12). Remember that you don't have to enclose the zip code value in quotes since it's a number.

When you print merge this master form, Word will use the database DBBOARD, checking each record's zip code. If the zip is "22222," Word doesn't print a letter for that record and skips to the next record.

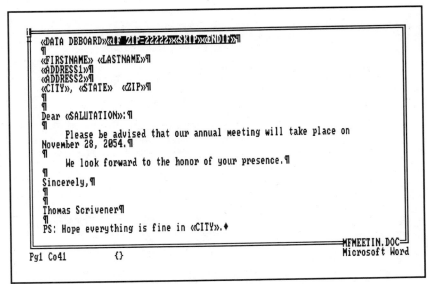

Figure 14.12: Excluding records that contain the zip code "22222"

On the other hand, you could instruct Word to print letters only for people with the zip "22222." Just replace the equals sign with not equal to (see Figure 14.13).

By using the SET statement, you could have Word request the zip code you want when you run the Print Merge command, rather than typing in the chosen zip as part of the master form. This way, you wouldn't have to change the document text to change the selection process. The merging instruction at the top would then be

«DATA DBBOARD»«SET SPECIFIEDZIP = ?Enter zip to print»
«IF ZIP < >«SPECIFIEDZIP»»«SKIP»«ENDIF»

With these instructions, Word will again use the DBBOARD database; this time, however, it will set the specified zip to the one you enter when prompted with "Enter zip to print." If a record's zip does not match the specified zip, Word will skip to the next record.

As you can see, you can handle complex situations with Word's Print Merge feature. For instance, here's a challenging problem. Suppose that you've set up your database to accommodate two full

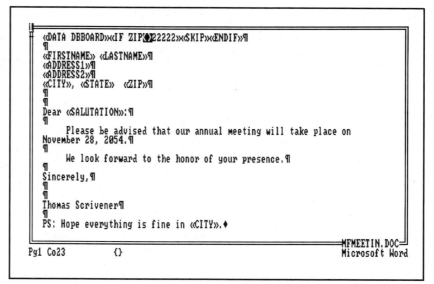

Figure 14.13: Printing only records containing the zip code "22222"

names for each address and that you've entered some records with one name, some with two, and some with no names. The object of the game is, first, to get Word to print "Dear So-and-so" for those with one name. Second, we want Word to print "Dear" with both names if the record has two names. Lastly, Word should leave out the entire salutation, *including* the "Dear," for records without names. To complicate the situation further, suppose you inadvertently entered some records' single name in the spot for the *second* name. Can Word possibly handle such a complicated but realistic situation?

Yes, it can. The trick is to get Word to print the text if there is no data specified for a name. We do so by immediately following IF statements with ELSE statements. Figure 14.14 shows you how to solve the problem.

Here's how we can paraphrase your instructions to Word. These steps coincide with the syntax given in Figure 14.14.

1. Test for records containing just a first name. If there's a second name, don't print anything yet; if the record doesn't have a second name and there's something for the first name, print "Dear," a space, the first name, a colon, and a paragraph mark.

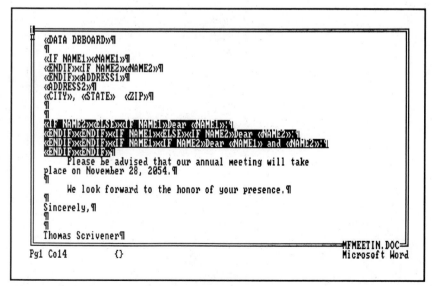

Figure 14.14: Printing text with no data present

2. Test for records containing a second name only. If there's something for the first name, don't print anything yet; otherwise, if there's something for the second name, print "Dear," a space, the second name, a colon, and a paragraph mark.

3. Test for records with both first and second names. If the first name has nothing in it, don't print anything on this line. If there's something entered for both names, print "Dear," a space, the first name, a space, the word "and," a space, the second name, a colon, and a paragraph mark.

Word's merging instructions cover many circumstances. As you gain experience with Word, you'll discover other ways to adapt these instructions for your needs. There is one other merge instruction, NEXT, that can assist you in an entirely different situation than the one we explored with our form letter. Let's see how you can use the NEXT instruction.

PRINTING MORE THAN ONE RECORD ON THE SAME PAGE

When you're using Print Merge, Word normally begins a new page each time it encounters a new record in the database. For some applications, such as directories, however, you'll want to have information from more than one record on the same page. In this case, you want Word to go to a new page only when it runs out of room on the current page.

For circumstances such as these, you'll need to include the NEXT instruction in the master form and create a master form that fills a printed page. The NEXT instruction tells Word to go to the next record and continue printing on the same page.

Figure 14.15 presents this type of master form in the top window. You have to include enough sets of field names, separated by NEXT instructions, in the master form to fill a printed page. (You could do this easily by using one of the copy techniques and checking the page number in the command area to verify the page depth.)

The second window in Figure 14.15 displays our sample database. When you merge this database with the new master form, you get the

```
‖‖«DATA DBBOARD»
‖‖Phone Directory

  «PHONE»        «FIRSTNAME» «LASTNAME»
  «NEXT»
  «PHONE»        «FIRSTNAME» «LASTNAME»
  «NEXT»
  «PHONE»        «FIRSTNAME» «LASTNAME»
  «NEXT»
  «PHONE»        «FIRSTNAME» «LASTNAME»
  «NEXT»
  «PHONE»        «FIRSTNAME» «LASTNAME»
                                                     ═MFPHONES.DOC═
2
‖‖ LASTNAME, FIRSTNAME, PHONE, ADDRESS1, ADDRESS2, CITY, STATE,
         ZIP, SALUTATION
  Eagle, Elaine, 111-1111, Chickenhawk Collection Agency, 1111
         Skyway Blvd., Soaring, OR, 11111, Ms. Eagle
  Sparrow, Samuel, 222-2222, Golden Egg Development
         Corporation, 2222 Parkview Terr., Movefast, MO,
         22222, Mr. Sparrow
                                                     ═DBBOARD.DOC═
  Pg1 Co1            {}                          Microsoft Word
```

Figure 14.15: Using the NEXT instruction to print records on the same page

printout shown in Figure 14.16. Because there are only five records
in the database, the printout occupies only one page. In a larger database, however, a new page would be started each time Word came to

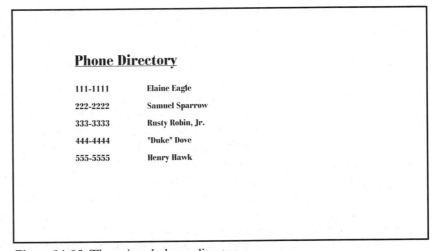

Figure 14.16: The printed phone directory

the end of the master form, as long as there were more records in the database.

PRINTING MAILING LABELS

The NEXT instruction is also an important component for creating some mailing label formats. Labels come on continuous paper (one long sheet of labels that is fan-folded in a box) or individual sheets, and you need to adjust how Word prints the labels, depending on their type. If you have a tractor-feed printer (commonly, a dot-matrix printer), you'll use continuous labels. With a laser printer, you'll use sheets of labels. Labels are side by side on the sheet and can be in one, two, or three columns. Let's examine how to use NEXT to create continuous three-across labels. Note that because this procedure is for continuous labels, it won't work with a laser printer as is. But later I'll explain how you can adapt the master form for use with this type of printer.

You can use Word's multicolumn layout with the Print Merge command to create continuous three-across mailing labels. Let's practice doing this using the same database that we've been working with. You can see the master form you need to create for this application and the Format Division Margins menu settings for it in Figure 14.17.

The strategy I employed in the figure may be a little difficult to follow, because I had to trick Word somewhat to get it to print the labels correctly. Here's how I did it. First, let's assume that you are using adhesive labels that come 33 to a page. If we set the page length option to 1 inch for this purpose, Word will consider each row of labels a page. To use the entire label surface, I eliminated the top, right, and bottom margins and narrowed the left margin considerably. Finally, I issued the Format Division Layout command, setting number of columns to 3 and space between columns to 0.

In the master form, I typed three sets of field names. Each of these prints one "column" (address label) on a "page" (row of address labels). The NEXT instruction in the master form tells Word to print the next record on the same sheet of labels instead of advancing the fan-folded sheet.

Note that when you register the settings after entering the text for the master form, the field name «LASTNAME» on the first line of the form

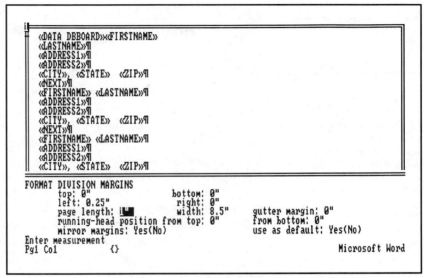

```
«DATA DBBOARD»«FIRSTNAME»
«LASTNAME»¶
«ADDRESS1»¶
«ADDRESS2»¶
«CITY», «STATE» «ZIP»¶
«NEXT»¶
«FIRSTNAME» «LASTNAME»¶
«ADDRESS1»¶
«ADDRESS2»¶
«CITY», «STATE» «ZIP»¶
«NEXT»¶
«FIRSTNAME» «LASTNAME»¶
«ADDRESS1»¶
«ADDRESS2»¶
«CITY», «STATE» «ZIP»¶

FORMAT DIVISION MARGINS
        top: 0"                    bottom: 0"
        left: 0.25"                 right: 0"
        page length: 11█           width: 8.5"      gutter margin: 0"
        running-head position from top: 0"          from bottom: 0"
        mirror margins: Yes(No)                     use as default: Yes(No)
Enter measurement
Pg1 Co1              {}                                  Microsoft Word
```

Figure 14.17: Creating three-across mailing labels with a master form and the Format Division Margins menu

will move to the second line, due to the narrowness of the column. Don't worry, though, Word will still print last names on the first line of the labels.

The printout resulting from this master form will have names and addresses printed on the adhesive labels, in order from left to right across the three columns and down the page. Be careful that the items in your database do not exceed the width of the columns. You may need to shorten company names, for instance.

To use this file with individual sheets of labels, you set up an 8½-by-11-inch page in a 3-column format and fill the page with sets of name and address fields. Issue the Format Division Layout command and set number of columns to 3. To make full use of the labels, set space between columns to 0. Then, with the Format Division Margins command, set page length to 11 and set the margins to account for any area where your printer cannot print. Finally, make numerous copies of the name-and-address fields, enough to fill the entire page.

OTHER PRINT MERGE OPERATIONS

The examples we've studied so far have all centered on the use of the master form and one other file at most—in our examples, this second file has been a database. The Print Merge command can also be used, however, to combine numerous other files with a master form in a variety of ways.

With Word, you can create a master form that might print little or no text, but serves instead to coordinate the printing of other files. An example of such a master form file is shown in Figure 14.18. You can use this sample form to print sections of a paper one after another. You might want to do this so that you can organize parts of a long document into separate files—it will then be easier to work with the different sections. Merging them together again with the master form would print these files as a seamless document.

The files in this example are named SECTIONA, SECTIONB, and so on. The first INCLUDE instruction tells Word to print SECTIONA. After printing this file, Word refers back to the master form, where the second INCLUDE instruction tells it to print SECTIONB, and so on. The whole procedure is called *file chaining*.

T I P

Word provides you with a macro, **chain-print.mac**, that prints one document after another according to a list you provide and numbers the pages in a continuous sequence (see Appendix C).

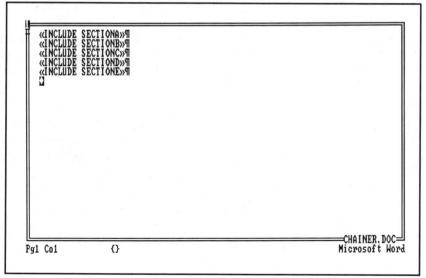

Figure 14.18: File-chaining instructions

The effect of file chaining is somewhat like that of Word's Print Queue command. In contrast to the Print Queue command, however, the master form file is permanent. You don't have to retype the names of the files to reprint them. Also, Word will treat the resulting printout as one document. Pages will be numbered accordingly, and footnote numbering will also be consecutive.

If you want one or more of the files to start at the top of a new page, be sure to enter a page-break character (Ctrl-Shift-Enter) either at the end of one file or at the beginning of the next file, or in the master form between INCLUDE instructions.

You can also have the included files call out other files themselves. Such an arrangement is often referred to as *file nesting*. For example, the SECTIONA file might contain the following merging instructions:

```
INCLUDE SECTIONA.1
INCLUDE SECTIONA.2
```

If you want to use a database with the included files and the master form, you add the DATA merging instruction to the master form and place the field names in the correct locations in the included files. The data in the database will then be referenced when you merge the files.

Although the merged included files are considered one document, you cannot create an index or a table of contents for the merged document (see Chapter 19). Instead, you must issue either the Transfer Merge or Print Merge Document command and combine the subordinate files into one before compiling those features.

The Print Merge command offers you a great deal of flexibility in selecting records to print and in personalizing your correspondence. In fact, you can even use data from other programs with this command, as you'll see in Chapter 18. We'll also see a lot of the merging instructions as we study Word's macro system in the next chapter, where they provide flexibility in automating commands.

15

Timesaving with Glossaries and Macros

Fast Track

WORD'S GLOSSARY FEATURE IS A CONVENIENT TOOL for writing documents. In this chapter, I will show you how to save time by using the NORMAL.GLY glossary as you initially type your text. In addition, Word provides three other glossaries and lets you create as many other glossaries as you need. We'll study why you might want that and how to manipulate multiple glossaries. Word also allows you to save time in performing repetitive operations by using *macros,* a specialized glossary application. We'll begin by examining the standard glossary's ability to enter text.

ENTERING TEXT QUICKLY

The concept of an electronic glossary is simple. In everyday usage, a *glossary* is a list of defined words—a vocabulary, if you will, for a particular book or field of knowledge that is prepared by an expert in the field. The glossary lists and defines the terms that are like code words to people who work in the given field.

Word's glossary is similar. With it, you are the resident expert. You create a list of code words or abbreviations to represent text that you would otherwise have to type over and over. Along with these codes, you supply their definition: the word, phrase, or even paragraphs that you want associated with each code.

In building the glossary, you can also assign abbreviations to hard-to-type text that you only need to use once in a while. Such text can be fully formatted, using any of the Alt codes or Format subcommands. Then, when you type an abbreviation (code) and tell Word to use the glossary, Word replaces the code with the entire corresponding text in your document. As a result, you type less and commit fewer typing errors.

What's an example of text that might be usefully placed in a glossary? A good glossary entry might be something as large as a standard legal paragraph or as complex as a scientific formula. You might also wish to put your return address in the glossary. If, for instance, you decided to abbreviate your return address as "ra," you could simply type "ra" and tell Word that "ra" is an abbreviation, anytime you wanted the return address to appear in your document. Thus, when you enter the glossary abbreviation (in this case, "ra") and press the Glossary key (F3), the entire glossary text (that is, the address) will be displayed in the document on the screen.

Your speed and accuracy both increase because the correctly typed address is permanently on file. All you have to do is type the short abbreviation correctly or select it from a list of abbreviations.

Table 15.1 lists some examples of glossary text along with abbreviations that could be used to represent the text. Because your glossary is your own personalized creation, you can use any abbreviations you want; those shown are just examples.

All glossary work in Word occurs internally; you can't inspect or edit the glossary directly. Instead, you input and gain access to glossary entries via their abbreviations. Even though you can't view the glossary as a file, however, it is stored in your hard disk directory, just like any other document. In fact, you can print out the complete contents of the glossary.

Glossary procedures closely parallel procedures Word uses elsewhere. You use the Copy, Delete, and Insert commands, for instance, to add entries to and extract entries from the glossary. As you will recall, Copy, Delete, and Insert usually operate with the

Table 15.1: Sample Glossary Entries

ABBREVIATION	TEXT
acd	asynchronous communication device
char	The characters depicted herein are fictitious. Any similarity to real persons living or dead is strictly coincidental.
dow	Dow Jones Industrial Average
hist	HISTORY OF PRESENT ILLNESS:
p1	party of the first part
price	Prices and availability subject to change without notice. California residents add $6^{1}/_{2}\%$ sales tax.
sop	standard operating procedure
tt	Telefriend Electronic Travel: We'll Phone You!

scrap area. It's not surprising, therefore, that your glossary entries are treated as so many scraps of text. Another parallel between the glossary and the rest of Word is the group of commands known as the Transfer Glossary commands. These commands (Transfer Glossary Load, Transfer Glossary Save, Transfer Glossary Clear, and Transfer Glossary Merge) act on the entire glossary—to move it to and from the disk, for instance—just as the corresponding Transfer commands operate on entire documents. First, though, let's consider how to add entries to the standard glossary.

CREATING GLOSSARY ENTRIES

You can place entries in the glossary with either the Copy command or the Delete command. There's no limit to the number of glossary entries that the computer can hold—no limit, that is, beyond the number imposed by the available space on your hard disk. If you use the Copy command, text you assign to an abbreviation will be sent to the glossary and remain on the screen as well. If you use the Delete command, the glossary text will be sent to the glossary and disappear from the screen; it will no longer be part of the displayed document.

Unlike operations involving the scrap area, you cannot use the Insert or Delete keys with the glossary. Only the Delete, Copy, and Insert commands operate with the glossary. Let's begin by deleting some text to the glossary.

USING THE DELETE COMMAND TO MAKE GLOSSARY ENTRIES

The process of making a glossary entry involves several steps. First of all, type and format the text for the glossary entry. It can be any length you want. Let's use this return address for our example:

1234 Easy Street
Facile City, OK 11111

You can type the text in any activated window, anytime you want. Type it just as you'd want it to appear whenever you use the abbreviation.

Format is as you like, assigning fonts, paragraph alignments, and so on. Press the Enter key at the end if you want a paragraph mark to be included.

Once the material is just as you want it, it's ready to be submitted to the glossary. As with so many other operations in Word, you must first designate the text that you want affected by highlighting it and then perform the appropriate procedure. Be sure to highlight the normally invisible characters, such as paragraph marks, that you want as well. If you're not sure where these characters are located, display them by issuing the Options command and changing show nonprinting symbols to Partial or All.

Once you've highlighted the text, you are ready to initiate the Delete command. Let's look at how the procedure is accomplished with our sample return address. You might want to practice now, using your actual return address, so that you begin to build your glossary.

MOUSE

Type the return address and highlight it. Click left on Delete (clicking right would send the text to the scrap area) and type the abbreviation for the glossary text ("ra"). Then click either button on DELETE to register the command.

1. Type in the text you want in the glossary: in this case, the return address.

2. Highlight the text. You can use the Paragraph key (F10) to do this, provided you pressed Shift-Enter to create new-line marks at the ends of all but the last line when you typed the address.

3. Press Esc and type D for Delete. Word then suggests deleting to the scrap area by displaying

   DELETE to: { }

4. Instead of accepting Word's suggestion, type the abbreviation you want in its place like so:

   DELETE to: ra

   The scrap symbol disappears as soon as you start typing.

5. Press the Enter key to register the command.

At this point the text will disappear from the screen; Word has deleted it to the glossary and recorded it there under the glossary abbreviation "ra."

You will want to delete to the glossary when you create entries that are unrelated to the document you're editing. Suppose, for instance, that you're typing along and suddenly you're reminded of an entry you've been wanting to add to the glossary. Even though the entry might have nothing to do with text that you're currently working on, you can type it and then delete it to the glossary. This removes it from the displayed document on the screen.

USING THE COPY COMMAND
TO MAKE GLOSSARY ENTRIES

The second way to send text to the glossary is by means of the Copy command. With the Copy command, the material remains on the screen, and an exact copy is sent to the glossary. This is a handy ability. Imagine, for example, that as you are typing along, you realize that you've just typed the same passage for the umpteenth time. You decide that it's time to assign this passage to the glossary. All you have to do is highlight what you've just typed and issue the Copy command to send it to the glossary. The text will remain in the document, and a copy of it will be entered in the glossary as well.

Using the Copy command, let's enter a phone number into the glossary under the abbreviation "ph." Here are the steps:

1. Type the material you want in the glossary. Use a fictitious number or your own phone number.

2. Highlight the phone number. In this case, you could expand the cursor to the left or press the Line key (Shift-F9) to highlight it.

3. Press the Esc key and then type C for Copy.

4. Type your abbreviation in place of the proposed scrap symbol like so:

   COPY to: ph

5. Press the Enter key to register the command.

This time, the text remains on the screen. In fact, everything looks just as it did before the glossary maneuver. Now, though, your glossary has two abbreviations in it, "ra" and "ph," along with their corresponding glossary text. We'll see how you can verify that it does contain these entries in a moment.

MOUSE

Type the material bound for the glossary and highlight it. Click left on Copy and type the abbreviation for the text, in this case, "ph." Then click either button on COPY to complete the command.

GUIDELINES FOR
FORMING GLOSSARY ABBREVIATIONS

When you assign a glossary abbreviation, it must be one word. You can simulate a space within the abbreviation by using the underline character (_). You can also use the period (.) and the hyphen (-). In addition, you can use letters or numbers, but you can't use any other symbols (for instance, no commas). You can also assign a Ctrl code to a glossary entry that allows you to insert it quickly. I discuss this technique, which is generally used with macros, in the "Using the Ctrl Codes" section, later in this chapter.

For example, you might want to use "now here" to represent "Now, here's a word from our sponsor, Telefriend Teleportation Travel Systems." You couldn't use "now here" because that's two words, but you could use this abbreviation:

    now_here

You can often just avoid using more than one word or run a two-word abbreviation together, unless such combining would result in confusion. In our example, for instance, uniting the words could make it appear that the abbreviation is "no where" instead of "now here."

Although you can include up to 31 characters in a glossary abbreviation, you will usually want to keep your abbreviations as short as possible to make the most efficient use of the glossary.

As you develop your glossary, be careful when assigning glossary names that you don't duplicate one that's already on file. If you do, Word will display the message

Enter Y to replace glossary entry, N to retype name, or Esc to cancel

Type Y if you want your new text to replace the text that's currently assigned to the abbreviation, type N if you want to use a new abbreviation, or press Esc if you no longer want to make an entry. Of course, there may be times when you want to substitute new text for the current glossary text: if a glossary phone number has changed, for instance. If you're not sure whether the abbreviation exists, you can look at a list of the abbreviations currently on file as you use the Copy or Delete command.

CONSULTING THE GLOSSARY LIST TO MAKE ENTRIES

For practice, let's call up the list of abbreviations while using the Copy command. After typing the text you wish to place in the glossary and highlighting it, issue the Copy command. When you see the prompt

COPY to: {}

press F1 to display the list of abbreviations. You'll see a listing such as the one shown in Figure 15.1. Note that the listing is presented in alphabetical order. Just check the listing for the abbreviation you want for the glossary entry and select it. When prompted, you can type Y to replace the existing glossary text with the highlighted text.

You are not committed to selecting from the list just because you displayed it; you can still type a response. If you want, you can display the list to verify that the abbreviation isn't already in use and then type it.

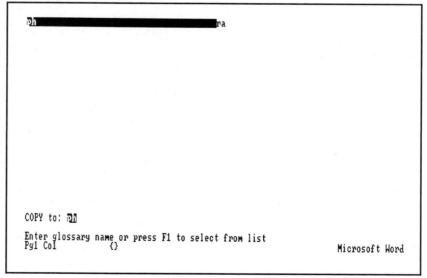

Figure 15.1: A sample glossary listing

SAVING GLOSSARY ENTRIES

Now that we've got some entries in the glossary, let's see how to save them. Adding entries to the glossary is only temporary at first—they are placed in the computer's RAM area but are not automatically stored on disk. This means that if you quit Word without saving the entries, they will be gone when you come back. For permanent storage, you must save the glossary. Word 5 has four Transfer Glossary commands, as shown in Figure 15.2. Transfer Glossary Save allows you to save entries on disk.

When you issue Transfer Glossary Save, Word proposes a name for the glossary: NORMAL.GLY. (The file name stands for the glossary—GLY—normally used—NORMAL.) Each time you start up Microsoft Word, the program automatically loads the NORMAL.GLY file located in the current directory when you start Word. Because of this, you can have a different NORMAL.GLY file in each directory that corresponds to the Word documents stored in that directory, and you can use the glossary right away to submit and retrieve text: you don't need to load it separately.

Follow these steps to save your glossary:

1. Press the Esc key to activate Command mode.

2. Type T for Transfer and type G for Glossary to display the Transfer Glossary subcommands.

3. Type S for Save. Word then displays the Transfer Glossary Save command, proposing the current directory's NOR-MAL.GLY file as the glossary to save to (see Figure 15.3).

4. Accept the suggestion and complete the command by pressing the Enter key.

M O U S E

Click left on Transfer and click left on Glossary to display its subcommands. Click right on Save to save your entries to NORMAL.GLY.

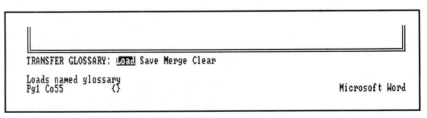

Figure 15.2: The Transfer Glossary command

```
 ┃
 ┃
 ┃
 ┃
 TRANSFER GLOSSARY SAVE filename: C:\WORD\NORMAL.GLY
 Enter filename
 Pg1 Co55          {}                              Microsoft Word
```

Figure 15.3: The Transfer Glossary Save command

New in
Word 5

In addition, you can save all displayed documents and the glossary at the same time by issuing the Transfer Allsave command. This command also saves the style sheets associated with the displayed documents. (For more on style sheets, see Chapter 17.)

If you don't use the glossary often, you might find that you don't remember to save your entries before quitting your session with Word. If this is the case, when you invoke the Quit command, you will see the message

Enter Y to save changes to glossary, N to lose changes, or Esc to cancel

To save your glossary, type Y at this point. If you decide that you don't want your glossary entries, type N and the glossary will remain as it was when last saved. If you decide that you don't want to quit after all, you can press the Esc key to cancel the command.

You could get the same message when you give the Transfer Clear All command because this command clears the glossary and reloads NORMAL.GLY (from the directory specified by the Transfer Options command). You can again choose to save the revised glossary, lose your changes, or cancel the command.

INSERTING FROM THE GLOSSARY

So far, we have only prepared the glossary; we have yet to use it to save time when creating documents. Let's practice adding glossary entries to a document now. First, clear the screen.

Word provides two ways to get material from the glossary: the Glossary key (F3) and the Insert command. Generally, you'll want to

T I P

Word supplies a macro, **repl_w_gloss.mac**, that replaces each occurrence of the specified text with the contents of a glossary entry you choose (see Appendix C).

use the Glossary key because it's fast and simple. Use the Insert command when you want to see the list of glossary abbreviations. We'll see how they work by trying them out on our glossary entries for the return address and phone number.

USING THE GLOSSARY KEY (F3)

One way to add a glossary entry to your document is to type the abbreviation and then press the Glossary key to indicate to Word that what you've typed is a glossary abbreviation. You would type the abbreviation in the spot where you want the full text to appear. In the case of the return address, you would type

ra

and then press the Glossary key (F3).

When you press the Glossary key, Word looks to see which word precedes the cursor and looks up that abbreviation in the glossary, provided the cursor is no larger than one character. The cursor and the word can be separated by spaces, but do not press Enter or the Tab key before pressing the Glossary key. If you have expanded the cursor to highlight more than one character, Word looks up all the highlighted text. In either case, the abbreviation must be one that the glossary has on file.

Suppose you forget which abbreviations are in the glossary. In this case, it would be best to use the other method of adding glossary text to your document: the Insert command.

USING THE INSERT COMMAND WITH THE GLOSSARY LIST

Let's use the Insert command to insert the phone number from the glossary into a document. This time, imagine that you want to insert your phone number after typing this phrase:

For additional information, please call us at

However, you can't remember the abbreviation you used to represent your phone number.

M *O U S E*

Type the regular text, leaving the cursor where you want the glossary text to appear. Click left on Insert. Click right on the from field to display the list of abbreviations and click right on the abbreviation you want (in this case, "ph").

1. With the cursor where you want the glossary text to appear (leave a space after "at"), press the Esc key.

2. Type I to display the Insert command.

3. To see the glossary abbreviations on file, press F1. You'll see a display similar to that shown in Figure 15.4.

4. Move the highlight to "ph" and press the Enter key to register your choice. The full glossary text—that is, the phone number—will appear in the document in the correct position, and Word will return to Document mode.

When you invoke the Insert command, you could type the glossary abbreviation if it came to you before displaying the list. Usually, however, you will only use the Insert command if you need to select an abbreviation from the list. If you already know the abbreviation, it's quicker just to type the abbreviation in the document and press the Glossary key (F3).

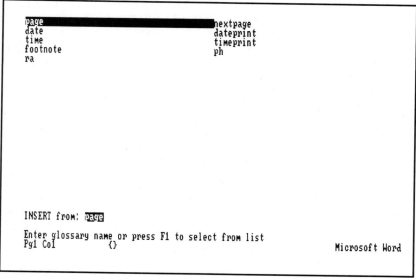

Figure 15.4: Inserting from the glossary

AUTOMATICALLY PRINTING THE DATE AND TIME

When you looked at the list of glossary abbreviations, you undoubtedly noticed several abbreviations that you didn't place in the glossary. Word uses the two entries "page" and "nextpage" to insert the page number and the number of the next page in your document. As you may recall, you added the "page" entry to your document in Chapter 9. You can also insert the footnote entry if you should accidentally delete a footnote reference while revising your document. To do so, type

footnote

and press F3 or use the Insert command to select it from the list.

Additional entries are "date," "time," "dateprint," and "timeprint." These entries allow you to date and time-stamp your documents automatically, using the operating system date and time.

For example, you can display the date in the document you're working on by typing the word

date

and pressing the Glossary key (F3). When you do this, "date" will disappear and in its place today's date will appear, spelled out in full. You can also use the Insert command and select "date" from the glossary's list to achieve the same end.

Using the "time" entry operates in the same fashion. Word displays afternoon and evening hours with PM, even though you enter them with 24-hour time.

The "dateprint" entry is similar, but it indicates the date a document is printed. Once you press the Glossary key (F3) or complete the Insert command, you won't see the date appear. Instead, you'll see the entry surrounded by parentheses, like so:

(dateprint)

When you print the document, Word will substitute the current date in place of this parenthetical code. This entry is particularly useful if you are working on a document over several days and want the final version to display the date it is printed. By comparison, the regular date entry shows the date that you typed the entry into the document. The glossary's "timeprint" entry works in the same fashion, with respect to the time at which you print the document.

Notice that the reserved abbreviations did not appear on the Copy menu. That's because you can't copy any text to them, as they are reserved for use by Word. Because Word inserts special material with these abbreviations, you'll receive the message

Reserved glossary name

if you attempt to assign glossary text to them.

You can also change the format of the date and time that Word displays and prints. Issue the Options command and change the appropriate option. Set date format to MDY (month, day, year format, as in January 1, 1990) or DMY (day, month, year format, as in 1 January 1990). You can set the Options command's time format option to 12- or 24-hour format.

Finally, note that if you are running Word under Microsoft Windows (see Chapter 7), you will see the "clipboard" reserved glossary entry. Use this entry to insert text from the Microsoft Windows clipboard.

SAVING FORMATS IN THE GLOSSARY

As I mentioned, the text you store in the glossary keeps its formatting. When you work with paragraph formatting, though, remember that it's the paragraph mark that stores the formatting for the paragraph. Thus, if you wish to store the paragraph formatting, you must include that mark as part of the text that you copy or delete to the glossary.

Since the paragraph mark stores the formatting, you can create a glossary entry that contains just the formatted paragraph mark and no other text. The mark can be formatted as justified, double-spaced, indented, and so on, as discussed in Chapter 5. After adding the entry to your glossary, type its abbreviation where you would normally press Enter and retrieve the paragraph mark by pressing the Glossary key (F3). This action formats the paragraph automatically.

You can also format the division mark, discussed in Chapter 9, and store it in the glossary. Thus, you could have various division-mark entries; for example, one for the first page of a document that prints the page number on the bottom center and has a large top margin, and another for printing the page number on the bottom right and using standard margins. Remember to insert the division mark at the end of the section you want to format.

I don't recommend that you save many format entries, as you may find it difficult to keep track of them, especially if you create highly customized formats. Your best bet is to use style sheets instead (see Chapter 17). If you only have one or two simple formats, however, you might prefer to use the glossary, especially if you're already using the glossary for other purposes.

Regardless of how many glossary entries you create for formats, you will occasionally need to review the contents of your glossary. Let's see how to do this next.

PRINTING THE GLOSSARY

You can print the contents of the glossary by using Word's Print Glossary command. The command is simple and straightforward. When you issue the command, it prints according to the settings specified in the Print Options command. If you have any trouble printing, be sure to check your established settings. The printout lists glossary abbreviations on the left and their corresponding glossary text to the right.

You may want to print your glossary periodically to keep track of your revisions to it. You can even refer to it to double-check an abbreviation or text entry if necessary.

CLEARING GLOSSARY ENTRIES

If you print the glossary and find that there is a glossary entry you no longer use, you can remove it from the glossary. You might want to do this to free up some disk space or so that you'll have fewer entries to view when you use the Insert command to choose an abbreviation. To clear out individual entries or the entire glossary, use the Transfer Glossary Clear command.

M_O U S E_

Save the glossary if
you have made
changes to it recently.
Then click left on
Transfer, click left on
Glossary, and click
either button on Clear.

1. Press the Esc key to activate Command mode.

2. Before clearing, you should save the glossary as it is with the Transfer Glossary Save command, in case you accidentally clear the wrong entries.

3. Press Esc to return to the main command menu and type T for Transfer.

4. Type G for Glossary and C for Clear to use this subcommand.

Once the Transfer Glossary Clear command appears (see Figure 15.5), you can type the abbreviation to be erased from the glossary and then press Enter. You can also press F1 or click right in the names field to display the abbreviation list and then select your choice from the list.

If you press the Enter key without displaying the list or typing an abbreviation, you will erase all the entries in the glossary at once. For this reason, exercise caution when using the Transfer Glossary Clear command: if you change your mind about clearing, press the Esc key to cancel the command—not Enter. (Even if you do delete entries unintentionally, though, the action won't affect the glossary on the disk until you save.)

Suppose, however, you want to delete several entries but not the entire glossary. You can specify multiple entries by alternately typing an entry and pressing the comma key, or by alternately selecting an entry from the list and entering a comma. Don't add spaces after the commas. You'll probably want to display the list even if you type the entries so that you know you're typing the abbreviations correctly.

M_O U S E_

To specify multiple
entries, alternately
click left on an entry
and press the comma
key. Do not add a
comma after the final
entry. Then click on
TRANSFER GLOS-
SARY CLEAR to
clear the selected
entries.

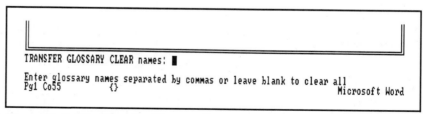

Figure 15.5: The Transfer Glossary Clear command

When you delete one or more entries or clear the entire glossary, Word requests verification from you by displaying the message

Enter Y to erase glossary names

You can cancel the deletions by typing N for No or pressing the Esc key. Both keys return Word to Document mode.

If you delete some entries by accident, the last version you saved on the disk will still be there. To ensure that accidental changes can be remedied, save the glossary regularly.

If you have only one glossary, you'll probably want to keep it active for the next document you work on. To do this, issue the Transfer Clear Window command and load the next document. The glossary will remain in RAM, ready to be accessed. On the other hand, if your next document is in another directory and is associated with a different glossary, change to the new directory with the Transfer Options command. Then issue the Transfer Clear All command, which removes the displayed document(s) and the active glossary and loads NORMAL.GLY from the new directory.

USING ADDITIONAL GLOSSARIES

If you find that you use Word's glossary capabilities extensively, you may want to have more than one glossary. You might find it useful, for instance, to set up a glossary for each field that you work in, placing each glossary in a separate directory. If there's more than one person using Word, each person could have a glossary saved under his or her name to differentiate it from other glossaries in the directory.

Before you create an additional glossary in Word, save NORMAL.GLY to store its most current version. Then consider its existing entries and decide whether you want any of them to be part of the new glossary. If you don't want to include these entries in the additional glossary, issue the Transfer Glossary Clear command, clearing away some or all of them. If you want all the entries, don't use the Transfer Glossary Clear command.

Next, construct the special glossary, adding entries as you see fit. Save the new glossary with the Transfer Glossary Save command. When you do, override the suggested name, NORMAL.GLY, by typing the name you want for the new glossary. You need only type the primary file name, not its extension. Word will automatically add .GLY to indicate that it's a glossary.

5 New in Word 5

To use a glossary other than NORMAL.GLY, you load it specially with Word 5's Transfer Glossary Load command; NORMAL.GLY is the only glossary Word loads automatically. The Transfer Glossary Load command clears the existing glossary and loads the glossary you specify. As with the Transfer Load command, you can change directories by pressing F1 or by clicking right on the filename field, and you can specify read-only status to ensure you don't accidentally change entries in the glossary you're using. (In Word 4 you can only merge glossaries, not clear one glossary and load another simultaneously.)

Although you can duplicate entries in your glossaries by borrowing entries from the last glossary you used when you create another, you don't have to. You especially don't want to retype glossary entries—if you later find that you need an entry from a glossary other than the one that is active, you can merge the two glossaries' entries to access it by issuing the Transfer Glossary Merge command. You must be cautious about which glossary you load first, however. If there are abbreviations with identical names in the two glossaries, newly loaded entries will replace previous ones without warning.

If you don't want to combine the glossaries permanently, don't save them after they are loaded and merged. They'll be left on the disk as they were before you merged them.

In addition to your own glossaries, you can load or merge any of the three glossaries Microsoft provides with Word: CONTRACT.GLY, MACRO.GLY, and SAFEKEYB.GLY. When you install Word, they are placed in your WORD directory. By merging them into the glossary that you create, their entries will be available to you as you work. Check first that you don't have entries with the same names as the supplied glossary's entries; if you do, load the glossary instead of merging it with your glossary. This way, your existing entries won't be overwritten.

CONTRACT.GLY contains legal-oriented entries. If you work with legal documents, you may wish to use its entries as boilerplates for those documents. You may want to use SAFEKEYB.GLY when running resident programs. This glossary and resident programs are examined in Appendix B.

T I P

The memo format created by memohead is the same as that created by the macro **memo_header.mac** (Ctrl-M-H); however, using the glossary entry inserts text slightly faster than the macro types it in.

MACRO.GLY contains several useful glossary entries as well as Word's supplied macros. (We'll study the macros in Appendix C and use their text as examples in the next section.) Its "legal_line_numbers" entry inserts double-spaced line numbers along the left edge of the page (with the Format pOsition command), accompanied by a vertical double-line. This format is sometimes necessary for legal applications. The "memohead" entry creates a memo template. You can press Ctrl- > and Ctrl- < to jump from one blank space to another in the memo and fill all the spaces in. Finally, "label" inserts field names, complete with enclosing chevrons, for use in creating mailing labels with the Print Merge command. The names it uses are «firstname», «lastname», «title», «company», «address», «city», «state», and «zip».

AUTOMATIC PROCEDURES WITH MACROS

As anyone who has done word processing knows, there are often tasks to be performed on a regular basis. For example, you might find that you need to write a letter to someone, save it, and then print out two copies of the letter. In addition, you need to create an envelope with an address that matches the inside address of the letter.

Word lets you automate procedures such as this with its macro feature. A *macro* is a sequence of recorded keystrokes that you can create and that Word will play back for you more or less at the touch of a button. Macros are for keyboard operations only, not mouse operations. They can automate commands and other procedures that Word performs, as well as store text and formatting for inclusion in a document. They can also allow you to add text that varies, such as the body of a letter, when you play them back. The result is less repetitive work for you, increased speed, and a greater degree of accuracy.

HOW MACROS RELATE TO THE GLOSSARY

Macros constitute a special kind of glossary entry. The chief distinction between macros and other glossary entries is that only

T I P

Although you can create macros for text-only applications, using the standard glossary entries for this purpose is generally quicker. Use macros for automating commands and other procedures, alone or with inserted text. To enter long passages as part of a macro, you may find it more efficient to insert a glossary entry in the macro itself.

macros store commands and other operating procedures. Macros may or may not include text.

In the previous example, for instance, the macro could address your letter, issue the Transfer Save command to save the letter, set the Print Options command's copies option to 2, and then print two copies of the letter. It could also retrieve an envelope template document, address the envelope with the same address, and print the envelope.

As you can see, macros can become very sophisticated. You can use them to run a long series of operations. Of course, the more complicated they are, the more time they'll take to construct initially. Word macros can range from the simple, such as reassigning a key to a more convenient location, to the complex, such as offering you choices and changing procedures depending on your response.

When you construct a macro, you must think through the procedures, considering all possible alternatives. You must also test the macro on some sample material. Otherwise your macro could fail unexpectedly, and you could lose valuable work. Even when you have tested your macro, there may still be times when it doesn't work because an unforeseeable situation arises. You then need to identify the problem and test your macro again. Creating macros can take up a lot of time; think of it as an investment. In the long run, it will save you time.

Fortunately, though, Microsoft provides you with the MACRO.GLY file, which contains a set of macros that are complete and ready to use. Word's supplied macros allow you to either modify or simplify the program's existing features. For example, you can change the way you cut and paste text or save a portion of a document as a separate document. You can also simplify the way you set tabs or create side-by-side paragraphs.

Because Word supplies many macros for you, we will use them to learn how to create professional macros. First, let's look at the fundamentals of constructing and using macros.

CONSTRUCTING MACROS

There are two methods that you can use to create macros. You can record the macro as you go or you can write the macro into the glossary. You can even record some of the macro and then revise what you recorded and add more steps. Let's begin by looking at macro recording.

RECORDING MACROS

The first and simplest method of creating macros is to record them. Just as you are about to perform a procedure that you want to save as a macro, you turn on the Recording-Macro mode, just like you'd turn on a VCR to record a show. Then you use the keyboard as you usually would, and Word records everything that you do. (You cannot record mouse operations.) When the procedure is finished, you turn off Recording-Macro mode.

Let's say, for instance, that you don't like the way pressing Ctrl-Page Down makes all the text above the new screen disappear when it brings the cursor to the end of the document. If you want to add new material, you can't see where you left off. As a result, there are five steps to perform whenever you want to get to the bottom of the document and still see the preceding text. Of course, you'd like to automate those steps, which consist of:

- Pressing Ctrl-Page Down to get to the bottom of the document
- Scrolling up one screenful with the Page Up key
- Going to the bottom of the screen with Ctrl-End
- Moving to the end of the line with the End key
- Moving to the end mark with the ↓ key

Let's see how you could record these steps as a macro, giving it the name

End_of_doc.mac

Note that the .mac extension is optional, although Word recommends that you include this extension to differentiate macros from text entries in the glossary. We will follow this convention in our examples. Capitalization in the macro name is also optional. Word treats uppercase and lowercase letters the same.

To record the macro, you need to have a document displayed; any sample text will do. Here are the steps you perform to record the macro I just described:

1. Turn on Recording-Macro mode by pressing the Record Macro key (Shift-F3). The letters RM appear in the bottom right of the screen.

2. Perform the steps in order, just as you usually would. (Press Ctrl-Page Down, Page Up, Ctrl-End, End, and ↓.)

3. Press Shift-F3 again to turn off Recording-Macro mode; the RM disappears. This automatically activates the Copy command and Word displays

   COPY to { }

4. Type End_of_doc.mac as the name for the macro. You can also provide an optional Ctrl code (which we'll examine shortly). The same rules for glossary abbreviations apply to macro names: they can have up to 31 letters, numbers, underline characters, hyphens, and periods. No spaces are allowed.

5. Press the Enter key to place the macro in the glossary.

WRITING MACROS

As I mentioned, you can also create a macro by writing it to the glossary. Writing a macro is not as easy as recording it, but by doing so you can include instructions that enhance the macro feature's capabilities. We'll examine such instructions later in the chapter. For now, let's look at how to create another macro by writing it to the glossary.

Suppose you have a table that's wider than the screen. You'll probably find it necessary to split the screen into two vertical windows to view the widely spaced columns in the table. When you do, though, the windows don't correspond as you bring new material on the screen, using the ↑ and ↓ keys. To keep the windows synchronized, you could create two macros, one to move the cursors up simultaneously in each window and one to move the cursors down.

You can create a macro for moving down that, when executed, is the same as pressing the ↓ key, F1, ↓ again, and then F1 again. It moves the cursor down in the current window, switches to the other window, moves the cursor down in that window, and then switches back to the window it was first in. All the steps take place very quickly, so the macro gives the impression that the two windows are scrolling together.

To write a macro on the screen, you type a representation of the keystrokes you want performed in the order that they occur. For the normal alphanumerical keys, you just type the letters and numbers. For other keys, you specify code words surrounded by angle brackets (< >). Table 15.2 shows how you represent these keys when you write a macro.

Table 15.2: Macro Codes for Keys

MACRO CODE	KEY REPETITION OR COMBINATION	KEY
0 to 9		0 to 9
A to Z		A to Z
a to z		a to z
<alt>	<alt *x*>	Alt key
<backspace>	<backspace 2>	Backspace key
<capslock>		Caps Lock key
<ctrl>	<ctrl *x*>	Ctrl key
<ctrl [> or «		Left chevron («)
<ctrl] > or »		Right chevron (»)
<del>	<del 2>	Delete key
<down>		↓ key
<end>		End key
<enter>	<enter 2>	Enter key
<esc>	<esc 2>	Esc key
<F1> to <F10>		Function keys, F1 to F10

Table 15.2: Macro Codes for Keys (continued)

MACRO CODE	KEY REPETITION OR COMBINATION	KEY
\<home\>		Home key
\<ins\>	\<ins 2\>	Insert key
\<left\>		← key
\<keypad *\>		* on numeric keypad
\<keypad +\>		+ on numeric keypad
\<keypad -\>		– on numeric keypad
\<keypad 5\>		5 on numeric keypad
\<numlock\>		Num Lock key
\<pgdn\>		Page Down key
\<pgup\>		Page Up key
\<right\>		→ key
\<scrolllock\>		Scroll Lock key
\<shift\>	\<shift *x*\>	Shift key
\<space\>‡		Spacebar
\<tab\>	\<tab 2\>	Tab key
\<up\>		↑ key
^ \<		\<
^ ^		^
!@#$% and so on		!@#$% and so on

‡ The Spacebar is used to move around command menus. When entering text, do not type \<space\>, just press the Spacebar as usual.

Note that you can abbreviate multiple entries for some keys. For example, \<backspace 2\> is the same as pressing the Backspace key twice. Simply substitute another number for the 2s listed in the table to provide another repetition. To code key combinations, enclose the two names within the brackets. For example, you can enter <shift F1> or <ctrl X>. You can substitute any letter for the Xs listed in Table 15.2. Two useful key combinations are <ctrl esc>, which activates the main command menu from another command, except from the Gallery subcommands (from which it activates Gallery), and <shift ctrl esc>, which activates the main command menu from all commands, including Gallery subcommands.

Here's how you would represent the sequence of keystrokes necessary for synchronizing two windows:

<down><f1><down><f1>

Once you type the macro, highlight it and issue the Delete or Copy command, providing a macro name, to add it to the glossary. Thus, you could use the Delete command to name this macro Sync_down-.mac. If you assign a name that is already in the glossary, Word will ask you to verify that you want to overwrite the existing entry.

When writing a macro, you must be certain to anticipate and allow for any eventuality. For instance, if you are loading a document, you should consider whether Word will ask to save an existing document. If so, you must include a response as part of the macro. However, Word 5 does allow you to circumvent such verification by using a reserved variable (see the following). As with recorded macros, you should always test your new written macro on sample material.

RUNNING MACROS

To run the macro, you can follow the procedure for inserting other glossary entries. That is, you type the glossary abbreviation and press the Glossary key (F3), or you issue the Insert command and select the abbreviation from the list. Word performs the operations recorded by the macro in order, starting at the current cursor position. If you need to interrupt the macro, press the Esc key and verify that you want to cancel by pressing Esc again.

T *IP*

The Undo command
will not undo the
effects of a macro.
Therefore, as a pre-
caution, always save
your document before
running a macro,
especially if you're
running the macro for
the first time. You can
then reload the docu-
ment, specifying N to
lose edits if something
goes wrong.

USING THE CTRL CODES

There is also a quicker method you can use to run a macro. When you provide the abbreviation for the macro, you can also include an optional Ctrl code. This code is a form of shorthand that allows you to run the macro simply by pressing the Ctrl key combination. (You can create combinations using one or two other keys.) Not only is using the Ctrl code faster, but it also allows you to trigger the macro into operation at times when you could not enter the macro name with F3 or the Insert command; for instance, when Word is display-ing a subcommand menu. You might want to do this to establish your preferred settings in an extensive menu like the Options or Format Character menu quickly.

When you name a macro, specify the Ctrl code after the macro name by typing a caret (ˆ) and then the code; for example, you could have pressed Shift-6 and then Ctrl-E for the End_of_doc macro. Word would have then displayed the code as

ˆ <ctrl E>

(You could also type the caret, brackets, and letters directly.)

If you plan on constructing many macros, you may want to use a two-letter Ctrl code for your macros' names. This way, you won't run out of unique Ctrl codes for each macro, as you might if you just used one-letter codes. To do this for End_of_doc.mac (assuming you haven't created and named it yet), you could enter

End_of_doc.mac ˆ

then press Ctrl-E, and type d in the to field for the Copy command (which Word displays when you turn off Recording-Macro mode). Word automatically changes the Ctrl code you type to

ˆ <ctrl E>d

as shown in Figure 15.6.

Now that the macro is recorded, you activate the End_of_doc.mac macro by simply pressing Ctrl-E-D. That's all there is to recording and running a simple macro. Of course, to save the macro on the disk per-manently, you must use the Transfer Glossary Save command as you do

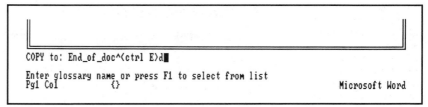

```
COPY to: End_of_doc^(ctrl E)d█

Enter glossary name or press F1 to select from list
Pg1 Col                {}                              Microsoft Word
```

Figure 15.6: Providing a macro name and ctrl code

with other glossary entries. (Note that this particular macro does not work when the end mark is initially visible on the screen because of idiosyncrasies in the way Word scrolls in this situation. However, if you immediately use it a second time, it will correct itself.)

In addition to the Ctrl key, you can use the twelve function keys, alone or with the Ctrl, Shift, and Alt keys, for coding macros. If you assign macros to the function keys, though, your macro will override the function key's normal operation. Therefore, only reassign function keys that you rarely use. The function key's normal operation will still be available if you press Ctrl-X first. For example, if your applications don't involve math, you probably won't need to use the Calculate key (F2), which makes it a prime candidate for a macro. Once you assign a macro to F2, you could still access the Calculate function by pressing Ctrl-X-F2.

You can use any scheme you can devise to assign macro codes, although I recommend using mnemonic codes for the Ctrl key. For example, I chose Ctrl-E-D for "end of the document."

Note that Ctrl codes are not reserved strictly for use with macros. By following these same steps, you can assign them to standard glossary text entries as well.

RUNNING MACROS IN STEP MODE

Another way you can run macros is in Step mode. When you run a macro in Step mode, Word runs the macro haltingly, pausing at the end of each command or procedure. For instance, if the macro issues the Transfer Load command, running it in Step mode will pause it after Word displays the Transfer command and after the Load command.

Running a macro in Step mode is handy for diagnosing a problem or for examining an unfamiliar macro. You might want to activate Step mode to analyze Word's supplied macros, for instance.

You run a macro in Step mode as follows:

1. Turn on Step mode by pressing Ctrl-F3. ST appears in the bottom right of the screen.

2. Invoke the macro by using its abbreviation (with F3 or the Insert command) or by entering the assigned code. Word will pause after the first step.

3. When the macro pauses, you have three alternatives. You can cancel the macro with the Esc key, you can turn off Step mode by pressing Ctrl-F3 again (which allows the macro to finish running in the usual manner), or you can proceed to the next step in Step mode by pressing any other key (the Spacebar is handy for this purpose).

4. When the macro has finished running in Step mode, you press Ctrl-F3 to turn Step mode off. Otherwise, the next time you run a macro, Step mode will still be activated.

You can also turn Step mode on and off as part of a macro's procedure by including <Ctrl F3> in the macro's text.

RUNNING MACROS AUTOMATICALLY

You can create a macro that will run automatically when you start Word or load a particular glossary by simply naming the macro AUTOEXEC (without a .MAC extension). You can have only one AUTOEXEC macro per glossary. When you load the glossary that contains AUTOEXEC, Word will execute it automatically.

If you include the AUTOEXEC macro in the NORMAL.GLY glossary that's in the current directory when you start up Word, Word will load the NORMAL.GLY glossary and execute the macro each time you start up Word or use the Transfer Clear All command.

EDITING MACROS

One strategy you may wish to follow as you start to develop more sophisticated macros is to record a macro's basic procedure and then enhance it by writing additional material in it. Alternatively, you may wish to revise the sample macros that Word supplies. You may also find that there is something wrong with a macro that you need to correct. In all of these cases, you will have to edit the macro.

To edit a macro, you display the macro text on the screen, make your changes, and then copy or delete it back to the glossary. To display macro text, you specify the macro's name with a caret (^) after it using the Insert command or the Glossary key (F3). Don't forget the caret, or Word will run the macro instead. For instance, to choose a macro that you want to edit from the list, proceed as follows:

1. Initiate the Insert command.

2. Press F1 in the from field or click right on it to display the list of macros.

3. Highlight the macro you want but don't press Enter.

4. Press F8 to move the cursor to the space following the entry's name.

5. Type a caret and press Enter or click right on INSERT to register the command.

Word then presents the macro text on the screen for you to edit. To retrieve the sample end_of_doc.mac macro, you'd make the entry you see in Figure 15.7.

Once you've made the necessary changes to the macro, you may want to save the edited macro under a new name so that you have both versions on disk. Add it to the macro glossary by highlighting it and issuing the Delete or Copy command. You can enter the macro's original name (by typing it or choosing it from the list), and press Enter to overwrite the existing macro text, or you can specify a new name and press Enter. In either case, save the macro by issuing the Transfer Glossary Save command.

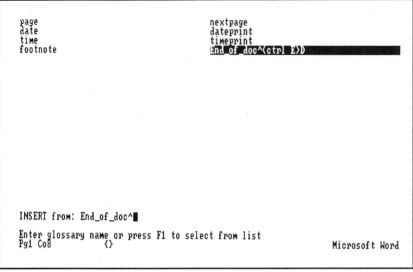

Figure 15.7: Displaying macro text

USING MACRO INSTRUCTIONS

When you are editing macro text or writing it from scratch, you can also include macro instructions to tell the macro how to perform as it's running. These instructions can make macros operate in sophisticated ways. You may recognize some of these instructions from working with the Print Merge command. Their operation is similar here.

To create a macro instruction, you enclose the instruction in chevrons (« and »). You create these chevrons by typing Ctrl-[and Ctrl-] respectively. Although we'll show the instructions in all caps, you can type them in upper- or lowercase letters since Word does not differentiate between case for macros.

Macros make use of *variables,* which are similar to fields in print merge operations. They act as receptacles that hold text or values that the macro places in them as it runs. Variable names can include letters and numbers only and must begin with a letter. Word reserves some variables for its use only. We'll examine them later in the chapter.

T I P

One of the easiest errors to make in working with macro instructions is confusing chevrons and angle brackets. Remember, use chevrons («») for macro instructions and angle brackets (< >) for the names of keys.

Strings of text are enclosed in quotes. You can use the Search command's special characters as part of the text string (see Chapter 10). For example,

«IF answer = "N ^ p"»

checks whether the text in the variable "answer" is an N followed by a paragraph mark.

Always add a second caret (^) when you want to include a caret in the macro's text. For example, you may want to search for any occurrence of two sequential paragraph marks. If you were to perform this operation without a macro, you would activate the Search command and indicate two paragraph marks in the command like so:

SEARCH text: ^ p ^ p

Then you would press Enter to begin the search. To create a macro that accomplishes the same thing, you would record or type

<esc>S ^ ^ p ^ ^ p<enter>

In this macro, <esc>S activates the Search command, ^ ^ p ^ ^ p places ^ p ^ p in the text field, and <enter> begins the search.

As your work with macros becomes more complex, you may find you need to use numeric values and have your macros respond to them. For example, if you are churning out letters that answer the day's mail, you could have the macro ask for the date and then use one of several letters, depending on the response. You can use a variety of mathematical and logical operators with macros (see Table 15.3).

For each macro instruction, I normally use one of Word's supplied macros as an example, providing an extract from the macro and an explanation of it. Figure 15.8 presents the names of the supplied macros you can see using the Insert command. (I used a full-page display so you can see them all.) Word 5's supplied macros also appear in Appendix C, where I examine how they operate.

ASK

By including the ASK instruction in a macro's text, you can vary the operation of the macro. When the macro runs and encounters the

Table 15.3: Macro Operators

OPERATOR	FUNCTION
+	Add
–	Subtract
*	Multiply
/	Divide
>	Greater than
<	Less than
=	Equal to
> =	Greater than or equal to
< =	Less than or equal to
< >	Not equal to
()	Parentheses
AND	Logical and
OR	Logical or
NOT	Logical not

ASK instruction, it pauses and waits for you to provide a response (text, a number, or a date) and press Enter. In effect, it asks you to assign a value to the variable that follows the ASK. You can use ASK with or without a customized prompt, although having a well-turned prompt makes it easier to enter valid responses.

EXAMPLE

authority_entry.mac: Ctrl-A-E

«ASK scope = ? What is the source? 1 = Previous Case, 2 = Statute, 3 = Regulation, or 4 = Other»

This macro prompts you with the multiple-choice question for use in creating an entry for a table of authorities. It substitutes your response for the scope variable.

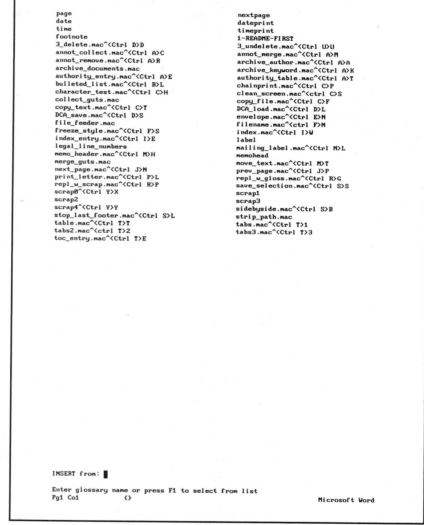

```
page                              nextpage
date                              dateprint
time                              timeprint
footnote                          1-README-FIRST
3_delete.mac^<Ctrl D>D            3_undelete.mac^<Ctrl U>U
annot_collect.mac^<Ctrl A>C       annot_merge.mac^<Ctrl A>M
annot_remove.mac^<Ctrl A>R        archive_author.mac^<Ctrl A>A
archive_documents.mac             archive_keyword.mac^<Ctrl A>K
authority_entry.mac^<Ctrl A>E     authority_table.mac^<Ctrl A>T
bulleted_list.mac^<Ctrl B>L       chainprint.mac^<Ctrl C>P
character_test.mac^<Ctrl C>H      clean_screen.mac^<ctrl C>S
collect_guts.mac                  copy_file.mac^<Ctrl C>F
copy_text.mac^<Ctrl C>T           DCA_load.mac^<Ctrl D>L
DCA_save.mac^<Ctrl D>S            envelope.mac^<Ctrl E>N
file_feeder.mac                   filename.mac^<ctrl F>N
freeze_style.mac^<Ctrl F>S        index.mac^<Ctrl I>W
index_entry.mac^<Ctrl I>E         label
legal_line_numbers                mailing_label.mac^<Ctrl M>L
memo_header.mac^<Ctrl M>H         memohead
merge_guts.mac                    move_text.mac^<Ctrl M>T
next_page.mac^<Ctrl J>N           prev_page.mac^<Ctrl J>P
print_letter.mac^<Ctrl P>L        repl_w_gloss.mac^<Ctrl R>G
repl_w_scrap.mac^<Ctrl R>P        save_selection.mac^<Ctrl S>S
scrap0^<Ctrl Y>X                  scrap1
scrap2                            scrap3
scrap4^<Ctrl Y>Y                  sidebyside.mac^<Ctrl S>B
stop_last_footer.mac^<Ctrl S>L    strip_path.mac
table.mac^<Ctrl T>T               tabs.mac^<Ctrl T>1
tabs2.mac^<ctrl T>2               tabs3.mac^<Ctrl T>3
toc_entry.mac^<Ctrl T>E



INSERT from: █

Enter glossary name or press F1 to select from list
Pg1 Co1              {}                      Microsoft Word
```

Figure 15.8: Supplied macros in MACRO.GLY

COMMENT

The COMMENT instruction allows you to enter a comment in the macro text. The comment has no effect on the macro, but aids in making the text more understandable as you work with it. For example, you can use comments as placemarkers that indicate where one procedure ends and another begins.

EXAMPLE

tabs2.mac: Ctrl-T-2

«COMMENT Get line length»

This comment in Word 4's version of the macro indicates that the procedure that follows it calculates the line length.

IF, ELSE, ENDIF

As with print merge operations, the IF, ELSE, and ENDIF instructions allow you to specify conditional procedures. With IF you specify what the macro should do when a condition is true. The ELSE is optional; with it you can provide an alternate procedure to perform if the condition is not true. You can specify multiple ELSE instructions to cover several possible circumstances; this occurs in the tabs2.mac macro.

EXAMPLE

strip_path.mac

«IF found»<shift Ctrl PgUp><del>«ENDIF»

If the macro finds the text (with the Search command), it extends the highlight to the beginning of the document and then deletes the highlighted text.

MESSAGE

You can include the MESSAGE instruction in a macro to display a message in the screen's message area. The message stays on the screen until it is replaced with one of Word's messages or another macro message.

EXAMPLE

annot_remove.mac:Ctrl-A-R

«MESSAGE All annotations removed successfully»

After successfully removing annotations from a document as instructed, this macro informs you that the procedure is finished.

PAUSE

The PAUSE instruction temporarily halts the running of the macro so that you can take some action, such as making an entry for the Search command or highlighting text. Provide a prompt to remind yourself what you should do. To restart the macro after you take some action, press Enter.

EXAMPLE

repl_w_gloss.mac: Ctrl-R-G

«PAUSE Enter text to replace, choose desired options, press Enter when done»

The macro pauses to allow you to specify the text and establish settings for the Search command.

QUIT

The QUIT instruction ends the macro's operation. You normally use it to end the IF and ENDIF or WHILE and ENDWHILE loops.

EXAMPLE

save_ascii.mac: Ctrl-S-A

«IF printer< >plain»«PAUSE Cannot find PLAIN.PRD, press Enter to end macro»«QUIT»

If the macro finds that the text in the printer field is not "plain" (you have not selected the PLAIN.PRD printer driver), it pauses, displays a message, and quits the macro when you press Enter. (This macro appears only in Word 4. Word 5 does not supply a macro using QUIT.)

REPEAT, ENDREPEAT

You can use the REPEAT and ENDREPEAT instructions to perform the same procedure or procedures for more than one element. You provide the numeric value with the macro's REPEAT instruction to perform all the operations between REPEAT and ENDREPEAT that many times. The value can be contained in a variable, such as "limit" as in the following example, or it can be a numeric expression.

EXAMPLE

    tabs2.mac: Ctrl-T-2

    «SET limit = cols − 1 »
    «REPEAT limit»
    «SET tabpos = tabpos + incr»
    «tabpos» <ins>
    «ENDREPEAT»

In this example, the macro takes the value from the cols variable; for example, the value "8," subtracts "1" from it, and substitutes the result, "7," for the limit variable. It then repeats the cycle between the REPEAT and ENDREPEAT instructions seven times—the result's value.

SET

The SET instruction works like ASK in that it assigns the value or text string provided by the macro when the macro runs. The value remains in place until it is reset. Enclose only text strings in quotes, not numeric values and variables.

5 New in Word 5

Word 5 provides two additional uses for the SET instruction. First, it allows you to assign values to some of Word's reserved variables to perform one of their possible actions, such as activating a window.

For more on this use, see this chapter's "Using Reserved Variables" section.

Second, you can concatenate two or more strings into one with this instruction. By doing so, you can insert the combined string anywhere—in a document or in a message, for example. Just list the strings (or variables) one after another, separating each with a space.

EXAMPLES

chainprint.mac: Ctrl-C-P

«SET document = selection»

The macro treats whatever text is highlighted as the document variable.

None of the supplied macros make use of the concatenated strings. However, you could create a macro that tests whether its operations were successful and then uses a concatenated string to display a message that informs the user accordingly. Depending on the success of a procedure, make the macro assign the string "successful" or "not successful" to a variable. For example, you could assign "successful" as follows:

«SET successindicator = "successful"»

The following instructions would then use that variable to display the appropriate message:

«SET successdisplay = "The operation was " successindicator»
«MESSAGE «successdisplay»»

WHILE, ENDWHILE

The WHILE instruction allows you to specify a condition, such as whether text can be found with the Search command, and procedures for that condition. The macro reissues the procedures between WHILE and ENDWHILE, creating a loop that repeats like a broken record, as long as the condition remains true (for example, as long as the text can be found).

EXAMPLE

repl_w_scrap.mac: Ctrl-R-P

«WHILE found»<shift ins><shift f4>«ENDWHILE»

This macro searches for the text to be replaced. Whenever it finds the text, it presses Shift-Insert and then Shift-F4. (Shift-Insert deletes the highlighted text, replacing it with the text in the scrap area, and Shift-F4 repeats the last edit.) When it cannot find the text, it does not perform these steps and goes on to its next step.

USING RESERVED VARIABLES

When you include one of the instructions we just examined in your macros, you will often need variables to determine how it operates. Although you can make up your own variables, Word reserves the following variables for its use only—you cannot use them for purposes other than those shown here. I provide an example and explanation for each reserved variable to illustrate its use. Some of the reserved variables allow you to assign numeric values or text to them directly with the SET instruction.

ECHO

New in
Word 5

When you run a macro, Word normally displays what's happening as the macro runs, just as if you were executing the macro's steps yourself. You can use SET to turn off such screen updating and to later turn screen updating back on. Thus, the echo variable can be set to on or off. Turning off screen updating can help to speed up the operation of macros.

EXAMPLE

«SET echo = "off"»

If the screen was being updated as usual, this instruction turns off the updating while the macro executes.

FIELD

Word assigns to the field variable whatever the current field is set to. For example, if the macro has initiated the Format Paragraph command, the alignment option is highlighted, and alignment is set to Justified, then Word would assign Justified to the field variable. Similarly, if the macro has initiated the Format Division Margins command, the top option is highlighted, and top is set to 1", then the contents of field is 1. (Word does not include the measurement unit, such as ", Cm, Pt, and so on, in the field variable.)

Use the field variable to determine the setting of a particular command's option and to direct the macro's subsequent operations accordingly. You cannot use SET to assign a value or string to the field variable.

EXAMPLE

«IF field = C:\WORD»

If the Transfer Options command's setup option is current and is set to C:\WORD, the field variable equals C:\WORD, and the IF statement is true.

FOUND

When the macro reaches the found variable, it checks whether the last search operation (as a result of the Search or Format sEarch command) successfully located material. The found variable can be 1 or 0. If the search was successful, Word sets found equal to 1; if the search was unsuccessful, Word sets found equal to 0.

Use the found variable after searching for text or formats to determine whether the material was found and to direct the macro's subsequent operations accordingly. You cannot use SET to assign a value to the found variable.

EXAMPLE

«IF found»

If the macro's previous search was successful, found = True (1), and the IF statement is true. If the macro didn't find the specified search string or format, found = False (0), and the IF statement is false.

NOTFOUND

As with the found variable, the macro checks whether the last search operation (as a result of the Search or Format sEarch command) successfully located material when it encounters the notfound variable. The notfound variable can also be 1 or 0. If the search was successful, however, Word sets notfound equal to 0; if the search was not successful, Word sets notfound equal to 1.

Use the notfound variable after searching for text or formats to determine whether the material was not found and to direct the macro's subsequent operations accordingly. You cannot use SET to assign a value to the notfound variable.

EXAMPLE

«IF notfound»

If the macro's previous search was successful, notfound = False (0), and the IF statement is false. If the macro didn't find the search string or format, notfound = True (1), and the IF statement is true.

PROMPTMODE

New in
Word 5

When you run a macro, the macro may perform procedures that require verification before being executed. For example, when you save to an existing file name, Word requests confirmation before overwriting the existing file.

Normally, Word looks to the macro for responses to such verification prompts. However, you can insert a SET instruction with the promptmode variable to redirect Word in its handling of such verification prompts.

You can set the promptmode variable to user, ignore, or macro. Setting promptmode to user makes Word direct subsequent verification prompts to the screen, so the person who is running the macro can respond to them. Ignore causes Word to execute the macro without verification prompts. If you set promptmode to user or ignore, you can later set it back to macro so that Word again looks to the macro for responses to its prompts.

EXAMPLE

«SET promptmode = "ignore"»

If you have created a macro that requests you to verify a procedure when it runs, including this instruction tells the macro to disregard the instruction that creates the prompt; the macro will no longer request verification.

SAVE

5 New in Word 5

When you create macros that perform complex operations, you may need to check that Word has sufficient memory for them. To do this, you can rely on the SAVE indicator. Remember that Word prompts you with a flashing and then a steady SAVE indicator when it runs out of memory; this generally occurs after a complex operation. If you include the save variable in an IF statement after complex operations in your macro and follow it with the Save command, the macro will look for the SAVE indicator and save documents as necessary. If you don't include this procedure and the SAVE indicator appears, Word will abort the macro.

Note this does not help when Word runs out of memory while a command is executing. For example, should this happen in the middle of a complex replace procedure, Word will abort the macro even if you added the save variable after the Replace command in the macro. (To correct such a problem, simplify the replace procedure by replacing in steps rather than all at once.)

EXAMPLE

«IF save»

If Word is displaying SAVE in the message area, save = True, and the IF statement is true. If SAVE is not showing, save = False.

SCRAP

On encountering the scrap variable, Word places whatever text is in the scrap area in the scrap variable. Any amount of highlighted text, including non-printing characters such as paragraph marks, can be assigned to the scrap variable. You cannot use SET to assign text to the scrap variable.

EXAMPLE

«IF scrap = "leftovers"»

If the word "leftovers" appears in scrap, the IF statement is true.

SELECTION

When Word reaches the selection variable, it substitutes whatever text is highlighted for the variable. Any amount of highlighted text, including non-printing characters, can be assigned to the selection variable. You cannot use SET to assign text to the selection variable.

EXAMPLE

«IF selection = "Times Square"»

If the words "Times Square" are highlighted, they are the string for the selection variable, and the IF statement is true.

WINDOW

5 New in
Word 5

When Word encounters the window variable, it assigns the number of the currently activated window to the window variable. Because Word can open up to eight windows at a time, the window variable can become a number from 1 to 8.

You can also use SET to assign a value to the window variable; doing so activates the specified window. If the SET instruction specifies a number greater than the number of open windows, Word activates the window with the largest window number.

EXAMPLE

«IF window = 3»

If window 3 is active, then the window variable has a value of 3, and the IF statement is true. If window 2 is active, however, the IF statement is false.

To have a macro change the active window, include in it this instruction:

«SET window = 4»

When you run the macro, this instruction activates window 4.

WORDVERSION

New in Word 5

When the macro encounters the wordversion variable, it checks the version number of Word (for example, 5 for Word 5, 4 for Word 4) and assigns that number to the wordversion variable. Because the highest version of Word is currently 5, the wordversion variable can become a positive number up to 5.

If you plan to use your macros in different versions of Word, you can include this variable in them to determine which version is in use. Then you can have the macro terminate or change its procedures as necessary.

EXAMPLE

«IF wordversion = 5»

If you are using Word 4 when you run the macro, wordversion = 4, and the IF statement is false.

ZOOMEDWINDOW

New in Word 5

When the macro reaches the zoomedwindow variable, it checks whether the activated window is zoomed. Zoomedwindow can be equal to 1 or 0. If the window is zoomed, zoomedwindow equals 1; if the window is not zoomed, zoomedwindow equals 0.

Use the zoomedwindow variable to determine whether a window is zoomed and to direct the macro's subsequent operations accordingly. For example, you may have a macro that compares the contents of two documents in windows split side by side. To enable the macro to work on a zoomed window, you could have it check whether the user has turned zoom on and, if so, turn it off. You cannot use SET to assign a value to the zoomedwindow variable.

EXAMPLE

«IF zoomedwindow»

If zoom is turned on, then zoomedwindow = True (1), and the IF statement is true. If zoom is turned off, then zoomedwindow = False (0), and the IF statement is false.

ADDING MATH AND STRING FUNCTIONS TO YOUR MACROS

5 New in Word 5

Word now provides three math and string functions for use with macros. To include them in a macro, you enter the name of the function, followed by one or more applicable parameters in parentheses. Separate multiple parameters with commas and don't add a space between the function and the opening parenthesis.

You can try out the following examples by creating them as macros and running them.

INT()

The INT() function truncates a number (or the value of a variable) to the next lowest integer; that is, it removes a number's fractions. Use the INT() function when you need to change a fractional value to a whole number.

EXAMPLE

«ASK temperature»«INT(temperature)»

The macro asks the user for a value to insert in the temperature variable. If the response is 99.6, the macro would insert 99. If the response is −99.6, the macro would insert −100.

To add a value to the calculated temperature, simply enter

«ASK temperature»«INT(temperature + .5)»

in the macro. When you run it, it will round the response to the closest integer. For example, if the response is 99.6, the macro would insert 100. If the response is −99.6, the macro would insert −100.

LEN()

The LEN() function determines the length of characters in a string. Normally, you use it with a variable, and it determines the length of the text that's assigned to that variable.

EXAMPLE

«LEN(scrap)»

This macro inserts the length (in characters) of whatever text is in the scrap. For example, if the number "20782" is in scrap, the macro would insert "5" since the scrap text is five characters in length. If "20782-1111" is in scrap, the macro would insert "10."

MID()

The MID() function extracts characters from a string. Use it when the macro must handle part of existing text or part of a variable's text. Provide the variable or text, the beginning character position, and the ending character position, separating these values with commas.

EXAMPLE

<del>«SET phone = scrap»«MID(Phone, 1, 3)»

If "800-555-1212" is highlighted in the document, the macro would delete this number and insert "800" in its place. On the other hand, if you enter

<del>«SET phone = scrap»«MID(Phone, 5, 12)»

and "800-555-1212" is highlighted, this instruction would delete it and insert "555-1212" in its place.

USING ARRAYS IN YOUR MACROS

5 New in Word 5

Word 5 allows you to create *arrays,* which are ordered collections of elements of the same type, in your macros. Using arrays allows you to assign variables in a automated fashion. An array's elements can come from a data file or from a document whose paragraphs are demarcated the same way—in short, this versatile feature can take any repeated pattern for its elements.

For example, suppose you had a database file, like the DBBOARD file from the previous chapter, and you wanted to get an idea of the relative size of each record in the file to determine how much disk space they require. To do this, you could create a macro like that shown in Figure 15.9. This macro counts the number of characters in each record and assigns the count from each record to a variable in the recordlength array. Recordlength0 holds the length of the header record, recordlength1 holds the length of the first record of data, recordlength2 holds the length of the second record of data, and so on. The macro then creates a document that lists the character count for each record.

> **TIP**
>
> When you write a macro, you can indent the text in WHILE and REPEAT loops to make them easier to read (see Figure 15.9). If you do this, use the Tab key, not the Spacebar, to create the indents.

Go ahead and create this macro. When you run the macro, it will pause for you to provide the name of the file to load; specify the DBBOARD file. Should you need to change directories at this point, select the new directory with the F1 and directional keys or click left on it. Don't use the Enter key. Enter will terminate the pause, so only use it after you select the file. Once you have selected a file, a document like the one shown in Figure 15.10 will be displayed.

T IP

Remember, to create indenting in the macro's text, use the Tab key or formatting (such as Alt-N); do not add spaces with the Space bar.

```
«SET promptmode="user"»
«SET recordcount=0»
<shift ctrl esc>TL<F1>
«PAUSE Enter or select file for calculating paragraph lengths»
<enter><esc>TS«SET title=field»<esc>
<F10>
«WHILE len(selection)<>0»
     «SET recordlength«recordcount»=len(selection)»
     <F10>
     «SET recordcount=recordcount+1»
     «ENDWHILE»
<esc>TCW
Character count for the file «title»<enter>
date<F3><enter><enter>
<esc>FTS1.75"<down>R<enter>
«SET printnumber=0»
«WHILE printnumber<>recordcount»
     Record «printnumber»:<tab>«recordlength«printnumber»»<enter>
     «SET printnumber=printnumber+1»
     «ENDWHILE»
<enter>Note: Record 0 is the header record
```

Figure 15.9: Creating an array for counting characters in records

```
Character count for the file A:\DBBOARD.DOC
March 15, 1990

Record 0:       78
Record 1:      106
Record 2:      118
Record 3:       99
Record 4:      101
Record 5:       73

Note: Record 0 is the header record
```

Figure 15.10: A summary report created by the macro's array

Figure 15.11 shows a listing for another helpful macro. This macro prints out all the entries in whatever glossary is loaded. Naming this macro "1" and adding the instruction "SET movenumber = 8" will ensure that the macro does not print its own listing nor the listing of the reserved glossary entries ("date", "dateprint", and so on).

Word's glossaries and macros are handy if you are typing the same text and commands over and over. Another Word timesaver is its outliner, which allows you to organize and rearrange material quickly. We examine the outliner as we embark on our study of Word's desktop publishing features in the next chapter.

```
«SET promptmode="user"»
«SET movenumber=8»
«SET oldglossname=0»
<shift ctrl esc>TCW
<esc>TGS
«SET glossfile=field»<esc>
«SET promptmode="ignore"»
Glossary: «glossfile»<enter>
Date: date<F3>
<esc>PP
<esc>TCW
<esc>I<F1>
«REPEAT movenumber»
     <right>
     «ENDREPEAT»
«SET glossname=field»
«WHILE glossname<>oldglossname»
     <F8>^^<enter>
     <ctrl pgup>
     Glossary name: «glossname»          Page page<F3><enter>
     <up><F10><alt X>P<alt X><space>
     <esc>FRT<tab 3>Y<enter>
     <esc>PP
     «SET movenumber=movenumber+1»
     «SET oldglossname=glossname»
     <esc>TCW
     <esc>I<F1>
     «REPEAT movenumber»
          <right>
          «ENDREPEAT»
     «SET glossname=field»
     «ENDWHILE»
```

Figure 15.11: The 1 macro that prints glossary listings

PART IV

Desktop Publishing in Word

16

Organizing Your Material with the Outliner

Fast Track

PERHAPS THE MOST IMPORTANT COMPOSITIONAL tool Microsoft Word provides is its outliner. Word's outline processor enables you to organize and reorganize your thoughts easily so that your document makes sense and its structure supports the ideas that you wish to convey. In addition, the outliner allows you to look at your material both in detail and in general. You can see just the headings of your document, or you can view each paragraph in it.

Additionally, you can use the outliner in combination with Word's style sheets to create a formatting structure. You can make the headings for your outline become the headings for the document, fully formatted according to typeface, alignment, indents, and so on (see Chapter 17). Also, you can compile a table of contents from the outline headings automatically (see Chapter 19).

These and other Word tools work together to make Word the first word processor that allows you to take a document from initial conception and organization all the way through to the final desktop-published results. As we work through the remaining chapters in this book, you'll see how Word's abilities complement each other, seamlessly integrating to handle your desktop publishing needs.

CREATING AND VIEWING YOUR OUTLINE

As you work on large documents in Word, you'll find it helpful to use the two views that Word affords you. First, you can look at the document in its detailed view, or Document mode. Or you can look at just the headings of the document, in much the same way that you might regard the table of contents in a book, using the *Outline* view. The Options command's show outline option allows you to switch between Document mode (Outline view off) and Outline view:

M*OUSE*

Click either button on Options to display the Options menu. For show outline, click right on Yes or No to turn Outline view on or off.

1. Press Esc and type O for Options.

2. Press the ↓ key four times to move to show outline.

3. Type Y for Yes to turn Outline view on. Reset show outline option to turn Outline view on or off.

Shortcut:

Shift-F2 toggles Outline view on and off.

Figure 16.1 presents an outline that we'll create in this chapter. The outline is the basis of a manual for the fictitious Telefriend Foundation.

When Outline view is turned on, Word displays the level designation for the cursor's current position in the bottom-left corner of the screen, like so:

Level 1

The displayed level number indicates the relative importance of the heading the cursor is in. The major headings are Level 1, their immediate subheadings are Level 2, and so on.

In Outline view, Word indents each heading an additional four spaces from the previous level. It's important to note that you cannot change this spacing for outlines and it does not necessarily reflect the indentation that will occur when you print your finished document. Rather, your formatting operations in Document mode will govern the amount of that indentation.

Along the left edge of the outline, three symbols or nothing may appear in the selection bar. These codes indicate the status of material to their right as listed in Table 16.1. You'll only see these symbols

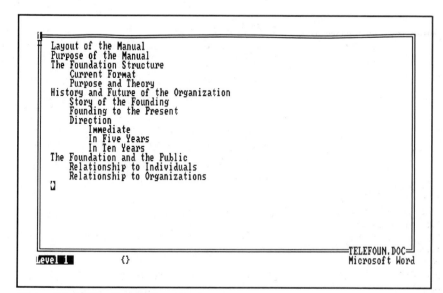

Figure 16.1: Word's Outline view

Table 16.1: Outline View Codes

SYMBOL	MEANING
+	A heading with one or more additional headings collapsed below it
t	A heading with only body text collapsed below it
T	Body text
[*none*]	A heading with no material collapsed below it

when you have Outline view turned on. You won't see them in the normal view (Document mode). Thus, whether you see the symbols also indicates which view of Word is operational.

CHANGING OUTLINE LEVELS

In Word, material you type that is not an outline heading is called *body text* or simply *text*. You can type text with Outline view either on or off. However, you can only change text into headings in Outline view or with a style sheet (see Chapter 17).

When you press Enter while entering text, the view that is operating determines the heading or text status of the paragraph, provided the cursor is on the end mark. If Outline view is *on* when you press Enter, the paragraph will become a heading. If Outline view is *off,* the paragraph will become text. You can transfer a paragraph's format to the subsequent paragraph, however, by pressing Enter when the cursor is on the paragraph mark, not the end mark. (This holds true regardless of whether Outline view is on or off.)

With Outline view on, you change the level of your outline headings with two keys, Alt-9 and Alt-0. A new heading has the same indent level as the heading just above it. Once you have created the heading, you can change its level. To add an indent, decreasing the heading level in importance, you press Alt-0. To maintain proper outlining structure, Word will not allow you to decrease a heading

T I P

Word supplies the OUTLINE.STY style sheet that allows you to apply outline formats to text easily (see Chapter 17).

more than one indent level from the heading above it. For instance, a main heading can have a subheading but not a secondary subheading immediately below it. To decrease the amount of indent, increasing a heading's importance, you press Alt-9. You also press Alt-9 to establish a heading from existing body text.

For practice, enter the outline shown in Figure 16.1. (I set the Options command's show non-printing symbols to Partial to display the paragraph marks in the figure.)

1. Turn on Outline view by issuing the Options command and setting show outline to Yes or by pressing Shift-F2.

2. Type the first three headings. When you press Enter after each line, the paragraph (line) takes on level 1 formatting.

3. With the cursor at the beginning of line 4, press Alt-0 to decrease the next heading to level 2. Word creates a paragraph mark to store the formatting, and the end mark moves down a line.

4. Type the fourth and fifth lines. Don't press Enter after "Purpose and Theory"; instead, leave your cursor on the paragraph mark at the end. Your screen should look like that shown in Figure 16.2.

FORMATTING TEXT AS OUTLINE HEADINGS

If you type text in Document mode and then change to Outline view, Word will indicate such text by a capital letter T in the selection bar, which is just inside the left border of the window.

You can reformat this text as an outline heading by moving the cursor to it and pressing Alt-9. The cursor can be anywhere in the paragraph to become a heading. Try this for the next two headings. (Notice that when you change text to a heading, Word initially assigns the same indent level to the new heading as to the heading just above it.)

1. Press Shift-F2 to switch to Document mode, turning Outline view off. The heading indents will disappear.

2. Move to the end mark.

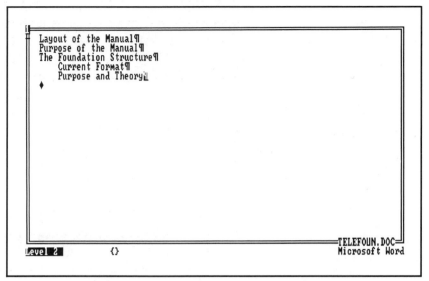

Figure 16.2: Creating an outline in Outline view

3. Type the sixth line ("History and Future . . ."), press Enter, type the seventh line ("Story of the Founding"), and press Enter again. Your document should now resemble that shown in Figure 16.3.

4. Press Shift-F2 again to return to Outline view. The indents reappear and T indicates body text (see Figure 16.4).

5. Move to the "History and Future . . ." heading and change it from text to a heading by pressing Alt-9. Initially, the heading has the same level as the "Purpose and Theory" heading above it, that is, level 2. Decrease the amount of indentation by pressing Alt-9 again. Word now displays Level 1 in the bottom-left corner.

6. Move the cursor to the "Story of the Founding" line, which is still text, and change it into a heading by pressing Alt-9. The indentation now is the same as for "History and Future . . .", which isn't enough, so press Alt-0 to change the heading to level 2. The revised outline should look like the one shown in Figure 16.5.

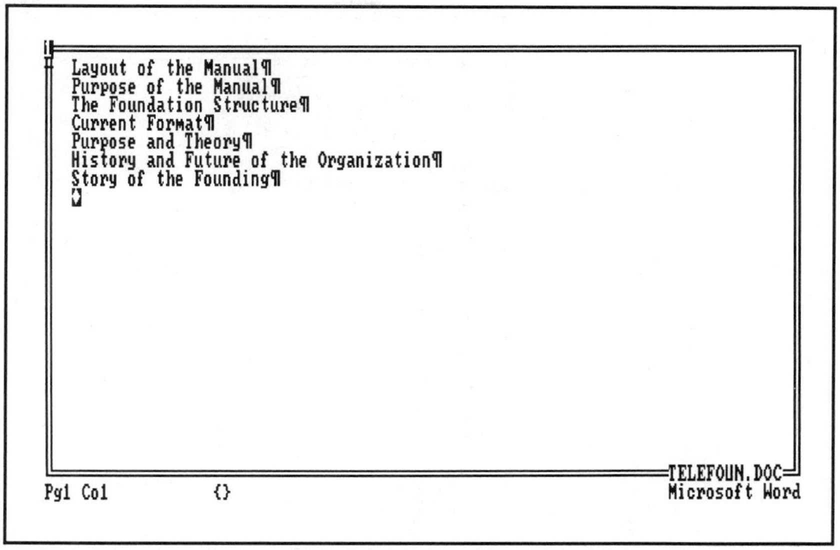

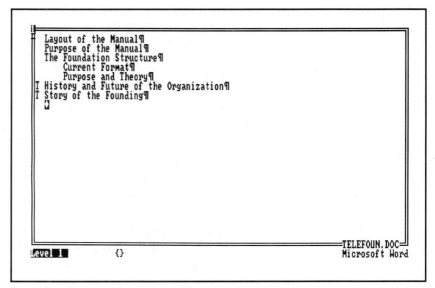

Figure 16.3: Headings and text in Document mode

Figure 16.4: Headings and text in Outline view

```
┌─────────────────────────────────────────────┐
│ ║                                             │
│ ║ Layout of the Manual¶                       │
│ ║ Purpose of the Manual¶                      │
│ ║ The Foundation Structure¶                   │
│ ║    Current Format¶                          │
│ ║    Purpose and Theory¶                      │
│ ║ History and Future of the Organization¶     │
│ ║    Story of the Founding¶                   │
│ ║ ♦                                           │
│ ║                                             │
│ ║                                             │
│ ║                                             │
│ ║                                             │
│ ║                                  ═TELEFOUN.DOC═ │
│ Level 2          {}                Microsoft Word │
└─────────────────────────────────────────────┘
```

Figure 16.5: Text changed to headings in Outline view

Continue in this manner, entering the entire outline shown in Figure 16.1. You can type with Outline view on or off. However, set and change levels with the Outline view on. After completing the outline, save the file as TELEFOUN.

COLLAPSING AND EXPANDING HEADINGS

Once you've created your headings, you can reveal them or make them invisible to whatever degree you choose. In other words, you can view as much or as little of your document's structure as necessary for analyzing and modifying it.

To perform these operations, Outline view must be on and you use three keys on the keypad on the right side of the keyboard. Move to the heading you want collapsed and press the minus key (–) to make its subheadings disappear, up to the next heading with the same indent level as the selected heading. This process is called *collapsing* the outline. Press the plus key (+) to reveal collapsed headings in the next indent level. This is called *expanding* the outline. If you want to reveal all levels below a heading, not just those immediately below it, press the asterisk key (*). (Do not use the asterisk key above the number 8.) Table 16.2 reviews these and other special keys that are used for outlining purposes. Note that you can use the additional function keys, F11 and F12, that are provided on some keyboards.

Practice collapsing and expanding the example as follows:

1. Move the cursor to anywhere in the heading "The Foundation Structure."

Table 16.2: Special Keys for Outlining

KEY	EFFECT
Shift-F2	Turns Outline view on/off
Shift-F5	Turns Outline Organize on/off (Outline view must first be on.)
Alt-9	Establishes headings Raises headings
Alt-0	Lowers headings
Minus or F11 or Alt-8	Collapses headings and text
Shift-minus or Shift-F11 or Shift-Alt-8	Collapses text only
Asterisk	Expands all headings below
Plus or F12 or Alt-7	Expands the next level of heading only
Shift-plus or Shift-F12 or Shift-Alt-7	Expands body text only
Ctrl-plus	Allows you to enter a level number from 1 to 7 that Word then expands headings to
Alt-P	Changes to unformatted body text

Note: Use the plus, minus, and asterisk keys on the keypad only.

2. Collapse the heading by pressing the minus key.

3. Move the cursor to the "History and Future . . ." heading and press the minus key to collapse it as well.

Once you do this, the screen should look like Figure 16.6. The plus signs to the left of these two lines indicate that there are more headings collapsed below them. They also remind you which key you push to make that material visible.

Now try your hand at making material visible by expanding the outline:

1. Move the cursor to "The Foundation Structure." Expand the heading by pressing the plus key on the keypad.

2. Move to "History and Future . . ." and expand the heading by pressing the plus key on the keypad. Notice that the "Direction" heading does not expand.

3. Collapse the "History and Future . . ." heading again and then expand it with the asterisk key on the keypad. This time, all its subsidiary levels expand fully.

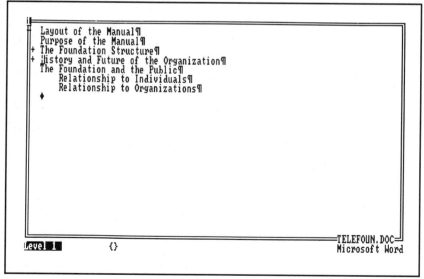

Figure 16.6: A partially collapsed outline

T IP

You may have considered collapsing and expanding the entire outline by highlighting it with Shift-F10 and then pressing the appropriate key (+ or −). Be aware, however, that highlighting with Shift-F10 in Outline view automatically activates Outline Organize. We'll look at Outline Organize later in the chapter.

You can also expand headings to a specified level by pressing Ctrl-plus (on the keypad). Word prompts you to specify a level number from 1 to 7 and then expands the outline to that level.

Besides collapsing and expanding headings, you can also make revisions in Outline view. The process is much like editing in Document mode. However, in Outline view you can only highlight one heading at a time or the entire document (with Shift-F10), not several headings. In addition, you cannot delete paragraph marks with the Delete key (though the Backspace key will still erase). Word imposes these restrictions to keep the proper outline form in order. They don't apply when Outline view is off.

FLESHING OUT WITH BODY TEXT

Once you have finalized your document's structure, you'll need to compose body text. You can add body text to the outline with Outline view on or off. In either case, when you press Enter to create a blank line for the new material, the paragraph mark will initially have the same heading level or text status as the paragraph from which it came. You can turn off the heading format with Alt-P. (This is the same code we used to turn off paragraph formats in Chapter 5.) After you press Alt-P, the paragraph mark will store the plain text format.

Let's type some text below the heading "Layout of the Manual."

1. With the Outline view on (Shift-F2), move to the paragraph mark at the end of the "Layout of the Manual" line and press Enter to create a new paragraph.

2. Turn off the heading format by pressing Alt-P. Word then displays T on the sidebar and the word Text in the message area.

3. Type the text shown in Figure 16.7.

Like headings, text can be collapsed and expanded with the minus key on the keypad. If you choose, though, you can collapse just the text by pressing Shift-minus with the cursor on the heading. This way, headings remain expanded.

The plus and asterisk keys on the keypad will not expand text, only headings. To expand text below a heading, you must press Shift-plus.

```
┌─────────────────────────────────────────────────────────┐
│ │                                                         │
│ ├ Layout of the Manual¶                                   │
│ │T This manual is divided into three major sections. The first│
│ │  is entitled THE FOUNDATION STRUCTURE.  It looks at the │
│ │  current organizational format of the Telefriend Foundation│
│ │  and examines the purpose and theory behind that structure,│
│ │  and how it serves to benefit so many.  The section entitled│
│ │  HISTORY AND FUTURE OF THE FOUNDATION documents the     │
│ │  organization's evolution from its historic founding and also│
│ │  discusses the direction in which we are now heading.   │
│ │  Finally, THE FOUNDATION AND THE PUBLIC addresses our   │
│ │  relationship to the individuals and organizations that make│
│ │  use of our philanthropic services.▓                    │
│ │  Purpose of the Manual¶                                 │
│ │  The Foundation Structure¶                              │
│ │      Current Format¶                                    │
│ │      Purpose and Theory¶                                │
│ │  History and Future of the Organization¶               │
│ │      Story of the Founding¶                             │
│ │      Founding to the Present¶                           │
│ │      Direction¶                                         │
│ │          Immediate¶                                     │
│ │          In Five Years¶                                 │
│ │                                         ╤TELEFOUN.DOC╤  │
│ └Text█████████       {}                    Microsoft Word │
└─────────────────────────────────────────────────────────┘
```

Figure 16.7: Adding text to the outline

Practice these commands on the "Layout of the Manual" heading. Notice that when you collapse the text, a lowercase t appears to the left of it. This code indicates that the heading has body text (and *only* body text) collapsed below it. If it also had headings collapsed below, a plus sign would appear instead.

You can adhere to your outline's structure easily by entering your text in Document mode and pressing Shift-F2 to switch to Outline view whenever you need to check your placement in the outline. This is more efficient than displaying your text in Document mode in one window and in Outline view in another window, because text you enter in one window is automatically entered in the other, regardless of which mode is activated. Thus, to view your complete outline, assuming you are working in the Document mode window, you have to switch to the other window, scroll up, and condense the body text. Conversely, pressing Shift-F2 presents the outline on the entire screen, showing exactly where you are in it. You then press Shift-F2 to go back to Document mode and continue revising.

CREATING AN OUTLINE FROM A DOCUMENT

Although it is helpful to check your document's outline while you are entering its text, you might not use the outliner for every document. In this case, you could find yourself losing track of a document's structure as you create the document unaided. Provided you have divided the body text into sections with headings, you can easily focus your attention on the overall structure by converting these section headings to outline headings by pressing Shift-F2 and then pressing Alt-9 the appropriate number of times on each heading. In other words, you can reverse the process—create an outline from body text, rather than create body text from an outline. Both techniques are simply tools for clarifying your thoughts.

Even when you work with a completed outline, you will often need to restructure the document at varying points. To enable you to accomplish this easily, Word provides its Outline Organize feature (Shift-F5). Let's examine this feature next.

REVISING YOUR OUTLINE

T I P

With Outline view turned on, you can also activate Outline Organize by pressing Shift-F10.

The advantage of revising your document in Outline Organize mode is that moving a heading moves the rest of its subsection—subheadings, body text, and all. For instance, you can view your collapsed outline and delete and move headings, secure in the knowledge that a deleted heading's unwanted body text will not get left behind and that text associated with a relocated heading follows along. To activate this mode, first press Shift-F2 to turn on Outline view and then press Shift-F5.

With Outline Organize on, Word takes on a new look. First of all, the word Organize appears in the bottom-left corner of the screen. Additionally, the cursor expands to highlight no less than an entire heading or text paragraph at a time.

JUMPING LEVELS

The movement of this expanded highlight is also different than normal. When you use the ← and → keys, the highlight moves from one paragraph (heading) to the next, regardless of the level of the heading. When you use the ↑ and the ↓ keys, the highlight jumps to the next heading with the same indent level. The Home and End keys move the highlight to the beginning and end of a level.

Collapsing and expanding, on the other hand, operate the same with Outline Organize on or off. Practice expanding and collapsing the entire outline by highlighting it with Shift-F10 and clicking both buttons on the selection bar.

To collapse a heading in Outline Organize using the mouse, click both buttons on it. Expand a heading by clicking right on it. Clicking left on a heading only relocates the highlight to it.

Our outline is small, but you can imagine how handy Word's ability to jump headings and collapse outlines is with a large document. Not only can you easily move around the document, but with Outline Organize you can perform major surgery on it as well.

MOVING OUTLINE MATERIAL

When you are working in Outline Organize, you can highlight more than one heading. Any action you then take for the highlighted headings affect their subsections as well. For instance, let's say that we want to move "The Foundation Structure" section to a point later in the document. Follow these steps:

M O U S E

Click left on Option and click right on Yes for show outline. Then press Shift-F5 to turn on Outline Organize. Click either button on "The Foundation Structure" and then press Ctrl-either button on "The Foundation and the Public."

1. If you haven't already, turn on Outline view (Shift-F2) and then turn on Outline Organize (Shift-F5).

2. Highlight the heading "The Foundation Structure."

3. Delete the heading to scrap with the Delete key or the Delete command. Notice that this action deletes its subheadings, "Current Format" and "Purpose and Theory," as well.

4. Move the cursor to "The Foundation and the Public."

5. Copy the text to its new location by pressing the Insert key or issuing the Insert command. Your screen should look like that shown in Figure 16.8.

When you move text, Word doesn't require you to keep its same indent level. If you move it to a different indent, Word will

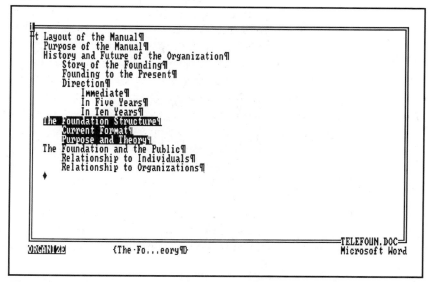

```
t Layout of the Manual¶
  Purpose of the Manual¶
  History and Future of the Organization¶
        Story of the Founding¶
        Founding to the Present¶
        Direction¶
             Immediate¶
             In Five Years¶
             In Ten Years¶
  The Foundation Structure¶
        Current Format¶
        Purpose and Theory¶
  The Foundation and the Public¶
        Relationship to Individuals¶
        Relationship to Organizations¶
     ♦
```
```
ORGANIZE          {The·Fo...eory¶}                    TELEFOUN.DOC
                                                      Microsoft Word
```

Figure 16.8: Restructuring your document with Outline Organize

automatically adjust its subsidiary headings. Thus, you could relocate "The Foundation Structure" as a subsection under "History and Future of the Organization." Just highlight the "Direction" heading before inserting "The Foundation Structure" section. The results appear in Figure 16.9.

Practice these and other block moves with your headings. Then see if you can return the outline to its original shape.

REFORMATTING LEVELS

If you like, you can format your major headings identically by collapsing the outline so that only those headings show. Then highlight all the headings and use the Format commands. You can also highlight subheadings and format them together, as long as they are under the same major heading. For best formatting results, though, I recommend you use a style sheet with your outline (see Chapter 17).

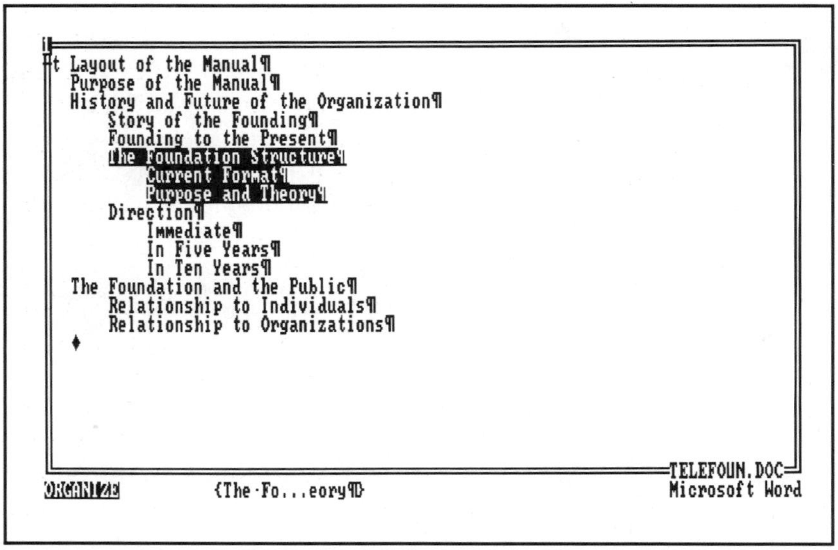

Figure 16.9: Relocating a heading to a different indent level

PRINTING YOUR OUTLINE

T *I P*

You can use the short-cut for printing, Ctrl-F8, to print your outline.

You can print outlines just as you do any document. Word is flexible in that it prints only the material that would appear in the window. If you only want certain subheadings to print, collapse or expand the headings, as appropriate, before you print. If you want certain text passages to appear, expose them as well by pressing Shift-plus. Of course, to print all the regular text in Document mode, turn Outline view off before printing by using the Options command or by pressing Shift-F2.

NUMBERING AND SORTING YOUR OUTLINE

Word can number all your outline headings automatically. To use this automatic feature, simply turn on Outline view and issue the Library Number command, which we studied in Chapter 12. You can number your outline with either Outline view or Outline Organize on, and the cursor can be anywhere in the outline except on the end mark. Word will number the outline in proper outline format. That is, Roman numerals will designate the first level, capital letters the next level, followed by Arabic numerals, and finally lowercase letters. Word will not number headings that begin with a hyphen (–), an asterisk (*), or a square bullet (■). (You can create a bullet by holding down the Alt key and typing 254 on the numeric keypad.) Figure 16.10 shows how our sample outline would appear after being numbered, along with the Library Number command, which accomplished this.

If you number your outline with Outline Organize (Shift-F5) on, the highlight should be no larger than one line. Otherwise, Word will only number the highlighted section.

When you issue the Library Number command for your outline, Word numbers it automatically; with regular documents, the command can only renumber existing numbers. If your outline does contain numbers, though, Word will update them. However, these numbers must follow Word's rules for spacing and punctuation. That is, you must enter a number, followed by a period or a closing parenthesis. If you use the closing parenthesis, you can also precede the number with an opening parenthesis. After the punctuation,

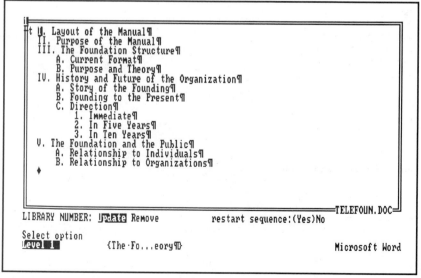

Figure 16.10: Numbering an outline automatically

there must be a space or a tab character. As with text renumbering, Word takes its punctuation cues from the first item with the same indent.

To remove numbers, issue the Library Number command and select the Remove setting. Do this now before proceeding, so that you can try alphabetizing.

When using the Library Autosort command for your outline, you must sort with Outline Organize on. You can't sort with just Outline view on, because Word won't allow you to highlight across levels. With Outline Organize, Word sorts only the highest indent level that's highlighted. It leaves deeper levels as they are, keeping them with their major heading. Figure 16.11 shows how alphabetizing only level 1 headings affects the sample outline. (The figure also presents the Library Autosort command.)

In this chapter, we've focused our attention on Outline view. However, since the outline headings' formats become the formats for the document's headings as well, you may want to establish their formats with a style sheet and then select them in your outlines. This way, you only create the formats once, and you will have no trouble maintaining consistency in your documents. You'll see how that's done in the next chapter.

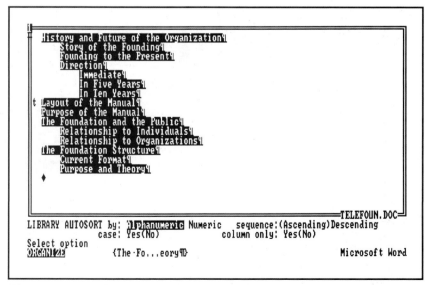

Figure 16.11: Alphabetizing the sample outline by its main headings

17

Achieving Polished Results with Style Sheets

Fast Track

DESKTOP PUBLISHING IS CURRENTLY ONE OF THE MOST popular uses for the PC. It involves using your personal or desktop computer to format material for publication. We've seen how Word can print fonts of various sizes (Chapter 7), newspaper-style columns, and a variety of lines and boxes (Chapter 11). In Chapter 18, we'll see how you can incorporate graphics into your documents. Traditionally, such procedures would be handled by a typesetter, and pasteup would be done manually. Now, Word, in conjunction with other programs, does the typeset and pasteup work for you.

When we studied the process for formatting paragraphs and characters in Chapter 5, we saw that there are two ways to produce many formats. In most cases, you can format with Alt codes, or you can format characters and paragraphs by using the Format Character and Format Paragraph commands. Although the command method is more complicated, it allows you to make more precise settings. It also gives you access to effects for which there are no equivalent Alt codes.

As your work with Word becomes more sophisticated, you may find yourself drawing on the capabilities of the Format commands more and more. You may wish that there were more Alt codes so that you didn't have to use the cumbersome Format commands so often. This especially holds true for desktop-published documents in which you use different-sized fonts. If you create many documents that are formatted similarly, you may find yourself repeatedly making the same series of format changes, even within the same document. It would certainly be convenient to have the settings automatically in place as you begin work on similarly formatted documents, and at least easily accessible for long documents.

USING WORD'S STYLIZING FEATURE

One method we've examined for speeding up the formatting process is the use of template files. At the end of Chapter 9, you learned how to create structured, formatted forms (templates) that you fill in, such as the memo in our example. In addition, Word enables you to stylize formats. You would want to stylize applications less structured than those for which you'd use template files. When you stylize, you create your own palette of personalized Alt codes or style formats—a *style sheet*. The Alt codes you create can correspond to settings that normally do not have equivalent Alt codes, such as those for the Format Division or Format Border command. You can also conjure up Alt codes that duplicate the effects of multiple settings; in this way, for instance, you could assign an Alt code to a series of tab settings to set up a complete table format.

5 New in word 5

When you load Word, it establishes its default format settings with the NORMAL.STY style sheet in the directory that's active. In Word 5 the active directory is the directory that's current when you start Word, unless you've set the Transfer Options command's save between sessions option to Yes and specified another directory with its setup option. In any case, you can add to and change the settings in NORMAL.STY. You can also create additional style sheets.

If you do create additional style sheets, you can change the style of a document simply by switching the style sheet associated with that document. For example, you might want to create one style sheet for the rough draft of a document and another for the final version. While the final-version style sheet might specify single-spacing and other formatting elements that will give your document polish, the rough-draft version might double-space the document and add wider margins, so that you can easily make notations and changes on a printed copy. The rough-draft style sheet might also eliminate changes in font sizes so that printing is quicker.

Another reason you may want to use style sheets is to accommodate changes your company makes in the way documents are formatted. Suppose, for example, that your company specifies that running heads should be five lines from the top of the page and flush with the left edge of the text. You could establish a standard running-head style for this. Later, if you need to change the specifications for running heads for any reason, you would only have to change the specifications in the style sheet. In other words, you wouldn't need to memorize the new specifications and remember to apply them each time: they would be put in place automatically whenever you create a running head. The result is less effort on your part and a greater degree of accuracy.

A third reason for using style sheets is simply to change the standard settings in NORMAL.STY. Suppose there are some settings that you always want to be initially different from those provided by Word, regardless of which document you're working with. Without changing NORMAL.STY, you would have to reset the options in each document, one document at a time. By changing the standard settings in NORMAL.STY, however, the changes will be in place automatically each time you start a new document. Because Word can use the NORMAL.STY in the directory that's active when you start Word, you can vary your standard setup by organizing categories of documents in separate directories.

Finally, by combining the style sheet with the outliner and its table of contents generator, you'll be able to format all parts of your publication consistently. That is, major headings will look the same throughout your document, subheadings will look similar, and secondary subheadings will likewise have a matching format. For instance, if you have an Alt code that provides both italics and a larger font for your major headings, you know all major headings will have this formatting—you won't find an instance where you remembered to italicize but forgot to change the font size. Word can then extract these formatted headings to create a table of contents.

There are three main components in Word you use to create style sheets and stylize your documents. Before we actually create a style sheet and attach it to a document, let's survey these three areas.

AN OVERVIEW OF THE STYLIZING OPERATION

The components of Word that you use to stylize documents are the gallery, the Alt codes, and the Format Stylesheet command. They each perform an integral part in stylizing, and they operate very differently from each other.

THE GALLERY

Think of the gallery as a special area within Word, like the document-retrieval system or Help. To access it, you issue the Gallery command from the main command menu. The gallery operates according to its own rules until you leave it by invoking its Exit command. The function of the gallery is to store style formats for the style sheet. As you use the gallery, in effect, you hang and then paint each of the customized Alt code formats in a gallery, one after another.

While it may seem odd to hang a picture first and then paint it, hanging is analogous to the process of establishing a style format in the gallery, which is accomplished with the Gallery's Insert command. You must always insert a style format in the gallery before you specify the exact characteristics of that element—that is, paint the picture. This step is accomplished with the Gallery's Format command.

To change a style format that you have already established in the gallery, you use the Name command. Other operations you can perform in the gallery require its set of Transfer subcommands. These operations are similar to the transfer operations you perform with the main Transfer command. In the gallery, you issue Transfer Load to load a different style sheet, Transfer Clear to clear the screen so that you can work on a new sheet, Transfer Delete to delete style sheets from the disk, and so on.

ALT CODES AS STYLE FORMATS

Generally, you assign an Alt code to each style format that you insert in the gallery. The Alt codes that you create through the style sheets may consist of two characters, unlike the one-character Alt codes used in formatting without style sheets. The two-character Alt code for your style format can be anything you want, but it's usually best to select a code that will remind you of what the style format does. For example, a particular style for headings might be designated by the code Alt-H-E to stand for headings.

Once you use a style sheet with its own Alt codes on a document, you cannot access a standard Alt code in the normal fashion if you've assigned its letter as the first character of any style format's Alt code. For example, if you create a style format called Alt-U-C, you won't be able to press Alt-U to turn on underlining. Instead, you add an X in the code to use it. In other words, you would press Alt-X-U to underline. If you avoid using the standard Alt codes as the first letter in your style formats' Alt codes in Word 5, you don't have to add an X to the standard codes. In Word 4, however, you must add an X to any standard Alt code when you use it in a document attached to a style sheet containing Alt codes.

Once you have created your style format Alt codes, you implement them in the standard fashion. For instance, say you created the

5 New in
Word 5

code Alt-B-I for boldface and italics. To format your document's text with this code, you first highlight the characters you want formatted and then you press Alt-B-I. To format paragraphs and divisions with their respective Alt codes, you can place the cursor anywhere in the paragraph or division you want formatted and then press the Alt code. Word will then implement all the effects you have specified as belonging to that particular code.

THE FORMAT STYLESHEET COMMAND

The Format Stylesheet command, the third component in the creation of style sheets, enables you to attach the style sheet to the document. This process, which is accomplished by invoking Format Stylesheet Attach, instructs Word to reference the style sheet for formatting specifications while you compose, edit, and print the document.

The Format Stylesheet Record command allows you to record a sample style format in the gallery. With this capacity, Word offers you another way to add formats to your style sheets. You can set up formats in your document using standard methods and then transfer those formats to the gallery.

You can use the other Format Stylesheet subcommands, Character, Paragraph, and Division, to list your personal Alt codes for those elements. If you have a mouse, you may prefer to select Alt codes from the lists displayed with these subcommands, rather than type the Alt codes.

CREATING A STYLE SHEET

Now that you know what a style sheet does, we can create one. We will begin by creating a style sheet containing three style formats: a standard paragraph format, a page layout, and a special format for a quotation paragraph. Later in the chapter, we will attach these style sheet formats to a document we create.

In setting up your hypothetical style formats, let's assume for a moment that you normally type using single-spacing, that you indent the first line of each paragraph, and that you like to have a blank line between paragraphs. In addition, you generally prefer to have your material justified on both the left and right edges. To obtain these effects in a document, you usually press Alt-F, Alt-O, and Alt-J as you begin to work with it. You always have to be careful not to lose the formatting as you work with the document. If, for instance, you should press Alt-P, the formats will be turned off and you will have to reenter their codes.

Let's also suppose that you find Word's left and right margins (usually 1¼ inches) too narrow—you are accustomed to using 1½-inch margins. To duplicate such a layout without using a style sheet, you could establish the layout with the Format Division Margins command and set its use as default option to Yes (this would apply the format to all new documents), or you could set up the layout with Format Division Margins for each document requiring that format. The advantage of using a style sheet over these two methods is that you only set up the format once and you can apply it to documents selectively. By grouping all documents to receive this format in one directory and changing that directory's NORMAL.STY style sheet, for example, the settings for this format will be in place each time you create a document in that directory.

Finally, suppose that you occasionally include indented quotation paragraphs in your documents, and when you do, you like to have them indented from the left and right. With stylizing, you can create an Alt code that will indent the right and left margins and assign italics and a smaller typeface, all at the same time.

To make these features available, we must first create these style formats in the style sheet by either inserting the style format into the gallery or adding a sample style format using the Format Stylesheet Record command. (We'll look at this second method shortly.)

DISPLAYING THE GALLERY

We will establish our style formats by using the TELEFOUN document we created in Chapter 16. Load TELEFOUN.DOC into Word. Once you've loaded TELEFOUN.DOC, issue the Gallery command so that you can insert a style format. Initially the gallery is empty (see Figure 17.1). When you have already attached a style sheet to the document, the gallery displays that style sheet.

Although the gallery screen looks similar to the screen for Word's Document mode, its window (where the style formats that you create will appear) cannot be split, and you can't edit the individual style

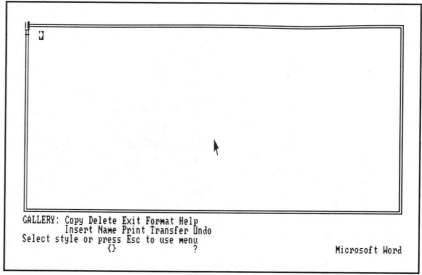

Figure 17.1: The Gallery command

formats directly. You can only add and delete entire style formats or change their formatting.

Below the command area are some old friends: the message line, the scrap area, and (with a mouse installed) the mouse's question mark. The scrap area operates as it did in Document mode, except that it moves style formats rather than text.

Now that you have the gallery displayed, you are ready to see how to change the standard paragraph shape and page composition. First, we must establish the style formats for the paragraphs and composition we want, and then we will format the style formats accordingly.

M O U S E

Click left on the Gallery's Insert subcommand to display this command menu. (Clicking right would instruct Word to insert a style format from the scrap area.)

CREATING THE STYLE FORMATS

To establish style formats, issue the Gallery's Insert subcommand by typing I from the Gallery command (see Figure 17.2). The first option, key code, is where you provide the Alt code for the style format you're creating. The curly braces, which Word initially displays in this option's field, indicate that you can insert style formats from the scrap area. You use this setting when you have placed style

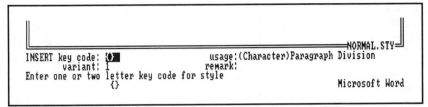

Figure 17.2: The Gallery Insert command

formats in scrap with the Gallery's Copy or Delete subcommand. Usually, though, you will need to create style formats from scratch, as we are doing now.

Because we want to create a standard paragraph shape for our documents, we'll use SP for our Alt code. (Note that if you enter the Alt code in lowercase, Word will change it to capitals in the gallery display.) As mentioned earlier, Alt codes can consist of one or two letters.

There are some points to consider before you assign a single letter as an Alt code. First, if you use a single-letter Alt code, you won't be able to use any two-character codes that begin with that same letter. For instance, if you established Alt-Q for one style format, you wouldn't be able to use Alt-Q-A through Alt-Q-Z or Alt-Q-1 through Alt-Q-0, for any others. Second, you won't want to assign Alt-X or a two-letter Alt code beginning with X since you may not be able to access Word's regular Alt codes if you do. (Remember, you add an X to a regular Alt code when the document's style sheet has an Alt code beginning with the same letter.)

When you create a new style format, you indicate whether the format will be used to format characters, paragraphs, or a division with the usage option. Once you register the settings, usage cannot be changed. You can change the Alt code, variant, or remark, however, with the Gallery's Name command. In this example, you'll set the usage option to Paragraph, as this style format applies to paragraphs.

Let's create these settings now.

M*OUSE*

Type SP as the key code setting. Then click left on Paragraph for usage.

1. Type SP in the key code field. (Note that the braces disappear when you start to type.)

2. Move to the usage option (using the Tab or → key).

3. Type P to set usage to Paragraph.

Next, you must assign a variant to each element. With variants,
Word keeps track of each style format for a particular text element
(character, paragraph, or division). Word allows you to number up to
55 paragraph variants and also provides reserved variants called
Standard, Footnote, Annotation, and Running Head. In addition,
Word sets aside 7 variants for headings in your document, plus 4 for
the index and 4 for the table of contents.

In the variant field, Word proposes the next number that's available. Since we haven't assigned any numbers yet, Word suggests 1.
As is often the case, you can accept Word's proposal, enter your own
setting, or select one from a list. Although you can assign numbers
out of sequence, I recommend that you use the order proposed by
Word. Because Standard is a special variant that automatically
defines the default format for paragraphs, Word presents it first in the
list of possible variants, and you should assign it first.

1. Move to the variant option and press F1 to see the possible
   variant choices (Figure 17.3).

2. Since Standard is already highlighted, press Enter to register
   the settings and establish the style format.

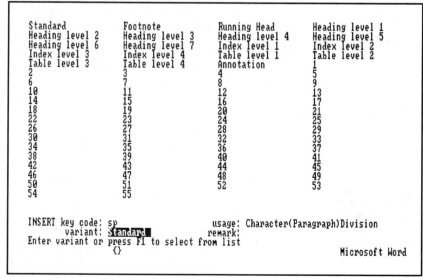

Figure 17.3: The list of paragraph variants

When you register the settings, you establish the style format in the gallery, as shown in Figure 17.4. Let's look at the parts of this display. Word provides the number 1 to show you how many style formats you have in the gallery. This number is not used to reference the format. SP indicates the Alt code you've assigned to the style format. The word Paragraph shows the usage, and Standard signifies the variant.

As you can see in Figure 17.4, the second line of the style format lists the default typeface, Courier (modern a), that's assigned to the style format. (It may vary, depending on your printer.) The font size is 12. Flush left is the standard paragraph format. These settings indicate that so far we have not reformatted the style format. We've only created its basic form. We'll learn how to format after we establish all three of our style formats.

You can insert additional style formats below or above those already on display in the gallery. The position of the highlight determines where Word will insert the new style format. You can move the highlight from one style format to another with the directional keys or

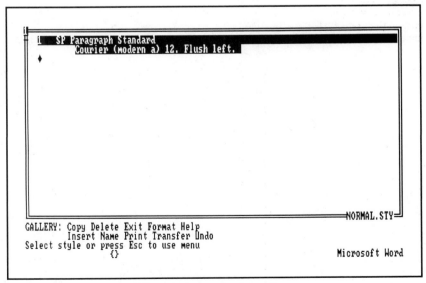

Figure 17.4: Establishing a style format in the gallery

by clicking left on it before you issue the Gallery's Insert subcommand. Word will then insert the new style format before the one highlighted.

To change the standard format of a page, we must create a style format for standard division, just as we created a style format for standard paragraph. Leave the highlight on the standard paragraph and follow these steps:

M*OUSE***

Click left on the Gallery's Insert subcommand. Type SD for the key code option and click left on Division for usage. Click right on variant. This displays the list of division variants and sets the variant to Standard. Click either button on the command name, INSERT, to register the settings.

1. Type I to display the Gallery's Insert subcommand.

2. Type SD in the key code field.

3. Move to the usage option and type D for Division.

4. Move to the variant and list the division variants by pressing F1 (see Figure 17.5).

5. Since Standard is already highlighted, press the Enter key to register the settings.

Two style formats are now displayed in the gallery; the standard division style format is above the standard paragraph format (see Figure 17.6).

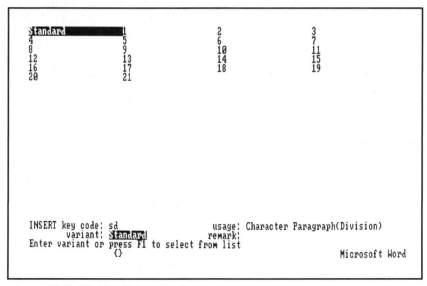

Figure 17.5: Word's division variants

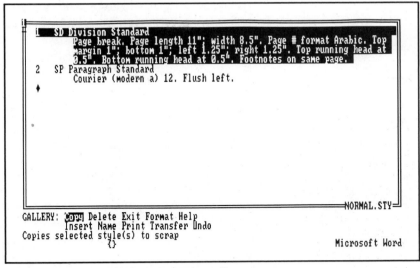

Figure 17.6: Two style formats in the gallery

Now let's establish the settings for our quotation paragraph. It's a good idea to keep the style format for standard division at the top of the gallery; this way, you can verify the standard page format of a document at a glance. To do this, move the highlight to the end mark by pressing the ↓ key twice. This will keep the standard paragraph format above other paragraph style elements you may enter.

Other cursor-movement methods work in the gallery as they do in Document mode. So you could also reach the end mark by pressing Ctrl-Page Down, pressing Ctrl-End, or clicking on it.

To add our quotation paragraph style element, follow these steps:

1. Issue the Gallery's Insert subcommand once again.

2. Type QP (for quotation paragraph) in the key code field.

3. Set the usage option to Paragraph.

4. For the variant option, Word suggests the number 1. This is what we want, so leave it as is.

5. For remark, type the comment

   Quotation

   and press Enter or click right on INSERT to register the settings.

T *IP*

Remember, you can change your key code, variant, or remark settings with the Gallery's Name command. You cannot change usage once you've assigned it with the Insert command.

The remark option lets you add a memo about the purpose of the style format. We haven't used it before because the usage and variant options described the previous style formats sufficiently.

At this point, however, we've only established the style formats; their formats are no different than those provided by Word. To give each one the characteristics we have in mind, we must format them one by one.

FORMATTING THE STYLE FORMATS

M_OUSE_

Click either button on any part of the standard division style format to highlight the entire style format. Then click either button on the Format command to display the Gallery's Format Division subcommand.

Let's first provide our page format. To do this, highlight the style format for the standard division by pressing ↑ twice or Ctrl-Page Up and then issue the Gallery's Format subcommand by typing F. Since the standard division style format is highlighted, choosing Format automatically initiates the Gallery's Format Division subcommand (see Figure 17.7).

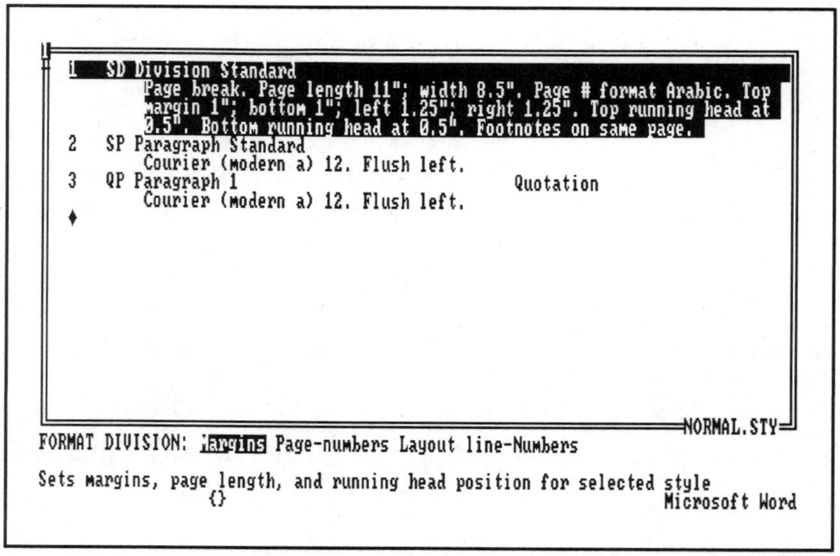

```
1   SD Division Standard
       Page break. Page length 11"; width 8.5". Page # format Arabic. Top
       margin 1"; bottom 1"; left 1.25"; right 1.25". Top running head at
       0.5". Bottom running head at 0.5". Footnotes on same page.
2   SP Paragraph Standard
       Courier (modern a) 12. Flush left.
3   QP Paragraph 1                              Quotation
       Courier (modern a) 12. Flush left.
↓

                                                          NORMAL.STY
FORMAT DIVISION: Margins Page-numbers Layout line-Numbers
Sets margins, page length, and running head position for selected style
              {}                                    Microsoft Word
```

Figure 17.7: The Gallery Format Division command

USING THE GALLERY'S FORMAT DIVISION COMMAND TO FORMAT YOUR PAGES Here are the subcommands you can use to establish the standard page format. Notice how the Gallery's Format Division subcommands are similar to those of the regular Format

Division command. Once registered, your changes will be reflected in the standard division style format.

Remember that we wanted to make our margins wider. Set the left and right margin options in the Format Division Margins command to 1.5. As long as inches are displayed, Word assumes that you mean inches unless you specify otherwise. Register your choices; the gallery will then reflect the new settings.

FORMATTING A PARAGRAPH STYLE FORMAT WITH ALT CODES
For the next style format, standard paragraph, we want to change the Flush left setting to Justified. With paragraph style formats, you can change settings (once the style format is highlighted) by using Word's standard Alt codes—in this case, Alt-J. We also want standard paragraphs to have the first line indented (Alt-F), and one blank line before each paragraph (Alt-O). Here are the steps:

1. Move the highlight to the standard paragraph style format.

2. Press Alt-J. Notice that Word replaces Flush left with Justified in the window.

3. Press Alt-F. Word adds

   (first line indent: 0.5″)

   to the gallery window.

4. Press Alt-O, which adds

   space before 1 li.

   Your gallery should now look like Figure 17.8.

Just as in Document mode, you can format paragraphs with the Gallery's Format subcommand as well as with the Alt codes. Let's format the quotation paragraph style format by using this subcommand.

USING THE GALLERY'S FORMAT PARAGRAPH AND FORMAT CHARACTER COMMANDS
When you issue the Format command with a division style format highlighted, Word moves directly to the Gallery's Format Division subcommand. When

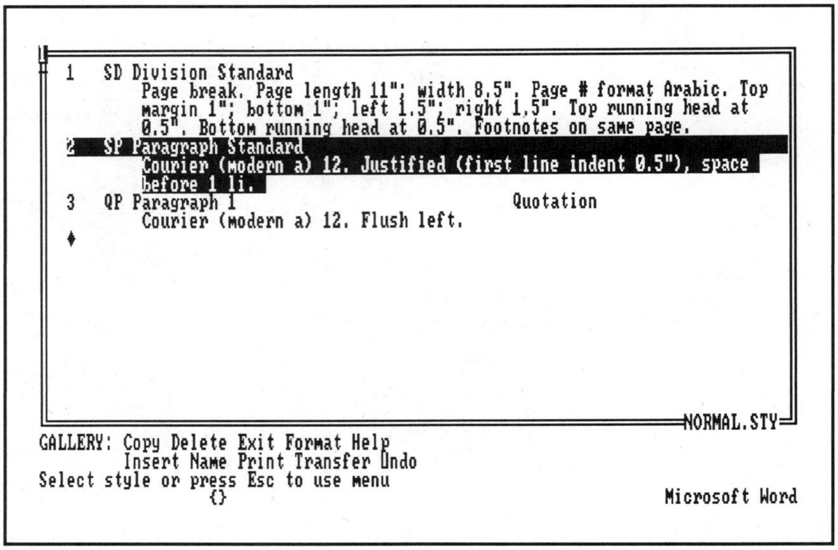

Figure 17.8: Reformatting two style formats

formatting a paragraph style format, however, you get these choices:

FORMAT: Character Paragraph Tab Border pOsition

When you format a paragraph style format, Word allows you to format characters, tabs, and border lines as well as the paragraph shape. This capability enables us to italicize our quotation paragraph. Let's begin by formatting the paragraph as follows:

1. Move to the quotation paragraph style format.

2. Type F for Format and P for Paragraph.

3. Adjust the Format Paragraph command's options as shown in Figure 17.9 and register them by pressing Enter.

The quotation paragraph will be justified for consistency with the rest of the document, indented ½ inch on both sides, and separated from the surrounding text by an additional blank line above and below it. We still need to add the italic format, however. With the keyboard, you can use the Alt code; with the mouse, you can use the Gallery's Format Character command.

M O U S E

Highlight the quotation paragraph style format by clicking either button on it and click left on Format. Click either button on Paragraph, reset its options, and click either button on FORMAT PARAGRAPH to create the quotation paragraph format.

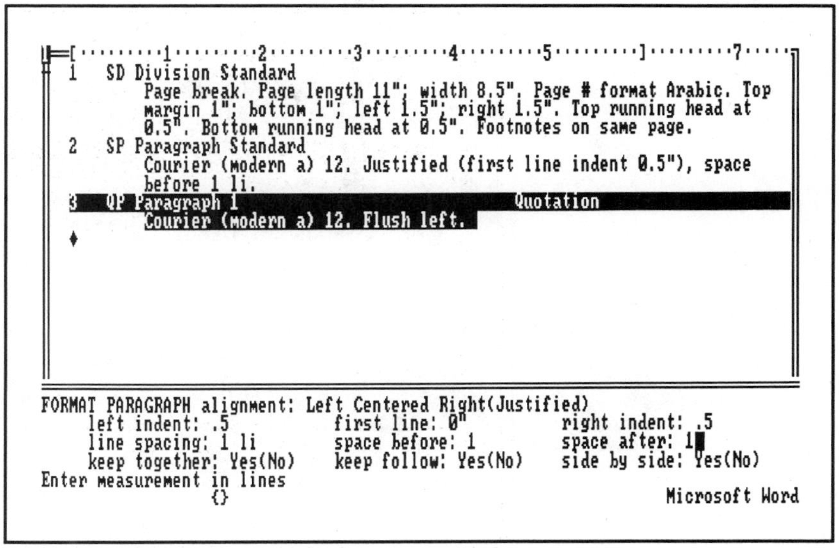

```
 ┌[·····+····1·····+····2·····+····3·····+····4·····+····5·····+·····]·······+·7····┐
 │ 1    SD Division Standard                                                         │
 │           Page break. Page length 11"; width 8.5". Page # format Arabic. Top     │
 │           margin 1"; bottom 1"; left 1.5"; right 1.5". Top running head at        │
 │           0.5". Bottom running head at 0.5". Footnotes on same page.              │
 │ 2    SP Paragraph Standard                                                        │
 │           Courier (modern a) 12. Justified (first line indent 0.5"), space        │
 │           before 1 li.                                                            │
 │▓3▓▓▓QP▓Paragraph▓1▓▓▓▓▓▓▓▓▓▓▓▓▓▓▓▓▓▓▓▓▓▓▓▓▓▓▓▓Quotation▓▓▓▓▓▓▓▓▓▓▓▓▓▓▓▓▓▓▓▓▓▓▓▓▓│
 │▓▓▓▓▓▓▓▓▓Courier▓(modern▓a)▓12.▓Flush▓left.▓▓▓▓▓▓▓▓▓▓▓▓▓▓▓▓▓▓▓▓▓▓▓▓▓▓▓▓▓▓▓▓▓▓▓▓▓▓│
 │ ♦                                                                                │
 │                                                                                   │
 │                                                                                   │
 │                                                                                   │
 │                                                                                   │
 ├──────────────────────────────────────────────────────────────────────────────────┤
 │ FORMAT PARAGRAPH alignment: Left Centered Right(Justified)                        │
 │      left indent: .5           first line: 0"          right indent: .5           │
 │      line spacing: 1 li        space before: 1         space after: 1█            │
 │      keep together: Yes(No)    keep follow: Yes(No)    side by side: Yes(No)       │
 │ Enter measurement in lines                                                        │
 │                {}                                      Microsoft Word              │
 └──────────────────────────────────────────────────────────────────────────────────┘
```

Figure 17.9: The Gallery Format Paragraph command

MOUSE

Leaving the quotation paragraph style format highlighted, click right on the Format to display the Format Character menu. Click right on Yes for italic to change the setting and register the command (see Figure 17.10).

1. Make sure that the quotation paragraph style format is still highlighted.

2. Press Alt-I to turn on the italic format. The word Italic then appears as part of the style format's description in the gallery.

ALLOWING FOR PLAIN PARAGRAPH FORMATS

There's one more paragraph format that we should include in our style sheet. As you know, pressing Alt-P normally turns off paragraph formats, creating a plain paragraph. Because you have redefined the standard paragraph (plain paragraph) in the style sheet, however, pressing Alt-P (Alt-X-P in Word 4) gives the paragraph the characteristics you've assigned to the standard paragraph. We need to create a style format for the times when we truly want unformatted paragraphs.

We can use the Insert command to assign UP as the Alt code for unformatted paragraphs. To add this code to the gallery, display the Insert menu and enter UP as the key code setting. Next, set usage to

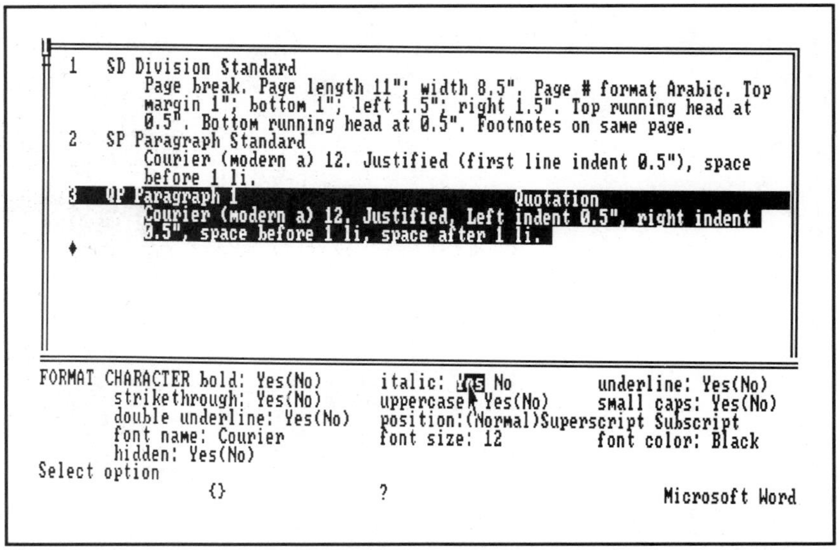

Figure 17.10: The Gallery Format Character command

Paragraph. For the remark option, type the comment

Unformatted

and register the settings by pressing Enter.

When the gallery reappears, notice that Word has automatically assigned the variant number 2 to the new style format since that was the next available number for a paragraph variant.

The newly inserted style format initially has the same format as a standard paragraph; that is, it is justified with a first-line indent. To turn off all paragraph formatting for this highlighted style format, press Alt-P.

ADJUSTING SEVERAL STYLE FORMATS SIMULTANEOUSLY

T I P

Alt-F8, the shortcut to the font name field, works on style formats in the gallery as it does with text in a document.

If you have a laser printer, you will probably want to establish a new default font for your documents' text, even when you use unformatted paragraphs. You can highlight all these paragraph style formats by pressing F6 and then press Alt-F8 to change the font name for them simultaneously (see Figure 17.11). You could select from the

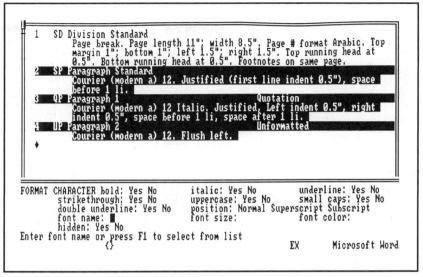

```
1   SD Division Standard
       Page break. Page length 11"; width 8.5". Page # format Arabic. Top
       margin 1"; bottom 1"; left 1.5"; right 1.5". Top running head at
       0.5". Bottom running head at 0.5". Footnotes on same page.
2   SP Paragraph Standard
       Courier (modern a) 12. Justified (first line indent 0.5"), space
       before 1 li.
3   QP Paragraph 1                              Quotation
       Courier (modern a) 12 Italic. Justified, Left indent 0.5", right
       indent 0.5", space before 1 li, space after 1 li.
4   UP Paragraph 2                              Unformatted
       Courier (modern a) 12. Flush left.



FORMAT CHARACTER bold: Yes No       italic: Yes No         underline: Yes No
       strikethrough: Yes No        uppercase: Yes No      small caps: Yes No
       double underline: Yes No     position: Normal Superscript Subscript
       font name: ■                 font size:             font color:
       hidden: Yes No
Enter font name or press F1 to select from list
       {}                                           EX      Microsoft Word
```

Figure 17.11: Formatting multiple style formats simultaneously

available choices by pressing F1 or clicking right on the font name field. I used Garamond for the font in our example. (Your font choices may vary.) After selecting a font name, move to the font size option and select the appropriate font size (say 12). To have Word adjust line spacing to a font automatically, keeping all the paragraph formats highlighted, issue the Format Paragraph command and set line spacing to Auto.

You may also wish to make the typeface smaller for quotation paragraphs. To do this, register the settings, highlight only the style format for quotation paragraph, and reissue the Gallery's Format Character subcommand, specifying 9 for the font size.

We have now completed our style sheet (for the moment). We have defined four style formats: a standard page layout, a standard paragraph, a quotation paragraph, and an unformatted paragraph. In addition, we've selected a standard font for all of them.

RECORDING SAMPLE STYLE FORMATS

The Format Stylesheet command has a subcommand that provides an alternative way to add style formats to your style sheet. With

T *IP*

Alt-F10 is a shortcut
for the Format
Stylesheet Record
command.

Format Stylesheet Record, you can transfer sample formats from
your document's text to the gallery. This feature is an easy way to
create style formats and eliminates unnecessary shuttling between
your document and the gallery.

To record a new style format, you highlight a sample format (paragraph, character, or division) in your document that you want to
save. Then you invoke the Format Stylesheet Record command.
You'll see a menu that looks just like the Insert menu in the gallery.
Use it to specify the Alt code, usage, variant, and remark for the style
format. Register the command with the Enter key or the mouse;
Word then establishes the style format in the gallery. As we are not
quite ready to leave the gallery yet, we'll practice this method shortly.

If you've previously recorded or inserted the same usage, variant,
and Alt code combination to the gallery, Word will ask you to enter Y
if you want to replace the existing style format with the sample's format. If the new combination conflicts with part of the existing style
format, Word will not allow you to record it, informing you of the
conflict so you can make adjustments.

As always with Word, the work you do is only temporary until you
save it on disk. Let's save the style sheet now.

SAVING YOUR STYLE SHEETS

To save your style sheet permanently, you must use the Gallery's
Transfer Save subcommand. Ctrl-F10, the shortcut for saving, also
saves style sheets in the gallery. Because it saves the style sheet under
the same name, though, you couldn't use it here since we want to
assign a different name to the style sheet.

M *OUSE*

In the gallery, click left
on Transfer. Then
click left on Save, type
the file name, and
click either button on
TRANSFER SAVE.

1. Type T for Transfer. Word displays the Gallery's Transfer
   subcommand (see Figure 17.12).

2. Type S for Save. Word proposes the name NORMAL.STY
   for the style sheet. However, we don't want to change NOR-
   MAL.STY, which would affect other documents you create
   in this directory. Let's have the name of our style sheet agree
   with that of our document, so enter

   TELEFOUN

   and press Enter to register the command.

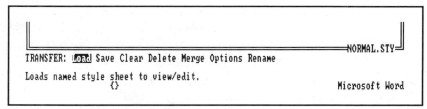

Figure 17.12: The Gallery Transfer command

Although Word automatically assigns the .STY extension to the style sheet name that you specify, you could override the extension by typing your own (that is, you would type a period and then a three-character extension). I advise, however, that you always use the .STY extension since style sheets with this extension are normally the only ones displayed if you list style sheets at Word's menus.

PRINTING AND EXITING FROM THE GALLERY

Now that you have saved the style sheet, our next major step is to create a document that uses it. As you work on a document that uses a style sheet, you may want to refer to a list of the style formats you've created, along with their associated Alt codes, until you have the style formats memorized. To print the style sheet displayed in the gallery, just get the printer ready and issue the Gallery's Print subcommand. For the printout, Word will follow the main Print Options command's settings that you've established. Once you have printed the style sheet (see Figure 17.13), keep it handy as you proceed to create your document.

To get back to Document mode, issue the Gallery's Exit command. If you loaded the sample document before entering the gallery, Word will display the message

Enter Y to attach new style sheet, N to keep old one, or Esc to cancel

when you exit.

Type Y to attach the TELEFOUN.STY style sheet to TELEFOUN.-DOC. The "old one" refers to the previously attached style sheet; in this

```
1    SD Division Standard
        Page break. Page length 11"; width 8.5". Page #
        format Arabic. Top margin 1"; bottom 1"; left 1.5";
        right 1.5". Top running head at 0.5". Bottom running
        head at 0.5". Footnotes on same page.
2    SP Paragraph Standard
        Garamond (roman m) 12/Auto. Justified (first line
        indent 0.5"), space before 1 li.
3    QP Paragraph 1                              Quotation
        Garamond (roman m) 9/Auto Italic. Justified, Left
        indent 0.5", right indent 0.5", space before 1 li,
        space after 1 li.
4    UP Paragraph 2                           Unformatted
        Garamond (roman m) 12/Auto. Flush left.
```

Figure 17.13: Printing the style sheet

case, it means NORMAL.STY, the default. Remember that Word applies the style formats in the NORMAL.STY style sheet to your document, unless you specify a different style sheet.

USING THE STYLE SHEET WITH DOCUMENTS

The document that we will produce with the style sheet we've just created is shown in Figure 17.14. You entered the text for the "Layout of the Manual" section in Chapter 16.

After exiting the gallery, you'll notice as you enter the rest of the text that the settings of the style sheet are in effect. Namely, paragraphs are automatically indented without your having to press the Tab key or Alt-F. Paragraphs are also automatically justified left and right.

Move to the end of the second heading, "Purpose of the Manual," and press Enter. As you do, you'll notice that the cursor skips a line automatically, indicating that the Alt-O effect has been activated. Type the paragraph of text (turning bold on, where indicated, with Alt-B and turning it off with Alt-Spacebar or Alt-Z) and press the Enter key to end it.

For the indented quotation, press Alt-Q-P, our Alt code for a quotation paragraph. As you type, you'll see italics displayed, and Word will wrap the text at the indented right margin for quotation paragraphs. After you type the quotation paragraph, press Enter.

For the next sentence, we will use our unformatted paragraph style. This way, Word will not indent the text after the quotation. To

Layout of the Manual

This manual is divided into three major sections. The first is entitled The Foundation Structure. It looks at the current organizational format of the Telefriend Foundation and examines the purpose and theory behind that structure, and how it serves to benefit so many. The section entitled History and Future of the Foundation documents the organization's evolution from its historic founding and also discusses the direction in which we are now heading. Finally, The Foundation and the Public addresses our relationship to the individuals and organizations that make use of our philanthropic services.

Purpose of the Manual

Recently, the esteemed president of **Telefriend Teleportation, Inc.,** made the following significant remarks at a banquet of notable dignitaries and highly respected members of the community:

The Telefriend Foundation is indeed one of the finest groups of good-deed doers active in this country today. Their work directly assists in a wide range of areas, too numerous to mention except in a cursory manner. Moreover, their activities repeatedly serve as an inspiration to anyone fortunate enough to come within their sphere of influence.

To help maintain the high standards of our foundation, the activities of the board have been compiled in this formidable document.

The first paragraph of the manual is to act as an introduction to the Telefriend Foundation, for those of you whom we have approached with the honor of serving on our board of directors. The manual should give you an idea of the Foundation and show you what would be expected of you if you became a member of the board.

The manual is also designed to serve as an ongoing reference tool for those who become board members. It provides a convenient means for keeping records of activities and decisions made during the course of the year. Because of its loose-leaf format, it can be updated regularly and used to store additional information that you may receive throughout the upcoming year.

Finally, the manual is designed to act as a resource for staff members and others. Thus, if you are aware of someone who has a legitimate need for information about the Telefriend Foundation, the manual may be made available to that person.

Figure 17.14: Producing the TELEFOUN document with the style sheet

select the unformatted paragraph style format, press Alt-U-P and enter the text.

After you type the paragraph, however, you might notice that it isn't justified on the right like the other paragraphs. That's because Alt-U-P has now taken away all formatting, including justification. It's easy enough to justify this paragraph, however. With the cursor anywhere in the paragraph, press Alt-J (Alt-X-J in Word 4). As you work with style sheets, however, you'll probably find that it is easier to create a style format to handle this type of situation.

Before you enter the next paragraph's text, you could press Alt-S-P to activate the style sheet's standard paragraph format once again. Suppose, however, that you can't exactly recall your Alt codes. If you made a printout of the codes, as we did earlier, you could consult the sheet. But there's also another way to view style sheet formats and choose from among them—namely, with the Format Stylesheet command.

VIEWING AND CHOOSING STYLE FORMATS WITH THE FORMAT STYLESHEET COMMAND

The Format Stylesheet command actually has several functions, one of which is attaching style sheets other than NORMAL.STY to documents. It also allows you to list the available style formats and assign style sheet formats in the same way as the Alt codes. Let's practice using this aspect of the Format Stylesheet command now.

1. Press the Esc key to activate Command mode.

2. Type F for Format and S for Stylesheet. The Format Stylesheet menu then appears (see Figure 17.15).

3. Type P for Paragraph since we can't recall the Alt code for standard paragraph. The Format Stylesheet Paragraph menu appears.

4. Press F1. The screen displays the three types of customized paragraphs that are available (see Figure 17.16).

5. Highlight the style format—standard paragraph—and press the Enter key to register your choice.

Now type the rest of the document.

As you may have noticed, you can use the Format Stylesheet command to assign style sheet formats to characters (Format Stylesheet

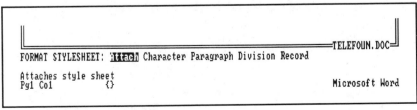

Figure 17.15: The Format Stylesheet command

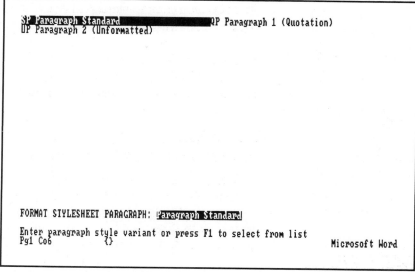

Figure 17.16: The Format Stylesheet Paragraph menu

Character) and divisions (Format Stylesheet Division) as well. Each of these commands displays its respective style formats.

ATTACHING STYLE SHEETS

Although we have no immediate use for the Format Stylesheet Attach command since we already attached the TELEFOUN.STY style sheet to our sample document, it's important for you to know how to use this subcommand of Format Stylesheet. If you have a style sheet other than NORMAL.STY that you want your document to follow, you'll need to attach the style sheet when you exit the gallery or use the Format Stylesheet Attach command. To use the command, simply invoke it and type the name of the style sheet (without the .STY extension) or select it from the list.

You can do this at any point in the preparation of a document. Changing the style sheet that's attached will reformat the document immediately. We'll look at how you would go about creating multiple style sheets at the end of the chapter.

T I P

Before converting a document for use in telecommunications, you must freeze the style sheet formats to make them part of the document; otherwise, the formats won't be converted. Word provides a macro, **freeze_style.mac**, that accomplishes this procedure automatically. See Chapter 18 for more on document conversion.

Format Stylesheet Attach also allows you to delete style sheets from documents. If you want to remove a style sheet from a particular document (but not from the disk), issue the Format Stylesheet Attach command. The name of the style sheet that's attached to the document will be listed. Press the Delete key to delete the highlighted name and then register the deletion with the Enter key. You can even remove NORMAL.STY from documents in this manner. By deleting the style sheet, you turn off all formats in the document that were established with the style sheet.

When you remove a style sheet from a document, formats that you set with the regular Format command or the standard Alt codes will remain in effect. Figure 17.17 shows what would happen if you deleted the style sheet assignment from our TELEFOUN document. Notice how the paragraph that begins ''To help maintain'' is still justified, as a result of pressing Alt-J, and ''Telefriend Teleportation, Inc.,'' is still bold as a result of Alt-B. To reattach a style sheet to the document later, you may have to remove these directly applied formats. You can even create a macro, as described in the next section, to search and replace direct formats with style formats.

SEARCHING FOR AND REPLACING STYLE FORMATS

Word can search for a style and, optionally, replace it with a different style. Although Word does not provide you with an automatic means of replacing standard formats with style formats, you can use a macro to accomplish this.

SEARCHING AND REPLACING STYLE FORMATS ONLY

Word's search and replace procedures use Alt codes to identify the styles. The techniques and reasons for searching for style formats are similar to those for standard formats. For example, if you decide you want to eliminate subheadings, which you've assigned with Alt-S-H, from your document, you can search for Alt-S-H and replace them with the heading style, Alt-H-E.

To search for style formats and not replace them, issue the Format sEarch Style command (see Figure 17.18). Provide the Alt code you

```
Layout of the Manual
This manual is divided into three major sections.  The first
is entitled The Foundation Structure.  It looks at the
current organizational format of the Telefriend Foundation
and examines the purpose and theory behind that structure,
and how it serves to benefit so many.  The section entitled
History and Future of the Foundation documents the
organization's evolution from its historic founding and also
discusses the direction in which we are now heading.
Finally, The Foundation and the Public addresses our
relationship to the individuals and organizations that make
use of our philanthropic services.
Purpose of the Manual
Recently, the esteemed president of Telefriend
Teleportation, Inc., made the following significant remarks
at a banquet of notable dignitaries and highly respected
members of the community:
The Telefriend Foundation is indeed one of the finest groups
of good-deed doers active in this country today.  Their work
directly assists in a wide range of areas, too numerous to
mention except in a cursory manner.  Moreover, their
activities repeatedly serve as an inspiration to anyone
fortunate enough to come within their sphere of influence.
To help maintain the high standards of our foundation, the
activities  of  the  board  have  been  compiled  in  this
formidable document.
The first paragraph of the manual is to act as an
introduction to the Telefriend Foundation, for those of you
whom we have approached with the honor of serving on our
board of directors.  The manual should give you an idea of
the Foundation and show you what would be expected of you if
you became a member of the board.
The manual is also designed to serve as an ongoing reference
tool for those who become board members.  It provides a
convenient means for keeping records of activities and
decisions made during the course of the year.  Because of
its loose-leaf format, it can be updated regularly and used
to store additional information that you may receive
throughout the upcoming year.
Finally, the manual is designed to act as a resource for
staff members and others.  Thus, if you are aware of someone
who has a legitimate need for information about the
Telefriend Foundation, the manual may be made available to
that person.
```

Figure 17.17: Printing the document after removing its style sheet

are seeking in the key code field. Choose Up or Down for the direction option to tell Word which way to search from the cursor's current position.

To search for a style format and replace it with a different style format, issue the Format repLace Style command (see Figure 17.19). Enter the Alt code you're searching for and the one you want to replace it with. If you're sure of the switch in all instances, set the

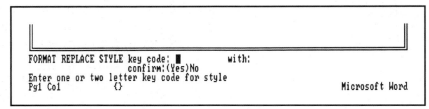

Figure 17.18: Searching for style formats

Figure 17.19: Replacing style formats

confirm option to No. Otherwise, leave it set to Yes so that you can check each occurrence before changing its format.

REPLACING STANDARD FORMATS WITH STYLE FORMATS

Word's inability to replace standard formats with style formats can cause trouble when you create a document using standard formats and attempt to switch to style formats later. For example, suppose a co-worker prepares a document for you without concern for fonts, because he has been using a simple dot-matrix printer. Initially, Word assigns Courier 12, a fixed-pitch font, to the text. Your co-worker has italicized text, every now and then, by pressing Alt-I. You receive the document, and it's your job to make it typeset-quality by using attractive fonts, changing heading sizes, and so on. The best way to handle the job is by attaching a style sheet. But when you select a different font, using your standard paragraph style format, you'll find that the text in italics remains formatted with Courier 12. This is because using normal Alt codes, such as Alt-I, freezes all character formats, including the font name. The same holds true when you use the Format Character and Format Paragraph commands directly.

In place of these normal codes, you'd like to add a character style format to your style sheet (perhaps Alt-I-T); this would specify the same font name as you're using for the standard paragraph format, but in italics. Having such a style format would also be important should you later decide to adjust the font size: you could easily match the font size for the italicized text to standard paragraph format's size.

TIP

Remember, to create indenting in the macro's text, use the Tab key or formatting (such as Alt-N); do not add spaces with the Space bar.

Figure 17.20 presents a simple macro you can create in Word 5 (or in Word 4, with some adjustments) that can replace Alt-I with Alt-I-T automatically. It allows you to replace any standard character or paragraph format with a corresponding style format. Before running the macro, load the appropriate document (with the style sheet attached) and place the cursor at the point where you want the searching to begin.

First, the macro asks you to indicate the format you are replacing by entering C for Character or P for Paragraph. The subsequent WHILE loop ensures that you've entered only a C or a P. Then the macro displays the Format sEarch Character or Format sEarch Paragraph menu as appropriate, so you can indicate the standard format to be searched for. Once you respond, the macro locates the first instance of the format and displays the list of available style formats. It pauses for you to highlight the one that you want, and then it substitutes that style format for the first found standard format. Finally, another WHILE loop repeats the search (<Shift F4>), substituting the style format (<F4>) for the standard format as long as it is found. (With Word 4, you can create the equivalent by eliminating the first WHILE loop and replacing <Shift Ctrl Esc> with <Ctrl Esc>.)

```
«ASK CP=? Search for: C=Character format; P=Paragraph format»
«WHILE CP<>"C" and CP<>"P"»
     «ASK CP=? Press only C or P and Enter: C=Character; P=Paragraph»
     «ENDWHILE»
<shift ctrl esc>FE«CP»
«PAUSE Indicate format to search for and press the Enter key»<enter>
<shift ctrl esc>FS«CP»<F1>
«PAUSE Highlight format to replace with and press the Enter key»<enter>
«WHILE found»
     <shift F4>
     <F4>
     «ENDWHILE»
```

Figure 17.20: A macro for replacing standard formats with style formats

USING THE STYLE BAR
TO DISPLAY PARAGRAPH ALT CODES

As you use style sheets more, you might forget which formats you have assigned to paragraphs in your document. Word provides a handy way to view your Alt code assignments. You can see them in an area of the window called the *style bar*. It's to the left of your document, between the border and the selection bar. To display the style bar in a window, activate the window and issue the Options command, changing show style bar to Yes. Figure 17.21 presents the document we've been working on with its style bar.

If the paragraph has a style that's not defined on the style sheet currently attached to the document (this could happen if you switched style sheets, for instance), an asterisk will appear in the style bar. If the paragraph is a running head, the code in the style bar will indicate its location on the printed page. It uses t for the top of the page, b for bottom, e for even pages, and o for odd pages. Thus, a running head that appears on the top of even pages will show up in the style bar as te.

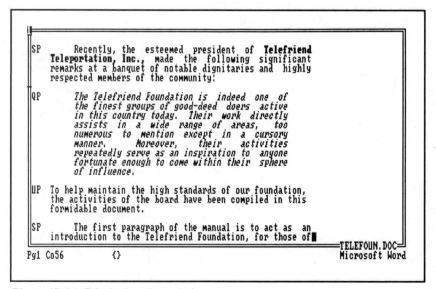

Figure 17.21: Displaying the style bar

ADDITIONAL STYLE SHEET ENHANCEMENTS

Now that you have an idea of what style sheets can accomplish, let's enhance our style sheet. You may have some ideas of your own by now.

Consider headings. Let's suppose that you like to have three blank lines before headings in your documents and that you like to italicize and underline all your headings. Without a style sheet, you would have to use the Format Paragraph command each time you typed a heading, changing the space before setting to 3. When typing the heading, you would have to turn on the italics and underlining and remember to turn off these formats when you're done. You'd probably like a bigger font for headings as well. You would have to choose the same font each time. Finally, when printed, your heading could end up at the bottom of one page with the information that follows it printed on the next, unless you thought to set the keep follow option in the Format Paragraph menu to Yes. You can handle all these chores automatically by making a style format for headings.

While we're at it, let's create a style format for footnotes. Suppose you always like to have footnote reference marks raised (superscripted) and set in a smaller typeface than the rest of the text. Without a style sheet, accomplishing this would be tedious. You would have to type the appropriate Alt code or issue the Format Character command every time you made a footnote reference.

Finally, let's consider our use of multiple divisions. In Chapter 9, I explained how to make the layout of your first page different from the rest of the document by making two divisions. To create the page layout without a style sheet, you add a division and format it with the Format Division command's numerous options for each document. With a style sheet, we can set up division formats once and then just use Alt codes to format the divisions for different documents.

CREATING A STYLE FORMAT FOR HEADINGS

We'll create our style format for headings using the sample recording method. First, we'll format a sample paragraph, setting up the alignment, indent, line spacing, keep follow, and font characteristics with the Format Paragraph command, and specify that we want italicized and underlined headings with the Format Character command. Then we'll establish a new style format for headings, using Alt-H-E as the Alt code, and observe the results.

Word has variants reserved for seven headings, and they work together with the outliner. When you set up a style format using one of these variants and then apply that style format to text (using the Alt code you assigned to it or the Format Character command), the text becomes the formatted heading and adjusts automatically in Outline view. You needn't press Alt-9 or Alt-0 to establish a heading level in Outline view when you use a style sheet—the style format determines the level, as well as its format.

If your document has an attached style sheet, you can still print the document in Outline view; Word will maintain the outline and character formats but ignore the established paragraph formatting. (The headings' complete formatting can only be printed in Document mode.)

When we establish the format for headings, we'll set the alignment option to Left, specify no first-line indent, and set the keep together option to Yes. Although these settings would be relevant only if there were more than two lines in the heading, by setting them now we can prepare for some heading in the future that might take up two or more lines.

1. Move the cursor to a sample heading. For this example, use the "Layout of the manual" heading at the beginning of the document.

2. Format the heading. Issue the Format Paragraph command and set alignment to Left, first line to 0, space before to 3, and both the keep together and keep follow options to Yes.

3. Highlight the entire paragraph and issue the Format Character command to set italics and the font name. Because you're providing all characters in the paragraph with the same format, Word will associate this character format with the paragraph style.

4. Initiate the Format Stylesheet Record command (or press Alt-F10).

5. With the menu that appears, type HE in the key code field. Set usage to Paragraph. In the variant field, press F1 and choose the reserved variant for Heading level 1 (see Figure 17.22). You can leave the remark option blank—the variant says it all.

6. When the settings are in place, register them with the Enter key or the mouse. Word will then record the style format in the gallery.

Once you have recorded the style format, you can check that the gallery contains the established style format (Figure 17.23). You can then use Alt-H-E to format additional headings exactly like this first heading (see Figure 17.24).

If you later want to format your headings additionally, you would only need to change the style format for headings by entering the gallery and using the Format command. You could also update a sample heading in Document mode and issue the Format Stylesheet Record command again, replacing the existing style with the new version.

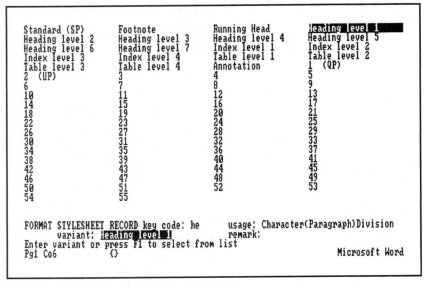

Figure 17.22: Recording a heading style format

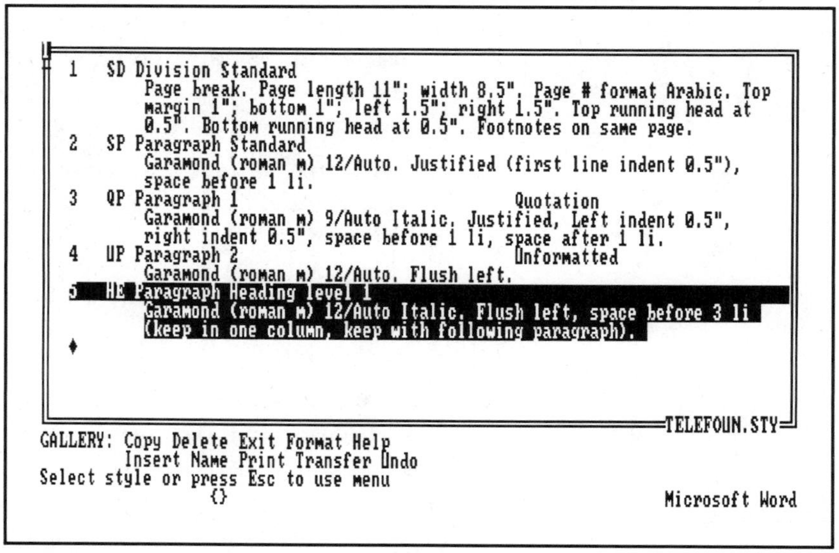

```
1   SD Division Standard
       Page break. Page length 11"; width 8.5". Page # format Arabic. Top
       margin 1"; bottom 1"; left 1.5"; right 1.5". Top running head at
       0.5". Bottom running head at 0.5". Footnotes on same page.
2   SP Paragraph Standard
       Garamond (roman m) 12/Auto. Justified (first line indent 0.5"),
       space before 1 li.
3   QP Paragraph 1                                      Quotation
       Garamond (roman m) 9/Auto Italic. Justified, Left indent 0.5",
       right indent 0.5", space before 1 li, space after 1 li.
4   UP Paragraph 2                                      Unformatted
       Garamond (roman m) 12/Auto. Flush left.
5   HE Paragraph Heading level 1
       Garamond (roman m) 12/Auto Italic. Flush left, space before 3 li
       (keep in one column, keep with following paragraph).
♦

                                                      ═TELEFOUN.STY═
GALLERY: Copy Delete Exit Format Help
         Insert Name Print Transfer Undo
Select style or press Esc to use menu
              {}                                      Microsoft Word
```

Figure 17.23: The heading style format in the gallery

STYLIZING FOOTNOTES

To produce stylized footnotes, you must create two style formats. One format will specify the format of the character that's used for the footnote reference mark, while the other will specify the paragraph formatting for the footnote paragraph. You won't need to specify Alt codes when creating footnotes, because Word will assign the formatting by using the style sheet's reserved variants automatically.

To create a style format for the reference marks, enter the gallery, issue the Insert command, and specify Character for usage. Move to the variant setting and list the character variants. Select the reserved variant Footnote ref (reference) for the variant, as shown in Figure 17.25. Register the command and format the style format as a superscript that will appear in a smaller typeface.

When you insert the style format for the footnote paragraph, specify usage as Paragraph. Display the paragraph variants and choose Footnote as the variant. Format it as you would like your footnote paragraph to appear.

Layout of the Manual

This manual is divided into three major sections. The first is entitled The Foundation Structure. It looks at the current organizational format of the Telefriend Foundation and examines the purpose and theory behind that structure, and how it serves to benefit so many. The section entitled History and Future of the Foundation documents the organization's evolution from its historic founding and also discusses the direction in which we are now heading. Finally, The Foundation and the Public addresses our relationship to the individuals and organizations that make use of our philanthropic services.

Purpose of the Manual

Recently, the esteemed president of **Telefriend Teleportation, Inc.,** made the following significant remarks at a banquet of notable dignitaries and highly respected members of the community:

The Telefriend Foundation is indeed one of the finest groups of good-deed doers active in this country today. Their work directly assists in a wide range of areas, too numerous to mention except in a cursory manner. Moreover, their activities repeatedly serve as an inspiration to anyone fortunate enough to come within their sphere of influence.

To help maintain the high standards of our foundation, the activities of the board have been compiled in this formidable document.

The first paragraph of the manual is to act as an introduction to the Telefriend Foundation, for those of you whom we have approached with the honor of serving on our board of directors. The manual should give you an idea of the Foundation and show you what would be expected of you if you became a member of the board.

The manual is also designed to serve as an ongoing reference tool for those who become board members. It provides a convenient means for keeping records of activities and decisions made during the course of the year. Because of its loose-leaf format, it can be updated regularly and used to store additional information that you may receive throughout the upcoming year.

Finally, the manual is designed to act as a resource for staff members and others. Thus, if you are aware of someone who has a legitimate need for information about the Telefriend Foundation, the manual may be made available to that person.

Figure 17.24: Using the heading style format

Once you're back in the document, just establish footnotes as needed with the Format Footnote command. Word will apply your formats to them automatically.

Figure 17.26 shows our completed document, labeled with the numbers that correspond to the style formats I selected from its style sheet. Notice how I've added two style formats for footnote paragraph and footnote reference.

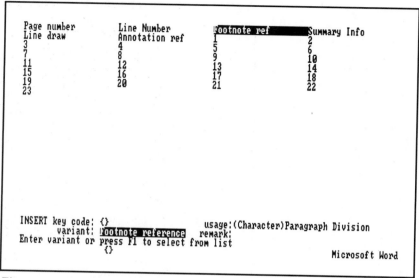

Figure 17.25: Listing the character variants

FORMATTING AN ADDITIONAL DIVISION

You can insert style formats in the gallery for other divisions as well—for example, to set up a different layout for the first page. You might use LD for the Alt code (to stand for letterhead division) and establish its style format to fit your company's preferred format. You would press Alt-L-D as you work on the document, which would initially establish the letterhead layout for the document. Keep the text above the division mark that Alt-L-D creates. To format the second division, go to the beginning of the second page—you can use the Jump Page command to do so—and insert a division mark by pressing Ctrl-Enter. Then, with the cursor after this new division mark, enter the division Alt code for the remaining pages of the document.

The page break between the first and second pages should initially be above the division mark, and it will disappear shortly after you insert the division mark. Should you later add text to or remove text from the first page, you would have to preview your document and move the division mark so that the second division starts at the top of the second page, not before or after.

T I P

Word 5 supplies the macro **print_letter-.mac**, which prompts you to set up margins for the first page that are different from the subsequent pages, and then it prints the letter (see Appendix C).

T I P

When adding divisions, you need to adjust forced page breaks (Ctrl-Shift-Enter). Delete the page break and allow the division

⑤ ## *Layout of the Manual*

This manual is divided into three major sections. The first is entitled The Foundation Structure. It looks at the current organizational format of the Telefriend Foundation and examines the purpose and theory behind that structure, and how it serves to benefit so many. The section entitled History and Future of the Foundation documents the organization's evolution from its historic founding and also discusses the direction in which we are now heading. Finally, The Foundation and the Public addresses our relationship to the individuals and organizations that make use of our philanthropic services.

②

Purpose of the Manual

Recently, the esteemed president of **Telefriend Teleportation, Inc.,** made the following significant remarks at a banquet of notable dignitaries and highly respected members of the community:

③ *The Telefriend Foundation is indeed one of the finest groups of good-deed doers active in this country today. Their work directly assists in a wide range of areas, too numerous to mention except in a cursory manner. Moreover, their activities repeatedly serve as an inspiration to anyone fortunate enough to come within their sphere of influence.*

④ To help maintain the high standards of our foundation, the activities of the board have been compiled in this formidable document.

The first paragraph of the manual is to act as an introduction to the Telefriend Foundation, for those of you whom we have approached with the honor of serving on our board of directors. The manual should give you an idea of the Foundation and show you what would be expected of you if you became a member of the board.[1] ⑦

The manual is also designed to serve as an ongoing reference tool for those who become board members. It provides a convenient means for keeping records of activities and decisions made during the course of the year. Because of its loose-leaf format, it can be updated regularly and used to store additional information that you may receive throughout the upcoming year.

Finally, the manual is designed to act as a resource for staff members and others. Thus, if you are aware of someone who has a legitimate need for information about the Telefriend Foundation, the manual may be made available to that person.

⑦
⑥ ---

[1] For those who are considering joining us, we hope to welcome you aboard in the near future!

1   SD Division Standard
        Page break. Page length 11"; width 8.5". Page #
        format Arabic. Top margin 1"; bottom 1"; left 1.5";
        right 1.5". Top running head at 0.5". Bottom running
        head at 0.5". Footnotes on same page.
2   SP Paragraph Standard
        Garamond (roman m) 12/Auto. Justified (first line
        indent 0.5"), space before 1 li.
3   QP Paragraph 1   Quotation
        Garamond (roman m) 9/Auto Italic. Justified, Left
        indent 0.5", right indent 0.5", space before 1 li,
        space after 1 li.
4   UP Paragraph 2   Unformatted
        Garamond (roman m) 12/Auto. Flush left.

```
5    HE Paragraph Heading level 1
          Garamond (roman m) 18/Auto Italic Underlined. Flush
          left, space before 3 li (keep in one column, keep
          with following paragraph).
6       Paragraph Footnote
          Garamond (roman m) 10/Auto. Justified, Left indent
          0.5" (first line indent -1"), space before 1 li.
7       Character Footnote reference
          Garamond (roman m) 9 Superscript.
```

Figure 17.26: Selecting footnote and other style formats in the document

mark to break the page, or keep the page break below the division mark. Otherwise, Word will apply the first division's top margin settings to the second division's first page.

You could also create division style formats for legal-sized paper (8½" by 14") and for different page number formats. Then you'd just have to type an Alt code when you want to put one of these division formats into effect. For example, suppose you always use the same paper size but change the position and format of the page number. Sometimes, you don't use a page number at all. To handle such situations, you can attach ACADEMIC.STY, one of the style sheets supplied with Word 5, to your document. It has three division formats in it.

Figure 17.27 shows the last three style formats that are in this style sheet. By simply applying one of these division formats (with its Alt code or the Format Stylesheet command), you can change a document's

T IP

After merging style sheets, you could easily end up with more than one style format that has the same variant, which Word does not allow. Delete one of the conflicting style formats or provide a different variant for it before you save the style sheet or exit the gallery. Otherwise, you'll get the message "Style already defined."

```
9   ND Division 3                          NO PAGE NUMBERS
        Page break. Page length 11"; width 8.5". Page # format Arabic. Top
        margin 1"; bottom 1"; left 1.5"; right 1". Top running head at
        0.5". Bottom running head at 0.5". Footnotes on same page.
10  RD Division 2                     CENTERED ROMAN NUMERALS
        Page break. Page length 11"; width 8.5". Page # format lowercase
        Roman at 10.5" from top, 4.25" from left. Top margin 1"; bottom 1";
        left 1.5"; right 1". Top running head at 0.5". Bottom running head
        at 0.5". Footnotes on same page.
11  AD Division 1                          ARABIC NUMERALS
        Page break. Page length 11"; width 8.5". Page # format Arabic at
        0.5" from top, 7.5" from left. Top margin 1"; bottom 1"; left 1.5";
        right 1". Top running head at 0.5". Bottom running head at 0.5".
        Footnotes on same page.



GALLERY: Copy Delete Exit Format Help
         Insert Name Print Transfer Undo
Select style or press Esc to use menu
             {}                              Microsoft Word
```
ACADEMIC.STY

Figure 17.27: Style formats for numbering pages, in Word's ACADEMIC-.STY style sheet

numbering system. To add these style formats to an existing style sheet, issue the Gallery's Transfer Merge command. You can then delete ACADEMIC.STY's other style formats if you don't want them in your TELEFOUN style sheet.

Figure 17.28 shows how applying style format #10 would number our document. Compare it to Figure 17.29, which shows the results of using style format #11.

USING MULTIPLE STYLE SHEETS

The purpose of multiple style sheets is to allow you to create different formats for a document easily. Then you can attach one style sheet or another to the document, depending on the way you want your document formatted. If you wanted a draft copy of our TELEFOUN document, for instance, you could create a style sheet called DRAFT.STY. This style sheet might call for more white space so that it would be easier to indicate changes in the rough document. For instance, you might want to increase the margin width to 1.75 inches. You might also want to double-space the rough draft and change to a wider character pitch so that you could make notations between words more easily. All of this information could be specified within the DRAFT style sheet.

For style formats to take effect once a new style sheet is attached to a document, the new variants for each usage must coincide with those of the first style sheet; the Alt codes are not the coordinating factor. To design a new style sheet for a document, you can load the first style sheet and then just reformat the style formats to your new specifications. Then save the new style sheet under a different name.

To change the style sheet that's attached to a document, use the Format Stylesheet Attach command. Type the name of the style sheet that's desired or select it from the list. Then print the document.

For example, after printing the outline of your document, you may find that the character formatting, such as a font size, that you've assigned to the heading variants is desirable for your standard document but inappropriate for outline format. Assuming you used the reserved variants for headings correctly, you could simply attach either Word's SAMPLE.STY or OUTLINE.STY style sheet, as they both have

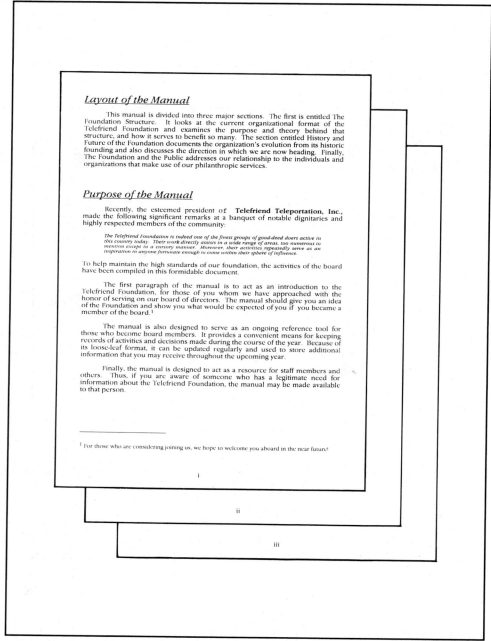

Figure 17.28: Applying division format #10, Centered Roman Numerals

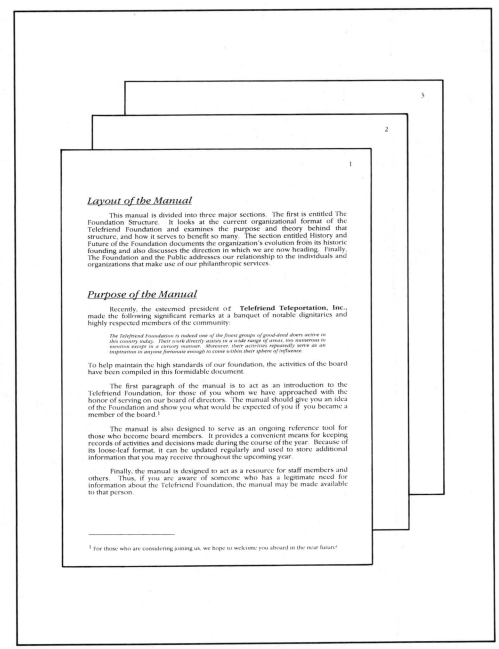

Figure 17.29: Applying division format #11, Arabic Numerals

outline style formats already set up. Here's how you would proceed to get the outline formats shown in Figures 17.30 and 17.31:

1. Activate Outline view (with Shift-F2 or the Options command).

2. Highlight the entire document, collapse the text by pressing Shift-minus on the keypad, and expand all headings by typing an asterisk (using the keypad).

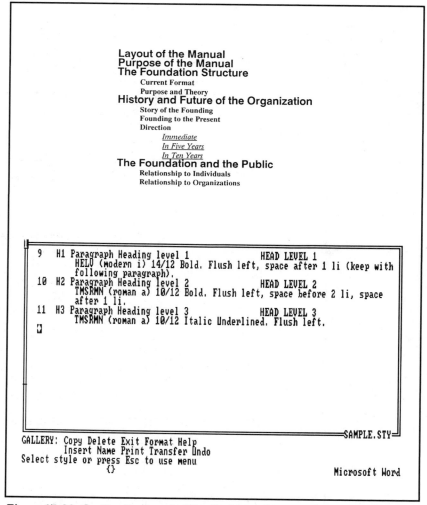

Figure 17.30: Outline formats in Word's SAMPLE.STY style sheet

3. Issue the Format Style Attach command to attach SAMPLE.-STY or OUTLINE.STY to your document.

4. Print the outline.

Once you've printed the outline, issue the Format Style Attach command to reattach your original style sheet.

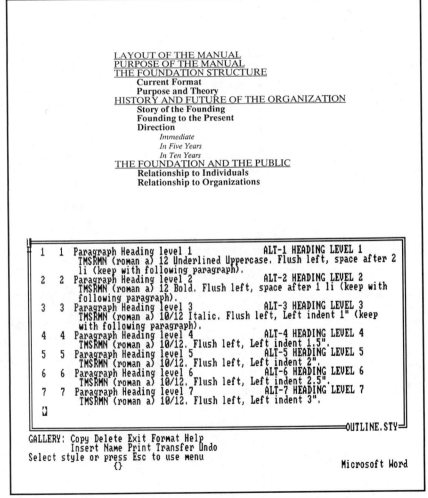

Figure 17.31: Outline formats in Word's OUTLINE.STY style sheet

USING WORD'S
SAMPLE STYLE SHEETS

Word 5 comes with nine sample style sheets. You can use them as they are, adapt them to suit your needs, or use the Gallery's Transfer Merge command to add their style formats to one of your style sheets. Microsoft delivers these style sheets on the Utilities 2 disk except for FULL.STY and SEMI.STY, which are on the Program 1 disk. The Setup program copies them, along with the Word program, to your hard disk when you install Word (see Appendix A).

You can look at these sample style sheets by loading them with the Gallery's Transfer Load command or by pressing Ctrl-F7 in the gallery. You can then print out their specifications if you want.

SAMPLE.STY is a simple, general purpose style sheet. There are large font styles for a bold, centered title (applied with Alt-T-I) and an underlined subhead (Alt-S-H). There are also two style formats for side-by-side paragraphs, one each for the left and right paragraphs (Alt-L-1 and Alt-R-1). This style sheet uses reserved styles for an italicized, centered running head (Alt-R-H) and for three heading levels with graded amounts of space before and after them (Alt-H-1, Alt-H-2, and Alt-H-3). There is also a style format for creating lists with a left indent and a negative indent for the first line. This format creates a hanging indent for each paragraph in the list.

SIDEBY.STY is a style sheet that has five paragraph styles for creating side-by-side paragraphs. The first two (Alt-2-L and Alt-2-R) create the left and right paragraphs in a two-column arrangement of paragraphs. These style formats create paragraphs of equal width. The other three (Alt-3-L, Alt-3-C, and Alt-3-R) create left, centered, and right paragraphs, respectively, in a three-column layout.

RESUME.STY is another style sheet that provides a two-column layout. Its two style formats, which can be easily interchanged with SIDEBY.STY's Alt-2-L and Alt-2-R style formats, establish a narrow left paragraph and a wide right paragraph.

OUTLINE.STY is a style sheet targeted for use with Word's outliner (see Chapter 16). It has seven paragraph styles, which are assigned to the seven reserved heading levels. You select these styles with Alt-1 through Alt-7. The Alt code corresponds to the level of importance. For example, level 1 is underlined, in a larger font than usual, and has

T I P

Word also provides a macro, **sidebyside-.mac**, for automatically formatting paragraphs side by side (see Appendix C).

New in Word 5

2 lines of spacing after it. Level 2 is bold and has 1 line of spacing after it. Level 3 appears in italics, while Level 4 is unformatted.

FULL.STY is a style sheet for typing a left-justified letter. There are paragraph styles for the parts of a letter, such as the inside address (Alt-I-A), the salutation (Alt-S-A), and so on. All parts of this letter format begin at the left margin, although some paragraph styles, such as the inside address, accomplish this by providing a hanging indent.

SEMI.STY is a style sheet that assigns a semiblock format to letters. Although it's similar to FULL.STY, this format indents appropriate parts of the letter (the return address, the date, the complimentary closing and so on) 3.2 inches so that they start in the middle of the page.

FULL.STY and SEMI.STY sheets probably don't represent the best way to handle the repetitive formatting of letters that you send regularly. A better approach is to use a document template (see Chapter 9) or the Print Merge command (see Chapter 14). Document templates allow you to include properly positioned text, such as the return address and closing as well as formats. They're more efficient because you have less text to type and fewer Alt codes to apply. Use Print Merge when the bulk of the letter, especially the body, remains the same from one letter to another.

New in
Word 5

ACADEMIC.STY has centered formats for the title page (Alt-T-1), which is also centered vertically on the page), chapter title (Alt-T-2), and section titles (Alt-T-3). There is a style format for double-spaced text (Alt-D-P), quotes, indented left and right (Alt-Q-T), hanging paragraphs for a bibliography (Alt-B-P), and footnotes. As I discussed previously, it also contains three division formats for different page-numbering arrangements.

New in
Word 5

APPEALS.STY has a standard paragraph with a first-line indent (Alt-H-1). Its style formats for standard paragraph (Alt-S-P), lead-in (Alt H-1), and quotes (Alt-Q-T) are progressively indented from the left. Although one style format is called Standard Paragraph in its remark, it doesn't use the standard variant so it's not applied to text automatically. The lead-in style format is set for uppercase, and the quotes style format is set for italics. It also has a standard division for a left margin that's wider than the right.

New in
Word 5

STATE.STY has the same Alt codes assigned to the same variants as APPEALS.STY, which means that you can swap these two style sheets to reformat the same document quickly. With this style sheet, standard paragraphs are double-spaced, lead-in text is uppercased, and quotes are underlined. All three formats have double lines on the left and on the right. Like APPEALS.STY, STATE.STY has a standard division for a left margin that's wider than the right.

Style sheets are an advanced word processing feature—a feature that allows you to streamline your work. To make it even easier, you can order a disk containing the examples we created in this and other chapters. The last two chapters are devoted to Word's hidden text feature. It gives you the ability to import graphics and create automatic forms, an index, and a table of contents. Like the style sheet and outline features, Word's hidden text capabilities set it apart from many other word processing systems.

18

Linking Spreadsheets, Documents, and Graphics

Fast Track

AS YOU CREATE MORE AND MORE DESKTOP-PUBLISHED documents in Word, you'll probably want to incorporate tables, graphics, and text from outside sources. Microsoft Word, especially release 5, meets these increasingly sophisticated needs.

FLAGGING WITH HIDDEN TEXT

T I P

Because you can format text as hidden, you can also use this feature to type notes to yourself or to your colleagues in your documents.

To provide these capabilities, Word uses *hidden text,* which acts as a code that indicates where to reference a worksheet, graphic, or another Word document in your document. We'll examine these applications in this chapter, along with methods for sharing Word documents with other programs. In the next chapter, you'll see how you can use hidden text to create entries for an index, a table of contents, or other lists, such as legal citations or a list of illustrations.

You can format text as hidden by using the Alt-E code or the Format Character command's hidden option. You can also enter your own Alt code if you've created a style format that's formatted as hidden.

Although text disappears from the screen when you format it as hidden, you can also display it on the screen and print it, just like any other text. To display hidden text, which you'll want to do when you are revising a document, issue the Options command and set its shown hidden text option to Yes. In Graphics mode, you'll see a dotted line below hidden text made visible.

If show hidden text is set to No, what you'll see depends on the Options command's show non-printing symbols option. If it's set to None, there is no indication of hidden text on the screen, and it's easy to delete the hidden text unintentionally. For instance, if you simultaneously delete the characters before and after the hidden text, Word will delete the hidden text as well. Similarly, pressing the Backspace key with the cursor on the character following hidden text deletes the hidden text.

When you set show hidden text to Partial or All, a small double-headed arrow pointing left and right

$$\longleftrightarrow$$

indicates the position of hidden text. If you delete this marker, your hidden text will be deleted as well.

Even if hidden text is displayed on the screen, Word will only print it when the Print Options command's hidden text option is set to Yes. So, unless you want the hidden text to appear in print, leave this option set to No.

Now that you know how to create, view, and print hidden text, let's put this feature to use.

LINKING LOTUS 1-2-3 TO WORD

With hidden codes and the Library Link command, you can incorporate spreadsheets, other documents, and graphics directly into your text. Let's begin by examining this command's use with spreadsheets.

Besides being able to pull data from an electronic spreadsheet such as Lotus 1-2-3, Word also allows you to keep the data current. The process is simple.

First, to add the spreadsheet's data to your document, create a paragraph mark (¶) by pressing Enter where you want the data to appear. This will make the incoming table its own paragraph. With the cursor on that paragraph mark, invoke the Library Link command (see Figure 18.1).

Select Spreadsheet to display the Library Link Spreadsheet menu. As always, you can type the name of the file you want in the filename field (including its path, if necessary), or you can select the spreadsheet file from a list (after pressing F1 or clicking right on filename).

When you link a spreadsheet to a Word document, you can indicate the portion of the spreadsheet that you wish to import (that is, pull into the Word document) by using the area field. Press F1 in it to see a list of the spreadsheet's named ranges and then choose from

T I P

You may find it useful to type a wild card specification before displaying the file names. For example, entering C:\123\T*.WK1 and pressing F1 will display only the files in drive C's 123 directory that begin with the letter T and have the .WK1 extension.

T I P

Do not delete the new-line character (↓) after the code line or replace it with a paragraph mark (¶); otherwise, Word won't be able to update the data.

```
LIBRARY LINK: Document Graphics Spreadsheet
Lets you import a bookmarked region from another document
Pg1 Co1            {}                                    Microsoft Word
```

Figure 18.1: The Library Link command

among them. You can also enter a range by providing the top-left corner followed by double dots (..) and the bottom-right corner.

After you register the command, Word imports the data, inserting

.L.

at the beginning of the table. This code is the link that Word uses in updating the table. After this code, Word provides the path, the file name, and a new-line character (the new-line character places this information on a line separate from the spreadsheet). If you provided a range, Word adds the range to the .L. code line after the spreadsheet's file name. There is also a .L. code on a separate line at the end of the document. Word formats all this information as hidden, so it doesn't normally appear in the printed document.

It also inserts tab characters between columns and places a new-line character at the end of each row, thereby making the entire table one paragraph. This makes it easy to format the table with the Format Tab Set command.

Figure 18.2 shows the Library Link Spreadsheet command and a table that's been imported from Lotus 1-2-3. For this figure, I set the Options command's show non-printing symbols option to All. Notice how Word inserts tab characters, as indicated by the → symbol. Also, notice how it doesn't repeat the hyphens (created with /- in 1-2-3).

As you work with a document containing a linked spreadsheet, be careful not to erase any coded information or change its formatting from hidden, or Word won't be able to update the table. However, you can edit the coded information if you like. For example, should you move the spreadsheet file to a different directory, you can simply change the directory name on the .L. code line.

To update your spreadsheet information in a Word document, proceed as follows:

1. Highlight the entire document (with Shift-F10, for instance).

2. Issue the Library Link Spreadsheet command again but don't provide a file name or range. Word will search for the .L. codes and highlight the table, requesting verification before updating the spreadsheet data (see Figure 18.2).

3. To update the table, enter Y for Yes.

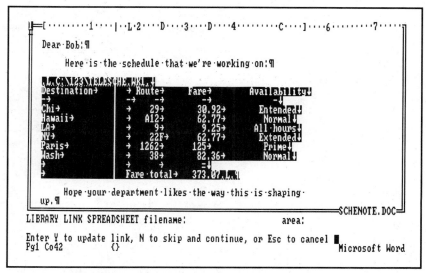

Figure 18.2: A table imported with the Library Link Spreadsheet command

You can have more than one spreadsheet in a document. When updating, you can highlight and update each table individually, or you can highlight all the tables and update them simultaneously. Be careful not to nest spreadsheets, however—you can't place one spreadsheet and its linking codes within another. The mismatched codes will confuse Word when it tries to update the table.

If you have Lotus 1-2-3 or another spreadsheet program that uses its format (such as Quattro), see if you can create Figure 18.2's example in the spreadsheet program and then link it into Word. Next, save the Word document, go back to the spreadsheet program, make some changes, and update your Word document. The Library Link Spreadsheet command also supports Microsoft Excel and Microsoft Multiplan.

LINKING WORD DOCUMENTS

5 New in Word 5

The Library Link Document command (Figure 18.3) imports one Word document into another and updates the linked document, just like the Library Link Spreadsheet command does for spreadsheets. As with

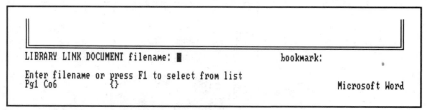

Figure 18.3: The Library Link Document command

spreadsheets, Word sets off the imported material with a hidden line of text—in this case the .D. code—which you should not erase.

Linking documents differs from merging one document into another with the Transfer Merge command in that merging the document incorporates it permanently. Subsequent changes in the original document file will have no affect on the document it was merged into. With the Library Link command, Word maintains an active link with the associated document, allowing you to quickly update the incorporated text whenever necessary.

Updating documents is similar to updating spreadsheets. Highlight the part of the document you want to update and issue the Library Link Document command without providing a file name. Word will highlight the imported material and ask for verification before updating it.

You can also incorporate only part of another document. To use this feature, you must first assign a bookmark name to the text to be imported. To do this, load the document containing the text and highlight it. Next, issue the Format bookmarK command and provide a bookmark name for the text. After saving the document, load the other document and position the cursor where you wish to incorporate the bookmarked text. Then, issue the Library Link Document command, move to the bookmark field, and enter the bookmark name or select it from the list. Only the designated material will be imported and later updated.

LINKING GRAPHICS TO WORD

When you import a graphic, Word allots a box of space (frame) to it, selecting a width and height for this frame. Word then places the graphic in its frame when you print the document.

By graphic, Word means any supported graph, line drawing, or image created with another software program. Because graphic formats can be complex, importing graphics often requires some adjustments on Word's and your part. For instance, you may want to change the size of the frame for the graphic or realign the graphic in its frame.

INSERTING A GRAPHICS CODE

The simplest way to import a graphic is simply to place the cursor on a paragraph mark where you want the graphic to go, invoke the Library Link Graphics command, and specify the graphic file in the filename field. Word will analyze the graphic and, assuming it can figure out its format, insert a .G. code into the text, which indicates where the graphic will be linked with the document when you print it. Like a spreadsheet, Word considers the graphic one paragraph.

For example, suppose you incorporated a TELESCHE.PIC file created with Lotus 1-2-3 into the schedule note we were working on. Word's resulting .G. code line indicates that the file is in drive C's 123 directory and has the name TELESCHE.PIC like so:

.G.C:\123\TELESCHE.PIC;5.5″;3.972″;Lotus PIC

The numeric measurements, 5.5″ and 3.972″, provide the size of the graphic. The first measurement, 5.5″, is the width of the column for the graphic. The graphic's height, 3.972″, preserves the ratio of its height to its width—its *aspect ratio*—so that the graphic is not distorted. Lotus PIC represents the format of the graphic.

If the graphic is in the same directory as the document, the .G. code line will only indicate the name of the file, not the entire path. This makes it easier to copy files and graphics together; you won't have to adjust paths in the .G. code line.

When the Options command's show layout option is set to No, this line of text is all you'll see in the document to indicate the presence of a graphic. However, when you set show layout to Yes, Word sets off the area that the graphic will occupy with dotted lines (see Figure 18.4).(Displaying the layout automatically hides text formatted as hidden unless you set the Print Options command's hidden text option to Yes.)

T I P

Word's supplied macro **copy_file.mac** will copy documents and their linked graphic files. It also automatically adjusts any path in the document's .G. code line (see Appendix C).

T I P

Press Alt-F4 to toggle the show layout option on and off.

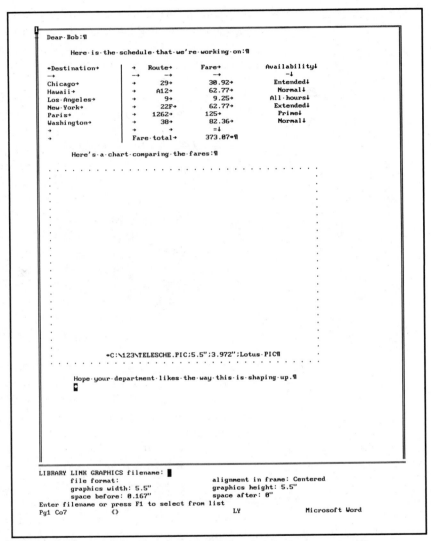

Figure 18.4: Linking graphics, with Options' show layout set to Yes

FINE-TUNING THE IMPORT
WITH LIBRARY LINK GRAPHICS OPTIONS

You can also see the Library Link Graphics command in Figure 18.4. When you import a graphic, you can use this command's options to

T I P

The latest information on the graphics software that Word supports appears in the GRAPHICS.DOC file, which comes on Word's Utilities 2 disk. You can load this file like any standard Word file and print it if you wish. For graphics packages that have more than one method of storing files, this document also tells you the acceptable format(s).

control the process. After you provide a file name for the graphic and tab to the file format option, Word will insert the file format that matches the file's extension. If Word is unable to ascertain the format, you can list the available formats by pressing F1 or clicking right on the field and then select the correct format.

To adjust the placement of the graphic in its frame, you use the alignment in frame and graphics width options. For the alignment in frame option, you can select Left, Right, or Centered from its list (or type one of these settings in). Word assigns this alignment to the graphic's paragraph, and you can later change it with this same command or with the Format Paragraph command.

Although Word normally fills the frame with the graphic (this is determined by the Format pOsition's frame width option, which is initially set to Width of Graphic), you can specify any width in the Library Link Graphics command's graphic width option to change this. Once you enter a value larger or smaller than the column, the graphic will be aligned according to the alignment in frame setting you specified.

You can specify any value for graphics height. You can also choose a value from its list, which provides the value that maintains the aspect ratio and the value that makes the graphic's height the same as its width.

You can set the graphic off from its surrounding text options with the space before and space after options. Values you enter here will also be noted in the paragraph's Format Paragraph menu, and you can later adjust them there or with the Library Link Graphics command.

PREVIEWING AND PRINTING THE GRAPHIC

Because printing graphics takes longer than printing text, you will probably want to preview your document with its imported graphic before you print it. Simply press Ctrl-F9 to issue the Print preView command; pressing Ctrl-F9 again returns you to Document mode. When you are satisfied with the way the previewed graphic looks, you can print the document by issuing the Print Printer command. Figure 18.5 shows how our sample document and its graph look so far.

Suppose that after previewing your graphic's placement and alignment, you decide that you want to move it. You can use Word's standard cut and paste techniques to relocate, copy, or delete the graphic

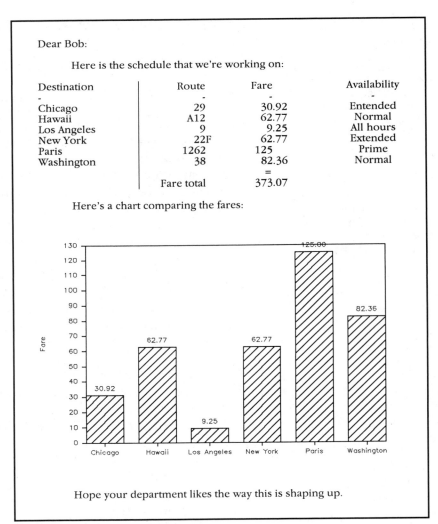

Figure 18.5: Printing your imported graphic

paragraph, or you can issue the Format pOsition command and adjust its options to place the graphic on the page. With Format pOsition, you can also specify how close neighboring text can get to the graphic. (For more on using this command, see Chapter 11.) You may even decide you want to refine the graphic's appearance; let's see how to do this next.

REFINING THE GRAPHIC'S APPEARANCE

You can place lines beside a graphic or a box around it by using the Format Border command. Try it with our sample memo:

1. Place the cursor anywhere in the .G. code line.

2. Initiate the Format Border command.

3. Set the type option to Box and register the command.

Word will then display a box around the .G. code line on the screen. The graphic will be enclosed in a box when you print or preview the document. You can also shade a graphic with this command.

You can even repeat a graphic on every page by applying the Format Running-head command to a graphic paragraph (see Chapter 9).

To add a caption to a graphic, move to its paragraph mark (at the end of the .G. code line), press Shift-Enter, which inserts a new-line code (↓), and enter the caption on the new blank line. The caption will remain with the graphic even if you move the graphic or use the Format pOsition command to relocate it on the page.

CAPTURING GRAPHICS

If you are using graphics software that Word doesn't support, you can still link its graphics with Word documents by first capturing the displayed graphic with the Capture program and then importing the captured screen. Microsoft supplies this resident program (CAPTURE.COM) on Word's Program 1 disk, and Setup copies it to your WORD directory.

To set up Capture, quit Word, change to the directory CAPTURE-.COM is in, and type

    CAPTURE /S

at the operating system prompt. The menu shown in Figure 18.6 then appears.

From Capture's setup menu, type D to configure Capture to the display adapter that your system uses. There are numerous display adapters available, and you indicate your choice by typing its

```
                          CAPTURE.COM
               Screen capture program version 1.0 for Microsoft Word
           (C) Copyright 1989 Jewell Technologies, Inc. - All rights reserved

        Use the menu below to select your display adapter and choose your options.
        When you press a letter for an option, a screen will appear to describe
        the option in more detail.

        ┌──────────────────────────────────────────────────────────────────┐
        │ TO                                                          PRESS  │
        ├──────────────────────────────────────────────────────────────────┤
        │ Select display adapter                                        D    │
        │ Enable/Disable text screens as pictures                       T    │
        │ Enable/Disable saving in reverse video                        U    │
        │ Enable/Disable clipping                                       P    │
        │ Enable/Disable 90 degree rotation                            R    │
        │ Enter number of text lines per screen                         N    │
        │ Quit and save settings                                        Q    │
        └──────────────────────────────────────────────────────────────────┘
```

Figure 18.6: Preparing Capture for your system

number and pressing Enter. For example, the first choice is

0 - Standard IBM and compatible adapters: CGA, EGA, MCGA, and VGA

Use the Page Down and Page Up keys to display the remaining available choices. After you make your selection, Capture's initial menu reappears. Use it to make additional settings, as per the following discussion; then enter Q to quit and save your settings. (Pressing Ctrl-X quits Capture without saving.)

Once you set up Capture, you can invoke it simply by typing CAPTURE without the /S switch at the system prompt. This makes the program resident; you can then run other programs and capture images from the screen by pressing Shift-PrtSc.

When you press Shift-PrtSc, Capture displays a file name to save the screen to and allows you to provide an alternative name. Capture begins with the name capt0001 and increments the number in the name by 1 with each capture. It also adds one of two extensions to this file name, depending on the display mode (unless you specify your own extension).

You can capture screens in either Text or Graphics mode. The display mode will affect which options on Capture's setup menu you can use and the way that Capture stores the screen. If you chose 0 for the display adapter, Capture will automatically detect the display mode and capture the screen accordingly. If not, you may need to reconfigure Capture, using its other menu options to indicate how screens should be captured. Let's examine capturing screens in each of these modes.

CAPTURING IN TEXT MODE When you capture a screen in Text mode, Capture adds the .LST extension to the file name and saves the text screen as a text file. You can then load the file into Word as you would any text file, with the Transfer Load or Transfer Merge command.

If you selected any display adapter other than 0, Capture will not be able to determine when the screen is in Text mode. To signal Capture that you want to capture a text screen in this case, press Shift-PrtSc as usual and then press the Esc key immediately.

If you chose 0 for your display adaptor and you prefer working in Text mode, you can still capture graphic screens by configuring Capture with its T menu option; this specifies that you want text screens to be saved as pictures.

In Text mode some display adaptors require that you specify the number of lines that appear on the screen. If so, use the N option on Capture's setup menu to provide that number before you capture any screens.

CAPTURING IN GRAPHICS MODE When you capture a screen in Graphics mode, Capture adds the .SCR extension to the file name. Capture saves the file as a graphics file that you can import to a Word document with the Library Link Graphics command.

Unlike capturing in Text mode, you can *clip* your images when you capture screens in Graphics mode. After you provide a file name for the screen, clipping lines appear, which you can move to indicate which part of the screen you wish to capture. Initially, the ← and → keys move the right-hand clipping line; pressing the Tab key makes them control the left line. Similarly, the ↑ and ↓ keys move the top clipping line until you press the Tab key to transfer their control to the bottom clipping line. Table 18.1 summarizes the keys you can use

Table 18.1: Keys for Clipping Graphic Screens with Capture

KEY	DESCRIPTION
← or →	Moves the right- or left-hand clipping lines.
↑ or ↓	Moves the top or bottom clipping lines.
Tab	Toggles the arrow keys between the top and bottom lines or the right and left lines.
+ on keypad	Makes the arrow keys move clipping lines in greater increments.
– on keypad	Makes the arrow keys move clipping lines in smaller increments.
Insert	Makes the arrow keys move the top and bottom or left and right lines toward one another.
Delete	Makes the arrow keys move the lines independently.

to clip a graphic. If you find that clipping does not operate with a particular program (Microsoft Windows, for example), you can disable it by using the P option on Capture's setup menu.

You can also have Capture reverse the screen's black and white colors in the captured graphic images by selecting the V option on Capture's setup menu. Finally, in Graphics mode you can have Capture rotate the screen image clockwise 90 degrees when it saves it. To do this, select the R option on Capture's setup menu.

For the latest information on using Capture, check the CAPTURE-.DOC file supplied on Word's Program 1 disk.

TRANSLATING WORD DOCUMENTS

In this chapter, we've imported files created with other programs into Word. In addition, Word enables you to save its files in various formats, so you can use them with other programs.

When you save a document on disk with Word, its file stores the information in ways that only Word can understand—in Word's own language, so to speak. This way, Word can format and print its files quickly. Because other programs don't speak Word's language, you have to convert a Word file to a more standard format to use it with other programs or to send it to another computer via telecommunications. You can convert that file into an ASCII, DCA, or RTF file. ASCII stands for American Standard Code for Information Interchange, and its format is probably the most common. RTF stands for Rich Text Format, a Microsoft format. DCA, an IBM format, stands for Document Content Architecture.

Word 5's Transfer Save command allows you to save a file in two kinds of ASCII formats or in an RTF format. Word also includes a program for DCA conversion. The method you choose depends on the requirements of the software you will use with the files. Check the software's documentation or experiment to find a format that works.

T I P

If you formatted the document in Word and want to save your formatting, save the document as usual before saving it in another format under a different name.

New in
Word 5

SAVING AS ASCII OR RTF

After creating or revising a file in Word, you can save it as an ASCII or RTF file with the Transfer Save command. Once you have issued the command for the displayed document, move to the format option, set it to the appropriate setting, and register the command.

ASCII WITH PARAGRAPH MARKS Use the format option's Text-only setting to create an ASCII file that has carriage returns only at the ends of paragraphs and no formatting at all. Word processing software generally uses this format. Running heads and footnote text will occur wherever you typed them in.

ASCII WITH LINE BREAKS When you choose the format option's Text-only-with-line-breaks setting, Word places carriage returns at the end of each line of text. It also leaves margins in place and replaces tab characters with spaces. It does not include character formatting (for example, no boldfacing or underlining). Data-communications software often uses this format.

CONVERTING TO RTF FORMAT With the format option's RTF setting, Word saves the file in Microsoft RTF format and replaces the .DOC extension with .RTF. If you have attached a style sheet to the document, Word converts it to .RTF format as well.

For the latest information on the abilities and limitations of the RTF format, see the WORD_RTF.DOC file supplied on Word's Utilities 3 disk.

CONVERTING WORD FILES TO DCA

T I P

Word provides you with two macros, **dca_load.mac** and **dca_save.mac**, that perform these conversions directly from Word (see Appendix C).

DCA is IBM's standard for converting documents among its word processors. Word documents can be changed to this standard, which Word also refers to as revisable form text (RFT). Be careful not to confuse RFT with Microsoft's RTF (Rich Text Format) discussed previously. Other word processing programs can then translate the DCA files into their own formats. Additionally, you can reverse the process. For instance, you can export Word documents to WordPerfect and Multi-Mate Advantage, or vice versa.

Don't expect your documents to be converted perfectly every time, though. You may need to do some adjusting either before or after you convert them. Small caps, for instance—as in A.M. or P.M.—aren't supported by DCA.

The conversion process results in three document files. First, there's the original file. Then, you make the DCA version of that file. Finally, you create the other word processor's version of the DCA file.

T I P

Word provides you with the macro, **freeze_style.mac**, that binds the formatting to the document automatically (see Appendix C).

When you convert a Word document to DCA format, you'll need to do some preparatory work if the document uses a style sheet. Otherwise, you won't get the formatting that's stored in the style sheet. To convert the formatting to DCA, you must first freeze it with the Format Character and Format Paragraph commands. Use formatting options that you're not using in the document to do this: I'll use uppercase and keep together to demonstrate. Start by highlighting the entire document (Shift-F10), then issue the Format Character command, set the uppercase option to No, and register the command. This binds all character style formats assigned to the document. With the document still highlighted, issue the Format Paragraph command, set keep together to No, and register the command. If you want to keep the original version of the document, save this altered version under a different name.

Follow a similar procedure if your document has a division formatted with multiple columns, because DCA doesn't recognize this

Word format. Highlight the entire document, issue the Format Division Layout command, and set the number of columns option to 1.

Once the preparation is complete, you run the WORD_DCA program provided on Word's Utilities 3 disk. The Setup program normally copies it to the WORD dictionary. From the operating system prompt, change to this directory if it is not already current, type

```
A:WORD_DCA
```

and press enter. WORD_DCA will ask if you want to go from Word to DCA or DCA to Word. After you specify the format, it will then ask you to enter the name of the document you wish to convert. Type the full name, including the disk drive, path, and .DOC extension. Press Enter, and WORD_DCA will ask you for the name of the output file. You might want to use the original file's primary name with .DCA as the extension.

Finally, run the other word processor and convert the DCA file to its format with its conversion program. You can then use the file in that word processor.

To convert another word processor's file to Word format, first use the other word processor's converting feature to change the document to DCA format. Be aware that there may be restrictions imposed by DCA and the word processor.

Once you have a DCA version of the file, run the WORD_DCA program again to convert the DCA file to a Word .DOC file. If the DCA version of the document contains any document comments, they won't appear in the Word version. Also, line drawings will not be converted to Word format. For more information on these and other restrictions, use Word to load and read the file WORD_DCA-.DOC located in your WORD directory. (Setup copied if there from Word's Utilities 3 disk.)

EASY TRANSLATION WITH WORD EXCHANGE

Perhaps the easiest way to convert Word documents is with a program called Word Exchange from Systems Compatibility Corporation. This program is designed exclusively for converting documents to and from Word. Formats that it supports include WordPerfect, WordStar, MultiMate, and DCA (although it only converts *to* DCA).

Like WORD_DCA, Word Exchange does not honor Word's style sheet formatting when it converts a Word document. You must first freeze the document's formatting as described in the previous section.

IMPORTING DATABASE FILES TO WORD

You can also use data from database management systems with Word. Such systems store data in a sophisticated filing format, somewhat like an electronic Rolodex file. The most popular system is dBASE.

The best way to import data is in a comma-delimited format. This is the format we used for the file that we created and used with the Print Merge command in Chapter 14. To output dBASE data, you copy it to a separate file in the comma-delimited format. From there, you can access it directly as a database for the Print Merge command. If you want to create a Word table from the data, load the file and issue the Replace command to change it from comma-delimited to tab-delimited format.

Thus, if you are using a dBASE file called CLIENTS.DBF and you wish to change it to comma-delimited format, type the following line next to the dBASE dot prompt:

```
COPY TO CLIENTS.CMD DELIMITED
```

Other database management systems will have their own methods for exporting comma-delimited data.

The data file from a database management system won't have a header record, so you will have to make a separate header file with Word and reference both files in the master form. For example, let's say that you created a database in dBASE called DBCLIENT.TXT. To use this database in Word, you would have to create a header file that you might call HECLIENT.DOC. The header file would contain only the header paragraph, for example:

```
LASTNAME, FIRSTNAME, PHONE, ADDRESS1, ADDRESS2,
CITY, STATE, ZIP, SALUTATION¶
```

The information in the header file must, as usual, match the order of the data in the database.

In your master form, your DATA merging instruction would be set up to reference first the header file and then the data file, like so:

«DATA HECLIENT, DBCLIENT.TXT»

Notice that because the header file has a .DOC extension, you do not need to type the extension.

DESKTOP PUBLISHING WORD DOCUMENTS IN VENTURA

As we've discussed throughout the book, Word has excellent desktop publishing features. With its fonts, style sheets, and graphics importing features, it may be all you need to become a desktop publisher. However, you may want to do more. Although you can preview your page layouts in Word, you may want to edit them when the fonts are displayed correctly (show layout doesn't do this).

When importing graphics (other than Capture screens) to Word, you can't crop them, and you can't specify the exact position or thickness of paragraph lines.

To accommodate more precise desktop publishing needs, you'll need additional software, such as Ventura Publisher from Xerox. Ventura can paste up pages and display the finished copy on the screen, which you can revise as needed. Not only can you include Word text in Ventura, but some Word formatting will also be converted. In addition, you can send text back to Word for reprocessing.

Ventura formats its documents as a whole, in much the same way as Word's style sheets do. In fact, Ventura has style sheets of its own and doesn't honor Word's style sheets. However, you can transfer formats by freezing them into the Word document, as you do when converting Word documents to the DCA format.

If you do purchase Ventura, you can learn Ventura's ropes by reading *Mastering Ventura*, written by yours truly, Matthew Holtz, and published by SYBEX. It contains a special section on using Word with Ventura.

Whether or not you take advantage of Word's importing and exporting features when you create desktop-published documents, you will always want your documents to be complete. Often, this entails adding an index or a table of contents to your long documents. In the next chapter, you'll learn how Word can compile an index or a table of contents for you.

19

Compiling an Index and a Table of Contents: The Finishing Touches

Fast Track

issue the Library Table command. You can format the table of contents with this command, the Alt codes and Format commands, or a style sheet.

use letter codes other than C, D, G, I, and L. These codes are reserved for use by Word.

AS DESKTOP PUBLISHING GROWS MORE POPULAR, the documents that it can accommodate grow larger and more complex. The more complex the document, the more important it is to include an index and a table of contents. Consider your readers. How can they find information quickly and easily? Suppose they remember its approximate location in the document. To find it, they could just thumb through the document, assisted by the running heads, but a table of contents would help them find the material more efficiently. On the other hand, they may know exactly what they're looking for and could simply find it alphabetically. If that's the case, they'll appreciate a good index.

Microsoft Word allows you to create an index and table of contents automatically. Once you code items that you wish included in your index, Word goes through the document, scanning it for your hidden codes, and constructs the index. You can use this same method to compile the table of contents, or you can have Word compile this reference source even more quickly from your document's outline. In either case, Word automatically puts items in the right order, eliminates duplicates as appropriate, structures the compilation, and inserts the proper page numbers. If you make changes to the document, you can easily have Word compile a new index and table of contents.

You can also create an automatically formatted index or table of contents with Word's justly celebrated style sheets. Let's begin by seeing how you can use Word to create an exemplary index.

CREATING AN INDEX FOR YOUR DOCUMENT

There are two steps to creating an index with Word. First, you must indicate the items you wish to include in the index. You do this by flagging them with codes formatted as hidden text. You can either create these flags as you type the document or insert them once you're done.

Second, you issue the Library Index command to compile the index. You do this when you have finished revising the document. When you issue this command, Word paginates the document, scans its text, and compiles an index at the end. You can specify formats with this command, and you can format the compiled list as well.

FLAGGING ITEMS FOR THE INDEX

To include items in the index, you must place a special code before each item in your document and format it as hidden text. Sometimes, you will need to place a code at the end of the entry as well.

To mark an item for inclusion in the index, type the code

.I.

before the item. (You can use either an uppercase or lowercase I.) If the item ends with a paragraph mark, that's all you have to type to flag it. But for the code to *operate* as an index flag, you must also format it as hidden by pressing Alt-E or issuing the Format Character command. If you have a style sheet attached, you can enter your own custom Alt code for a hidden text format.

Let's create an index entry for the "Foundation Structure" in our sample TELEFOUN.DOC file that we worked with in Chapter 17. Since we will be working with hidden text, issue the Options command and set show hidden text to Yes; otherwise, text formatted as hidden will disappear from the screen.

CREATING AN INDEX ENTRY WITHOUT A STYLE SHEET

To create the index entry and then format it when there isn't a style sheet attached to the document, you can activate Outline view or Document mode for the displayed document. Since we used an outline to create the TELEFOUN document, go ahead and press Shift-F2 to activate Outline view. Then follow these steps:

1. Bring the cursor to the "F" in "Foundation."

2. Type the index code

.I.

The existing text moves to the right.

3. Highlight the index code and format it as hidden text by pressing Alt-E (see Figure 19.1).

T I P

Word provides you with two macros, **index.mac** and **index_entry.mac**, that automatically place the index codes before and after text that you highlight (see Appendix C).

T I P

Always keep Overtype (F5) turned off when you are adding index codes to a document.

M O U S E

Highlight the code and click right on Format to initiate the Format Character command. Then click right on Yes for the hidden option to format the highlighted text and register the command.

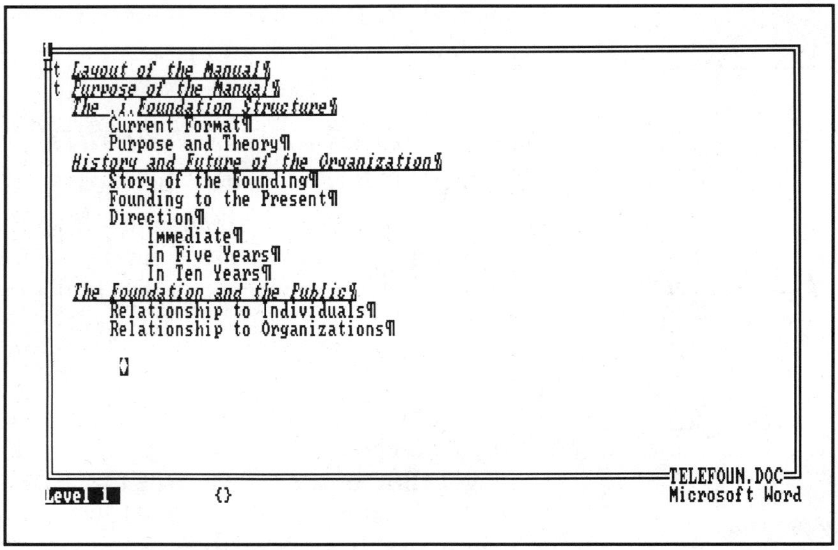

Figure 19.1: Viewing hidden text

This hidden-text designation will list "Foundation Structure" in the index once you compile it with the Library Index command. The .I. code marks the beginning point for the index entry, and the paragraph mark is the ending point. This works fine for index entries, like this one, that are part of the heading. However, you will also want to include entries that are embedded in a paragraph. To do this, you indicate the ending position with a semicolon that you format as hidden. Remember that to format just a single character after you enter it, you must press the Alt code twice.

Figure 19.2 shows how a reference to the president would be designated as hidden. (I highlighted it so you can easily spot it in the figure.) The figure also shows how you can insert hidden entries that you don't want to appear in the document. Look at the heading. Previously, it read "Purpose of the Manual." If you want the index to show "Manual, Purpose," however, prepare the index entry as shown. The first "Manual" and the comma following it are hidden. Make sure that you do not separate such hidden entries from their text references when you edit; always keep the entries in front so that the correct text and page numbers are referenced.

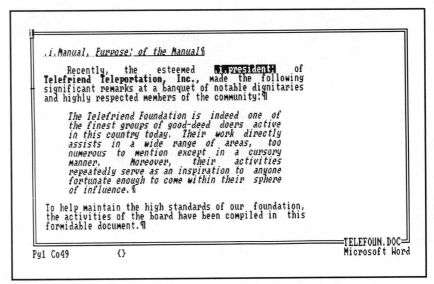

Figure 19.2: Indicating the end of hidden text with a semicolon

INDEXING SUBENTRIES

You can also create subentries in your index. Suppose you find that you have a lot of references to the word "manual" in the document. You may want to create a main entry for "Manual," and then beneath it list subentries with their categories. When you encounter text in your document that you want to designate as a subentry, insert the .I. code, the main entry, and a colon (:) before it and then add a semicolon after it. Follow this procedure for each subentry in the document, formatting it as hidden text (with Alt-E).

Thus, the "Purpose" subentry for "Manual" would appear in the document like this:

    .I.Manual:Purpose;

You would add a similar entry to classify "Layout of the Manual"; you can use the scrap area to copy the entry (see Figure 19.3). When

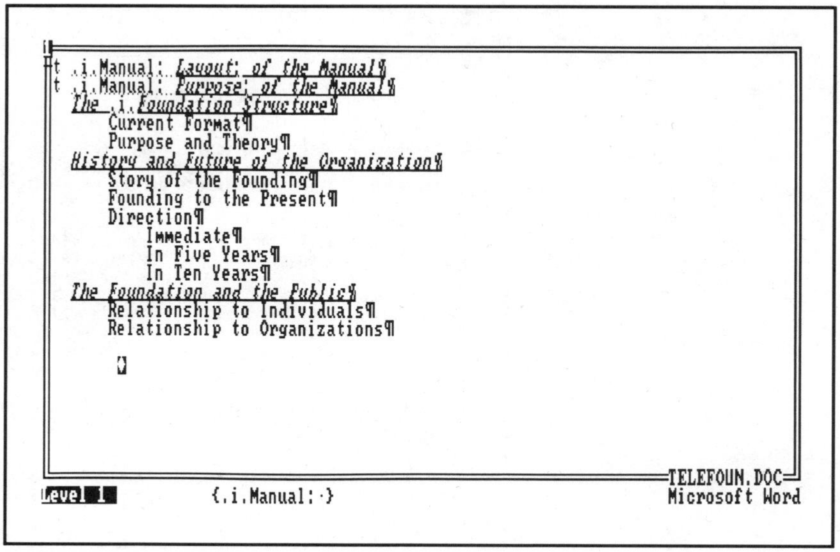

Figure 19.3: Creating subentries

you compile your index, these two entries would be

> Manual
> > Layout 1
> > Purpose 1

Of course, the appropriate page numbers would show up in place of the 1s.

In this example, the main entry doesn't have any page numbers directly after it; only its subentries have numbers. To add page numbers to the main entry, pinpointing its central discussion, establish "Manual" as a regular index entry in that part of the document. That is, include the .I. code and semicolon, not a colon or a subentry.

PUNCTUATING ENTRIES Colons and semicolons that are part of the entry require special handling because of the way Word uses them to compile an index. If the entry includes one of these punctuation marks, you must put the entire entry in quotes. This makes quotation marks a special form of punctuation as well, so they, too, require special treatment. To print quotes in the entry, you must type a pair of quotes and then, as with colons and semicolons, enclose the entire entry in quotes. Thus, if you have an entry that you want listed in the index as

Teleporting: "Nightowl"

you'd type

.I."Teleporting: ""Nightowl"""

in the document.

PREPARING STYLE FORMATS FOR AN INDEX

After you've flagged your index entries in the text, you can set up the format for your index with a style sheet. Word will then automatically format the index each time you compile it.

In the gallery, issue the Insert command to establish your style formats for the index. Delete the scrap symbol in the key code field since you don't need to assign an Alt code to your index formats. Set usage to Paragraph, move to the variant field, and press F1 or click right on it to display the list of reserved variants (see Figure 19.4). Select Index level 1 for this paragraph variant and register your settings. Word has three other reserved variants for index entries. You can set up each one in turn.

As Word compiles the index, it will automatically format the levels according to their assigned reserved variants. Needless to say, this is quite a convenience.

With the Index level 1 style format listed in the gallery, you can use the Gallery Format subcommands to format it. For the purpose of illustration, let's make the first level entries in our index all uppercase. To do this, leave the cursor on the Index level 1 style format, issue the Format Character command, and set uppercase to Yes. Then insert a style format for Index level 2 in the gallery. Use the Format Paragraph command to provide it with a left indent of 0.2" and press Alt-I to italicize it.

When you create your index entries and subentries using the document's style sheet, compiling the index is the last step—your formatted index will be ready, and you will just need to print the completed

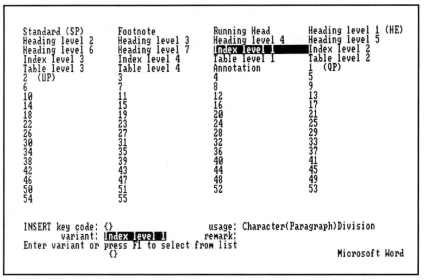

Figure 19.4: Word's reserved variants for the index

document. If you don't use a style sheet, you can either specify the index's formatting as you compile it or format it after you compile it. The advantage in using a style sheet is that you are assured of a consistent format and you won't ever have to reformat the index, which you might have to do if you use one of the other methods. Regardless of which method you choose, you should learn how to compile the index now.

FORMATTING AND COMPILING THE INDEX

Once you've specified all your index entries in the document and you have prepared your style sheet, if desired, it's time to create the index with the Library Index command. Before you run it, however, set the Options command's show hidden text option to No. If you left hidden text showing, Word considers it standard text and allots space for it in the document's pages. If you then print the document after hiding the text, the page numbers may not agree with those in the index.

M_OUSE_

Click left on Library and click either button on Index. Then click right on Yes for the use style sheet option to initiate the operation. Reset show hidden text to Yes by issuing the Options command and clicking right on Yes for this option.

COMPILING A FORMATTED INDEX WITH A STYLE SHEET

If you are using a style sheet, follow these steps to compile the index:

1. Press Esc and then type L for Library and I for Index to display the Library Index menu (see Figure 19.5).

2. Set the use style sheet option to Yes.

3. Accept the settings by pressing Enter. Word creates the index and places it at the end of the document.

4. To see the identifying markers Word places at the beginning and end of the index, reset the Options command's show hidden text option to Yes. The formatted index will then resemble that shown in Figure 19.6. Don't delete the markers, as Word uses them to locate the index when you update it.

Since our document is short, Word created our sample index rather quickly. Be aware, though, that with a long document this process may take several minutes.

Now let's examine the Library Index options that you can use to create your index's format if you haven't established style formats for the index. Even if you have index style formats, these options can assist you in formatting your index.

FORMATTING AND COMPILING YOUR INDEX WITH THE LIBRARY INDEX COMMAND

When you issue the Library Index command, you can reset its options to format your index. With the first option, entry/page # separated by, you can adjust the spacing between index entries and their page numbers in the index. If you don't enter anything, Word puts two spaces between the entries and their

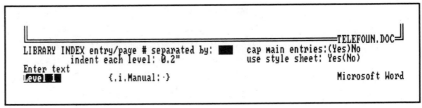

Figure 19.5: The Library Index command

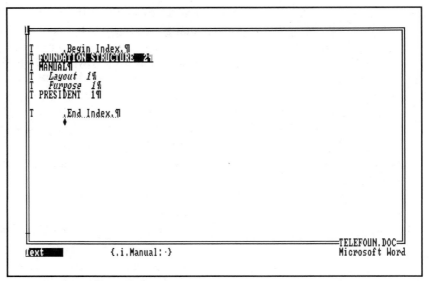

Figure 19.6: The newly created index

page numbers. You can type in more or fewer spaces in this option's field, or you can enter another character as the separator. For instance, if you'd like a tab character to be inserted, indicate this by typing ^t (pressing Shift-6 and then t).

The cap main entries option is usually set to Yes, which means Word will capitalize the first letters of all main entries. If you want the main entries' case left as you entered it, set this option to No. (Alternatively, you could change the entries on a case-by-case basis once the index is compiled.) However, if you have attached a style sheet containing an uppercase format to your document (as in the previous example), the style sheet's format will override the cap main entries option's No setting—you will need to adjust the style sheet to lowercase the entries.

The indent each level option determines how far subentries are indented from the main entries and how far subentries of subentries are indented from the primary subentries. You can adjust this option, which is initially set to 0.2 inches, to your liking. (This option has no effect when you use a style sheet; set indents with the style formats instead.)

After you have specified the settings for the Library Index command's options, press Enter to compile the index. Word separates the index from the rest of the document with a row of colons, placing it in a separate division. This is what enables you to format the pages of your index differently from the rest of your document.

Although you have already created a general format for the index, you may still want to format it directly so that you can set up a two- or three-column layout, boldface certain page numbers for each entry—in other words, format it in ways that the Library Index command's options don't permit. Let's see how to do this next.

FORMATTING
THE INDEX AFTER COMPILING IT

You can format this new division with or without a style sheet. Unfortunately, Word does not have an index division that's applied automatically, so using a style sheet does not offer a significant advantage over formatting it directly. Furthermore, with or without a style sheet, the division settings you apply remain with the index even when you recompile it. Be aware, though, that if you should later recompile the index, Word will overwrite the old index along with any directly applied character or paragraph formatting. Therefore, be sure that your work is complete before you format characters or paragraphs in the index directly.

To format the index directly, place the cursor in the index division. Then you can use the Format Division Layout command to format the index as multiple columns and the Format Division Margins command to adjust its margins. You can also issue the Format Division Page-numbers command to change the page-number format of the index; for instance, assuming that you used the same command to number pages in the document, you could choose to not number the index pages by setting this command to No.

If you wish to use a style format for the index division format, issue the Gallery's Insert subcommand to set usage to Division and assign an Alt code to one of the numbered variants. Then, with the highlight on this new format, use the Gallery's Format subcommands to establish the formats you want. Exit the gallery and then format the index division with your assigned Alt code.

T *I P*

If you expect to
recompile the index
later, place the word
"Index" above the
.Begin Index. code
but below the division
mark. This way, Word
won't remove the word
when it recompiles the
index. You may want
to create glossary
entries of other format-
ted text so that you can
reinsert them in the
new index easily (see
Chapter 15).

You can also add text to a compiled index. You'll probably want to
add the word "Index" at the top, and you might want to include running heads as well. Just type them at the top of this division and format them, as you would elsewhere in the document.

MAKING CHANGES AND REINDEXING

It's easy enough to update an index with Word. After revising
your document or its hidden index entries, rerun the Library Index
command.

When you do, Word will require verification before it destroys the
first version of the index. It highlights the first index and displays
the prompt

Index already exists. Enter Y to replace or Esc to cancel.

Type Y to create a new version of the index and overwrite the old one.

If you want to keep the first version of the index, delete the markers ".Begin Index." and ".End Index." before recompiling your
entries. You might want to keep the old index on hand as a reference,
should the new index present unexpected results.

CREATING A TABLE OF CONTENTS

If you're using the outliner, Word can automatically create
the headings for your table of contents, or TOC, from your outline's
headings—you do not need to flag TOC entries. Perhaps best of all, you
can use a style sheet to assign formatted outline headings automatically,
which in turn become the formatted table of contents headings. I recommend this comprehensive approach strongly.

If you don't have an outline to work from, you can still create a
TOC by formatting codes as hidden text; the process is strikingly similar
to that used for indexing. You can establish different heading levels for
your TOC. Once you've created the entries, you compile the table with
the Library Table command. It can then be formatted directly, just as
the index can.

PREPARING STYLE FORMATS FOR A TABLE OF CONTENTS

As with the index, Word has four style formats reserved for use with a table of contents. As Word compiles the TOC, it will automatically assign these style formats—which you prepare—as long as you use the reserved variants (Table levels 1 through 4).

Figure 19.7 presents some typical style formats for a table of contents. Each level is progressively indented, and all three style formats have a right-aligned tab set at 5'' with leader dots. This format adds dots between each level's text and page numbers in the TOC.

Bear in mind the difference between the reserved variants for headings (Heading levels 1 through 7) and those for the TOC. The formats of the Heading variants control the appearance of the heading in the document and also assign an outline level, which allows you to collapse and expand the document with Outline view. On the other hand, the Table variants (Table levels 1 through 4) format the headings in the table of contents only.

T IP

Remember that you can format multiple entries in the gallery by highlighting them together (with F6 or by dragging the mouse). This is a handy way to set the right-aligned tab with leader dots for all three TOC formats at once.

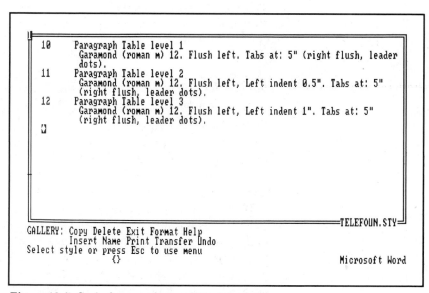

Figure 19.7: Style formats for a table of contents

T **I P**

Word provides a
macro, **toc_entry.mac**,
that automatically
inserts the hidden code
for table of contents
entries before and after
the highlighted material
(see Appendix C).

FLAGGING ITEMS MANUALLY

If you're not using the outliner or Table variants, you'll have to flag
entries for the table of contents with a hidden code. This approach is
time-consuming and is probably left over from the days before Word's
outliner was integrated with its TOC generator. The code is

.C.

As with the index code, you can format it as hidden text with Alt-E or
the Format Character command. You indicate the end of an entry
with a paragraph mark, semicolon, or division mark. You can format
the ending mark as hidden if necessary.

As with index entries, you demarcate subentries with colons. One
colon lowers the heading to the second level, two colons lower it to the
third level, and so on. Again, colons, semicolons, and quotation
marks require the same special handling as index entries do.

COMPILING THE
TABLE OF CONTENTS FROM YOUR OUTLINE

To compile the table of contents for the outline we were indexing,
load it and issue the Library Table command. When you select Outline and set use style sheet to Yes (see Figure 19.8), Word will compile
entries for the outline headings and format them with the style formats automatically. Once Word has compiled the TOC, it creates a
new division mark at the end of the document and places the TOC after
it (see Figure 19.9). Notice how the reserved Table variants have
indented the TOC subheadings and added leader dots before each
entry's page number. If you compiled an index first, the new TOC will
follow it. Likewise, the reverse is true: if you compile the TOC first, your
new index will follow it.

T **I P**

Don't number the
TOC division's page
numbers since you
will be moving the
pages after you print
the document.

Word places the TOC at the end so that the page numbering is not
upset when you print the document. If the TOC were at the beginning, it
would be included in the page numbering when you print the document. Thus, its page number references would be incorrect, as it didn't
exist when those numbers were compiled. So always leave the TOC at
the end, where Word places it. When you assemble the printed document, just move the TOC pages to the beginning.

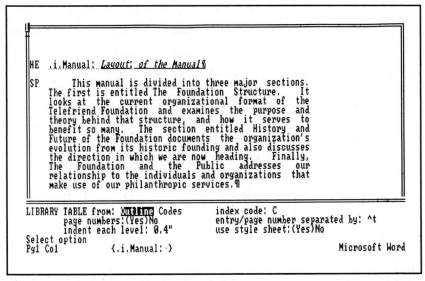

Figure 19.8: The Library Table command

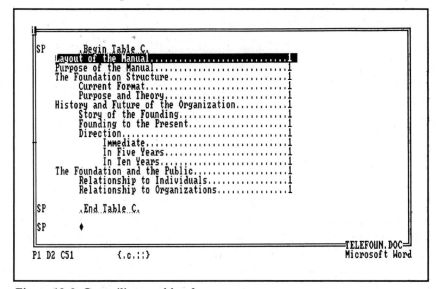

Figure 19.9: Compiling a table of contents

FORMATTING
THE TABLE OF CONTENTS DIRECTLY

You can format your TOC directly, as you do the index, if you haven't used a style sheet. You can accomplish some of the formatting with the Library Table command.

In the TOC, an entry and its page number are normally separated by a tab character. This is indicated by the ^t that appears in the Library Table command's entry/page # separated by field. To separate them in a different manner, replace this with your choice.

The indent each level option is initially set to 0.4 inch. You can increase or decrease the amount of indentation for each subsequent level. (This setting has no effect when you use a style sheet; the style formats dictate how much each level is indented.)

COMPILING CASE CITATIONS,
FIGURES, AND OTHER LISTINGS

In addition to a table of contents and an index, you can compile lists of other items in your document. To do this, use the Library Table command. Lawyers will find this feature useful for creating a list of case citations. Accountants could compile a list of various statistical tables that appear in their documents. In our example, you might want to list the pages that contain quotes from the president. With Library Table, you can also create a list of the pages that have figures.

To compile these various lists, you change the index code option in the Library Table command. Usually it reads

   index code: C

This indicates that Word will use the hidden .C. code as its flag for entries in the table of contents. Choose a single letter, such as F for figure, as the flag for your list. If you run the command after indicating some other letter, Word will look for entries you've made with the letter you specified. Do not use C, D, G, I, or L, which Word reserves for other operations we already examined in this and the previous chapter. (With Word 4 you cannot use P as well.) If you

T I P

Word provides you with two macros, **authority_entry.mac** and **authority_table-.mac**, that flag citations and compile a list of authorities, respectively (see Appendix C).

T I P

You can set the index code option to I to compile a listing of the index entries you've placed in the document. The listing is in the order in which the entries appear along with their page numbers, rather than in alphabetical order as they are in the index.

don't want page numbers to appear in your list, set the Library Table's page number option to No.

Once you've compiled a list, you can reorder it as necessary. You may find it handy to do this with the Library Autosort command (see Chapter 12), or you may wish to organize items individually.

These are the features of Word releases 4 and 5. Rest assured, though, that Microsoft will continue to add features to this extraordinary software program. You may not learn it all right away, but this book and future editions are ready to assist you with the features you need. Don't forget to consult the index, which makes this book something of an encyclopedia on Word.

There are, however, other abilities that Word has, depending on your particular setup. The operation of Word can change depending on your operating system and the supplied macros that you use. I examine these aspects in the appendices.

A

**Starting
Up Word**

BEFORE YOU BEGIN TO WORK WITH MICROSOFT Word, you need to install it on your computer system. After that, you can start up the program in a number of different ways. For example, you can make Word automatically load the last file you worked on.

PREPARING TO USE WORD

The Setup program takes care of the initial preparation of Word. In this section, I examine installing Word on a hard disk. To install Word on 5¼- or 3½-inch disks, see "Using Word without a Hard Disk" later in this appendix.

Setup copies Word to your hard disk so that you don't have to insert a disk every time you want to start up Word. For Word to take full advantage of your monitor, you indicate the kind of graphics adapter you have with the Setup program. Also, to enable Word and your computer to send data to your printer, you must place your printer's driver file on your hard disk. Printers differ from one another, and this file provides Word with the codes your printer needs to produce special effects, such as boldfacing. If you have font cartridges or downloadable fonts, you use the driver that contains information on them. The Setup program transfers this file from one of the original disks (depending on the printer) to the hard disk. Make sure you have all this information on hand before you run Setup.

To run Setup, start up your operating system and then insert the Utilities 1 disk in drive A. Then, simply type

    A:SETUP

and press the Enter key.

The Setup program first displays a screen explaining what it will accomplish. Then it will automatically analyze your system and present you with a menu of the different ways you can set up Word (see Figure A.1). Depending on your computer's configuration, this screen may vary slightly. Type H to set up Word on the hard disk; you can then specify the directory that you want to use for Word. (For more on directories, see Appendix B.)

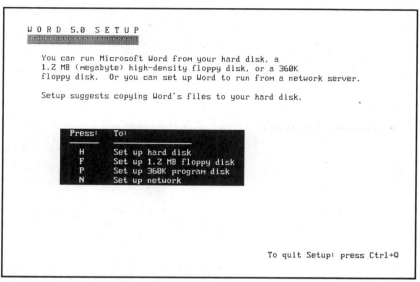

Figure A.1: The initial Setup screen

The Setup menu appears after you type H (see Figure A.2). Since this is the first time you are setting up Word, you will want to perform the procedures in the order listed. Start by typing W to copy Word. Follow the directions on the screen, inserting the appropriate disks as instructed. When Setup has completed the W procedure, it redisplays this menu and places an asterisk next to the W so you can keep track of what you have already done.

Continue with the other steps on this menu. Unlike the previous steps, the C procedure, which customizes particular Word settings, is optional. It allows you to specify Text or Graphics mode, whether the Word menu appears at the bottom of the screen, whether borders appear around the edges of the screen, and the default size of the paper. If you don't know what you want, skip this step—you can always adjust these settings later in Word. To create the screens for this book, I selected Graphics mode and chose to display the menu and screen borders. (See Chapter 2 for more on customization.) Select Q to end Setup once you have completed the steps.

Word then asks you to indicate whether it should change the AUTOEXEC.BAT and CONFIG.SYS files on your disk. Modifying AUTOEXEC.BAT adds your Word directory to the system

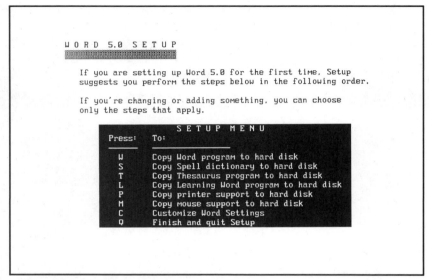

Figure A.2: The Setup menu

path, which allows you to start Word from any directory, and modifying CONFIG.SYS adds the FILES = 20 statement (at least), which Word requires to operate. It also configures the system for use with the mouse if you have one. There's more on these files in the CONFIG.DOC file, which is on the Utilities 3 disk. You can load and print this file with Word, if necessary.

Quitting also allows you to view the README.DOC file. This file contains the latest information about the version of Word that you purchased. Peruse the document to see if there is anything that you need to know before running Word.

There are many other files of interest on the Word disks, which I list in Table A.1. It also shows which of the Word 5 disks contain these files as of this writing.

Congratulations! Word is now ready for use. Restart or reset your computer before loading Word.

METHODS OF LOADING WORD

I describe the plain vanilla way to load Word first, and then I discuss how you can customize the startup procedure. Note that for any

Table A.1: Document Files Included with Word 5

File	Disk	Purpose
CAPTURE.DOC	Program 1	Explains capturing screens with CAPTURE.COM (Program 1 disk).
CHARTEST.DOC	Utilities 2	Provides the complete character set.
CONFIG.DOC	Utilities 3	Describes adjustments the Setup program makes to the CONFIG.SYS and AUTOEXEC.BAT files.
GRAPHICS.DOC	Utilities 2	Lists the graphics packages Word supports.
MACROCNV.DOC	Spell	Explains converting Word 4 macros to Word 5 format with MACROCNV.EXE (Spell disk).
MAKEVID.DOC	Utilities 2	Discusses using MAKEVID.EXE (Utilities 2) to make a second screen driver.
OS2_NOTE.DOC	Utilities 1	Provides latest information for running Word in OS/2.
PRINTERS.DOC	Printers 1	Lists all printers that Word supports.
README.DOC	Utilities 1	Gives updates on Word's features.
TYPOS.DOC	Spell	Is a practice file for use with the spelling checker.
WORD_DCA.DOC	Utilities 3	Explains DCA conversion using WORD_DCA.EXE (Utilities 3).
WORD_RTF.DOC	Utilities 3	Explains RTF conversion with the Transfer Save command.

procedure you choose, you can type either capital or lowercase letters. It makes no difference to Word.

LOADING WORD WITHOUT OTHER INSTRUCTIONS

Begin by starting the computer and loading the operating system. Next type the program name, like so:

WORD

The operating system will load Word without any special instructions (other than copyright messages), and a blank screen will appear.

LOADING A PARTICULAR FILE ALONG WITH WORD

You may often find that you want to load a particular file when you start Word (instead of using the Transfer Load command to do so from inside the program). To do this, simply type

WORD *filename*

where *filename* is the name of the file you want to load. Be sure to type a space between WORD and the name of the file. When you press Enter, the operating system will load Word, and Word will automatically load the file you specified, displaying it in the window.

The usual rules for a file name apply: Word assumes a .DOC extension unless you specify otherwise. Also, you can provide a complete path as part of the file name if you want (see Appendix B). If you don't provide a path, Word will look for the file in the directory that's active when you load Word. If it can't find the file there and you've previously established a different directory for the Transfer Options command's setup option (setting save between sessions to Yes), Word will check that directory for the file. If Word still can't find the file name, it displays the message

File does not exist. Enter Y to create, or Esc to cancel

Instead of telling Word to load a particular file, you can tell Word to load whatever file you were working on the last time you used Word. To do this, type

WORD /L

The /L here stands for last. This /L and other characters we'll look at are called *switches*. The space between WORD and /L is optional.

When you include /L, not only will Word display the file you were last working on, but the cursor will also be located in the same position it was in when you quit. (This information is stored in the MW.INI file.) In addition, the document's read-only status, which was recorded when you quit, will be the same. Of course, the document file you were working on in your last Word session must be available on the disk. If Word can't find the document, it will simply display a clear window.

SPECIFYING WORD'S MEMORY USAGE

New in
Word 5

Word 5 has two switches that affect the manner in which it uses memory. The /X switch instructs Word to not use expanded memory, even if your computer has it. Because Word normally uses expanded memory automatically, you would include this switch if you have resident programs that require your expanded memory.

You can also provide the /B switch, with a number from 4 to 1500, to indicate how many 512-byte buffers (chunks) of memory (RAM) Word should allot to documents that you work with. For example

WORD /B1000

assigns 1000 buffers of 512 bytes each to RAM. The larger the documents you work with, the more memory you'll probably want to assign to document memory; this expedites your word processing. However, if you perform memory-intensive operations (such as elaborate Replace and Library commands, or complex math calculations and macros), assigning a lot of memory to your documents may produce "out-of-memory" errors. Experiment to find the distribution of memory that best suits your needs.

CHANGING YOUR KEYBOARD'S SETUP FOR WORD

Some compatible systems, such as Tandy, have enhanced keyboards that do not operate properly with Word. If some of your keys are not working, you can disengage the keyboard enhancements by starting Word with

WORD /K

This will make the keyboard behave like a standard keyboard. The extra function keys, F11 and F12, will not operate.

CHANGING WORD 5'S SCROLLING

New in Word 5

If you've worked with an earlier release of Word, you'll notice that the method of scrolling in Word 5 occasionally differs. When the cursor is on a paragraph mark (¶) on the last line of the screen and you add more text, Word 5 simply scrolls the screen's text upward and creates a new, blank line at the bottom of the screen. Because Word 5 scrolls like this for each line, you may find such repeated scrolling annoying. In earlier releases, adding more text makes Word scroll the text up by half a screen. The cursor then appears in the middle of the screen which makes for less scrolling. To make Word 5 scroll as it did in earlier releases, start Word 5 with the /Y switch like so:

WORD /Y

Once you do, Word will continue to scroll in this manner, even when you quit Word and start it up later. To return Word 5 to its normal scrolling method, start Word with the /Z switch:

WORD /Z

You can combine Word's switches when you start up, provided the switches' instructions do not conflict. For instance, you can tell Word to use half-screen scrolling and load the last file by typing

WORD /Y/L

USING WORD WITHOUT A HARD DISK

If you do not have a hard disk, you must have at least two formatted disks on hand before running Setup. If you're using 360K disks, Setup will copy the Program 2 disk to one of them. (Use your operating system to copy the Program 1 disk.) Setup will also create a disk containing the printer driver, help, and hyphenation files. With higher-capacity disks, Setup will combine copies of the program files on one disk. By making copies and storing the original disks separately, you will still be able to reinstall the program if the copies becomes damaged.

You will want to store your documents on separate disks if you have a floppy disk system. Depending on your system, you can use 5¼- or 3½-inch disks, which you format from the system prompt. The blank, formatted disks will then be ready for use when you run Word.

To load Word, restart your computer system. Then, insert the copy of your program disk in drive A. If you've placed drive A on the system path, type

WORD

to start the program. If you have not placed drive A on the path, start Word by typing

A:WORD

at the system prompt. If you have a 360K floppy disk drive, insert the Program 2 disk in drive A when prompted.

SETTING UP A SERIAL PRINTER WITH A BATCH FILE

To print from Word, your printer must be set up before you run Word. Your printer is either a parallel or serial printer, and setting it up requires that you identify its type. Parallel printers, which are the most common, are relatively easy to set up; just follow the instructions in your printer's manual. Because setting up a serial printer is more difficult, I explain the general procedure and provide an example.

To allow Word to work with a serial printer, you must use the operating system MODE command (which must be on the disk) every time you start up Word. You can automate the procedure by putting it in a batch file. First, however, you must locate the following information in your printer's manual:

- Baud rate (you will enter the first two characters).
- Parity (you will enter N for no parity, O for odd parity, or E for even parity).
- Number of data bits (you will enter 7 or 8).
- Number of stop bits (you will enter 1 or 2).

Once you've located the specifications for your printer, you're ready to create the batch file. To do this, start up Word (without loading a document) and enter the system MODE command. The command begins with MODE COM1:, followed by a space and then the baud rate, parity, number of data bits, and number of stop bits, with each specification separated from the next by a comma. Finally, you would type P to indicate that you are configuring the port for a printer and press the Enter key. For example, if your printer manual specifies 1200 baud, no parity, eight data bits, and one stop bit, you would enter

MODE COM1: 12,N,8,1,P

You can also start up Word from the batch file. Suppose, for example, that you want Word to load the last file that you worked on. To do this, type

WORD /L

on the next line and press Enter. Note that there should be one and only one paragraph mark after each line.

To save this file as a batch file, folow these steps:

1. Initiate the Transfer Save command.

2. For the file name, enter

   START.BAT

   All batch files must have the .BAT extension.

3. Move to the format option, set it to Text-only, and press Enter. Word will then prompt you to

   Enter Y to confirm loss of formatting

4. Type Y for Yes. Since this file is going to be used by your operating system directly, it can't have any Word formatting.

5. Invoke the Quit command to leave Word and return to the system prompt.

You can run this batch file's commands, setting up your serial printer and starting Word, by typing

START

at the system prompt. If you do this now, you will see the START.BAT file displayed on the Word screen since that is the last file you worked with.

RUNNING WORD ON A RAM DRIVE FROM YOUR BATCH FILE

To use Word with a RAM drive, you copy the Word programs, along with the printer files for your printer(s), to the RAM drive every time you run Word. Then you log onto the RAM drive. Since you'll need to do this whenever you use the RAM drive, it's a good idea to add this procedure to your batch file.

In addition, if you want to keep your established Options and Print Options command settings for each Word session, which are recorded in the MW.INI file, this file must be copied to the RAM drive as well. In this example, I assume that you wish to copy all the .PRD files and their corresponding .DAT files to the RAM drive (which will also copy HYPH.DAT, the hyphenation file). I also assume that you've installed the Word program on drive C in the

WORD directory, that you have a serial printer, and that you're using drive D for the RAM drive.

If your START.BAT file is not displayed on the screen, reload it. To revise it so that it handles all the tasks involved in running Word 5 on a RAM drive, include the following lines in it in order:

```
COPY C:\WORD\*.OVL   D:
COPY C:\WORD\WORD.EXE   D:
COPY C:\WORD\MW.HLP   D:
COPY C:\WORD\MW.INI   D:
COPY C:\WORD\*.PRD   D:
COPY C:\WORD\*.DAT   D:
COPY C:\WORD\SCREEN.VID   D:
MODE COM1: 12,N,8,1,P
D:
WORD /L
COPY D:MW.INI   C:\WORD
```

You can adjust the second-to-last line to customize the way that Word starts up as you like. Once you have verified that your batch file's contents match these lines, invoke the Transfer Save command, double-check that the format option is still set to Text-only, and press Enter. When you run this batch file from the system prompt, each system command is performed automatically, one after the other, and Word runs from the RAM drive.

Creating a batch file to start up Word is efficient—it starts Word up quickly, exactly the way you want it to every time. In the next appendix, you'll learn other efficient ways of using your operating system with Word.

B

Understanding Your Operating System

Because Microsoft Word relies on your computer's operating system to run, understanding it makes Word easier to use. You can even use the operating system to perform some tasks more efficiently than you can with Word alone. In this appendix I discuss some fundamental system commands that you may need. You can enter these commands at the operating system's prompt or with Word's Library Run command.

THE OPERATING SYSTEM AND WORD

Whenever you initiate a task at the computer, the operating system directs the hundreds or even thousands of steps needed to accomplish it. Like so many nerve cells that fire when you raise your hand, these initiated steps take place automatically. Although different operating systems may have unique procedures, the two operating systems you can use with Word, DOS (Disk Operating System) and OS/2 (Operating System/2) share many standard procedures.

Microsoft and IBM introduced their first joint venture, DOS, in 1981 to control the first IBM personal computers. Another joint venture, OS/2, runs on the IBM PC/AT computers (and compatibles) and on IBM's Personal System/2 (PS/2) machines. It is designed to take advantage of the advances in technology that these computers provide. However, much of the way OS/2 looks and interacts with you, the user, remains the same as that of DOS.

In either case, the operating system operates like an efficient stage manager. It keeps the show going and remains largely unnoticed. For each letter you type, the computer needs to know where to display the letter on the screen and its size and shape. It must know how long the letter should stay on the screen, and whether it should be changed under certain circumstances. The computer must also be able to instruct the disk drives and the printer.

These common procedures are handled by the operating system so that the program designer doesn't need to reinvent the wheel for each program. The operating system also provides a common ground for exchanging information between programs.

RUNNING YOUR OPERATING SYSTEM

If you have a hard disk system, you place the operating system on the hard disk. Starting the computer then automatically invokes the operating system.

On a 5¼- or 3½-inch disk system, you put the operating system in charge by placing its system disk in drive A before you turn on or reset the computer. When you turn on the computer with a disk in drive A, the computer searches the disk for instructions. If it's a system disk, the computer reads the disk, and the operating system takes over.

When you start up the operating system, you will see the system prompt. If you are using DOS, you see C> or A>, depending on which disk drive is active. The term prompt isn't exactly descriptive, however, because it doesn't give you a clue as to what's next. When you see it, though, you know that you've come back to the operating system.

If you are using OS/2 (version 1.1), however, you will see the Program Selector screen instead of the prompt. Unlike the initial startup procedure discussed in Appendix A, to start Word in OS/2, you highlight Word in the Start Programs portion of the screen and press Enter. Later, if you have left Word running in the background while you work with another program (thus taking advantage of OS/2's *multitasking* capability), you can return to Word by highlighting it in the Switch to a Running Program portion of the Program Selector screen (and pressing Enter). In this book, however, I use the more common term, prompt, to refer to the operating system's screen.

If you see something radically different, it probably means that the computer's AUTOEXEC.BAT file has been altered (see Appendix A). You may need to get assistance from whoever made the changes.

RESETTING THE COMPUTER

If you had the Setup program make changes to your CONFIG.SYS or AUTOEXEC.BAT file when you prepared Word, you will need to reset the computer to incorporate those changes.

Resetting does essentially the same thing as turning the computer off and on—it takes you to the operating system. It's quicker, though, because your computer does not have to run the self-checking test it runs every time you turn it on. This procedure, also known as a *warm boot,* uses three keys. Simply press Ctrl-Alt-Delete and release all three keys at once to reset your computer.

Resetting is one of the most potentially dangerous procedures in your computer. Performing a reset erases everything that's in RAM, including any unsaved changes you might have made to your documents. It's intentionally awkward so you don't perform it accidentally. Except when all else fails, *never* reset the computer to leave Word: always use Word's Quit command (see Chapter 2).

PROGRAMS AND THE OPERATING SYSTEM

There are a myriad of programs that work with the operating system. There are word processing programs, like Word; electronic spreadsheet programs; database management programs; educational programs; and game programs, among others.

When you run a program, it's as though you are entering a wing in the system mansion. The password you use to enter this wing is the program's file name. To prepare the Word program for running, for instance, we used the Setup program.

CHANGING THE LOGGED DRIVE

The drive you are logged onto is the activated or current drive. This is the one to which the operating system will direct your commands. To perform the system commands described in this appendix, you will need to know how to activate the correct drive.

When you start up the operating system on a hard disk,

```
C>
```

is displayed on the screen. This indicates that drive C is the activated drive. To activate drive D instead, type

```
D:
```

prompt and press the Enter key. The computer will respond by displaying the prompt

```
D>
```

which indicates that drive D is now current. You can reactivate drive C by typing

C:

at the prompt and pressing Enter.

SETTING THE DATE

If your computer contains a battery-operated clock, it will keep track of the date and time for you automatically—you need not set them. If necessary, you can reset date and time by using one of the techniques that follow.

You can establish the date and time for your operating system in one of three ways. If your computer doesn't have a clock, the operating system asks you to enter the date and then the time when you start it up. To set the date, enter it in the order of month-day-year. (For example, November 5, 1990 would be 11-05-90.) For the time, be sure to use the 24-hour format. Thus, 9 P.M. would be 21:00.

You can also enter the date by typing

DATE

at the system prompt and pressing the Enter key. The operating system displays the date that it's set to, and you can enter a different date if necessary. You can set the time in a similar fashion with the TIME command.

In addition, you can use Word's Library Run command, which I describe later in this appendix, to work with the operating system temporarily. Initiate this command and type DATE or TIME as before.

ORGANIZING WITH DIRECTORIES

To make it easier to find and organize files on your hard disk, the operating system allows you to divide the disk's contents into directories. (You can even do this on floppy disks, although it is of greater benefit for organizing hard disks.) Directories can be broken into other directories (sometimes called subdirectories). You can then group related files as you choose.

CREATING DIRECTORIES

Originally, your operating system has only one directory, which is called the root directory. You create additional directories that branch off the root, and you assign their names.

To create a directory, you activate the proper drive and use the MD system command. Type the letters MD (for make directory), followed by a space and the name you want to assign to the directory. Thus, to create a directory called CLIENTS (for holding client information), you'd enter the following at the system prompt:

MD CLIENTS

You can use any name for the directory, provided it has no more than eight characters for its primary name. You can also add an optional period and extension of up to three characters.

Once you've created the directory, you may wish to make it current before you start up Word. The advantage in this approach is that if you load Word from one of the directories, Word will automatically load the NORMAL.GLY glossary and NORMAL.STY style sheet stored in that directory (unless you have set the Transfer Options command's save between sessions option to Yes, in which case Word will use the directory specified by that command's setup option). This feature allows you to create different versions of the default glossary and style sheet that correspond to the stored documents in your directories.

To change to a directory, type CD, a space, and the name of the directory you want to change to. Thus, to change to the CLIENTS directory, you'd enter

CD CLIENTS

To change back to the root directory, you enter

**CD **

SPECIFYING DIRECTORIES WITH A PATH

You create a path to identify the directory or drive that the operating system or Word should use for a particular operation. For instance, you change to a directory at the operating system level by providing its path with the CD command. A path in the Transfer Options command indicates which directory Word should normally use for the Transfer commands. You also use a path with the Setup program to indicate where Setup should store the Word program files on the hard disk.

To specify a path, type the disk drive letter, a colon, a backslash (\), and then the directory's name. If the path includes a directory within the directory, type another backslash and the name of the next directory.

Suppose you want to store your files for Microsoft Word in a directory called MSWORD on drive C. When you run the Setup program, you'd indicate it with this path:

C:\MSWORD

Suppose, too, that you want to store your Word documents in a subdirectory of this MSWORD directory. Assuming you called this subdirectory DOCUMENT when you created it, specify the following path for the Transfer Options setup option:

C:\MSWORD\DOCUMENT

You can type this path or select the drive and directory from Word 5's list.

By setting up the path for Word to use with the Transfer commands like this, you need only specify the name of the file, not the path, when you use one of the Transfer commands (say, Transfer Load). However, you can still enter a path when you issue Transfer Load, if you so choose. This ability would come in handy if most of your work is directed toward one directory, but you want to load a particular file from another directory.

When you use some of the Transfer commands, Word displays the path along with the file name. You can use the command-editing capabilities of the F7 through F10 function keys to edit the path and file name if necessary.

Just as you can set up a path for some of Word's commands to avoid having to reenter it each time, so too can you set up a path for running programs, such as Word, from the operating system. Let's learn how to do this next.

RUNNING PROGRAMS EFFICIENTLY WITH THE PATH COMMAND

By specifying a default path with the PATH command, you can tell your computer where to look for programs you want to run. When you want to run a program, you then only have to enter the name of the program, not its complete path. The PATH command remains in effect until you turn off or reset the computer.

To issue the PATH command, type PATH at the system prompt, followed by the drive and directory of the first location where you want the operating system to check, a semicolon, the next drive and directory, another semicolon, and so on. (You can have your system automatically type this information each time you start the computer by including it as part of your AUTOEXEC.BAT file.)

Thus, if you want the system to check for programs in drive C's root, DOS, and MSWORD directories, you'd enter the following:

    PATH C:\;C:\DOS;C:\MSWORD

You can then start Word simply by entering

    WORD

at the system prompt, regardless of which directory you're at. (You can also have this PATH command executed from a batch file; see Appendix A.) The operating system will check the directories listed in the PATH command and run Word when it finds it (in the WORD directory). This loads the current directory's NORMAL.GLY glossary and NORMAL.STY style sheet or those in the directory established with the Transfer Options command.

Without a system path, you can run Word from a directory by typing the full path leading to Word. To do this, you enter the drive letter, a colon, a backslash, the directory name, another backslash, and WORD, without entering any spaces. Thus, to start Word, which is located in the MSWORD directory on drive C, you'd enter

C:\MSWORD\WORD

DISPLAYING THE DIRECTORY

The point of displaying the directory of a drive is to see the names of the files that are in it. To list the file names, follow these steps:

1. Change to the directory you want to see by using the CD command with the directory's path.

2. At the prompt, type

   DIR

   and press the Enter key.

If the directory display is so long that it scrolls off the screen, you can stop it by pressing Ctrl-S or Ctrl-Num Lock as the screen scrolls. Alternatively, you can enter

DIR /W

to display the directory in a wide format, which accommodates more file names on the screen. You can also enter

DIR /P

which pauses the display when the screen fills up. To restart one of these displays, press any key.

You can also use the DIR command with wild cards. The asterisk represents any group of characters, while the question mark represents any single character. Thus, to see a display of all the backup files in the current directory, you would type

DIR *.BAK

TIP

You can cancel a long display by pressing Ctrl-C or Ctrl-Scroll Lock. The scrolling will stop, and the operating system prompt will reappear.

RENAMING A FILE ON THE DISK

As you know, you can rename a loaded document with the Transfer Rename command in Word. To change the name of a file at the operating system level (and thus avoid having to load the file), you can use the system's RENAME command. Because the operating system knows nothing about Word's .DOC convention, you must type out all file names in full. For example, if you have a Word document named DATED that you wanted to rename as MODERN, follow these steps:

1. Change to the drive and directory that the DATED document is in.

2. Type

   RENAME   DATED.DOC   MODERN.DOC

   and press Enter.

FORMATTING A DISK

Even if you own a hard disk, you may wish to store your documents on floppies; for example, you can keep copies of your files on floppies as a safety measure or to share them with other people. When you buy floppy disks from the store, you must format them for your particular computer before they can store any information. To format a disk with the operating system, you must have a copy of its FORMAT.COM program in a directory listed in the PATH command (or change to the appropriate directory first).

1. At the system prompt, type FORMAT, a space, and the drive letter (usually A) followed by a colon, like so:

   FORMAT A:

2. Press Enter. The operating system will invoke FORMAT.COM and prompt you to

   Insert new diskette for drive A:
   and strike ENTER when ready

4. Put a new disk in drive A. Generally, you'll want to use a disk that is new and does not have anything already recorded on it. If the disk does contain any files, they will be erased by the formatting process.

5. Press the Enter key to begin formatting. If you'd rather cancel formatting at this point, press Ctrl-C or Ctrl-Scroll Lock instead.

When you finish formatting one disk, the operating system will ask

Format another (Y/N)?

If you wish, insert another disk, type Y for Yes, and press Enter. You can format a whole box of new disks this way. To indicate that the disks in the box are formatted, attach their blank labels. Once you do, though, be sure to use only a felt-tip pen to write on the labels; otherwise, the pressure of your pen on the disk may damage it when you write on its attached label.

COPYING A FILE

You can use the operating system to make an exact copy of a file in the same directory as the original but with a new name. This would be useful if you wanted to create a document that resembled another but was not identical. Once copied, you could revise the copy. You may also wish to copy files from your hard disk to floppies if you don't expect to use the files again and you want to free up space on your hard disk. The copying procedure is similar to loading a file with Word and saving it under a different name.

To copy a file with the operating system's COPY command, proceed as follows:

1. Change to the drive and directory containing the original file (say, it's called PROTO.DOC).

2. Using DITTO.DOC as the copy's name, type

   COPY   PROTO.DOC   DITTO.DOC

   and press Enter.

With this command, you're telling the operating system to make a copy of PROTO.DOC and call the copy DITTO.DOC.

USING WORD'S LIBRARY RUN COMMAND

You can invoke a system command, including COPY, FORMAT, RENAME and so on, from within Word by issuing the Library Run command. After the command has run, you are returned to where you were in Word. That is, the document, windows, scrap, and so on would all be exactly the same.

Be careful when you use the Library Run command, though, as things can go wrong. You could find that Word can't be restarted or that the keyboard freezes up. This is especially true if you use resident programs (discussed later in this appendix). For this reason, save all the documents that you have on display before you issue this command. Then, if you have to reset the computer or turn it off and back on to get it started, your documents will be safe. (These steps should be avoided if at all possible. Always try to use Word's Quit command to end a Word session.)

With Word, you can use any of the system commands we've studied in this appendix so far. Just invoke Library Run and type the command. You can also run other programs, such as an electronic spreadsheet.

Once your operation is complete, Word will ask you to

Press a key to resume Word

Doing so brings Word back to the screen.

If you have a number of chores to perform with DOS, you can temporarily invoke DOS itself. You do this by loading a second command processor with the Library Run command (the first is automatically loaded when you load DOS). Then you can perform as many operations as you want. When you're done, you can resume your session with Word. This technique also works with a hard disk, but without all the swapping of disks.

1. For safety, issue the Transfer Save command on all the displayed documents.

2. Invoke the Library Run command. You'll see the prompt

   Enter DOS command

   with Word 5 proposing the response

   COMMAND

   Simply press Enter to call up the operating system and display the prompt. (With OS/2 you can invoke a command processor in Protected mode by typing CMD instead.)

4. Issue the system commands as needed.

5. When you're through with the operating system, type

   EXIT

   and press Enter.

6. You will then be prompted to

   Press a key to resume Word.

   Press any key, and Word will start up again, where it left off.

USING RESIDENT PROGRAMS

Resident programs are popular these days. They get around some system restrictions so they can be operated at the same time as other programs, such as Word. Generally, they work well with Word, but there are a few points to be aware of.

First, you should never use the Library Run command to load a resident program. Doing so may force you to quit Word, and you could lose work that you haven't saved. Word's other Library commands may also be unavailable while resident programs are loaded. If you need to use these commands, quit Word, end all resident programs, and restart Word.

When used from within Word, some resident programs leave garbage on Word's screen after they're done. To remove it, press Ctrl-Shift-\; Word then repaints the screen correctly without the garbage.

New in
Word 5

Sometimes, resident programs interfere with Word's more unusual keystroke combinations. To get around this problem, Word 5 provides a special keyboard driver and a set of macros that can invoke those keystrokes. To use these tools, do the following:

1. Rename or erase the SCREEN.VID file in your WORD directory.

2. Run Setup again.

3. Using the W procedure, select Safe keyboard support for TSRs, 3270 emulators for your type of computer. (You won't need to reinstall printer drivers and other files.)

4. Start up Word and issue the Transfer Glossary Load command to load the SAFEKEYB.GLY glossary, which Setup copies from the Utilities 2 disk to your WORD directory. (Alternatively, you can merge this glossary with one you are already using.)

5. For the troublesome keystrokes, substitute the Ctrl codes listed in Table B.1. For example, to create a column break, press Ctrl-C-B instead of Ctrl-Alt-Enter.

Table B.1: Safe Key Substitutions

STANDARD KEYSTROKES	PURPOSE	SUBSTITUTE KEY CODES
Ctrl-Alt-Enter	Breaks a column	Ctrl-C-B
Ctrl-plus (on keypad)	Expands the outline	Ctrl-E-O
Ctrl-5	Jumps to another column	Ctrl-J-C
Ctrl-Alt-hyphen	Creates a long hyphen	Ctrl-L-H
Ctrl-period	Moves to the next field (chevron)	Ctrl-N-F
Ctrl-comma	Moves to the previous field (chevron)	Ctrl-P-F

Table B.1: Safe Key Substitutions (continued)

STANDARD KEYSTROKES	PURPOSE	SUBSTITUTE KEY CODES
Ctrl-↓	Moves to the next paragraph	Ctrl-N-P
Ctrl-↑	Moves to the previous paragraph	Ctrl-P-P

Notice how the Ctrl codes are mnemonically related to their purpose. For this reason, you may wish to use them even if you aren't having problems with a resident program. To do so, simply load the SAFEKEYB.GLY glossary; you don't need to reinstall Word.

There are many other system commands, as well as additional variations on the commands we've discussed, that you might find useful. You may wish to consult *The ABC's of MS-DOS*, by Alan Miller, or *Essential OS/2*, by Judd Robbins, both published by SYBEX. These are excellent books for the beginner and experienced alike.

C

Exploring
Word's
Macros

IN THIS APPENDIX I LIST THE MACROS MICROSOFT supplies in Word release 5's MACRO.GLY glossary. As a precaution, save your files and close additional windows before running the macros; several open horizontal windows themselves, and some may not work with more than one window open. With other macros, you can have at most two vertical windows on the screen, since the macros open a vertical window and Word allows only three vertical windows.

In this listing I describe the macros as they are, including any drawbacks. However, you can overcome most limitations easily by adapting the macro to suit your needs. Many supplied macros use the function keys as configured by Word, so you can't assign other macros to the function keys (unless the macro lists the function key preceded by Ctrl-X).

Some macros are designed for use by other macros, and you should not run these macros directly yourself. I do not list these macros here separately, but rather with the macro that uses them. The consequences of running one of these macros vary—unexpected characters may appear in your document, or the macro may be aborted because of unknown fields.

Remember that you can display a macro's text in a window to study it there or print it. With a clear screen, issue the Insert command, type the name of the macro (or select it from the listing) followed by a caret (^). Don't forget to provide the caret before pressing the Enter key, or Word will run the macro instead of displaying it.

3_DELETE.MAC: CTRL-D-D

This macro deletes text, assigning the deleted text to a glossary entry so that you can restore up to three deletions with the next macro, 3_undelete.mac (Ctrl-U-U).

The 3_delete.mac assigns text to the glossary entries named scrap0, scrap1, scrap2, scrap3, and scrap4, so don't use these names for other purposes or invoke them yourself. As it also requires the Ctrl codes Ctrl-X-Y and Ctrl-X-Y, don't use these Ctrl codes either.

PROCEDURE

Highlight your text to be deleted and run 3_delete.mac. The macro first turns off the display of the command menu if it's showing. It then calculates the scrap number using a field in the Format Division Margins command. It inserts the number from the glossary into the field momentarily, and then it deletes the text, assigning it to the appropriate glossary entry in rotation.

ASSOCIATED MACRO

3_undelete.mac: **Ctrl-U-U**

3_UNDELETE.MAC: CTRL-U-U

This macro undeletes text that has been deleted with 3_delete.mac (Ctrl-D-D). You can undelete up to the last three deletions.

PROCEDURE

Position your cursor where you want the deleted text to appear and invoke 3_undelete.mac.

Specify which deletion you want after the macro prompts you with

Undelete which scrap? 1 = last edit, 2 = second to last edit,
3 = third to last edit

The macro then asks you for verification with

Is this correct? (Y)es or (N)o

Typing Y ends the macro. If you type N for No, the macro deletes the text again and returns to step 1. If you change your mind about restoring deletions, you can abort this macro by pressing the Esc key.

ASSOCIATED MACRO

3_delete.mac: **Ctrl-D-D**

New in
Word 5

ANNOT_COLLECT.MAC: CTRL-A-C

This macro collects annotations from documents that you specify individually or collectively with a query and saves them in a file. This is handy when you have created multiple copies of a document and distributed them to others so they can insert comments with the Format Annotation command; you can then use this macro to compile their comments. The macro will create a list of all the annotations from page 1 of each copy, followed by those for page 2, and so on. Of course, each person should use a unique annotation mark so you can identify the comments' source. Additionally, an annotation can't be inserted at the very beginning of any document, or it will not appear correctly in the list.

The annot_collect.mac macro uses the macros collect_guts.mac and file_feeder.mac, which you should not run directly.

PROCEDURE

Close all but one window before running annot_collect.mac or make window 1 active.

After initiating the Transfer Load command, the macro prompts you to

Type the name of the annotations destination document and press Enter

Specify the document's name. If the file is not already on disk, Word prompts you to enter Y to create a new file. The macro then invokes the macro file_feeder.mac, which asks

Do you want to be prompted for each source file (y/n)?

Type N if you want to reference a group of files or type Y if you want to specify each file name individually.

If you typed Y, the macro invokes the Transfer Load command in window 2 and prompts you to

Enter the name of a source document and press Enter

If you typed N, the macro issues the Library Document-retrieval's Query command and displays the prompt

Enter search information for source files; press Enter when done

Specify the query the macro should use to find and load the documents one by one. While each document is on the screen, the macro displays the message

Collecting annotations from source document

including the document's number, and collects its annotations in window 1.

If you are specifying each file name when prompted, the macro asks

Add another source document (y/n)?

after collecting the annotations from the loaded document and repeats the process if you respond with Y for Yes.

After combining all the annotations in the document in window 1, the macro closes window 2 and leaves the annotation document on the screen.

ASSOCIATED MACROS

annot_merge.mac: Ctrl-A-M

annot_remove.mac: Ctrl-A-R

ANNOT_MERGE.MAC: CTRL-A-M

New in
Word 5

This macro collects annotations from multiple documents and combines them in one document. Generally, you use it to gather comments from copies of a document that you've distributed to others, so that all the comments appear in just one copy. This macro's operation resembles that of annot_collect.mac, except it actually inserts annotations in the document, rather than listing them. The annot_merge.mac macro uses the macros file_feeder.mac and merge_guts.mac, which you should not run on your own.

PROCEDURE

Close all windows except one before running the macro or make window 1 active. When you run the macro, it prompts you to name the file it should merge the annotations with and then loads that file. You can then choose to collect annotations from documents specified individually or collectively with a query expression.

After loading each file and gathering its annotations (using the same procedure annot_collect.mac uses), annot_merge.mac runs the merge_guts.mac macro, which automatically inserts the annotation in its proper place if possible. If the macro can't find where the annotation belongs (if you're not using copies of the same document, for example), it asks you where it should insert the annotations, one by one, with the prompt

Move highlight to where annotation should go, then press Enter.

The annot_merge.mac macro leaves the document containing the merged annotations on the screen when it's done.

ASSOCIATED MACROS

annot_collect.mac: Ctrl-A-C

annot_remove.mac: Ctrl-A-R

ANNOT_REMOVE.MAC: CTRL-A-R

5 New in Word 5

This macro removes all the annotations from the loaded document and saves the document under a new name. You can use it when you need a "clean" copy of a document—without annotations—to provide to others so they can insert their comments.

PROCEDURE

Load the document whose annotations you wish to remove. If it's a new document, save it to keep a copy of the file with the annotations intact.

When you run annot_remove.mac, it repeats the Jump Annotation command until it has deleted all the annotations. It then displays the message

All annotations removed successfully

prompts you to

Save the document with a new name

and completes the save.

ASSOCIATED MACROS

annot_collect.mac: Ctrl-A-C

annot_merge.mac: Ctrl-A-M

ARCHIVE_AUTHOR.MAC: CTRL-A-A

 New in Word 5

This macro copies each document by the same author (as specified by the summary sheet) to the author's directory. It determines which directory to use with the AUTHLIST.DOC file; this file lists authors and their corresponding directories. Use archive_author.mac to reorganize your hard disk if several authors have stored their documents in the same directory and have used the summary sheet feature. This way, each author can then set the Transfer Options command to his directory, and it will show only his files.

To complete this process, archive_author.mac uses the macro archive_documents.mac, which you should not run directly.

PROCEDURE

If you want to store the authors' documents in new subdirectories, create them at the operating system level. If you don't have a AUTHLIST.DOC file, run Word and specify the directory in which it should create this file with the Transfer Options command's setup option. Before invoking archive_author.mac, you can set up a query with the Library Document-retrieval command to find all the files you wish to archive.

When you run archive_author.mac, it invokes the macro archive-_documents.mac, which opens a vertical window (it will use the window to display AUTHLIST.DOC), and issues the Library Document-retrieval's Query command. The macro then attempts to locate and load the author list. If it can't, it displays the prompt

Can't find author list. Create new list (y/n)?

If you don't want to create AUTHLIST.DOC in the directory you've specified with the Transfer Options command, type N for No. The macro then initiates the Transfer Load command and prompts you to

Please locate the file AUTHLIST.DOC and press Enter when ready

If you need to change drives or directories, press F1, highlight the drive or directory, and press F1 again.

After loading an existing author list, archive_author.mac asks if you want to add an author's name to the author list. If you do, you are then prompted to give the path of the directory you want to copy that author's files to. The archive_author.mac macro adds the information, asks you if you want to add another author to the list, and repeats the process until you type N when prompted to add another author.

Once you have completed the AUTHLIST.DOC file, the macro finds its listed authors' files and copies them to their respective directories with the Library Document-retrieval's Copy command. It then resets the query settings that were in place before it ran and closes the window containing AUTHLIST.DOC.

ASSOCIATED MACRO

archive_keyword.mac: Ctrl-A-K

ARCHIVE_KEYWORD.MAC: CTRL-A-K

5 New in Word 5

This macro copies each document with the same keyword (as specified by the summary sheet) to the keyword's directory, which it identifies by referring to the KEYLIST.DOC file. If necessary, it creates this file in the current directory. Its procedure is similar to that of archive_author.mac.

The archive_keyword.mac macro invokes archive_documents.-mac, which you should not run directly.

PROCEDURE

Assuming you have already created the necessary subdirectories, issue the Library Document-retrieval's Query command to find all the files to be archived, and invoke archive_keyword.mac.

The macro then loads KEYLIST.DOC, prompts you to add keywords and their directory names to the list, and copies each keyword's files to its directory.

ASSOCIATED MACRO

archive_author.mac: Ctrl-A-A

AUTHORITY_ENTRY.MAC: CTRL-A-E

This macro flags citations for legal purposes so you can use the next macro, authority_table.mac (Ctrl-A-T), to compile a table of authorities automatically. It allows you to assign the citation, along with its hidden codes, to the glossary so you can make subsequent citations easily.

PROCEDURE

When you invoke authority_entry.mac, it turns off Word's display of hidden text so the citation codes don't appear. It prompts you with the message

Type the new citation, highlight it & press Enter

Specify the source that will become the entry in the table after the prompt

What is the source? 1 = Previous Case, 2 = Statute, 3 = Regulation, or 4 = Other

If you respond with 4 for Other, it prompts you to provide a custom category for the citation's source.

The macro then inserts hidden codes before and after the citation. It prompts you to make the citation a glossary entry with the following message:

Move the cursor to the character before this citation

Press Esc to cancel the macro if you don't want to reassign the citation to the glossary. Otherwise, move the cursor and press Enter. You are then asked to assign a glossary abbreviation. Doing so ends the macro.

ASSOCIATED MACRO

authority_table.mac: Ctrl-A-T

AUTHORITY_TABLE.MAC: CTRL-A-T

This macro compiles a table of authorities at the end of your document, categorizing it by source and giving the page reference. An existing index will be deleted, unless you first remove its identifying markers (see Chapter 19).

PROCEDURE

After flagging your entries with authority_entry.mac (Ctrl-A-E), run this macro to compile your table of authorities.

ASSOCIATED MACRO

authority_entry.mac: Ctrl-A-E

BULLETED_LIST.MAC: CTRL-B-L

This macro allows you to enter a list of items. It automatically places hyphens (-) as bullets in front of each item as you enter it and indents the list according to your specifications.

PROCEDURE

Invoke the bulleted_list.mac macro when you're ready to begin entering items for the list. The macro responds with the prompt

Enter desired indent in inches for bulleted list

Provide a value and press Enter. It then prompts you to enter the items. The macro adds hyphens and indents them one by one. After entering the last item, press Esc instead of Enter and verify that you want to end the macro with another Esc.

CHAINPRINT.MAC: CTRL-C-P

This macro prints one document after another according to a list of document names that you provide. It also numbers the documents sequentially.

PROCEDURE

Prepare a list of document names by entering one name on each line. Save the list under a file name of your choice. Set up the Print Options command with your printer name and other standard settings. Make sure that you've saved all your files and that you have only one window open before you run the macro.

When you run chainprint.mac, it prompts you to

Enter filename of document which contains list of files to be printed

Give the name of the file that holds your list. The macro then opens a vertical window on the right of the screen and loads the list into it.

To determine whether to add page numbers, it asks

Is a running head used to print page numbers, Y/N ?

If you reply with N for No, it prompts you to specify the page number position from the top of the page and from the left edge of the page. The macro then uses the Format Division Page-numbers command to place the number on the page and asks you to indicate which number to begin numbering the first document with. Type the number and press Enter.

After you have provided the necessary information, the macro loads the first document in the first window and prints it. The macro then loads the second document, sets the page numbering to begin with the next number after the first document's last page number, and prints the second document. The macro proceeds in this fashion until it has printed all the documents on the list.

CHARACTER_TEST.MAC: CTRL-C-H

New in Word 5

This macro prints out samples of the fonts for the printer. It uses the CHARTEST.DOC file, which has all of IBM's extended character sets in it, and prints a character set in five newspaper-style columns.

PROCEDURE

Before running character_test.mac, set up your printer with the Print Options command. Also, it's best to first issue the Transfer Options command to provide the location of CHARTEST.DOC with its setup option. (The Setup program copied this file to your WORD directory.)

When you run the macro, it clears the window, allowing you to save a displayed document if necessary, and then loads CHARTEST.DOC. If it can't find the file, it prompts you to enter CHARTEST.DOC's full path. You can type the path name, or you can select it from a list by first pressing F1.

The macro formats the file in five newspaper-style columns and adds a running head containing the font name. Then it asks

Do you want to print a sample of every font (y/n)?

If you respond with Y, it highlights the document, formats it, and prints it for each font in turn, using 12 points for the font size.

If you choose not to print a sample of every font, the macro displays the Format Character's font name field and lists the available fonts. After you select the font you want, character_test.mac sets up, formats, and prints CHARTEST.DOC with that font. You can then choose another font to print or end the macro.

CLEAN_SCREEN.MAC: CTRL-C-S

5 New in Word 5

This macro issues the keystroke combination for refreshing the screen, Ctrl-Shift-\. Refreshing the screen is sometimes necessary after using a resident program (see Appendix B), and this macro allows you to use Ctrl-C-S to do so, which is easier to remember than Ctrl-Shift-\.

PROCEDURE

The quickest way to invoke the macro is by pressing Ctrl-C-S. The macro then issues the keystrokes Ctrl-Shift-\, which cleans the screen.

COPY_FILE.MAC: CTRL-C-F

5 New in Word 5

This macro copies a file and its imported graphics to a drive and directory you specify. Additionally, it adjusts the .G. code lines in the document to reflect the graphics' new paths.

The copy_file.mac macro uses the macro strip_path.mac, which you should not run directly.

PROCEDURE

Load the document you wish to copy and close other windows. Set the Options command's show layout option to No, as show layout doesn't display hidden text, which the macro needs to change the .G. code lines.

When you run copy_file.mac, you are first prompted to

Specify the drive and directory to which files should be copied.

Provide the complete path, such as

C:\WORD

After verifying the original file's path and name, copy_file.mac searches the file for the .G. code lines, replacing their path with the new path and issuing the Library Run command to copy their indicated graphics files to the new directory. It then copies the document file to the new directory and reloads the old file.

COPY_TEXT.MAC: CTRL-C-T

This macro prompts you at each step in a copy operation. It copies text from one part of a document to another or between documents. Unless you want to automate all your Word procedures, you'll probably find it easier to copy the text yourself, without using copy_text.mac.

PROCEDURE

Activate Document mode and invoke the copy_text.mac macro. It then asks you to

Select text to be copied, press Enter when done

Highlight the text that you want to copy and press Enter. The macro responds by prompting you to move the cursor to where you want the text to go and to press Enter.

ASSOCIATED MACRO

move_text.mac: Ctrl-M-T

DCA_LOAD.MAC: CTRL-D-L

This macro converts a file in IBM's Document Content Architecture (DCA) format, also known as Revisable Form Text (RFT), to Microsoft Word format and loads the document into Word. Be careful not to confuse RFT with RTF (Rich Text Format).

PROCEDURE

The Microsoft program file, WORD_DCA.EXE, which converts programs between Word and DCA, must be in the directory that's active when you start Word or in a directory specified with the PATH command (see Appendix B). Normally, the Setup program copies this program to your WORD directory. Save any displayed document before you run this macro.

After you invoke dca_load.mac, it asks you to

Enter the full name of the DCA document to be loaded

Include the file's extension (and path if the file is not in the current directory).

The macro then issues the Library Run command to suspend Word and run WORD_DCA.EXE, converting the document to Word format. It adds the extension .MSW to the converted file and loads it in Word.

ASSOCIATED MACRO

dca_save.mac: Ctrl-D-S

DCA_SAVE.MAC: CTRL-D-S

This macro converts the displayed Word file to IBM's DCA format, also known as Revisable Form Text (RFT). Be careful not to confuse RFT with RTF (Rich Text Format).

PROCEDURE

Save the displayed Word document before you run dca_save.mac; you must assign a name to the document. The Microsoft program file, WORD_DCA.EXE, which converts programs between Word and DCA, must be in the directory that's active when you start Word or in a directory specified with the PATH command.

When you run dca_save.mac, it issues the Transfer Save command to check the name of the file. It then converts the document to DCA format, using the Library Run command WORD_DCA.EXE. It adds the extension .RFT to the converted document and returns you to Word.

ASSOCIATED MACROS

dca_load.mac: Ctrl-D-L

freeze_style.mac: Ctrl-F-S

New in
Word 5

ENVELOPE.MAC: CTRL-E-N

The macro allows you to highlight an address and, optionally, a return address in a document, which it then prints on an envelope. As this macro sets the Print Options command's paper feed option to envelope, you can only use it if your printer has an envelope feed (unless you edit the macro).

PROCEDURE

Load the document that you want an envelope addressed for; then measure your envelope's size. As this macro opens a vertical window and Word allows only three vertical windows, make sure you have no more than two vertical windows open before running the macro.

When you invoke envelope.mac, it lists five envelope sizes, including Other, in a vertical window and prompts you to select a size. If you select Other, the macro asks for the size of the envelope with the two prompts

How wide is your envelope?
How tall is your envelope?

The macro will use the size you specify to format a new document for the envelope.

Then the macro asks you to highlight the address in the document for the envelope. At this point, you can choose to print a return address. If you indicate that you want to, the macro prompts you to highlight the return address.

After using calculations and the Format Paragraph, Format pOsition, and Format Division Margins commands to place the information correctly on the envelope page, the macro prints the address(es).

FILENAME.MAC: CTRL-F-N

New in
Word 5

If you have saved the displayed document, this macro inserts its file name, complete with its drive and directory, at the cursor. You can use this macro to identify your document. By placing the cursor in your header text, for example, you will then be able to determine where your file is on the disk by checking its printed version's header.

If the document has not yet been saved, the macro inserts the word "Untitled."

PROCEDURE

Load the file in the window, position the cursor where you want the file name, and run filename.mac. If the file is new, save it, assigning a file name, before you run the macro, or "Untitled" will appear in the document instead of the file name.

FREEZE_STYLE.MAC: CTRL-F-S

This macro freezes the style formats of a document attached to a style sheet so that its formats become a permanent part of the document and the document no longer refers to the style sheet for them. Freezing a document prepares it for conversion to other formats (such as DCA).

PROCEDURE

Load the document whose style formats you wish to freeze. Before running the macro, make a copy of the document by saving it under a different name if you wish to keep a version of the document that still uses the style sheet.

You freeze a document by setting a character and a paragraph format to the entire document. The freeze_style.mac macro does this by setting the double underline and keep together options to No. Hence, your document should not have double-underlined text or paragraphs kept together: the macro will turn off these formats if they do exist.

After highlighting the entire document, the macro issues the Format Character command and sets double underline to No. It then issues the Format Paragraph command to set keep together to No.

When the macro ends, the entire document is highlighted, and you see the end of the document. You can then use the associated macro, dca_save.mac, to convert the document to DCA.

ASSOCIATED MACRO

dca_save.mac: Ctrl-D-S

INDEX.MAC: CTRL-I-W

This macro uses a list you provide to code words in your document as index entries. It only codes individual words, not phrases.

PROCEDURE

Prepare your list of words for indexing by typing each word on a separate line, with a paragraph mark at the end of the line. Save the list, specifying a file name. Load the document you want to index. Move the cursor to the beginning of the document, if necessary, before you run the macro to ensure that the macro searches the entire document for the index entries.

Invoke index.mac; it first prompts you to provide the name of the file containing the list. After you enter the file name, the macro splits the window vertically and loads the specified file into the second window.

It then searches for the first list word in the document to be indexed. When it finds the word, it runs the index_entry.mac macro (Ctrl-I-E), which places indexing codes before and after the word.

It then switches back to the second window, checks the next word on the list, switches to the first window, and searches for this word, repeating this procedure until all the words on the list are indexed in the document. When the macro ends, it leaves window 2 open with the list file in it. If you need to run the macro again, be sure to close this window before doing so.

ASSOCIATED MACRO

index_entry.mac: Ctrl-I-E

INDEX_ENTRY.MAC: CTRL-I-E

This macro places index codes before and after the highlighted text. The macro index.mac (Ctrl-I-W) runs this macro to create entries, and you can run it, too.

PROCEDURE

Highlight the text you wish to index. The Options command's show non-printing symbols option should be set to Partial or All before you run the macro. Otherwise, the index code disappears when it's formatted as hidden, and the macro isn't constructed to allow for this.

When you invoke index_entry.mac, it deletes the highlighted text to scrap. It then types the .I. code, highlights it, formats it as hidden (with Alt-X-E), and inserts the text from scrap back into the document (following the .I. code). Next, the macro types a semicolon and formats it as hidden (Alt-X-E twice) to complete the coding of the entry.

ASSOCIATED MACROS

index.mac: Ctrl-I-W

toc_entry.mac: Ctrl-T-E

MAILING_LABEL.MAC: CTRL-M-L

The macro automates the printing of labels, allowing you to print one, two, or three labels across the page. It sends the output to a file.

PROCEDURE

The mailing_label.mac macro uses the template specified in the "label" glossary entry. Set up your database, and, if necessary, a header file that references the names it contains, for example:

«firstname» «lastname» «title» «company» «address» «city» «state» «zip»

Clear the screen before you invoke the macro. When you run the macro, it prompts you with

How many columns across the page: 1, 2 or 3 ?

Using your response, it sets up side-by-side paragraphs on the screen with the Format Division Margin command, the Format Paragraph command, and the "label" glossary entry.

The macro then asks you to specify your database file (including its extension). After you provide a name, it issues the Print Merge Document command, displaying the prompt

Enter name of document to merge to, then press Enter

The macro ends once it has merged the label format with your database, and you can print the resulting file with the Print Printer command.

MEMO_HEADER.MAC: CTRL-M-H

This macro creates a memo template. Because memo_header.mac includes hidden chevrons (created with Ctrl-[and Ctrl-]) wherever you will need to fill in text, you can jump quickly from one chevron to another by pressing Ctrl-> or Ctrl-<.

The memo will also include the date you print the memo in it since it uses the "dateprint" glossary entry.

PROCEDURE

On a clear screen, invoke memo_header.mac. The macro types out the template that you can fill in and save under a new name. You can run this macro whenever you need to create a memo—you can even experiment and revise the macro's text so that the macro formats the memo according to your company's standards.

MOVE_TEXT.MAC: CTRL-M-T

This macro uses prompts for moving text in a file or between displayed files. If you want to automate everything you do in Word with macros, you may want to use move_text.mac; otherwise, you'll probably find it just as easy to move the text yourself.

PROCEDURE

In Document mode, invoke move_text.mac. It first prompts you to select the text you want to move and press Enter. The macro then prompts you to designate the text's new location and press Enter.

ASSOCIATED MACRO

copy_text.mac: Ctrl-C-T

NEXT_PAGE.MAC: CTRL-J-N

This macro jumps to the next page. By using it repeatedly from the beginning to the end of a document, you can quickly check how text is breaking between pages.

PROCEDURE

The next_page.mac macro examines the setting in the Jump Page command to determine the current page number and adds 1 to it. It then issues the Jump Page command to jump to that page. You must have the pagination option set to Auto or have printed or repaginated the document at least once before running this macro.

ASSOCIATED MACRO

prev_page.mac: Ctrl-J-P

PREV_PAGE.MAC: CTRL-J-P

This macro jumps to the previous page, enabling you to move backward through a document quickly.

PROCEDURE

The prev_page.mac macro examines the setting in the Jump Page command to determine the current page number and subtracts 1 from it. It then issues the Jump Page command to jump to that page. You must have pagination set to Auto or have printed or repaginated the document at least once before running this macro.

ASSOCIATED MACRO

next_page.mac: Ctrl-J-N

PRINT_LETTER.MAC: CTRL-P-L

5 New in
Word 5

This macro allows you to assign margins to the first page of a document (typically for letterhead) that are different from the rest of the document.

PROCEDURE

Load the document and issue the Format Division Margins command to set the margins for the document from the second page on.

When you run print_letter.mac, it initiates the Format Division Margins command, assigns its margins to variables, and then pauses with the prompt

Set the desired margins for the first page and press Enter

Provide the margins for the first page, which the macro applies to the entire document temporarily.

It then repaginates the document, jumps to the beginning of the second page, and creates a division mark there. It uses the variables to reformat the new division (the second page on) with the initial margins.

REPL_W_GLOSS.MAC: CTRL-R-G

This macro searches for specified text and replaces it with the contents of a glossary entry whose abbreviation you provide. If you find that you make a particular replacement frequently (say you always change the header text on documents passed on to you), you can assign your version of the text to a glossary entry and use repl_w_gloss.mac to place it in different documents. The macro replaces the original text without confirmation from you, but you can specify other search criteria (such as direction, case, and whole word).

PROCEDURE

The repl_w_gloss.mac macro invokes the Search command and prompts you to specify the text to be replaced and set the command's options.

It then asks you to

Enter glossary name to replace with, press Enter when done

After you enter the name, the macro searches for the original text, deletes it, and inserts the glossary text you specified in its place.

ASSOCIATED MACRO

repl_w_scrap.mac: Ctrl-R-P

REPL_W_SCRAP.MAC: CTRL-R-P

This macro replaces the text you specify with the text in scrap. You can use it to repeat an edit that you already made when you discover that the same replacement needs to be made throughout a document. It replaces the text without confirmation, but you can specify other search criteria (such as direction, case, and whole word).

PROCEDURE

The repl_w_scrap.mac macro first invokes the Search command and prompts you to

Enter text to replace, choose desired options, press Enter when done

It then locates the text, deletes it, and inserts the text from scrap in its place.

ASSOCIATED MACRO

repl_w_gloss.mac: Ctrl-R-G

SAVE_SELECTION.MAC: CTRL-S-S

This macro saves highlighted text as a separate file under the file name you specify.

PROCEDURE

Before running this macro, you must first highlight the selection you wish to save. The location of the highlight on the screen is important because the macro uses it to open the window. If it's too near the bottom, for instance, the window will not open.

Invoke save_selection.mac, and it copies the highlighted selection to scrap. It then opens a cleared horizontal window at the cursor location and inserts the text from scrap in the window. The macro invokes the Transfer Save command for the new window and prompts you to provide a name for the new file, saving the file and closing the window when you're done.

SIDEBYSIDE.MAC: CTRL-S-B

The macro creates side-by-side paragraphs on the screen according to the criteria you specify.

PROCEDURE

When you run sidebyside.mac, it displays the following prompts to obtain the necessary information from you:

> How many paragraphs do you want to place side by side (2 or 3)?
> How wide do you want the left paragraph to be (in inches)?
> How wide do you want the center paragraph to be (in inches)?
> How wide do you want the right paragraph to be (in inches)?

The macro then calculates widths for the paragraphs and creates style formats in the document's attached style sheet, like those in the SIDEBY.STY style sheet.

You can format paragraphs as side by side with these style formats.

STOP_LAST_FOOTER.MAC: CTRL-S-L

5 New in Word 5

This macro prevents a footer (bottom running head) from appearing on the last page of a document. This arrangement is necessary for some legal applications.

PROCEDURE

Load the desired document, provide it with the standard footer you want, and run stop_last_footer.mac.

The macro repaginates the document, jumps to the beginning of the last page, and enters a paragraph mark. It then formats the empty paragraph as a bottom running head. This blank footer overrides the standard footer on the last page, so no footer appears on the last page when you print the document.

TABLE.MAC: CTRL-T-T

This macro allows you to set evenly spaced tabs, beginning at a specified position.

PROCEDURE

Place the cursor in the paragraph to receive the tabs before invoking the macro.

When you run table.mac, it prompts you to

Enter position of first tab in inches, then press Enter

It then prompts you for the remaining tab positions with

Enter desired distance between tabs in inches, then press Enter

The macro calculates the tab positions according to the settings in the Format Division Margin command and sets them with the Format Tab Set command.

ASSOCIATED MACROS

tabs.mac: **Ctrl-T-1**

tabs2.mac: **Ctrl-T-2**

tabs3.mac: **Ctrl-T-3**

TABS.MAC: CTRL-T-1

This macro allows you to set tabs one at a time, by character position.

PROCEDURE

Before invoking tabs.mac, place the cursor in the paragraph where you want the tabs set.

The macro first displays the prompt

Enter tab position in # of characters, (0 to stop)

so you can provide the position of one tab. It then prompts you to

Enter alignment: L(eft) C(entered) R(ight) D(ecimal) V(ertical)

Type the letter for the alignment you want.

The macro sets the tab with the Format Tab Set command and repeats the entire process, allowing you to provide another tab setting. The macro continues until you enter 0 for the tab position.

ASSOCIATED MACROS

    table.mac: Ctrl-T-T

    tabs2.mac: Ctrl-T-2

    tabs3.mac: Ctrl-T-3

TABS2.MAC: CTRL-T-2

This macro sets evenly spaced tabs according to the number of columns you indicate, giving all tabs the same alignment.

PROCEDURE

When you run tabs2.mac, it obtains your requirements with the prompts

    How many columns in your table?
    Enter position of first column in characters
    Enter alignment: (L)eft (C)entered (R)ight (D)ecimal

If you specify decimal alignment, it then asks

    How many decimal places?

After calculating the length of your document's lines and restoring the standard tab settings, the macro calculates the first tab position. It takes alignment and the space to the next tab position into consideration. It then sets the tab and repeats the process to accommodate the number of columns you specified.

ASSOCIATED MACROS

    table.mac: Ctrl-T-T

    tabs.mac: Ctrl-T-1

    tabs3.mac: Ctrl-T-3

TABS3.MAC: CTRL-T-3

5 New in
Word 5

This macro creates a table, complete with lines drawn between columns and around the table. You indicate the page alignment for the entire table. Once the macro has created the table, you can fill it in.

PROCEDURE

Invoke tabs3.mac, and it first obtains information it needs to construct the table with the prompts

How many columns are there in the table?
How is the table aligned between the margins: (L)eft, (C)enter, (R)ight?

It then allows you to decide the method of construction by asking

Do you want to specify column widths by measure or longest entry (m/l)?

Type M for measure or L for longest entry.

If you specified measure, the macro asks how wide column 1 is (in inches). If you specified longest entry, it asks you to type the widest entry in column 1.

The macro then prompts you to specify the first column's alignment. If you choose decimal, the macro asks you to provide the number of digits that should appear after the decimal place. It then prompts you for the next column's width and alignment, repeating the process for each column. Once the macro has all the necessary information, it calculates the measurements for the page layout and inserts the formatted table.

Fill in the table. Press Enter to create blank lines (paragraph marks) between rows of the table; use new-line marks (Shift-Enter) to keep lines from appearing between the rows.

ASSOCIATED MACROS

table.mac: Ctrl-T-T

tabs.mac: Ctrl-T-1

tabs2.mac: Ctrl-T-2

TOC_ENTRY.MAC: CTRL-T-E

This macro codes entries for a document's table of contents. It places codes before and after the text you highlight. Use it if you did not create an outline for the document you want to add a TOC to; otherwise, you can have Word automatically generate a TOC from your document's outline (see Chapter 19).

PROCEDURE

The Options command's show non-printing symbols should be set to Partial or All before you run the macro. Otherwise, the TOC's codes disappear when they are formatted as hidden, and the macro isn't constructed to allow for this.

Highlight the text to be included in the table of contents and invoke toc_entry.mac. After deleting the highlighted text to scrap, the macro types the .C. code, highlights it, and formats it as hidden (with Alt-X-E). It then reinserts the text from scrap in the document after the .C. code. It ends the entry with a semicolon and formats it as hidden (Alt-X-E twice).

ASSOCIATED MACRO

index.mac: Ctrl-I-W

D

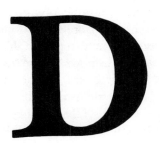

Printing IBM's Character Sets

AS YOU LEARNED IN CHAPTER 11, YOU CAN INCLUDE special characters in your Word documents by entering their Alt codes (pressing the alt key and typing the code number on the keypad). The characters assigned to the Alt codes can vary from font to font. As a reference, I have provided two standard character sets in Tables D.1 and D.2. Table D.1 presents the characters assigned to the Alt codes when you use the Courier font, while Table D.2 presents the assigned characters in the CourierPC font. I printed these files with Word's character_text.mac macro, which uses Word's CHARTEST.DOC document. You can print samples of the characters for any font with this macro (see Appendix C).

Table D.1: IBM's Character Set in Courier

ALT CODE NUMBER	CHARACTER	ALT CODE NUMBER	CHARACTER	ALT CODE NUMBER	CHARACTER
33	!	47	/	61	=
34	"	48	0	62	>
35	#	49	1	63	?
36	$	50	2	64	@
37	%	51	3	65	A
38	&	52	4	66	B
39	'	53	5	67	C
40	(	54	6	68	D
41	)	55	7	69	E
42	*	56	8	70	F
43	+	57	9	71	G
44	,	58	:	72	H
45	−	59	;	73	I
46	.	60	<	74	J

Table D.1: IBM's Character Set in Courier (cont.)

ALT CODE NUMBER	CHARACTER	ALT CODE NUMBER	CHARACTER	ALT CODE NUMBER	CHARACTER
75	K	97	a	119	w
76	L	98	b	120	x
77	M	99	c	121	y
78	N	100	d	122	z
79	O	101	e	123	{
80	P	102	f	124	|
81	Q	103	g	125	}
82	R	104	h	126	~
83	S	105	i	127	▓
84	T	106	j	128	Ç
85	U	107	k	129	ü
86	V	108	l	130	é
87	W	109	m	131	â
88	X	110	n	132	ä
89	Y	111	o	133	à
90	Z	112	p	134	å
91	[	113	q	135	ç
92	\\	114	r	136	ê
93	`	115	s	137	ë
94	—	116	t	138	è
95	ˇ	117	u	139	ï
96	[	118	v	140	î

Table D.1: IBM's Character Set in Courier (cont.)

ALT CODE NUMBER	CHARACTER	ALT CODE NUMBER	CHARACTER	ALT CODE NUMBER	CHARACTER
141	ì	164	ñ	187	£
142	Ä	165	Ñ	188	î
143	Å	166	ª	189	§
144	É	167	º	190	ï
145	æ	168	¿	191	ì
146	Æ	169	`	192	û
147	ô	170	^	193	ù
148	ö	171	½	194	ú
149	ò	172	¼	195	þ
150	û	173	¡	196	—
151	ù	174	«	197	±
152	ÿ	175	»	198	ó
153	Ö	176	—	199	ú
154	Ü	177	Ý	200	à
155	¢	178	ý	201	è
156	£	179	°	202	ò
157	¥	180	À	203	ù
158	£	181	Â	204	ä
159	ƒ	182	Ã	205	ë
160	á	183	È	206	ö
161	í	184	Ê	207	ü
162	ó	185	Ë	208	Å
163	ú	186	¤	209	î

Table D.1: IBM's Character Set in Courier (cont.)

ALT CODE NUMBER	CHARACTER	ALT CODE NUMBER	CHARACTER	ALT CODE NUMBER	CHARACTER
210	Ø	225	ß	240	Þ
211	Æ	226	â	241	±
212	å	227	Đ	242	·
213	í	228	ð	243	µ
214	ø	229	Í	244	¶
215	æ	230	µ	245	¾
216	Ä	231	Ó	246	—
217	ì	232	Ò	247	~
218	Ö	233	Õ	248	°
219	Ü	234	õ	249	·
220	É	235	Š	250	·
221	ï	236	š	251	˙
222	ß	237	ø	252	■
223	Ô	238	Ÿ	253	¨
224	Á	239	þ	254	■
				255	

Table D.2: IBM's Character Set in CourierPC

ALT CODE NUMBER	CHARACTER	ALT CODE NUMBER	CHARACTER	ALT CODE NUMBER	CHARACTER
33	!	55	7	77	M
34	"	56	8	78	N
35	#	57	9	79	O
36	$	58	:	80	P
37	%	59	;	81	Q
38	&	60	<	82	R
39	'	61	=	83	S
40	(	62	>	84	T
41	)	63	?	85	U
42	*	64	@	86	V
43	+	65	A	87	W
44	,	66	B	88	X
45	−	67	C	89	Y
46	.	68	D	90	Z
47	/	69	E	91	[
48	0	70	F	92	\
49	1	71	G	93	]
50	2	72	H	94	^
51	3	73	I	95	_
52	4	74	J	96	`
53	5	75	K	97	a
54	6	76	L	98	b

Table D.2: IBM's Character Set in CourierPC (cont.)

ALT CODE NUMBER	CHARACTER	ALT CODE NUMBER	CHARACTER	ALT CODE NUMBER	CHARACTER
99	c	121	y	143	Å
100	d	122	z	144	É
101	e	123	{	145	æ
102	f	124	|	146	Æ
103	g	125	}	147	ô
104	h	126	~	148	ö
105	i	127	▓	149	ò
106	j	128	Ç	150	û
107	k	129	ü	151	ù
108	l	130	é	152	ÿ
109	m	131	â	153	Ö
110	n	132	ä	154	Ü
111	o	133	à	155	¢
112	p	134	å	156	£
113	q	135	ç	157	¥
114	r	136	ê	158	₧
115	s	137	ë	159	ƒ
116	t	138	è	160	á
117	u	139	ï	161	í
118	v	140	î	162	ó
119	w	141	ì	163	ú
120	x	142	Ä	164	ñ

Table D.2: IBM's Character Set in CourierPC (cont.)

ALT CODE NUMBER	CHARACTER	ALT CODE NUMBER	CHARACTER	ALT CODE NUMBER	CHARACTER
165	Ñ	187	╗	209	╤
166	ª	188	╝	210	╥
167	º	189	╜	211	╙
168	¿	190	╛	212	╘
169	⌐	191	┐	213	╒
170	¬	192	└	214	╓
171	½	193	┴	215	╫
172	¼	194	┬	216	╪
173	¡	195	├	217	┘
174	«	196	─	218	┌
175	»	197	┼	219	█
176	░	198	╞	220	▄
177	▒	199	╟	221	▌
178	▓	200	╚	222	▐
179	│	201	╔	223	▀
180	┤	202	╩	224	α
181	╡	203	╦	225	β
182	╢	204	╠	226	Γ
183	╖	205	═	227	π
184	╕	206	╬	228	Σ
185	╣	207	╧	229	σ
186	║	208	╨	230	μ

Table D.2: IBM's Character Set in CourierPC (cont.)

ALT CODE NUMBER	CHARACTER	ALT CODE NUMBER	CHARACTER	ALT CODE NUMBER	CHARACTER
231	τ	240	$\equiv$	249	$\cdot$
232	Φ	241	$\pm$	250	$\cdot$
233	Θ	242	$\geq$	251	$\sqrt{}$
234	Ω	243	$\leq$	252	η
235	δ	244	$\lceil$	253	²
236	∞	245	$\rfloor$	254	$\blacksquare$
237	ϕ	246	$\div$	255	
238	ϵ	247	$\approx$		
239	$\cap$	248	$\circ$		

INDEX

MASTERING MICROSOFT WORD
DISK OFFER

One of the best ways to understand Microsoft Word fully is by studying examples and adapting them to your needs. Now, direct from the author, you can receive a disk of professionally prepared samples to expedite your work with *Mastering Microsoft Word* and to help you develop your own applications. These samples, which are designed to complement the material in this book, come ready for you to use.

Samples include:

- Text of the examples in this book
- Style sheets shown in the chapter on style sheets
- Document templates to streamline repeated text
- ALPHAMAC, a glossary of macros that I created to provide access to Word's features with push-button ease
- Other macros for automating procedures

To order, simply fill out the coupon below or print the information on a separate piece of paper. Mail to Matthew Holtz, Word 5 Disk, 455 Hyde Street, Suite 93, San Francisco, CA 94109. Include a check for $22.50, payable to Matthew Holtz. (California residents please add appropriate sales tax.) Please allow 4–6 weeks for delivery.

Please send me _____ copies of the *Mastering Microsoft Word* samples disk for Word 5.

_____

Name

_____

Address

_____

City   State   Zip

_____

Phone

SYBEX®

TO JOIN THE SYBEX MAILING LIST OR ORDER BOOKS
PLEASE COMPLETE THIS FORM

NAME _____ COMPANY _____

STREET _____ CITY _____

STATE _____ ZIP _____

☐ PLEASE MAIL ME MORE INFORMATION ABOUT **SYBEX** TITLES

ORDER FORM (There is no obligation to order)

PLEASE SEND ME THE FOLLOWING:

TITLE	QTY	PRICE
_____	_____	_____
_____	_____	_____
_____	_____	_____
_____	_____	_____

TOTAL BOOK ORDER _____ $_____

CUSTOMER SIGNATURE _____

SHIPPING AND HANDLING PLEASE ADD $2.00
PER BOOK VIA UPS _____

FOR OVERSEAS SURFACE ADD $5.25 PER
BOOK PLUS $4.40 REGISTRATION FEE _____

FOR OVERSEAS AIRMAIL ADD $18.25 PER
BOOK PLUS $4.40 REGISTRATION FEE _____

CALIFORNIA RESIDENTS PLEASE ADD
APPLICABLE SALES TAX _____

TOTAL AMOUNT PAYABLE _____

☐ CHECK ENCLOSED   ☐ VISA
☐ MASTERCARD   ☐ AMERICAN EXPRESS

ACCOUNT NUMBER _____

EXPIR. DATE _____ DAYTIME PHONE _____

CHECK AREA OF COMPUTER INTEREST:

☐ BUSINESS SOFTWARE

☐ TECHNICA!. PROGRAMMING

☐ OTHER: _____

**THE FACTOR THAT WAS MOST IMPORTANT IN
YOUR SELECTION:**

☐ THE SYBEX NAME

☐ QUALITY

☐ PRICE

☐ EXTRA FEATURES

☐ COMPREHENSIVENESS

☐ CLEAR WRITING

☐ OTHER _____

**OTHER COMPUTER TITLES YOU WOULD LIKE
TO SEE IN PRINT:**

_____

_____

OCCUPATION

☐ PROGRAMMER ☐ TEACHER

☐ SENIOR EXECUTIVE ☐ HOMEMAKER

☐ COMPUTER CONSULTANT ☐ RETIRED

☐ SUPERVISOR ☐ STUDENT

☐ MIDDLE MANAGEMENT ☐ OTHER:

☐ ENGINEER/TECHNICAL _____

☐ CLERICAL/SERVICE

☐ BUSINESS OWNER/SELF EMPLOYED

CHECK YOUR LEVEL OF COMPUTER USE

☐ NEW TO COMPUTERS

☐ INFREQUENT COMPUTER USER

☐ FREQUENT USER OF ONE SOFTWARE
  PACKAGE:
  NAME _____

☐ FREQUENT USER OF MANY SOFTWARE
  PACKAGES

☐ PROFESSIONAL PROGRAMMER

OTHER COMMENTS:

_____

_____

_____

_____

_____

_____

_____

_____

PLEASE FOLD, SEAL, AND MAIL TO SYBEX

SYBEX, INC.
2021 CHALLENGER DR. #100
ALAMEDA, CALIFORNIA USA
94501

SEAL

SYBEX Computer Books are different.

Here is why . . .

At SYBEX, each book is designed with you in mind. Every manuscript is carefully selected and supervised by our editors, who are themselves computer experts. We publish the best authors, whose technical expertise is matched by an ability to write clearly and to communicate effectively. Programs are thoroughly tested for accuracy by our technical staff. Our computerized production department goes to great lengths to make sure that each book is well-designed.

In the pursuit of timeliness, SYBEX has achieved many publishing firsts. SYBEX was among the first to integrate personal computers used by authors and staff into the publishing process. SYBEX was the first to publish books on the CP/M operating system, microprocessor interfacing techniques, word processing, and many more topics.

Expertise in computers and dedication to the highest quality product have made SYBEX a world leader in computer book publishing. Translated into fourteen languages, SYBEX books have helped millions of people around the world to get the most from their computers. We hope we have helped you, too.

For a complete catalog of our publications:

SYBEX, Inc. 2021 Challenger Drive, #100, Alameda, CA 94501
Tel: (415) 523-8233/(800) 227-2346   Telex: 336311
Fax: (415) 523-2373

Interaction of Special Keys in WORD

SPECIAL CHARACTER	CHARACTER'S FUNCTION	KEYS	DISPLAY ON SCREEN	DISPLAY IN SCRAP	SEARCH SYMBOL
New paragraph	Starts a new line and a new paragraph.	Enter	¶	¶	^p
New line	Starts a new line but not a new paragraph.	Shift-Enter	↓	↓	^n
New column	Starts a new column.	Ctrl-Alt-Enter	....	§	^c
New page	Starts a new page.	Ctrl-Shift-Enter	. . . .	§	^d
New division	Starts a new division (page format).	Ctrl-Enter	: : : :	§	^d
Optional hyphen	Creates a hyphen that won't print except at the end of a line.	Ctrl-hyphen	–	–	^-
Non-breaking hyphen	Creates a hyphen that keeps text on both sides of it on the same line.	Ctrl-Shift-hyphen	—	—	–
Non-breaking space	Creates a space that keeps text on both sides of it on the same line.	Ctrl-Spacebar	[space]	•	^s

The Directional Keypad

KEY	OPERATION
Top Row	
Home	Beginning of the line
Shift-Home	Extend to beginning of the line
Ctrl-Home	Top of the window
Shift-Ctrl-Home	Extend to top of the window
↑	Up one line
Shift-↑	Extend up one line
Ctrl-↑	Beginning of previous paragraph
Shift-Ctrl-↑	Extend to beginning of previous paragraph
↑ with Scroll Lock on	Scroll up one line
Page Up	Up one windowful
Shift-Page Up	Extend up one windowful
Ctrl-Page Up	Beginning of the document
Shift-Ctrl-Page Up	Extend to beginning of the document
Middle Row	
←	Left one character
Shift-←	Extend left one character
Ctrl-←	First character of the previous word
Shift-Ctrl-←	Extend to first character of the previous word
← with Scroll Lock on	Left 1/3 of the window
Ctrl-5-←	Previous object (in show layout)
Ctrl-5-→	Next object (in show layout)
→	Right one character
Shift-→	Extend right one character
Ctrl-→	First character of the next word
Shift-Ctrl-→	Extend to first character of the next word
→ with Scroll Lock on	Right 1/3 of the window
Bottom Row	
End	End of the line
Shift-End	Extend to end of the line
Ctrl-End	Bottom of the window
Shift-Ctrl-End	Extend to bottom of the window
↓	Down one line
Shift-↓	Extend down one line
Ctrl-↓	Beginning of next paragraph
Shift-Ctrl-↓	Extend to beginning of the next paragraph
↓ with Scroll Lock on	Scroll down one line
Page Down	Down one windowful
Shift-Page Down	Extend down one windowful
Ctrl-Page Down	End of the document
Shift-Ctrl-Page Down	Extend to end of the document